To My Father and Mother

Preface

This essay was originally written in the course of my service as "law clerk" to Judge Charles Edward Wyzanski, Jr. of the United States District Court of Massachusetts. He appointed me as "law clerk" so that I could act as his economic assistant in connection with the trial before him of the United Shoe case. I served for two years, and the material that comprises the bulk of this study was my major work product for him. It was completed in October 1952, but became available for publication only after the final decision of the Supreme Court in the case in May 1954. All of the present book except the first, ninth, and tenth chapters is identical, save in minor details, with my original memorandum for the Court. The first chapter serves as an introduction, presenting the earlier history of the United Shoe Machinery Company as reflected in previous anti-trust suits. Chapter IX discusses the final decree of the Court, and whatever information was available at the time of writing on developments in the industry since the decision. The final chapter contains some reflections on the economic standards of the anti-trust law and the problems of its enforcement. Chapters II through VIII, and a somewhat different version of Chapter I were used as a dissertation for the Ph.D. degree at Harvard University in February 1954.

As its title indicates, this study is an analysis of the issues in a particular anti-trust case, rather than an industry study in the more conventional pattern. For this reason, I have left the narrative of Chapters II through VIII in the present tense, as they were in my original memorandum, to describe the situation as it stood when the case was before the Court. It is my hope that the value of the study as an example of what can be achieved by the economic analysis of a court record, without the use of other materials, as well as its interest as a study which was before the Court when its decision was made will outweigh the shortcomings of this form.

It is my duty and pleasure to record two great debts, intellectual and personal, which I have incurred in the course of writing this study. They are owed to Charles E. Wyzanski, Jr. and Edward S. Mason. To Judge Wyzanski I am indebted for the opportunity of a unique educational experience, for his generosity in permitting me to use for my own purposes the memorandum I wrote for him, for insights into problems of administering the Sherman Act that only a teacher of his gifts and experience could provide, and for an association that continues to be full of the highest intellectual and personal rewards. My debt to Dean Mason has been growing over ten years of association with him as a student and colleague, and continues to grow. Whatever there is of value in the analytical scheme used here, and in my conception of applying economic analysis to the determination of the issues in an anti-trust suit, I owe chiefly to his teaching. What I owe to the stimulus of my personal association with him and to the influence of his example as a teacher and a man is not so simply defined.

I am indebted to Morris A. Adelman, Joe S. Bain, Robert L. Bishop, Kingman Brewster, Jr., Robert R. Bowie, David F. Cavers, Kermit Gordon, John V. Lintner, and James W. McKie for their contributions to the development of my ideas on the law and economics of anti-trust policy. With Dean Mason, we were members of a continuing discussion group on the problems of public policy in the field of monopoly and competition while I worked on this study. The nature of my responsibilities to the Court precluded my discussion with them of the specific issues of the case, but our general discussions contributed greatly to my legal and economic education.

I am indebted to the Merrill Foundation for the Advancement of Financial Knowledge, which, through a grant to the Littauer School of Public Administration of Harvard University for the study of monopoly and competition in the American economy, financed the discussion group on public policy.

At various times over the long period during which this manuscript has been typed and retyped, Barbara Prentice Broad, Ann Drachman, Norma Shoolman, and my wife have borne the burdens of typing cheerfully and efficiently.

For what I have written, I alone am of course responsible. Those who have read this study have not thereby assumed any share of that responsibility.

Carl Kaysen

Cambridge
June 1955

Contents

Table of Cases

I. Introduction

This study is an economic analysis of the issues in the civil anti-trust suit brought by the United States against the United Shoe Machinery Corporation under Sections 1 and 2 of the Sherman Act.[1] The problems it examines are substantially those set forth as issues in the Complaint, reproduced as Appendix A.[2] The analysis is made in terms of the issues as they were presented to the Trial Court for decision: only the record of the case is used as a source of factual material. The analysis was originally made during the course of the trial. Thus it can fairly claim to provide an example of what economic analysis can do when applied to the facts of a concrete anti-trust proceeding as they appear to the Court before which they are tried.

The application of economic analysis to an anti-trust case in this fashion has a claim to interest arising partly from its novelty, partly, and more fundamentally, from the relation of economic criteria to the basic policy which the anti-trust laws embody. Of course, there are other ways in which the application of economic analysis to the conduct of a suit under the Sherman Act is possible. The Attorney General might require his staff to make an economic study of an industry before bringing suit against a firm or firms in it. After the

[1] Civil No. 7198, District Court of Massachusetts. Filed 15 December 1947.

[2] There are two exceptions. The restrictive agreements charged between United and other producers, Complaint, paras. 52-59, are not treated since the Court ruled that no sufficient basis in the evidence existed to justify the admission of documents of the alleged co-conspirators. See Order of Court, March 10, 1950. The monopolization of parts charged in para. 89 of the Complaint presents no problem separate from the monopolization of shoe machinery, and therefore requires no separate analysis. See comments of the Court, Tr. 6088-9.

initiation of a suit, counsel for a defendant firm might make a similar study to help them decide what points they should and should not contest, as well as to plan their defense. On the whole, it seems fair to say that in the case examined here, neither of these two courses was followed. The presentation of the Government's case shows no signs of the systematic utilization of the concepts and techniques of economics. While the defense brought economists to testify as expert witnesses,[3] this appears to have been more a response to the developments of the case in the course of trial than the original plan of the defense. It is clear that a case which had been shaped by the application of economic analysis from its earliest stages as a proposed Complaint in the Department of Justice might well have a vastly different form than one not so influenced; indeed, it can be argued persuasively that the social product of such application will be far higher than that which can be achieved by bringing the economist in as aid to the judge after a case comes to trial. Be that as it may, the author's experience as economic aid to a judge is still unique; and systematic recourse to the aid of trained economists in the earlier stages of the process of anti-trust enforcement is still rare.[4]

THE PRESENT CASE

The defendant in the present case was the United Shoe Machinery Corporation, a New Jersey corporation organized in 1917. It is the successor in business of the United Shoe Machinery Company, created in 1899 by the merger of several shoe machinery manufacturers.[5] The headquarters of the corporation are in Boston, and its major manufacturing operations in Beverly, Massachusetts. Since its original formation the company has expanded in a variety of ways, both in the fields of shoe machinery and shoe factory supplies. When the suit was begun, United and its wholly owned subsidiaries[6] had total

[3] See Tr. 10706–911, 12930–975, testimony of Prof. R. S. Merriam, Harvard Business School; and Tr. 13040–185, testimony of Prof. Joel Dean, Columbia Business School.

[4] At the present writing, the recently decided suit against the investment bankers, US v. Henry S. Morgan, et al (Civil No. 43–757, S. District of New York), is the only completed case known to the writer in which the defense was planned with the aid of economic analysis, ab initio. As yet, the use of economic analysis by the Government is rudimentary.

[5] Appendix A, "Complaint," paras. 3, 17.

[6] See Complaint, para. 24, for a list of these. This list is incorrect in a few minor particulars; see United's Answer, para. 24.

assets of some $105 million, net worth of some $80 million, gross revenues of some $70 million, and net income before taxes of some $15
million.[7] United was clearly the largest seller in the field of shoe
machinery and shoe factory supplies. The major issue of the case,
baldly stated, was whether United was a monopolist in the shoe
machinery and shoe factory supplies markets, as the Government
alleged. Subsidiary were questions as to the bases and consequences
of its monopoly, if there was one.

The present case is the third major anti-trust proceeding in which
United has been involved. In 1911, a civil suit charging it with combination in restraint of trade and monopolizing in violations of
Sections 1 and 2 of the Sherman Act was brought by the Government. United won this suit. In 1915, another suit was started, directed
against United's leasing system, under the newly enacted Clayton Act.
This the Government won, and in 1923 United modified its leases
to meet the Court's decree. Thus the present case embraces United's
activities and situation over the period 1923–1947, from the time the
leasing system was first modified to the filing of the complaint in
this case.

TECHNIQUE OF SHOE MACHINERY AND SHOE MANUFACTURE

The manufacture of shoe machinery in essentially a large-scale
foundry and machine-shop operation in which techniques common
to all the machinery manufacturing trades are employed. As will
appear in the course of the discussion, shoe machinery manufacture
presents special problems of precision and complexity, but ones which
differ in degree rather than in kind from those of the machine-tool
trade and other trades manufacturing industrial machinery.

The special problems of technology which are relevant to this
study are those of shoe manufacture, which determine the nature of
shoe machinery, rather than those of machinery manufacture. Shoe
manufacture was a handicraft operation until the Civil War. The
stimulus of military orders led to the first introduction of machinery,
which has progressively displaced hand operation for all but a small
quantity of expensive shoes. But down to the present, mechanization
has taken the form, more or less, of substituting a machine for each
hand operation, or for each combination of a few hand operations,

[7] Moody's Industrials, 1949.

rather than transforming the nature of the product in such a way as to adapt it to continuous or semi-continuous machine production. Three reasons contribute to this relative backwardness of shoe manufacturing technology. First is the non-uniform nature of the chief raw material, leather: different skins and different pieces of the same skin show different tensile strengths, different grain qualities, different degrees of flexibility. Thus, nearly every machine operation must in some way be under the control of an operator who can "feel" and handle the specific material on which he is working. The typical mass production industries, by contrast, work with uniform raw materials. Second, the shape of a shoe is extremely complex; this means that the working parts of machines must describe motions which do not lie in one plane or in a pair of perpendicular planes, but which follow involved space curves. This makes the automatic guidance of machines difficult. Third, the wide range of shoe sizes, shoe constructions, and shoe styles, and the variability of styles and constructions from year to year taken together mean that the average run of an identical product in any one factory is short. Economical production of many short runs of differing products requires flexible machines, operator-controlled, rather than specialized machines which can be run automatically, once they are set up for their tasks.

The operations of a shoe factory can be divided into eight stages.[8] These are upper cutting, upper fitting, stock fitting, lasting, bottoming, making, finishing, and treeing. Upper cutting is the cutting of leather and other materials (gabardine, felt, satin, duck) of which shoe uppers are made into appropriate shapes for the parts of the upper. Upper fitting is the assembly and stitching and gluing together of these parts to make a complete upper. It also includes decorating the upper by means of perforations, bindings, etc. Stock fitting includes the preparation of the material for the soles and insoles of shoes, and in some cases, heels as well. Small shoe manufacturers generally buy rough-cut soles; larger ones cut their own. In lasting, the shoe upper is drawn tightly over the last—the wooden form on which the shoe is assembled and which gives the shoe its shape—and fastened to the insole. Bottoming is the fastening of the outsole to the lasted shoe; making, the fastening of the heel to heel-seat of the lasted and bot-

[8] This description is drawn from Exhibit A annexed to the Defendant's *Answer*, entitled "Outline of Shoe Making Procedures." The general characterization of the shoe manufacturing process above is repeated frequently in the Record.

tomed shoe. The two final stages, finishing and treeing, involve various surface treatments of the shoe, removal of the last, and finally boxing the finished shoes. Of these stages, it is lasting, bottoming, and making which involve most of the characteristic complex machines specialized to shoe manufacture. Upper fitting is performed chiefly on sewing machines essentially similar to those used in apparel manufacture. While machines for cutting leather and machines used in finishing operations are to some extent specialized, they are relatively simple in comparison with the machines used in the operations of pulling the assembled upper over the last, and temporarily fastening it to the last; attaching the insole to the lasted upper; preparing and attaching the outsole to the insole; and attaching the heel to shoe and trimming it to its final shape—the fundamental operations in lasting, bottoming, and making.

Shoes can be constructed in a variety of ways. Constructions vary in the way the outsole is attached to the insole, and in the way the insole is attached to the upper, the lasting method. Some of the more important sole-attaching methods are:

Goodyear welt—a strip of leather, the welt, is sewn to the insole on one edge and the outsole on the other. This is used for most men's shoes.

Cemented—the insole and outsole are cemented together, with the lasted over margin of the upper between the insole and the outsole, likewise cemented (usually). Used chiefly for women's shoes.

Littleway lockstitch—the insole is sown directly to the outsole, with the lasted-over margin between. Unlike the Goodyear construction, the seam is inside the shoe, and the last must be removed before the shoe can be sewn. Chiefly women's shoes.

McKay chainstitch—similar to above, but stitch is different. An obsolescent construction.

Stitchdown—the lasted-over margin of the upper, the insole and the outsole are fastened in that order, with a lock-stitch seam lying outside the shoe. Important in children's shoes.

As the above descriptions show, different sole-attaching methods involve different lasting methods. These in turn differ not only in the structural relations between insole, lasted-over margin and last, but also in the fastening means used to attach insole to upper: staples, tacks, cement, or thread. Enough has been said here to indicate the variety of operations, and consequently the variety of machines involved in shoe manufacture. These simple categories will be expanded and embroidered in more than sufficient detail in the course of the discussion.

EARLY HISTORY OF UNITED, PREVIOUS ANTI-TRUST SUITS

United Shoe Machinery Corporation began its corporate existence as the United Shoe Machinery Company of New Jersey on 7 February, 1899. It was created to take over the business of five shoe machinery manufacturers:

Goodyear Shoe Machinery Corporation (and its marketing subsidiary, International Goodyear)
Consolidated and McKay Lasting Machine Company
McKay Shoe Machinery Company
Davey Pegging Machine Company (owned by Consolidated and McKay)
Eppler Welt Machine Company (and its marketing subsidiary, International Eppler)[9]

Three of these companies—Goodyear, Consolidated and McKay, and McKay—were dominant companies in their respective branches of the industry at the time. Davey, owned by one of these three, also occupied an important position; but the pegged shoe construction in which its machines were applied was already obsolescent and has long since disappeared. Eppler was a small newcomer, just breaking into business.

The important constituents of United, Goodyear, Consolidated and McKay, and McKay Shoe Machinery, produced different types of machines, for the most part. Their major fields were:[10]

Goodyear	Welting and welt outsole sewing machines, lasting machines for women's shoes (Ideal).
Consolidated and McKay	Lasting machines for men's shoes (Chase). The CHM (Consolidated Hand Method) lasting machine, which was adaptable to women's as well as men's shoes, was being produced on an experimental basis.
McKay Shoe Machinery	Heeling and metallic fastening.

[9] See *Record* on appeal from the District Court of Massachusetts, in the Supreme Court of United States, No. 545, Oct. term 1916, *Brief for United States*, pp. 4 ff. (This is hereafter cited as Record on Appeal, 247 US 32.)
[10] *Brief* for United, pp. 6–7.

Eppler Welt was producing welt inseamers and outsewers, similar to those of Goodyear. It was a new company, backed and managed by shoe manufacturers.[11] At the time of the merger, when it was seven years old, it had succeeded in selling fewer than 50 machines.[12]

The merger achieved a very high degree of market control in the major fields of shoe machinery, since the constituent companies dominated their respective fields. The precise extent of domination is not made clear in our source, but it appears safe to say that the new company's market share in each major field was 70 per cent or greater.[13]

Following the merger, the new company grew at a fairly rapid rate. At its formation, it issued nearly $15 million worth of stock in exchange for the companies it acquired and some cash.[14] By 1910, the total assets of the company had reached $40.8 million;[15] this represents an annual rate of growth of nearly 10 per cent. This growth was financed from retained earnings; over the period 1905–1911 the average annual profit rate on total assets was 14 per cent. About half of this was paid out in dividends, and half reinvested.[16]

[11] *Brief* for the Government, pp. 34 ff.

[12] *Brief* for United, pp. 27–34.

[13] *Brief* for United, p. 6, gives the following figures:

Goodyear	60 per cent welt inseamers and sewers
	10 per cent lasters
Consolidated and McKay	60 per cent lasters
McKay	70 per cent heeling
	80 per cent other metallic fastening
Eppler	10 per cent inseaming and welt sewing
Davey Pegging	7 per cent pegging machines

These figures are cited from the *Complaint* (Part III), except that the Complaint showed 80 per cent for Goodyear's share in welt inseamers and sewers. Their reproduction in the United Brief, with the change noted, may indicate that United accepts them as correct, or merely that it considers them not worth arguing about. Note that the 10 per cent figure for Eppler is not consistent with the figure of fewer than 50 machines attributed to Eppler elsewhere in United's brief, and cited on the page above. Elsewhere, United's brief quotes with approval (p. 27) the opinion of the Supreme Court in US *v.* Winslow, 227 US 202, that there was " '. . . no objection to one corporation's manufacturing 70% of 3 non-competing group of machines.' " The Government Brief characterizes Davey Pegging and McKay Shoe Machinery as constituents having a substantial monopoly (pp. 49–50), but it gives no market-share figures for the constituent companies other than those cited already.

[14] Opinion, 247 US at 79–81.

[15] See Record on Appeal, 247 US 32, VI, p. 358 ff., testimony of USMC auditor.

[16] *Ibid.*

The process of growth involved a series of acquisitions of machine businesses, patents and inventions, sometimes along with the services of the inventor, and businesses in shoe findings and supplies. There were 59 acquisitions of one sort or another over the whole period 1899–1911 (excluding the original merger).[17] Only one of these was major in size and significance. Of the minor ones, 32 were of some significance; these involved an acquisition cost of $1.6 millions.[18]

The major acquisition was that of Thomas G. Plant Shoe Co., made in September 1910.[19] Thomas G. Plant was a shoe manufacturer who had undertaken experimentation on shoe machinery. By May of 1910 Plant claimed to have a complete line of shoe machinery; he canceled his leases on United's machines, substituting his own and began to advertise his machines to the trade. After various negotiations, initiated in June, interrupted and completed in September, United purchased Plant's machinery, patents, and inventions along with a covenant by Plant covering any inventions in the field he might make for fifteen years, as well as his majority stockholding in the Plant Shoe Co. The total price was $6 million; for this United received 206 US patents, 28 patent applications, machines, tools, and jigs, and 60 per cent of the stock of the Shoe Co. The

---

[17] *Brief* for United, p. 44. The number of acquisitions by years is given as follows:

1899	11	1904	9	1908	3
1900	8	1905	1	1909	1
1901	6	1906	3	1910	6
1902	6	1907	1	1911	1
1903	3				

Their distribution by type (except for the Plant acquisition, q.v. below), is:

20 new machines not previously made by United
11 improved machines to enable United to supply better machines
15 findings and supplies businesses
} These appear to involve going businesses, though this is not certain.
3 contracts of employment with inventors
3 patent acquisitions
3 " " to settle litigation
2 employment contracts arising out of transactions of constituent companies
1 exclusive license under patent on supplies

The *Brief* for United States, pp. 60 ff., lists 56 acquisitions, ex Plant, for the same period. Of these 32 appeared significant; 26 of these appeared to involve going businesses.

[18] *Brief* for United States, pp. 60 ff. See footnote 17.

[19] See *Brief* for United States pp. 97–120; *Brief* for United, pp. 48 ff.; Record, VI, pp. 577 ff. for details of this acquisition.

nominal value of the stock was $2.25 million; but Winslow in his testimony stated that it was worth $3.5 million. Taking this figure as correct, $2.5 million is thus left as United's valuation of the patents and inventions.[20] This gives a total figure for acquisitions over the period of 4.1 millions, a substantial sum in relation to the total growth in assets of some $25 million.

The new company concentrated all manufacturing activities in one new plant, in Beverly, Massachusetts. It created a service organization; by 1911 the service department employed over 600 men, had 27 branch organizations in 13 states, and an annual operating expenditure of $1.2 million.[21] United continued the practice of its major predecessors of leasing rather than selling most of its machines. From

[20] The significance of the acquisition, and United's motivation therefor were much argued in the anti-trust case of 1911. Much remains obscure, but an examination of arguments and testimony makes the following clear:

(1) The initiative for the transaction came from Plant;

(2) United initiated infringement suits against Plant before the purchase negotiations were begun. When the negotiations were interrupted, activity on the infringement suits continued.

(3) In September, Plant was negotiating with a combination of St. Louis shoe manufacturers. He asked $1.6 million for an undivided half-interest in the shoe machinery business alone, and gave them only 12 hours to consider the offer. They did not accept in time, and Plant made the arrangements described above with United. The record offered no evidence to show United knew of the Plant proposition to the shoe manufacturers before it closed the deal.

(4) The valuation placed by Winslow on the shoe business of Plant appears somewhat high. The shoe company's profits had been running $500–$700 thousand per year; one year they did exceed one million. United had been earning about 14 per cent per year on its capital; on this basis, the total stock would be worth some $3.5–$4.9 million; and 60 per cent of it, some $2.1–$2.9 million. This leaves then at least $3 million as the valuation of Plant's patents and inventions.

(5) If United's contention that the Plant machines all infringed United patents be accepted at face value, $3 million becomes a high price for United to pay. It is worth noting that Plant asked the St. Louis shoe men for more than that— $1.6 million for a half interest.

(6) However obscure United's intent, and the relations of infringement suits to bargaining for acquisition, the effects of the Plant acquisition are not at all dependent on United's intent. The acquisition certainly removed potentially important competition from the field. The competition cannot be described as more than potential, since it is likely (though not certain) that the machinery was not yet commercial, and would have required further development before it became so. But, given the fact that Plant had experience and capital, it is likely that such further development on at least some of the machinery would have taken place in the absence of the acquisition.

[21] *Brief* for United, pp. 32 ff.

the first, service was provided as an incident of the lease, without a special charge. United also created an experimental department (later the research department). Expenditures for research during the period averaged about $0.5 million per year. About 150 new machines were brought out in the period 1899–1914.[22]

By 1911, United appears to have increased somewhat its share of the shoe machinery market, compared with the 70 to 80 per cent share it had at its formation; but accurate information on this point is lacking. The Complaint presents figures which show shares greater than 95 per cent for all machines except the welt outsole stitcher; and 78 per cent for that machine.[23] Substantially the same figures are cited in the dissenting opinion of Mr. Justice Clarke, and characterized by him as "results . . . from which all elements seriously disputed by counsel for the defendants have been excluded."[24]

Market-share figures, presumably referring to United's position in 1915, were presented in the District Court opinion in the Clayton Act case (1915).[25] All of these estimates suffer from two rather serious limitations: first, figures are shown only for a relatively small number of the most important machine types; and second, no basis for weighting the market shares of individual machine types is provided.[26]

In 1911, the United States filed a civil suit against United Shoe Machinery Co. in the District Court of Massachusetts. The Complaint charged United with violating Sections 1 and 2 of the Sherman Act. The original merger which created United was cited as a combination in restraint of trade in violation of Section 1; both the creation of

---

[22] *Brief* for United, p. 195. The new machines brought out during the period were distributed by types as follows:

Eyeletting	5	Metallic	7
Goodyear	41	Pulling over	15
Heeling	11	Fitting room	3
Lasting	4	Miscellaneous	64

The most important developments were the Rex-pulling-over machine, the Clicking machine and the Stapling machine.

[23] Appendix B to the Complaint.

[24] 247 US at 89.

[25] See US *v.* United Shoe Machinery Co., 234 Fed. Rep. 127 at 134.

[26] The discussion below, Ch. II, of United's market share in 1947 indicates that these limitations are less important in practice than they appear to be in the abstract, since a small number of important machines account for a very large share of United's revenue, and different weighting systems make little difference in the estimate of over-

United, and the leasing system, with its tying clauses, were cited as monopolizing activities in violation of Section 2.[27] The three-judge

---

all market share. The actual figures presented in the various sources are shown in the following table:

Machine Type	Market Share in % (Date and Source)	
	1911 Complaint, App. B, Sherman Act Case and Clarke Dissent	1915 (?) DC Opinion District Court Case (Corrected)[a]
Goodyear welt and turn sewing	95	95
Goodyear welt outsole stitching	78[b]	81
Lasting	100	99+
Heeling	99+	95
Pulling over	100*	100
Heel slugging	99+ *	99+
Loose nailing	99+	99+
Clicking	not shown	99+
Eyeletting	not shown	under 65[c]
Tacking[d]	not shown	99+
Standard screw[e]	100	100
Pegging[e]	100	96

*Indicates machines not shown in Mr. Justice Clarke's table. The omission of the pulling over machines is puzzling, since there was no question, at that time, of the existence of competing machines to this newly invented and patented machine.

[a]The corrections applied to the District Court tabulation are those suggested in the Brief on Appeal for United (258 US, United States *v*. United Shoe Machinery Co. Record on Appeal), pp 41 ff. The figures for eyeletting and tacking machines were the only ones corrected.

[b]Probably an underestimate, since the figure for competitive Union Lockstitch machines includes all those known to have been manufactured, some of which are used elsewhere than in shoe factories.

[c]This is the corrected figure. The correction both lowered the number of United machines outstanding, and raised the number of competitive machines. It is quite possible that the higher number of competitive machines refers to all in use, in other factories as well as in shoe factories. If this is the case, the original uncorrected figure of 81 per cent may be nearer the mark.

[d]In terms of revenue, this was a relatively unimportant machine, not to be compared with those listed above.

[e]These two machines were obsolescent at the time, and therefore of little importance.

The tabulations support a guess of 90–95 per cent for the average market share of United about 1911–14.

---

[27] See 1952 CCH Blue Book of the Anti-Trust Laws, #101, and 247 US 32. The Government initiated a criminal case against Sidney Winslow and other officers on the same charges, in Sept. 1911. Some of the counts were dismissed on demurrer, *US v. Sidney W. Winslow et al.*, 195 Fed. 578, 227 US 202; the rest were nol-prossed. Blue Book, #95.

trial court unanimously found for United.[28] Their conclusion rested on three propositions: there was no showing of an intent to monopolize in the formation of United, rather, the intent was to realize efficiency and economy; the constituent companies were in fact noncompeting—only if they had been in competition with each other would their combination have been a restraint of trade; the leasing system, including the tying arrangements, was simply a valid exercise of the patent rights which United had. The Government appealed; the Supreme Court, in a divided opinion, affirmed the District Court's conclusions.[29] The opinion of the Court followed the line of the District Court argument; much emphasis was placed on the fact that the constituent companies merged in 1899 produced complementary rather than competitive machines. The two dissenting opinions attacked the character of the leases; and they asserted that the plain intent of the combination was monopoly, and that this intent was clearly achieved.

The concept of "competition" underlying the opinion of the Court and that of the District Court is clearly a much narrower one than would be applied in an anti-trust proceeding today. Whatever the merits of the finding that the products of the constituent companies were complementary machines rather than competitive machines,[30] it is clear that the very important indirect competition among machines through the competition between shoes of different constructions—e.g., welts and McKay's, or McKay's and turns—as well as the important potential competition among the constituent companies realizing itself through competing research programs and the development of new machines would justify the conclusion that the combination substantially lessened competition in the shoe machinery

[28] 222 Fed. Rep. 350. Each of the three judges wrote a separate opinion, examining part of the case, as well as concurring in the opinions of his colleagues.

[29] 247 US 32. The decision was 4–3, two justices abstaining.

[30] See the dissent of Mr. Justice Clarke 247 US at 81–82. Examination of the briefs suggests that there was some competition between the lasting machines of the Goodyear Company and those of Consolidated and McKay. The Chase and CHM lasters had been used and were capable of use on men's welt shoes (*Brief* for United States, pp. 30–34); though United argued that such use was "incidental" or "experimental" (*Brief* for United, pp. 28–30) it did not deny it. The examples of competing use quoted by the Government were supported by testimony. It is also clear that the Eppler machines competed with Goodyear's, whether or not they were "inferior." (See *Brief* for United States, pp. 34–49. The characterization is Winslow's. United's *Brief* does not deny the competition; it characterizes the Eppler machines as unsuccessful and infringing, p. 31.)

industry. It is safe to say that the reasoning of the majority opinion would not be reproduced by a Court today, as well as to point out that it was clearly erroneous on economic grounds becausse of the excessively narrow idea of competition on which it was grounded.[31]

In 1914, Congress passed the Clayton Act.[32] Section 3 of that act[33] forbade lease or sale transactions conditioned on an agreement not to use the goods of competitors when they tended to lessen competition. Soon after, the Anti-Trust Division of the Department of Justice filed a suit against United, charging that its lease provisions violated Section 3 of the Clayton Act. United's leasing system, as it then operated, had the following major features:

1. The lease term was 17 years.

2. Machines were classified as principal and auxiliary. In general, principal machines were paid for on a so-called royalty basis, so much per stitch or per pair of shoes processed, while auxiliary machines were let at a flat monthly rental. The rentals were described by United as nominal. Auxiliary machines were leased in "sets," with each appropriate principal machine, and their use was restricted to use in combination with the appropriate principal machines.

3. Leases were of two classes, "restricted" and "independent." The restricted leases embodied various clauses limiting the use of particular machines to shoes on which specified operations had been performed on other United machines; in effect, they tied together the use of various machines. The independent leases lacked these clauses. Lessees under the independent leases were required to make initial payments at the start of each lease; under the restricted leases, lessees made terminal payments on return of the machines. The initial payments averaged one and one-half times the terminal payments; for some machines they were twice as big. Royalty rates under the independent leases were in some cases higher than those on the same machines under the restricted leases. In practice, the option presented by the existence of the independent leases was not important.

4. There were a variety of clauses limiting the lessees' freedom in purchasing supplies, and in using non-United machines in his factory; these will be detailed below.[34]

[31] See for example, US v. *Columbia Steel Co.*, 334 US 495, and US v. *Du Pont* (Cellophane) 118 Fed. Supp. 41. Both of these indicate the breadth of the concept of competition and the definition of the market now applied in Sherman Act cases. The latter, of course, is only a District Court opinion, which may yet be appealed.

[32] Act of October 15, 1914, c 323, 38 Stat 730, 63rd Congress, 2d Sess.

[33] 38 Stat 731, 15 U.S.C. #14.

[34] This description is drawn from the Complaint and United's Answer. See Record on Appeal, United Shoe Machinery *v.* United States, 258 US.

The principal lease clauses of which the government complained were:

1. Prohibitive clause (restricted leases). Limits use to shoes on which a long list of basic operations have been performed only on United machines. (See footnote 36 for the machines to which this and other clauses apply.)

2. Exclusive-use clause. Requires exclusive use of United machines on work of given types.

3. Supplies clause. All supplies used in certain machines must be purchased from United.

4. Additional-machinery clause. Any requirements for additional machinery of certain types must be met by leasing United machinery.

5. Cancellation-of-all-leases clause. Any breach of any lease gives United right to cancel all leases; failure of United to exercise right in any particular instance not a waiver.

6. Factory-output clause. Royalty payable on all machine operations of specified types in lessee's factory, whether performed on United or other machines.

7. Patent-insole-restriction clause. United's patented insole (Economy insole) be reinforced only on United machines; shoes embodying this insole may be sewn only on United welting and outsole sewing machines.

8. Discriminatory-royalties clause. For certain machines, royalties are higher when used on shoes which have been made in part on competitive lasting, welting, outsole stitching, or metallic fastening machines.

9. Full-capacity clause. Required the use of United leased machines to full capacity whenever work was available on which they could be used.

10. Part-repairs-and-attachments clause. Required the purchase of repair parts and attachments exclusively from United. Required repair and service of machines exclusively by United.

11. Removal-of-unnecessary-machinery clause. Permitted United to order return of leased machines in excess of those required by lessee for volume of output he is producing.[35,36]

The Government argued that the effect of these clauses was to restrict the shoe manufacturer to the exclusive use of United machines and United supplies, operating in the context of United's

[35] The descriptions of clauses (1)–(8) are drawn from pp. 14 ff. of the United States *Brief* on reargument before the Supreme Court, Record on Appeal, loc. cit. The descriptions of (9)–(10) are in the opinion of the District Court on United's motion to dismiss, 234 Fed. Rep. 130 at 131. The Exhibits to the Complaint show examples of all the lease clauses here discussed.

[36] The various restrictive clauses apply to different machines. The *Brief* for United States on reargument, gives the following list of machines to which the various clauses

dominant position in shoe machinery. The District Court found substantially for the Government, ruling that clauses (1) to (8) above violated the Clayton Act. The Court found the last three clauses unobjectionable: (9) and (11) were necessary protections to United's revenue under a royalty system of payment; (10) was a reasonable protection of the functional efficiency of United's machines. The court also declared specifically that neither the leasing system in itself, nor the 17-year term of the lease was objectionable under the Act.[37] On appeal by United, the Supreme Court upheld the findings and the decree of the District Court.[38]

After the Supreme Court opinion, United met with representatives of the National Shoe Manufacturers Association, and conferred with them at length on the form and terms of new leases. In November 1922, leases of substantially the form prevalent during the period covered by the present case were adopted.[39] These leases will be dis-

---

apply, classified by machine type or department. Each classification has a separate lease form.

Clause	(1)	(2)	(3)	(4)	(5)	(6)	(7)	(8)
Department or type								
1. Eyeletting	x		x		x	x		
2. Buttonholing			x					
3. Lacing	x	x	x		x	x		
4. General dept.	x		x		x	x		
5. McKay sewing	x		x		x	x		
6. Clicking	x	x	x		x	x		x
7. Metallic	x		x	x	x	x		o
8. Goodyear	x	x	x	o	x	x		
9. Heeling	x	x	x	o	x	x		o
10. Lasting	x	x	x		x	x		
11. Pegging	x	x	x		x	x		
12. Pulling-over	x	x	x	o	x	x		
13. Gem insole	x		x		x	x	x	
14. Economy insole	x	x	x		x	x		
15. Insole tacking	x		x					
16. Loose nailing	x							

x indicates clause appears in all leases of machines of department or type.

o indicates clause appears in leases of some machine types of department but not all.

Note that the use of clause 5 in combination with clause 1 in effect applies other clauses to machines to which they do not directly apply.

[37] 264 Fed. Rep. 138.

[38] 258 US 451. The decision was 7 to 1, McKenna dissenting and Brandeis abstaining. The leases had been drafted originally by Brandeis.

[39] See Defendant's Requests for Findings of Fact, pp. 91–92, in the District Court trial of the present case.

cussed in detail below; here it suffices to say that they differed from the earlier ones in having a shorter term, in dropping all exclusive-use or restrictive-use clauses (such as (1), (2), (3), (7), and (8) above), in offering each machine separately rather than in groups of auxiliaries attached to principal machines, and in charging for supplies separately from machine charges.

THE ANTI-TRUST LAWS AND ECONOMIC ANALYSIS— A BRIEF STATEMENT OF THE VIEWPOINT OF THE PRESENT STUDY

The analysis of the present record in this study does not follow the organization of the Complaint. Rather, it utilizes two economic categories as organizing principles: market power and market performance; and it applies these to the two important markets (or sets of markets) in which United operates: shoe machinery and shoe factory supplies. For each market, the extent of United's market power and its bases are examined, and then economic characteristics of United's performance in the market are studied. Finally, measures for changing the structure of the markets are considered, and their probable impact on market performance forecast.

The economic concept of market power is the most convenient economic analogue to the legal concept of monopoly. In essence, it is the possession by a firm (or group of firms acting jointly) of the ability to behave over fairly long periods of time in a way different from the way a firm in the economist's model of a competitive market facing the same cost and demand conditions would be forced to behave by the pressures of competition. Market power is a matter of degree, not an absolute. Most—though not all—real firms in manufacturing industries possess some degree of market power, arising from imperfections in competition in nearly all real markets. Just as the lawyer is interested in finding not just monopoly, but illegal monopoly, the economist is interested in finding not just market power, but a substantial degree of market power. A substantial degree of market power rests on the existence of high barriers to the entry of the other firms into the market, whether they result from the activities of firms already in the market, or from the technical conditions of production and distribution, or both. In the last analysis, it is always the entry of other firms into the market which limits the power of existing sellers. Where substantial market power exists, the economist attempts to distinguish that which arises from the technical conditions of production or distribution, such as great economies of scale in manufacture, or localization of production combined with high transport costs, from that which arises because of the policy of firms in the market, e.g., the acquisition of competitors, or the use of exclusive-distribution agreements in situations in which distribution channels are limited.

A judgment on the degree of market power possessed by a firm or group of firms in a specific market usually involves three elements. First is the proper delimitation of the market. This involves a consideration of what set of near substitutes should be considered as the "product" traded in the market, and requires an inquiry into substitution both in production and in use of the items traded in the market. Second is an analysis of market structure. This is in effect an examination of the degree to which the market provides independent sellers and independent buyers, with relatively free access to each other, and gives each seller or buyer a wide choice of alternative customers or alternative suppliers as the case may be. The major elements of market structure are the number and relative shares of sellers and buyers, the nature of the products sold and the availability of substitutes therefor, the locational pattern of sellers and buyers, the minimum size of the efficient business unit on the selling side as determined by the techniques of production and distribution, the nature of the channels of distribution, the existence of patents, franchises, and other legal restraints on the entry of new producers, the existence and character of interfirm agreements. Third is an analysis of certain aspects of market performance. Market performance describes the actual behavior, in terms of certain economic criteria, of the firms in the market. These criteria for certain aspects of market performance are provided by the kinds of behavior which would be shown by a firm in the economists' model of a perfectly competitive market; the use of this standard thus merely repeats the standard on which the definition of market power is based. Competitive performance can be described in terms of price-cost relationships, the extent and nature of non-price competition, and the efficiency of resource use as indicated by the scale and utilization of facilities and the location of production.

Ideally, a judgment on market power could be made purely in terms of market structure. In practice, the ability of economists to

predict the performance of firms in the market from the structure of
the market is limited. So is their ability to draw conclusions on certain aspects of structure, such as the ease or difficulty of entry, on the
basis of purely structural data. Therefore, a judgment on market
power generally involves an examination of these efficiency aspects of
market performance as well as the facts of market structure.[40] The
rationale of using the competitive model as a basis for evaluating
these aspects of performance in order to form a judgment on the
existence of market power is twofold. First, only this model provides a definition of economic efficiency in an individualistic economy
with free consumer choice. Second, this model provides the back-
bone of the broader notion of "impersonal control by the market"
rather than control by powerful individuals in economic affairs.

There is, however, one very important aspect of performance for
which the competitive standard provides no useful basis of comparison, and the relation of which to market power is obscure: performance in research and development and the introduction of new cost-
reducing techniques and new goods. No hard and fast analytical
model which can serve as a standard of business performance in this
area has yet been provided by economists. All that is available is a
crude common-sense standard, resting on the comparison of actual
performance by the firms under study with performance which might
have occurred in other market situations, to the extent which this can
be predicted, and with performance which has been shown by firms
in other markets offering valid points of comparison. This standard
is filled with ambiguities, and its objectivity is low. Moreover, further
difficulties arise when the integration of performance measures under
this head with performance measures under the competitive standard
is attempted.[41] Fortunately, these difficulties need not be completely
resolved in order to apply economic analysis to anti-trust problems,
either in this case or in general.

As indicated above, the relevance of market performance to the

[40] Market power was defined on p. 16 above as the "ability" to behave over long
periods of time in a manner different from the behavior of firms in competitive market.
But since we depend on an examination of actual behavior for our conclusions as to
the existence of power, we cannot in fact detect "unexercised market power." Yet it is
conceivable that it could exist, although its existence would imply that firms pursued
other aims than profit maximization.

[41] See E. S. Mason, "The Current Status of the Monopoly Problem in the United
States," 62 *Harvard Law Review* 1265, for the best published discussion of these and
related problems.

n. This evaluation did not reflect dis-
ed witnesses, or lack of confidence in
ight not have been inappropriate), but
ce, in most cases, of statements of sub-
ve issue of the actual effects of the trans-

ttempted to maintain a sharp awareness
den of proof, and to distinguish between
e correct, but had not been proved, and
found as facts by a Court.
nited whose testimony is frequently cited

of the Board

Manager and Vice-President
neral Manager
neral Manager in charge of Sales (supplies)
sident in charge of Research
sident in charge of Manufacturing
Counsel (not an officer in the legal sense)

ployees are identified when their testimony is

kinds of documents cited can best be explained
al organization of United. Its machine business
operating departments, each corresponding to
s of machines, such as Cutting Die, Eyeletting,
ere is a Sales Department responsible for the dis-
ndise not sold directly by United's subsidiaries.
the General Manager. They operate in turn
ies, or field branches, scattered over the country,
y with the customers. Two important classes of
mmunications between branches and operating
oston, and the annual reports (AR's) which each
s to the General Manager. The Terms Committee,
President, the Vice-Presidents in charge of Research
ist is: Cutting Die, Eyeletting, Fitting Room, General, Littleway,
t Shoe, Goodyear, Lasting and Pulling-over, Heeling and Metallic.
12. The description of United's organization which follows is taken

legal judgments which courts must make under the anti-trust laws is indirect, and lies chiefly in the role evaluations of certain aspects of performance plays in judgments on market power. Whenever the facts of a market situation reveal a firm or firms possessing substantial market power arising in significant part from their policy, a legal finding of liability under the Sherman Act appears appropriate to the economist. (Here as elsewhere in this discussion, *per se* violations are excluded from the scope of the argument.) A determination of the existence of substantial market power must rest on analysis of performance as well as on market structure. The persistence of noncompetitive performance is the strongest evidence of the existence of market power. On the other hand, a market situation showing such structural features of market power as a high degree of output concentration in a single seller, but no deviations from competitive performance over long periods of time, would not warrant a finding of legal liability merely on a structural basis.

Note that the market power which justifies a finding of liability must arise from the policies of firms. If all market power is the result, say, of a very large minimum efficient size of production unit, then from an economic point of view there should be no liability, since there are no feasible—in the sense of economically worthwhile—alternative arrangements in the market which would lessen the power of the large firms.

This view of the relations between market power, market performance, and legal liability under the Sherman Act is not the only one possible. Some economists have advanced the view that an anti-trust trial (*per se* violations apart) should center on an analysis of all aspects of performance. If on balance, performance is "good," then there is no liability. Typically, such views give very heavy weight to progressiveness in technology and the introduction of new products, although they cannot be said to have articulated a clear standard for measuring progressiveness, or to have resolved the problems of compatibility between tests of progressiveness and other performance tests.[42] In the framework here presented, overall measures of performance are unnecessary, and "good marks" on some aspects of performance do not cancel "bad marks" on others, or on market structure tests. Rather, once a conclusion on liability is reached on the

[42] See, for example, Clare Griffin, *An Economic Approach to Anti-Trust Policy*, American Enterprise Association, 1951.

basis outlined above, the performance record, good and bad, is considered in framing the remedy. On the one hand, particularly poor
aspects of performance, e.g., price discrimination, or coercive practices, may become the object of injunctive remedies. On the other,
measures aimed at reorganizing the structure of the market, or plac-
ing future restrictions on the conduct of defendants must be considered in the light of their probable impact on the favorable aspects
of defendants' performance, as well as their probable success in
reducing the market power of these firms in the future. In other
words, remedial measures must be designed to make a net improvement in the whole market situation. Therefore, they must be scrutinized closely to see that the gains they make possible in one direction
are not counter-balanced by losses in another. It is chiefly in this
connection that evidence on efficiency in production and on progressiveness and similar topics becomes relevant.

The foregoing sketch of the relations between the economic categories of the market analysis and the standards of liability for offenses
involving monopoly, monopolization, and the like under the Sherman
Act is presented from a purely economic point of view. It thus avoids
discussion of some important jurisprudential problems. The question
of whether the standard of liability sketched has the degree of definiteness and predictability from the point of view of potential
defendants as to constitute what is usually called law and given to
courts to enforce is left without discussion. It might be argued that
the standard involves a degree of legislative discretion so wide as to
make its enforcement more appropriate for an administrative commission than for a court; if so, then a judge may be reluctant to use
such a standard. These questions are here ignored, as outside the
bounds of competence of an economist.

The raw material of the analysis presented below is the evidence
which constitutes the record of the case. A word on the canons of
evidentiary interpretation used in dealing with this record is in order.
The most outstanding characteristic of the record is its huge bulk.
The transcript of the oral testimony occupies some 12,000 pages; the
documents submitted in evidence number some 5000, many of which
are multi-volume tabulations and lists. One person cannot read all
of this in detail, even in two years, and the writer makes no such
claim. He has read the whole of the oral testimony at least once,
and many parts of it several times. He has looked at all the docu-

weight the writer gave to the
belief in the veracity of Unit
their candor (although this m
rested simply on the irreleva
jective intent to the substanti
actions.

In every case, the writer
of which party bore the bur
conclusions which might h
conclusions which could be

The major officers of U
are:

Winslow   Chairman
Brown   President
Wogan   General
Walker   Asst. Ge
Howard   Asst. Ger
Roberts   Vice-Pre
Palmer   Vice-Pr
Ashley   Patent

Other officers and em
cited.

The most importan
in terms of the inter
is conducted by ten
some functional clas
etc.[43] In addition, th
tribution of merch
All these report t
through the agen
which deal direct
documents are c
departments in I
department mak
consisting of the

[43] The complete
Rubber Shoe, Ceme
See GTB Part I, p.
from pp. 9–19.

si
ha
an
prir

Tl
great
throug
many
United
prepared
mony of
has accord
testimony
cers. Whene
of a global c
of some sort,
many matters,
individual tran
such matters co
from United's re
was not clear tha
material on these
these cases United
tion consisted of a
purpose, and result o
the oral testimony of
documents led to infe
writer relied on the do
ments of intent and pu

and Manufacturing, the General Manager, and the three assistant General Managers passes on machine lease terms. Terms Committee (TC) memoranda are addressed to the Committee by its secretary, and marshal information prepared by the Research Division that is considered relevant in pricing machines. Such memoranda typically contain estimates of research cost, manufacturing costs, probable demand (termed "estimated machine field"), and recommended lease terms. The Program Committee is a committee of the Research Department, which coördinates and plans research. Program Committee reports frequently survey possible markets for new machines and past revenue and cost data on existing machines. Outside Machine Installation Reports (OMIR's) are made by servicemen and other field men on the appearance of machines of competitive suppliers in shoe factories. These are the most frequently recurring United internal memoranda; others are identified when cited.[44]

This essay is an attempt to view an anti-trust record from the perspective of economic analysis as they are understood by the writer. While it would be plainly wrong to ignore the individual and subjective elements in the application of economic techniques to the record of the case, they can easily be exaggerated. With respect to the purely descriptive parts of the analysis, it does not seem too much to claim that the conclusions here set forth would command a wide measure of agreement among professionally competent economists experienced in the analysis of market structures and behavior. Where there was disagreement, it would probably reflect differences in the interpretation of the evidence, or the fallibility of the writer in collating and comparing all the evidence in the record on a given point, rather than fundamental differences in the use of the analytic tools here employed. Of course, the evaluation of the overall situation reflected in the conclusions on liability, and even more the proposals

[44] This discussion can be completed by indicating the method of referring to the record. All references are to the complete record as it is filed with the Clerk, Federal District Court of Massachusetts. Throughout, "United" is used to refer to the corporation and its subsidiaries collectively, unless the context indicates otherwise. References to the oral testimony are indicated by "Tr" followed by the page number in the stenographic transcript and the name of the witness. United's exhibits bear the designation S (for Shoe) and the Government's, G; followed by an identifying number. For Government exhibits both the G-number and the location in the Trial Brief, if printed, are given. These are indicated by Roman numerals for the 17 volumes of Part III of the Trial Brief, followed by page numbers for each volume. The brief proper, Part I, is referred to as "GTB Part I."

for altering the market structure by way of remedy, can make no such strong claim to objectivity. They depend much more on the particular framework within which the writer views anti-trust policy, which has been sketched briefly above—a framework for which general professional acceptance cannot be claimed. But though the application of other policy standards could lead to other judgments at this level, the picture of the working of the shoe-machinery and shoe-factory supply markets set forth may fairly be considered necessary to any broader conclusions.

Part One

The Shoe Machinery
Market

II. United's
Market Position

1. CHARACTER OF THE MARKET

The shoe machinery market in the United States consists of a relatively small number of machinery manufacturers leasing and selling machinery to a relatively large number of shoe manufacturers. The most important machines, and the great majority of machines are leased. It is without dispute that USMC has in some sense a dominant position on the supply side of the market; a detailed discussion of this position occupies the next section of this study. As of 1947, there were some 1650 shoe factories in the United States, operated by some 1460 firms.[1] The typical shoe factory is small,[2] but a few of the enterprises in the field are very large and one or two are of the same order of size as USMC.

The market has not been a rapidly growing one, compared to the markets for, say, consumers' durable good. The number of factories was about 1200 in 1915, 1550 in 1927 and about 1650 in 1947.[3] Shoe production increased more rapidly than the number of factories: from some 265 million pairs per year in 1915 to 367 million pairs per year in 1927 and 485 million pairs in 1947. Peak production so far was 529 million pairs in 1946.[4] The increase in productivity of shoe factories has been such, however, that the increased output has led to no increase in the *number* of machines needed to produce it—at least so far as figures relating to United are representative of the whole market. (See the following section in which it is argued that

[1] S-89.   [2] S-91, 92.   [3] S-92.   [4] S-87.

they are.) The number of USMC leased machines outstanding was in 1947 no higher than in 1917 and less than the peak figure for 1923: some 98,000 of all kinds for the latest of these years and about 101,000 for the earliest. Excluding clicking machines—a relatively simple machine leased in great and increasing numbers—machines on lease declined from some 90,000 after World War I to about 82,000 in 1947.[5] While these figures are for leased machines only and do not take account of those which are sold, the error introduced in this way is unimportant. This is true qualitatively, in that machines which are offered for sale are relatively simple ones which play a minor or auxiliary role in the shoe making process[6]—with the exception of a few nearly obsolete machines such as the McKay Sewer S, the last one of which was shipped in 1931. It is also true quantitatively: of the 342 machine types offered by United, only 42 are offered for sale and not for lease; and 122 are offered on optional sale or lease terms,[7] in which types nearly two-thirds of the numbers shipped have, in the past, been leased rather than sold.[8] Further, the sale of machines accounts for a very small part of United's machinery business income—about 2 per cent.[9]

The discussion so far has run in terms of "shoe machinery" in general, with only a hint of the wide variety of particular machines involved. Shoes are now manufactured by at least ten different major methods—distinguished by the method of attaching the bottom to the upper—and several of the methods are further divided into subcategories depending on the method of lasting the upper to the insole. Each construction requires the use of more or less machinery specially adapted to it. Moreover, within each process there is a great variety of sizes and styles, not all of which are turned out on the same machines. Thus, shoe machinery includes a wide range of different types of machines, some of which perform parallel functions, some sequential functions, in relation to others. Indeed, a pair of machines which are complementary in a particular manufacturing process may be competitive, considered in relation to alternative processes. If United made every variety of machine useful in a shoe factory, there would be no problem of defining the market for shoe machinery in the sense of what kinds of machines were considered "shoe machinery," in spite of the complexity in the relations among

[5] S-94.   [6] EX. B, C, D of Answer and testimony of Roberts, *passim*.
[7] S-322.   [8] S-243, summary.   [9] G-295, VI, 25; G-294, I, 18.

individual machine types. But United does not do so, the most important exceptions being dry-thread sewing machines used for stitching together the pieces of leather or fabric which compose the shoe upper, and some machines in the finishing, treeing, and packing departments of shoe factories.[10]

None the less, reasonable criteria for delimiting the market can be found, without an examination in detail of all possible complementary and competitive relations among all types of machinery found in shoe factories. The class of machines which can be reasonably selected from all these types and labeled "shoe machinery" is that class which shares two important characteristics: the use of these machines is unique to the manufacture of shoes, and the design and construction of these machines involve the application of a detailed knowledge of the art of shoemaking. The complexities of this art, and the difficulty of acquiring knowledge of it and embodying it in workable machinery have been detailed at great length in the oral testimony of United's witnesses.[11]

These criteria certainly lead to the exclusion of dry-thread sewing machines from the class of shoe-machinery. This exclusion is further justified by two other facts. First, it appears that the major manufacturers of dry-thread sewing machines—Singer Sewing Machine Co., and Union Special Machine Co.—do not now manufacture any machines which fall into the category of shoe machinery defined above.[12] This taken together with the non-manufacture of dry-thread sewing machines by United suggests that these machines are not in the same market, especially since United has denied in its Answer[13] and also through testimony[14] that it has ever engaged in a division of the market with Singer. Further, the fact that United in its OMIR's—which appear to be fairly complete and which, on their face, were kept diligently and systematically, made no provision for reporting dry-thread sewing machines[15] buttresses the judgment that dry-thread sewing machines are not shoe machinery.[16]

[10] Answer, paras. 11–16, 18, 20.   [11] See esp. Roberts, *passim*.
[12] Government *Summary* of Depositions of Shoe Manufacturers, including appendix tables I and II.
[13] Para. 55.   [14] Tr. 6596, 6837.
[15] See GTB Part III, V, 1, 2 for various exhibits containing compilations of the OMIR.
[16] The question as to whether manufacturers of such machines are potentially manufacturers of shoe machines will be considered below, in the section on United's market power.

The same criteria, especially the second one, justify the exclusion of certain of the machines in the finishing, treeing, and packing departments. It is true that a rigid application of these criteria would also justify the exclusion of some items now included in the market: such "minor" pieces of equipment as toe steamers or spraying booths, for instance, or even, speaking strictly, a "major" machine such as the clicker. In general, however, this wide definition of the market leads, if anything, to an understatement of United's position in it, rather than an overstatement; since it is mostly in these "minor" items which are marginal to the classification that other producers are active. The important exception is the clicker; again it will be shown in the following section that there is little difference made to the final result whether this is included in or excluded from the class of "shoe machinery."

Further, given United's position in the market, there may be real content to a definition of the market as being coextensive with the types of machines which United offers, in spite of the apparent circularity of argument involved. Stated more explicitly, the argument would run as follows: the class of shoe machines offered by United form a market legitimately separated from that for other types of machinery found in shoe factories because United's dominant position in the manufacture and distribution of those types of machines makes the conditions of entry for new firms, and of operation for existing firms, markedly different from the respective conditions in the supply of the other types of machinery. This argument is best considered in the context of the detailed examination of United's position in the market.

A digression might be added in respect to the burden of proof in the matter of market definition, and to what degree the parties have met it. It is clear, of course, that the initial burden of offering positive evidence as to the relevant market definition falls on the Government. The Government has attempted to meet this burden by the discussion in GTB, Part I, 19–25 and 112–136, and the evidence referred to and summarized therein. This discussion lacks clarity, and it treats the problem of market definition implicitly rather than explicitly. But even so, it appears that enough of an argument has been made that the defendant has to do more than point to the existence of other kinds of machinery in shoe factories to break down the Government's contentions as to the appropriate definition. In particular, a serious breach in the Government position would require that the defendant offer evidence either that machine types competitive to those described in the Government classification are produced by other manufacturers or that complementary machinery is produced by other producers who represent an important potential for producing competitive machinery. The defendant has offered no proof of either sort, and therefore the Government's view as to the relevant definition of the market should prevail.

The great number of machine types traded in the market are of widely varying importance, functionally, in terms of numbers and in terms of revenue.[17] United, in its business operations, classifies machines in terms of ten departments. The basis of this classification is technical: machines in the same class perform the same or a closely related group of functions—Pulling over, Lasting, Metallic, Heeling, Eyeletting, Rubber shoe, Cement shoe and Cutting die; or relate to the characteristic processes of a given shoe construction—Goodyear and Littleway; or are used at a particular stage of the manufacturing process—Fitting room. One department—General—is a miscellaneous class. The ten departments vary greatly in the number of machines they offer; 128 of the currently offered 342 machine types fall within the General department; four departments—Pulling over, Eyeletting, Rubber shoe and Cutting die—offer fewer than ten machines each.[18] The relative importance of the departments in revenue-producing terms varies just as widely and in quite a different way. It can be calculated[19] that the two most important departments in terms of lease revenue—Goodyear and Lasting—yield about 57 per cent of the total revenue from leased machines;[20] the four smallest departments in revenue terms—Rubber shoe, Eyelet, Littleway, and Metallic—produce only a little more than 7 per cent of total lease revenue from all machines.

The government presents a somewhat different system of classifying machine types. It divides all machines into "major" and "minor" machines.[21] Within the major group, machines are divided into 18 "fields," representing the major operations in making a shoe, with the parallel methods for attaching sole to upper in different shoe-

---

[17] In discussing this aspect of the market, United figures, rather than those of all sellers, are used chiefly for convenience. But, as will be shown below, the distortion arising from this approximation is in general small. [18] S-332.
[19] From G-4725 and G-4587. [20] Fiscal 1947. [21] GTB Part I, 20–21.

making processes as separate fields.[22] The minor machines are divided according to United's departmental classification and further subdivided according to function.[23] In general this classification appears justified: the major machines are those which perform important operations for which hand labor is a very poor substitute, which are out in large numbers, and have high aggregate and average revenue yields; they are the machines which United offers on unit-charge or rental and unit-charge basis; while a few are offered on optional sale or lease terms, none is offered on sale terms only.[24] Conversely, minor machines perform essentially auxiliary operations, for which, in many cases, hand labor offers active competition; they are used in relatively smaller numbers and yield much lower revenues per machine and in the aggregate; they are machines which United offers largely on optional sale or monthly rental terms or straight monthly rental terms; and all the machines offered on sale terms only (with the noted exception) are in this group.

Table 1 recapitulates the evidence for these assertions.

The classification of machines into "major" and "minor" has been attacked by the defendant;[25] but the foregoing evidence appears to justify the classification in general terms. The specific categorization of individual machines is another matter, however, and no case is made by the Government for its classification in detail. Thus, for example, the classification on the one hand of gearless sole cutters, which are offered on optional sale or lease terms, and yielded an average income of $300 per leased machine in 1947, as major machines, and on the other of Goodyear welt-butting and tacking machines, which are offered on unit charge and monthly rental, and brought in an average income of over $1000 in the same period, as minor machines, shows careless classification, at least. While no great reliance is placed on the details of classification in the following argument, it is convenient to speak broadly of major and minor machines, and the distinction appears to be justified.

The same wide variation noted above in the relative importance of different departments appears among the various major machinery

[22] GTB Part I, 22-25.
[23] GTB Part I, 112–114 and Part III, VII.
[24] Except the McKay Sewer, model S, which is essentially obsolete; cf. S-241.
[25] Answer, Paras. 11–16.

fields. The three most important fields in revenue terms—lasting, outsole stitching, and welt sewing—account for some 42 per cent of machine lease revenue; the next three fields in importance—pulling over, heel attaching, and clicking—account for another 17 per cent, making the total share for these six fields about 60 per cent. In contrast, machines in the six least important fields produce only about 3 per cent of total machine revenue. All major machines together produced 77 per cent of total machine revenue.[26]

TABLE 1
CURRENTLY OFFERED MACHINE TYPES (1947)*

	"Major" Machines	"Minor" Machines	
Monthly rental	9†	79	
Monthly rental and unit charge	39	46	
Unit charge only	4	2	
Lease only, total	52	127	
Optional sale or monthly rental	9	113	
Sale only	(1)‡	41	
Total types	61	281	
Total number of machines out§ (1,000)	54	61	Major—G-293 Minor—G-446 (II, 1)
Total machine lease revenue ($1,000)	17,153	5,099	G-4587

*Division by type of terms based on Answer, Ex. B, C, D, and S 332; Classification of "major" and "minor" machines on G-293 (I, 1 ff.).

†Includes 1 machine, Sole Sewer D, on which terms were withdrawn in Aug. 1947.

‡McKay Sewer S. This machine is essentially obsolete; the last one was shipped in 1931. See S-241.

§This total includes obsolete machines as well as the 342 machines currently offered. If anything, it is likely that the larger number of obsolete types, relatively, are included in the minor machine totals than the major machine totals. Cf. S-111.

[26] G-4587.

TABLE 2

USMC: Outstanding Machines 1 March 1947, Total Earnings
($1,000) in Fiscal 1947 and Per Cent Share of Total Machine
Lease Revenues, 18 Major Machine Fields and
Minor Machines

(Condensed from G-4587)

Field	Outstanding Machines*	Earnings	Relative Share of Earnings
Lasting	12,561	4,306	19.4
Outsole stitching	3,537	2,908	13.1
Welt sewing	1,470	2,222	10.0
Pulling over	3,145	1,369	6.2
Heel attaching	3,168	1,347	6.0
Clicking	16,346	1,258	5.7
Rough rounding	1,430	719	3.2
Outsole leveling	1,082	599	2.7
Cement sole attaching	870	577	2.6
Outsole laying	1,029	571	2.6
Inseam trimming	595	273	1.2
Loose nailing	1,224	260	1.2
Littleway lockstitch sole sewing	580	220	1.0
Eyeletting	2,296	145	0.6
Cutting press	3,319	104	0.5
Slugging	773	103	0.5
Fiber fastening	470	101	0.4
McKay chainstitch sole sewing	498	71	0.3
Total major machines	54,393	17,153	77.1
Total minor machines	61,394	5,099	22.9
All machines	115,787	22,252	100.0

*Including estimated outstanding sale machines as well as leased machines.

Examination of the relative importance in terms of revenue of
individual machines shows the same result: the high share of all the
business in the market accounted for by a relatively few machines.
There were 61 major machine models offered in 1947; counting as
one three models of pulling-over machines[27] and two models of bed
lasters[28] for which revenue was not recorded separately reduces this

[27] C, D, E.   [28] 6, 7.

number to 58 "models." One of these was offered on sale terms only—
the McKay Sewer S; subtracting this leaves 57 models offered on lease
or optional terms.[29] Twenty-five of these models each earned more
than $100,000 in revenue in 1947, and accounted in aggregate for
71 per cent of the total gross revenue from machinery leases. Four
models—the outsole rapid lockstitch machine, the Goodyear welt
sewer K, Rex pulling-over machine[30] and the bed-lasting machine[31]
—each earned over $1 million in 1947, and their total revenue was
35 per cent of total lease machine revenue. Eight machines—staple
side laster B, Goodyear universal rounder and channeler, McKay heel
loaded and attacher, heel seat laster D, Goodyear automatic sole
leveler, heel seat laster E, cement sole attacher, and wood heel nailer—
earned between $500,000 and $1,000,000 revenue; their aggregate
revenue was 23 per cent of total machine earnings. Thus the 12
largest revenue producers in 1947 accounted for nearly 60 per cent
of the total revenue from all leased machinery.[32]

The characterization of the market so far has run in terms of the
total stock of machines on lease, or the annual revenue yielded by this
stock. It is equally necessary to consider the annual flow of machines
into and out of the stock. In a sales market, of course, the annual
flow out of the existing stock would be the scrapping of worn out
and obsolete machinery; in addition, of course, there might be some
"recycling" of machines out of and back into the stock via a second-
hand market. In a lease market, the revenue figures relate to the total
stock, not to new additions; and new machines can be studied only
in terms of shipments in units. Old machines are returned to the
lessor, rather than scrapped by their users. The term of the lease is
typically ten years; given a stable total stock, annual flow and annual
returns might be expected to be about equal, and to amount to about
10 per cent of the total stock. As a first approximation, this would
serve to describe the actual situation in the market.

Considered in more detail, of course, there have been substantial
variations in this picture, as new machine types have made old ones
obsolete, and as the relative importance of different shoe constructions has changed over time.[33] For all leased machines, the 20-year

[29] Nine on optional terms, 48 on lease only.   [30] Models C, D, E.
[31] Models 6 and 7.   [32] Computed from G-294, I, 18 ff.
[33] See S-242, Tabulation of machines leased and returned, by models, 1920–50; and
S-88 and 93, showing changes in relative importance of various shoe constructions over
time.

TABLE 3
UNITED'S MOST IMPORTANT REVENUE-PRODUCING MACHINES,
FISCAL 1947*

Machine	Rank	Revenue, 1947f $1,000
Outsole rapid lockstitch	1	2,908
Welt sewer K	2	2,222
Rex pulling over (C and D combined)	3	1,369
Bed lasting (Nos. 6 and 7 combined)	4	1,197
Subtotal 1–4		7,696
Staple side lasting B	5	818
Universal rounding and channeling	6	720
McKay heel loading and attaching (includes very small revenue from a few Lightning nailers)	7	638
Heel seat lasting D	8	591
Goodyear automatic sole leveling	9	587
Heel seat lasting E	10	583
Cement sole attaching	11	577
Wood heel nailing	12	516
Subtotal 8–12		5,030
Goodyear improved sole laying	13	418
Goodyear inseam trimming	14	273
CHM McKay side laster	15	263
Loose nailing	16	260
Clicking C	17	259
Staple side lasting C	18	256
USMC Sole stitching	19	220
Toe lasting	20	205
Wood heel attaching	21	176
USMC Sole laying	22	143
Stitchdown thread lasting	23	104
Universal slugging	24	103
Fiber fastening	25	101
Subtotal 13–25		2,781
Total 1–25		15,507
Total machine lease revenue		21,752

*Computed from G-294, I, 18 ff.

period showed a moderate expansion, with total shipments exceeding total returns by some 11 per cent. Of the eleven United machine departments, four—eyeletting, metallic, heeling, and Goodyear—showed slight net declines over the period in outstanding machines; four showed small or moderate increases—Littleway, fitting room, lasting, and pulling over; and three showed fairly substantial increases—cutting die, general, and cement shoe.[34]

The large variety of machine types, and the small number of machines outstanding of many of these, mean typically that a year's shipments include a wide variety of types and rather small numbers of each type. And this is indeed the case, except that there are a few models for which annual shipments are substantial in number. The accompanying table, compiled from S-269, which shows the 1950 domestic shipments of unit charge machines illustrates the situation.

Number of Machines Shipped		*Number of Models*
Fewer than 25		48
25 and fewer than 50		13
50 and fewer than 100		11
100 and fewer than 200		9
200 and over		3
Total number of machines shipped	4888	
Total number of models	84	

The mean number of one model shipped was thus about 58; the modal and median numbers shipped were both less than 25. One model, the clicker C, accounted for 1411 shipments, more than one-third the total. The two other models of which 200 or more were shipped were the outsole rapid lockstitcher O, and the Rex pulling-over C, with 395 and 223 machines shipped respectively. The dozen models of which more than 100 were shipped, including the three above, accounted for about two-thirds of all shipments.

A similar picture, over a wider field, is presented by S-182 which shows expected domestic requirements of each machine model for calendar 1951. Shipments[35] were expected to total 11,355. Of these 1200 were to have been clickers. Only the clicker C was to have been shipped in 1000 or more units. Three models—the outsole rapid

[34] S-242. [35] Requirements.

lockstitcher O, Goodyear inseamer B, and the rapid folder J—were
to have been shipped in from 250 to 500 units. Thirty models were
to have shipments of 100 to 250 units. These thirty-four models,
roughly 10 per cent of the total number of models offered—were thus
expected to account for about 60 per cent of all machine shipments.

The tabulation of shipments of domestic shoe machinery from
Beverly over the period 1920–1947[36] offers a basis for a similar analysis based on sustained shipments over a period of years. This tabulation covers 701 machine models. Altogether some 273 thousand
machines of these models were shipped in the 28-year period. There
were among the 700 models only 29 for which average shipments
per year exceeded 100 for 10 consecutive years sometime during the
period. Aggregate shipments of these 29 machines during the whole
period totaled some 114 thousand machines, or 42 per cent of all
machines shipped. The clicker C showed a period of 10 consecutive
years in which average shipments exceeded 500. In fact, except for
one year during World War II, shipments were never smaller than
350; in six years they were between 300 and 600; in nine years between
600 and 1000; and greater than 1000 in twelve years. Aggregate shipments of the clicker C were about 25,000, or nearly 10 per cent of all
machines shipped. Of the 28 other machines with sustained periods
of relatively large volume, 16 were major machines and 12 minor.
The majors included: bed lasters 6 and 7, CHM McKay side laster,
staple side lasters B and C, McKay heel loader and attacher, Alpha
wood heeler, Ensign lacer, eyeletter B, outsole rapid lockstitcher O,
welt sewer K, automatic sole leveler D, staple fastener D, universal
slugger, Rex pulling over C and D.

In very broad terms, therefore, the shoe machinery market (as
represented by United's business) can fairly be characterized as one
in which, although a very wide and changing variety of machine
types are offered, a relatively small number of widely used and important machines account for the great bulk of the transactions.

Shoe machinery is, of course, a capital good. It might be expected,
therefore, that the shoe machinery market would show sharp cyclical
fluctuations. Perhaps because of the effects of leasing, fluctuations in
fact are not very great. In terms of relative changes from 1929 to
1931—the lowest of the depression years in the shoe machinery
market—the drop in shoe production was 16 per cent, in United

[36] S-241.

machine shipments 29 per cent, and in machinery income 15 per cent.[37]

2. UNITED'S SHARE OF THE MACHINERY MARKET

Any attempt to define United's position in the U. S. shoe machinery market quantitatively in terms of a single figure representing its share of the market is filled with difficulties; none the less it is not impossible, and a figure—a broad approximation to be sure—with a significant content can be calculated. This assertion is not self-evident, and a discussion of the conceptual problems of defining market share in the shoe machinery market seems an appropriate prelude to the examination of the evidence in the record on which such a calculation must rest.

The first problem raised by any measurement of market share is that of marking the boundaries of the whole market; this has already been treated to some extent above, and another aspect of the same problem, the competition between machinery and hand labor, will be considered in what follows. The bulk of the business in shoe machinery is done on a lease basis; this raises the question of what constitutes the appropriate dimension of the market to be measured: annual shipments of machinery, the total stock of outstanding machinery, or the annual flow of services from the existing stock of machinery? In an ordinary sales market, annual shipments are the "natural" measure of market share; in a lease market such as the present one, either the outstanding stock of machines or the annual flow of services from this stock is a more appropriate measure. The choice between the two presents issues of convenience as important as those of principle, but one important consideration weighs in favor of the stock measure. It incorporates a time dimension and corresponds to something like an average of the flow measure over a period of years determined by the average turnover period of the stock. Since the average share of the market over a period of years is more significant than the figure for any particular year, a figure based on the stock as of one time is in this respect superior to a flow figure for a single year in a situation, such as the present one, in which the annual turnover is relatively small compared to the total stock of machines outstanding.

---

[37] Computed from S-87, S-241, and S-246, respectively. For the latter, fiscal 1930 and 1932 were used instead of calendar 1929 and 1931.

Ideally, in measuring United market share, it would be desirable to divide up the whole machinery market into submarkets in such a way that all the machines in each submarket were substitutes for each other, and each submarket contained a group of machines which, as a group, was complementary to the groups contained in every other submarket. Then some average of the share in each submarket could be taken as the measure of the share in the aggregate market. As was pointed out above, the variety of shoe constructions and the varying relations of machines in terms of different constructions make this impossible. Thus, for example, the pulling-over machine and the welt sewer are complementary machines in making Goodyear welt shoes. But in relation to a shift in shoe constructions from welts to cements they become substitute machines in that the demand for pulling-over machines relative to the demand for welt sewers will increase with such a shift. Strictly speaking, therefore, a measure of aggregate market share can be defined only with reference to some given distribution of outputs among various shoe constructions. The use of the outstanding stock of machines rather than the annual flow of services as the basis of measurement minimizes the practical effects of this difficulty; as long as the variations in relative importance of several constructions fall within what can be met by varying the flow of services from existing machines, these variations need not affect the measurement of the existing share of the market of a given seller. The potentiality of such variations does, of course, limit the presumptive future validity of any aggregative measure of market share used independently of a measurement of its components.

Measurements of market share in either stock or flow dimensions present the issue of an appropriate choice of units: should the measure be in "physical" or in money units? Physical units for a stock measure would be numbers of machines of the various types outstanding; for a flow measure, the number of pairs of shoes processed on the various types of machines. Physical units of stock possess the advantage of concreteness and definiteness of record. Number of pairs of shoes processed, the flow unit, while perfectly clear conceptually, presents certain difficulties of measurement because of the complications presented by the varying relations among the several machine types. These difficulties make it hard to get meaningful figures.[38] Further-

[38] See S-432, a USMC attempt to make estimates of the general character, and examination thereon, TR. 13,379–88 (direct) and 13,390–96 (cross), Roberts.

more, there would be no reliable records for other than unit-charge machines. With either basis of measurement the problem of combining share measurements for each separate machine type into an aggregate measurement for the whole market presents serious conceptual difficulties. Either the "machine" or the "process" as a unit is essentially arbitrary; the statement that a 50 per cent share in a market of 10,000 welt sewers plus a 10 per cent share in a market of 10,000 staple side lasters is equal to an average share of 30 per cent in the whole market has no particular meaning. Nor would more clarity be achieved if "pairs of shoes sewn" and "pairs of shoes lasted" were substituted for "welt sewers" and "staple side lasters" in the foregoing. There is no meaningful sense in which one welt sewer equals one side laster, or one sewing operation equals one lasting operation.

The use of money units—value of stock of machines or annual revenue flow—instead of physical units avoids the arbitrariness inherent in the kind of averaging considered above. Moreover, the use of money units helps deal with the problem presented by the competition of hand labor and in part with that presented by the competition of homemade machines. No enumeration of machines can take account of the former, and the difficulties of handling the process concept in this respect would also be great. On the latter problem, accurate information is not available. With a measurement of market share in value units the hand labor problem falls into its appropriate place, and the difficulties in recording homemade machinery are seen in their true proportion. A machine is valuable essentially in so far as it saves hand labor; the more closely the machine is competitive with hand labor the less it is worth— a machine which saved no labor would be worth nothing. Thus the measurement of market share in value terms represents appropriately the contribution of different kinds of machines relative to hand labor. It is true, of course, that if all machines were very closely competitive with hand labor, the significance of any given large market share would be dubious. Though the discussion of this point falls appropriately into the following rather than the present section, it can clearly be asserted that this qualification is of no relevance to the situation under examination. Most hand-made machines are essentially of simple types,[39] and the machines with which they compete are of relatively small importance in value terms. There-

[39] See G-293, I, 3 ff. and G-446, II, 2 ff.

fore, the undoubted difficulties of tracing accurately such machines are of little significance in estimating aggregate market share.

The use of money units presents problems of its own in spite of the important advantages of these over physical units. With respect to a stock measurement the appropriate money measure would be the value of outstanding machinery. In the market as it exists, however, it is not clear what figure would represent this value for any machine type: "insurance value" as set forth in the lease and "Beverly cost" as figured for pricing purposes are the available value measures, and neither seems appropriate to the purpose. The insurance value figure is arbitrary; Beverly cost is not a total cost figure since it does not include general overheads, and of course even a cost figure would, unless defined to include profits, fail as an appropriate economic value measure. With respect to a flow measurement very full figures are available in the shape of revenues from leased machines. Given a market in which competition, or a workable approximation thereto, ruled, share of total revenues would provide a good measure of aggregate market share. Or put differently, revenue figures would be appropriate weights for combining the various market shares in different processes, free of the arbitrariness of averaging shares based on physical flow measures directly. But, as will be argued further below, such approximately competitive conditions do not exist in the shoe machinery market. In particular two kinds of departures from competitive pricing can affect a measure of aggregate market share based on machine revenues. First, the existence of market power which enables one seller to sell the services of his machines at a higher markup over cost than another will lead to an over-statement of the market share of the seller with great market power. Evidence on USMC's general level of profits in the machine business suggests that this factor may not be of great importance, but the existence of the machine servicing "bundle" makes this more an educated guess than a documented conclusion.[40] Since no separate figures on USMC's investment in the machinery as opposed to the supplies business is available in the record, even this guess is open to doubt. The second possible departure is again one on which exact statements are not possible. If market power leads to widespread price discrimination and in particular to higher markups in the sale of machine services for machines in which there is little competition and lower markups

[40] See S-335, S-412.

in the case of machines in which there is more competition, then a measure of aggregate market share based on machine revenues will overstate the share of the discriminating seller. As will be shown below, substantial discrimination of this kind clearly does exist in United's pricing structure, and thus an estimate of market share based on machine revenues will tend to overstate United's position.

The calculation of value measures of United's share in the shoe machinery market in stock and flow terms requires, for the former figures on the total value of machinery in the hands of shoe manufacturers and the part of this total represented by United machines and, for the latter, figures on the total value of current machine services per year and the part of this total represented by the services of United's machines. The data in the record do not permit the direct calculation of either of these share estimates. Estimates of United's share of the total machines in shoe factories, by machine types, and figures on annual revenues yielded to United by machine types are available; but appropriate value figures for valuing the stock of machines or process figures (or other figures) on which estimates of United's share of total value of current services could be based are both lacking.[41] The best estimate of aggregate market share than can be made on the basis of data in the record is a weighted average constructed by combining United's share of the number of machines in each field or department, weighted by the relative importance of each field or department as a source of machine revenue.

This estimate has one minor limitation which deserves mention before examination of its general character. Although sales machines are included in the count of outstanding machinery, they are not represented in the basic revenue figures from which the weights are derived—United's income from leased machinery. While the total of sale revenues is small,[42] the sales are concentrated in a few departments, especially the general and fitting room departments.[43] This omission, by understating the revenue importance of these two departments, leads to an underweighting of these two departments in the computation of the aggregate market share. Since United's share of the market in the machine types offered in these two departments is less than the average in all departments, this results in an overstatement of the aggregate share. The magnitude of this overstatement is very small, however, since machine sales revenues are

[41] See discussion above, pp. 39–40.   [42] See p. 28, above.   [43] S-243, summary.

about 2 per cent of total lease revenues; at most a difference of 1 per cent in the aggregate market share would result from this error.[44]

The general shortcoming of the method of computing aggregate market share which will be used is the essentially hybrid character of the result—it is neither an estimate of United's share of the value of the outstanding stock of machines nor an estimate of United's share of the value of current services provided by these machines, but something between them. Only if these two shares were the same would the measure presented in Table 4 below have a well-defined meaning. Since there may well be systematic differences in both the rate of utilization of United and non-United machines and in the price of the current flow of services relative to the value of the machines for the two categories, arising from the lack of effective competition in the market in general and from certain aspects of the leasing system, including the full capacity clauses in particular, it is unlikely that the measure of aggregate market share based on stock would be the same as that based on flow, if both could be computed. But the very fact that a choice of methods might be necessary, that the outcomes of the two methods might be different, and that no strong presumption founded in logic favors one rather than the other method, argues the virtues of a method yielding a number which is essentially an average of what the two conceptually clear-cut definitions would yield, could the computations be made.

In spite of the host of problems discussed above, the estimate of aggregate market share finally given below is lacking neither in meaning nor in applicability to the problem of judging United's position in the market. While the estimates are imprecise, the degree of precision is perfectly adequate to the judgment to be formed. Indeed, the only reason for the otherwise over-elaborate discussion of the problems of measurement in the preceding pages is to show that such difficulties as exist do not make a useful approximation to the ideally desired measurement impossible.

The basic data entering into the computation of aggregate market share are shown in Table 4 below. The classification of machines into major and minor and the division of these classifications into fields and departments follows the lines of the Government's presentation.[45] Column [2], the share of total USMC revenue from

---

[44] See Table 4 below, p. 46.
[45] An analysis of the merits of this classification appears above, pp. 31–33.

leased machines, was computed from G-4725 and G-4587; major
machine revenue in each field was arrived at directly by summing
revenues for the individual machines identified in G-293;[46] minor
machine revenue for each department was total revenue for that department less major machine revenue. This computation involved
an adjustment of the fiscal 1949 figures in G-4725 and the fiscal 1947
figures in G-4587 to the same basis, which was done by assuming
that the percentage distribution of revenue among the departments
for major and minor machines considered separately was the same
in both years. Column [3] merely repeats the figures presented by
the Government in its summary volume and contained in G-293
and G-446.[47] These figures, of course, are based on the tabulation of
the OMIR's found in United's files. Column [4] shows the proportion
of United to total machines found in the sample of 45 shoe manufacturers canvassed in the summer of 1949 in accordance with the
Court's directions.[48] This sample covered, according to the Government definition of the market, 1744 major and 3750 minor machines,
a total of 5495 machines. The computations of the Government excluded dry-thread sewing machines and general industrial machinery
not specialized to shoe manufacture, exclusions which have already
been justified. It also excluded machines in dead storage, presumably
consistently with United's treatment of such machines in its OMIR
reports,[49] and 618 machines, 314 of United manufacture, which
represent fields in which United does not now produce machines.
These exclusions seem reasonable, although in the first case an argument might be made that non-United machines (which they must
be, except for sale machines) in dead storage represent at least potential competition and deserve to be included in a stock, if not in a
current flow measurement of the market. But the numbers involved
in both cases are small, and the machines are almost all unimportant
in character and represent fields of little revenue importance. In any
event the quantitative difference in the outcome as far as the aggregate measure of market share goes which would result from the inclusion of these two categories of machines would be very small,
some 3 percentage points decrease in the aggregate at most.

[46] I, 1 ff.   [47] I, 1 and II, 1, respectively.
[48] See Government *Summary* of Depositions of Shoe Manufacturers, including appendix tables I and II.
[49] See G-293, footnotes pages 2 of I; but this point is certainly not explicit.

TABLE 4

1947 USMC SHARE OF THE SHOE MACHINERY MARKET

(1) Field or Department	(2) %USMC Total Machine Revenue	(3) (4) Share of Market (% of Outstanding Machines)		(5) (6) Weight	
		GTB	Sample	GTB	Sample
(Major)					
Clicking	5.7	97	98	5.9	5.8
Eyeletting	0.6	81	80	0.7	0.8
Cutting Press	0.5	91	78	0.5	0.6
Pulling over	6.2	99	100	6.3	6.2
Lasting	19.5	94	96	20.7	20.3
Welt sewing	10.0	97	100	10.3	10.0
Inseam trimming	1.2	99	100	1.2	1.2
Outsole laying	2.6	91	95	2.9	2.7
Rough rounding	3.3	98	100	3.4	3.3
Outsole stitching	13.3	92	96	14.4	13.9
*Cement sole attaching	2.6	40	24	6.5	10.8
Littleway lockstitch	1.0	91	91	1.1	1.1
McKay chainstitch	0.3	88	85	0.3	0.4
Loose nailing	1.2	98	100	1.2	1.2
Outsole leveling	2.7	97	93	2.8	2.9
Fiber fastening	0.4	100	100	0.4	0.4
Heel attaching	6.1	93	95	6.6	6.4
Slugging	0.5	91	62	0.5	0.8
(Minor)					
†Cement shoe	2.4	63	41	3.8	5.9
Cutting die	1.3	89	83	1.5	1.6
Eyeletting	0.3	100	100	0.3	0.3
Fitting room	4.0	58	45	6.9	8.9
General	3.9	71	76	5.5	5.1
Goodyear	4.4	88	83	5.0	5.3
Heeling	1.4	83	84	1.7	1.7
Lasting	1.5	88	89	1.7	1.7
Littleway	0.4	94	97	0.4	0.4
Metallic	1.0	77	54	1.3	1.9
Pulling over	2.1	97	96	2.2	2.2
Rubber shoe	0.3	48	—	0.6	(0.6)

Weighted averages		*Major*	*Minor*	*All*
GTB		90.5	74.6	86.3
Sample		87.5	64.8	81.0
GTB, corrected Cement (†)		90.9	73.9	86.3
Sample, corrected Cement (*†)		92.3	68.3	85.4

*†Cement sole attaching and cement shoe shares and weights computed from USMC and Compo data: (see text discussion).

	(2)	(4)	(5, 6)
Cement sole attaching	2.6	42	6.2
Cement shoe	2.4	59	4.1

It should be noted here that one reason for following the lines of the Government offer in computing share of the market (although, to be sure, an essentially different weighting system is used here) is that United has made no direct counter-offer in the record. While it might be possible, by a tabulation of the lists of machines in the inventory of the sample shoe factories presented by United,[50] to produce an estimate representative in some sense of United's views, the labor required is great. Perhaps this omission on United's part reflects a conclusion by counsel that the Government has failed to make a case for its views of United's market share. This view, in accordance with the argument here presented, is believed to be incorrect in the sense that a meaningful aggregate share estimate can be made with the data in the record, although the computation method differs significantly in detail from that used by the Government.

The major points that appear from the tabulation are clear. United's share of the market is very large in nearly every major field and minor department: in only 2 of the 18 major fields and 4 of the 12 minor machine departments is United's share of outstanding machines smaller than 75 per cent, as shown either by the tabulation of OMIR's or the inventory of sample shoe factories. In 14 of the major fields and 3 of the 12 minor machine departments United's share was more than 90 per cent on both tabulations. United's market share is greater in the major than in the minor machines; the aggregate market share in the major fields exceeds that in minor machines by 16 percentage points according to the OMIR tabulations and by 23 percentage points according to the sample. The aggregate market share of United—the weighted average share for all machines is very high—86 per cent on the basis of OMIR figures, 81 per cent on the basis of the sample figures.

The differences between the sample results and those based on the OMIR's are much less striking than the agreement between them. The differences in aggregates are small; the difference on major machines as a group even smaller. In the 18 major machine fields, differences between OMIR and sample figures well within what would be expected by chance from sampling fluctuations occurred in 15 fields: the sample showing a higher figure in 10 of these cases, a lower one in four, and no difference in one. There are significant differences which might be expected to occur as a result of sampling

[50] S-407.

fluctuations by chance fewer than 1 in 20 times in the cases of the cutting press and cement shoe fields where sample share falls short of OMIR share by 13 and 16 percentage points respectively. There is a significant difference in the slugging field—where the sample share falls short of the OMIR share by 29 percentage points, a difference which would occur by chance fewer than 1 in 100 times. In the 12 minor machine classes deviations between sample and OMIR were within the range of chance sampling fluctuations in 10 of the classes: the sample share was the same as the OMIR share in one of these, exceeded it in 5, and fell short of it in 4. For two classes, cement shoe and metallic, large differences which would result from chance sampling fluctuations fewer than 1 in 100 times appeared. The sample share was 18 percentage points less in the first case and 23 less in the second than the OMIR share.

In view of the continuous effort of United to cast doubt on the reliability of OMIR information, and indeed to picture the whole reporting system as essentially casual,[51] a certain interest attaches to the question of whether the divergences indicated above indicate shortcomings in the sample or shortcomings in the OMIR's. No firm answer to the question can be provided, but two indicators of some value are available, one indirect and one direct. They both point the same way.

A comparison of the distribution of shoe production among the various constructions in the sample with that in the total universe[52] indicates that the sample diverged substantially from the true picture in this respect: cement shoes were greatly over-represented, Goodyear welts under-represented, and stitchdowns, Littleway lockstitch, and nailed, pegged, screwed, greatly under-represented. This divergence does not, of course, directly indicate that the sample figures on the relative proportions of United and non-United machines of different types were also unrepresentative but simply suggests that the sample may in general fail to represent the universe faithfully, either because of sampling fluctuations or because of bias in sampling (in the technical statistical sense).

A more direct check on the relative merits of the sample and OMIR tabulations of outstanding machines, in the shape of an

---

[51] See Tr. *passim.*

[52] Depositions 1A, for the sample; and S-88, 433 for universe figures for 1947 and 1950.

independent estimate of the number of Compo machines outstanding, is available with respect to cement shoe machinery, where Compo is United's major competitor. This area is one in which the divergence between OMIR and sample figures was greatest: 40 per cent as against 24 per cent for the major machines and 63 per cent against 41 per cent for the minor machines were the respective estimates of United's market share. By a comparison of USMC figures of various types of cement shoe equipment on lease[53] with similar figures offered by the officers of Compo in their testimony as Court's witnesses,[54] a computation of the relative proportions of USMC and Compo machines outstanding as of 1 March 1947 can be made. This computation involves certain approximations—the most important of which is the necessity of arriving at 1947 figures for outstanding Compo machines other than conveyors by interpolation between the 1945 and 1950 figures—so that the resulting figures are estimates rather than complete counts. The magnitude of the errors involved in the approximations is not significant, and the resulting figures can be confidently used. The relative United-Compo proportions of outstanding machines were: for major machines, 51 USMC to 49 Compo; for minor machines, 59 USMC to 41 Compo. To pass from these figures to estimates of United's share of the whole market requires estimates of the share of outstanding machines of other manufacture. For minor machines, this is small enough in both the OMIR and sample tabulations to be neglected safely. For major machines, the tabulation shows the share of others to be 18 per cent; the sample, 4 per cent. On the former basis, United's share of the total market in major machines is 42 per cent; on the latter, 49 per cent. Using the smaller of these figures and the 59 per cent figure for minor machines, it is clear that the OMIR tabulation presents a much more accurate picture of United's market share in cement shoe machinery than does the sample:

	OMIR	Sample	Direct Estimate
Major: cement sole attaching	42	24	42
Minor: cement shoe department	63	41	59

Substitution of these "corrected" share estimates for the OMIR and sample figures respectively leads to a decrease in the difference between the aggregate market share measures based on the two tabula-

[53] S-313.   [54] C-35 for conveyors and C-39 and C-31 for other machines.

tions.[55] Using the OMIR figures as the better of the two, on the basis of the independent estimate of the shares in cement shoe machinery, and substituting the "corrected" cement figures, the "best" estimate of United's aggregate market share (indicated by an asterisk in the Table) is 86 per cent for all machines, 91 per cent for major machines and 74 per cent for minor machines.

Now that the estimates of United's share of the machinery market in aggregate and in each of the separate sub-markets have been presented, a further word on the problems of measurement is in order. The construction of an estimate of United's aggregate market share, in terms of a single number, involved procedures open to doubt for dealing with two problems. The first was the problem of classification of machines into groups such that the machines within one group were substitutes and the groups were complementary. The second was the problem of combining the measures for the various groups. Both are essentially weighting problems; if it were feasible to compute separately United's share for each outstanding machine type, and a corresponding set of weights for combining these shares into an aggregate estimate, the two problems would merge into one—the problem of selecting an appropriate set of weights. It is well known that a weighted average of a large number of items is insensitive to changes in the weights over a fairly wide range. The more nearly all the items to be averaged have the same value the greater can changes in weights be without affecting the value of the weighted average. In the limit, of course, if all the items have the same value, a weighted average will have that value whatever the weights. Since many of the items making up the estimates of aggregate market share vary within a rather small range—21 of the 40 shares which enter into the average lie between 80 and 100 per cent[56]—errors in the weights, arising either from inappropriate classification of machine types or from deficiencies in the revenue figures, will affect the estimate of aggregate market share very little. In sum, greater confidence can be put in the aggregate measure than in the parts which constitute it.

3. MARKET SHARE AND MARKET POWER

That USMC occupies some 85 per cent of the shoe machinery market is not in itself evidence that USMC has, in any economic

---

[55] Cf. Table 4, p. 46 last two lines.   [56] Cf. Table 4, p. 46.

sense relevant to a Sherman Act case, a monopoly position in that market. At most it suggests the possibility; to test the possibility requires an examination of USMC's market power. Market power is the most useful (but not the only) term in economic language with which the legal term "monopoly" can be identified. It is in essence a measure of the extent to which a firm can in the long run depart from the kind of behavior in respect to price-cost relations, capacity-output relations, and demand-capacity relations which would prevail in a competitive market. Market power so defined varies continuously from the theoretical zero of the perfectly competitive market to the equally theoretical infinity of the complete monopolist who controls the total supply of everything. In more practical terms it can be said that the legal problem of judging when a monopoly exists corresponds to the economic problem of judging when the degree of market power which some firm (or group of firms) has in a particular market is great. There are few, if any, markets in which no seller is without some positive degree of market power; the problem in this as in any particular case is not to detect its existence, but to estimate its extent relative both to the situation in other markets and to the possibilities in the shoe machinery market under other institutional arrangements.

In probing the extent of United's market power, two methods may be used. First, evidence of the actual exercise of such power in United's past behavior in the market may be examined. Second, the possible obstacles to such behavior should United attempt it can be considered. The first test is what economists have called the performance, the second the structural, standard of competition.[57] At this point it is appropriate to state summarily that on at least one major point an examination of United's behavior in the past shows results which could flow only from great market power: namely, continuing wide variations in the relations between prices and costs of different machines. This point, as well as other aspects of United's market performance, will be considered in detail in Ch. IV below. The rest of this section deals with the structural aspect of United's position in the market.

Monopoly power (market power) has been defined by Mr. Justice Burton, speaking for the Court, in the Tobacco Case, as the power

[57] See E. S. Mason, 62 *Harvard Law Review* 1265; also Ch. I, above, pp. 16–19.

to exclude.[58] This is indeed the essence of the matter, for without the ability to prevent competitors from entering the field a firm with a large share of the market must either behave in such a way as not to attract competitors—which means that its actions are hedged about by the threat of potential competition or indeed suffer the entry of competitors who will diminish its market share. Thus a general view of the character of United's position in the market can be achieved by considering it in relation to competitors, both actual and potential.

In both relations, the fact that United's market share is substantially greater in major than in minor machines—91 per cent as against 74 per cent—is important. The major machines are those which by and large are more essential in making shoes, are not easily substituted for either by hand labor or homemade devices, and constitute in terms of economic importance the bulk of the machinery market.[59] The demands in terms of knowledge of the shoemaking art and of manufacturing technique which a would-be competitor in major machinery must meet are high; the area not already occupied by United small. It seems fair to conclude that no competitor not prepared to compete in major machinery can offer a significant competitive threat to United or act as a substantial check on United's power in the market; yet it is in this area that United's position is strongest.

Existing rivals in the machinery market do not appear to constitute a significant limitation on United's power. The sample of shoe factories revealed 22 known competitors, the largest of which was Compo, with 3.4 per cent of the total number of major machines in the sample inventory and the second largest, International Shoe Machinery Corp., with 0.6 per cent of the total number of major machines.[60] The tabulation of OMIR's shows a similar picture.[61] Sixteen competitors in major machinery are shown, Compo and International again appear as first and second, respectively, with market shares of about 2 per cent and 0.5 per cent. As significant as their small market shares is the fact that these and other competitors offered only a few lines of machinery. International competes in only two major fields, lasting and outsole laying and in both only with respect to one relatively minor shoe construction—platform shoes. While Compo offers machines in four fields, its competition is substantial in only two—cement sole attaching and pre-welt lasting; in

---

[58] 328 U.S. 781.   [59] Cf. above pp. 31–33.
[60] Government *Summary* of Depositions.   [61] GTB Part I, 130–2.

UNITED'S MARKET POSITION 53

the other two, wood heel attaching and platform cover lasting, it is only a minor factor in the market.[62] Hamlin has outstanding machines in seven major fields, but its total position in the market is such as to rob this fact of any significance. Further, United's competitors are not only restricted to small shares of small parts of the market, they are in overall terms very small companies relative to United. Thus, for example, Compo, the largest and most important of United's competitors, has some 3.5 million dollars' total assets compared with United's 100 million and disposes of some $300-400 thousands of net earnings after taxes per year compared with United's $9-10 millions.[63] Neither Compo nor any other of United's competitors in the major machinery fields are large enterprises whose shoe machinery activities are only a small part of their total businesses. They are essentially shoe machinery or machinery-and-supplies businesses, and their small scale in the machine field indicates their overall smallness and weakness relative to United. Compo, and *a fortiori* other competitors, do not have the financial resources to operate on anything like the scale of United, in terms of the range of machinery offered, the scope of service and the general scale of business.

United's market share in the minor machinery field is lower than in major machinery, but even here United far outranks its nearest rivals. The sample of shoe manufacturers shows minor machines produced by 83 known manufacturers. The largest of these are Boston Machine Works, which accounted for nearly 6 per cent of the total number of machines, and Compo with about 5.5 per cent of the total number. United accounted for 64 per cent of the total number.[64] Only eight of the rival sellers, including the two mentioned above, were represented in the sample by more than 1 per cent of the total number of machines. Thus, even in the minor machine field, which alone could not support a serious competitive threat to United, there appears a similar picture: United dominant and a number of small and weak rivals in no way of comparable economic magnitude.

The consideration of potential rather than actual competition reveals no immediate threat of entry. Formidable barriers protect

---

[60] Government *Summary* of Depositions.   [63] C-1, 2, 4–6 and S-244, 245.
[64] Government *Summary* of Depositions of Shoe Manufacturers. The GTB gives no summary of competitive sellers of minor shoe machinery comparable to that for competitors in major machines; thus, for convenience, the sample figures are used.

United's existing position. The leasing system, the full line of machines, United's patent structure, United's resources, accomplishments and accumulated know-how in research all contribute significantly to United's market power. These and other factors are treated in the following section on the origins and sources of United's market power. Here the lack of potential competition in a narrower sense can be indicated—the fact that there are no manufacturers of close substitutes for shoe machinery other than the rivals already considered above. On the side of substitution in use the proposition is obvious: volumes of testimony have shown with a wealth of detail how specially and narrowly adapted to its range of tasks each shoe machine must be, how unlike each specific machine is from other shoe machines, not to speak of its distance (in a functional and technical sense) from the machinery used in other industries. But it is also true that there are no close substitutes in production, no manufacturers of other machinery who can easily and quickly turn to the production of shoe machinery, should it appear profitable to do so. This point was brought out in the testimony of Wilson Palmer, Vice-President in charge of manufacturing. Palmer testified that the manufacturing technique required in making a wide line of shoe machines is in general more advanced than that required in other branches of the machinery industry; the problems presented by the diversity and complexity of parts in each machine are unusual. In addition to this general opinion testimony, he offered an account of the difficulties United encountered in trying to contract out manufacture of certain machines in the immediate postwar period in order to meet the backlog of demand. Even though United provided drawings, in some cases parts, and the benefit of its own knowledge, United had difficulty in finding manufacturers who could produce what was required and who could meet United's cost figures.[65] These difficulties reflected, to be sure, the uncertainties on the part of the suppliers as to whether orders would be repeated and whether tooling and training investments were worthwhile, given the special circumstances of United's orders. But these uncertainties are not of a different order than a would-be new entrant might face as he first contemplated manufacture and distribution of a line of shoe machinery. Thus it appears fair to conclude that the threat of potential com-

[65] See esp. Tr. 6622–3, 6658–69, 6729–47, 6916–38, and 9296–8 and S-288, 291, and 292.

petition by the entry of other manufacturers into the shoe machinery market, irrespective of the height of other than technical barriers to such entry, does not represent a strong limit on United's market power, at least in the short run.

The significance of United's market share as an indicator of market power is further enhanced by the static character of the market.[66] This means that a new entrant to succeed must actually take away business from existing sellers; to succeed on any large scale he must take away business from United. This applies with the same force to the expansion of United's existing rivals. Since aggregate demand is nearly constant, an increased sale by one seller means a decreased sale by another. This proposition must be qualified in one respect: the fact that there is a substantial turnover of manufacturers, with new entrants (gross, not net) running as high as 10–12 per cent per year, does mean that there are new customers even though there is not new business.[67] Thus, while a new seller would face the active retaliation of rivals whose total business he was trying to diminish, he would not face the additional difficulty of having to break the tie of each individual customer to existing sellers in order to make any sales. Such ties would of course confront him in the great majority of cases, ties considerably strengthened by the leasing system, but they would not encompass the whole market.

On the basis of United's position in relation to those of its rivals and what might be called the "natural" barriers facing potential competition, even without an examination of the special features of United's marketing methods, pricing system and patent structure which might increase the barriers to entry, it can be concluded that United's high market share is an indicator of a substantial degree of market power.

[66] See above, pp. 27–28.   [67] Cf. S-445.

III. The Origins
and Present Bases of
United's Market Power

1. THE CREATION OF UNITED—THE
ORIGINAL MERGER

The single most important basis of United's present market position is the merger which created it (or, more exactly, its predecessor, United Shoe Machinery Corporation of New Jersey) and the acquisitions immediately following the original merger. The joining of the Goodyear and Consolidated companies took place in 1899, and the annexation in the newly formed United Shoe Machinery Company (successor to the New Jersey Company) to this combination of McKay Shoe Machinery Company and the Eppler Welt Machine Company followed soon after. Within the twelve-year period from the original merger to the filing of the complaint in the original Sherman Act case, United made 57 acquisitions, ranging from patent applications to a $6 million acquisition of a shoe manufacturer producing his own machinery. This history is discussed in some detail in the District Court opinion in the original Sherman Act case,[1] and in summary form in the Supreme Court opinions,[2] especially Mr. Justice Clarke's dissent. In this case, of course, the legality of the original merger and subsequent acquisitions was upheld, chiefly on two grounds: first, than the merged and acquired companies produced non-competing machines; second, the monopoly granted under the patent laws in respect of each individual machine. Comment on these two arguments, in the light of the present interpretation of the

---

[1] 222 Fed. Rep. 349.   [2] 247 U.S. 32.

Sherman Act and indeed in the light of simple logic, is unnecessary; it is sufficient to refer to the dissenting opinions of Mr. Justice Clarke and Mr. Justice Day in the Supreme Court. It is useful to note here that Mr. Justice Clarke found that the record showed clearly that the combination did achieve a monopoly, and that specifically, in respect to machines for lasting, welt sewing, attaching soles to lasted uppers and heeling, the combination had a "complete ascendancy" over the industry. Even today machines for performing these functions account for more than half of United's total machine revenue[3] and their relative importance was undoubtedly greater at the time of the merger, since many of the machines now in use had not appeared at that time.

If the original merger and acquisitions immediately following it were the sole source of United's present market power, a difficult legal problem would arise as to the appropriateness of the present proceeding against United, and one defense of United to the charge is indeed that the earlier Sherman Act suit had decided the major issues of the present case.[4] The defendant's market power may be no greater today than it was in 1911; there is little evidence in the present record on which to base a judgment on this point, except perhaps Mr. Wogan's testimony that United's market share has not declined since 1920, in the face of figures showing a decline in the number of outstanding United machines in relation to the number of shoe factories.[5] Even so, however, the problem remains as to whether in the absence of efforts to maintain it, the defendant's market power would not have been eroded away in the course of time. The means by which United's position in the market is maintained then becomes a relevant subject for examination even if the original decision,— clearly erroneous—that the mergers and asquisitions which created United's position were not in violation of the Act, is considered binding on the Trial Court.

2. SUBSEQUENT ACQUISITIONS

Acquisitions by United may be viewed in two ways. They can be considered in terms of their magnitude and character in relation to all other sources of growth of business and of new devices and ideas,

---

[3] See Table 4 above, p. 46.   [4] Third Defense, Answer, pp. 64 ff.
[5] Tr. 9599–9601.

with a view toward a conclusion on the relative importance of what might be called "external" and "internal" sources of growth. Or they can be examined as evidences of "intent to monopolize" by United, in the sense of deliberate reaching out to prevent the continuance of any probably successful effort at independent competition. The Government has discussed acquisitions chiefly in the second fashion; United's defense has necessarily run in similar terms. In view of United's position in the machinery market throughout the whole period under consideration (roughly 1915–1947), a question may be raised as to the usefulness of an examination into United's motives in search of a specific intent to monopolize as distinguished from an intent to avoid patent litigation or an intent to continue to make available to shoe manufacturers services or machines when the non-United provider thereof is about to fail. Given United's position in the market, United automatically becomes the major, if not the only, possible purchaser of failing businesses seeking to liquidate or businesses seeking to liquidate for other reasons; of new ideas in the form of applications or patents whose originators are not sure of their ability to develop them alone; of the services of inventors with talents in the shoe machinery field; of a whole host of similar items for sale which are for sale in every line of business. There is no need to seek out United's "intent" in making such acquisitions; rather the question should be asked, who else would be a likely purchaser? From this point of view, United's acquisitions are rather the consequence than the cause of its market power: if the latter is legitimate, the former are innocent; if market power in itself is condemned, then the acquisitions flowing from it are to be condemned too, whatever the "motives" of United's officers in making them.

Moreover, an acquisition viewed objectively makes the same contribution to the maintenance or increase of United's power whether the acquisition was made as a result of a "reaching-out" by United, or whether it was, so to speak, forced on United by an eager seller. Thus a judgment on the contribution of acquisitions to United's positions can be reached without consideration of intent. Nonetheless, such consideration is not without interest or irrelevant to judgment in the case. Since the acquisitions on their face cannot constitute evidence of intent, this must be sought in the practices surrounding particular acquisitions: in particular, evidence of oppressive practices, if it exists, might lead to the conclusion that United's acquisitions reflected a "specific intent" to monopolize. Examination of evidence bearing on United's intent in connection with acquisitions will be deferred to the general consideration of United's performance in the market; only the objective aspects of acquisitions will be considered here.

The Government, GTB, Part I, pp. 137–204, sets forth a list of 30 acquisitions in the period 1916–1937, inclusive. Three of these, numbers 13, 14, and 29, should be eliminated from consideration entirely. Number 13, the Standard Shoe Tying Machine Company, represents a case of United's agreeing to take over Standard's machines and parts on a consignment basis when the health of its chief officer failed.[6] This can hardly be termed an acquisition in any meaningful sense. Number 14, the Naumkeag Buffing Company, again does not represent an acquisition in a meaningful sense, since the company had previously been owned by Winslow since 1907. With respect to number 29, the Wilson Process Company, the evidence is inconclusive; what there is seems to show that Wilson was acquired by Littleway before United acquired the latter.[7]

The remaining 27 cases divide up as follows: 2 are acquisitions of inventors' services only; 3 are acquisitions of services plus patents and applications but without any going business; 11 are acquisitions of patents and patent applications without any going business; and 11 are acquisitions of going businesses, involving patents, patent applications, or experimental machines. For the 25 acquisitions in which there was some outlay on assets, total USMC expenditures were about $3.5 million in the whole 22-year period.[8] Since many of the acquisitions centered around patents and new ideas, this figure might appropriately be compared with research expenditures over the same period, which were at least $25 million.[9] The comparison suggests that acquisitions were quantitatively not very important; the absolute figure, standing alone, does likewise.

One alone of the 27 acquisitions stands out as being significant both in relation to United's general competitive position and in terms of its absolute size: the acquisition of the A. E. Little patents and pro-

[6] See Answer; no contrary evidence offered by the Government.
[7] G-1245-7, III, 160–1.
[8] Exact figures are not available for every transaction but this estimate is close enough.
[9] $15.2 million for 1928–1937 (S-401, 421); and an allowance of an average of $700,000 per year for 1916–1927, which seems conservative.

cesses.[10] This acquisition took place in two steps: first the formation of a corporation, the Littleway Process Company, which was jointly owned by Little and United; and second, the purchase of Little's interest in this corporation by United. The first step occurred in 1924 and Little received $1,000,000 from United for 49 per cent of the stock of the new corporation, all of whose stock Little had received in exchange for all rights in his patents and applications. In 1927 United bought the remaining 51 per cent of the stock from Little for another $1.4 million. Thus this single acquisition accounted for about two-thirds of United's total outlays on acquisitions during the whole period. What was acquired was not a going business in shoe machinery, but patents, applications, machines and parts for a new process of staple side lasting and sole sewing which came to be called the Littleway process. United asserts that it had undertaken developments in the same direction prior to the issuance of Little's patents and that it was its own developments and not Little's which formed the basis of the commercial Littleway process.[11] Acceptance of this assertion and the defendant's view of the evidence does not lead to a denial of the competitive significance of the Littleway acquisition. Little was a potential competitor with a new process which was either workable or sufficiently close to being workable to be worth $2.4 million to United. Not only did he have a process, he had a going shoe business which could have supplied funds for its development; he evidently had experience and competence as a businessman, so that the probability that he would succeed in commercializing his inventions could not be considered negligible. The fact that United chose to commercialize its own rather than Little's developments does not prove that Little's could not have been commercialized or that, if commercialized, they could not have offered serious competition to the United-developed processes, if non-infringing development of the latter had occurred.

Beside the Littleway acquisition the others are small, but a few of them deserve notice. The total outlay for the three acquisitions of patents and developments acquired in connection with the service of their inventors[12] was something more than $53,000, with the outlay

---

[10] Number 4 on the Government list.

[11] Answer, para. 36 and Tr. pp. 6478–88. But see below, pp. 83–84, for evidence pointing in a somewhat different direction.

[12] GTB Part I, numbers 5, 20, 25.

in connection with the Krentler-Pym patents[13] unknown. The latest of these acquisitions, that from Kamborian and the Northern Machine Company, took place in 1935.

The 11 acquisitions involving going businesses were numbers 6, 9, 10, 11, 12, 19, 21, 23, 27, 28, and 30 in the list of GTB, Pt. I. More of them occurred in the twenties than in the thirties, but some appeared in the closing years of the period. One acquisition shows clearly United's position as the important market, regardless of any desire on the part of United to reach out to acquire: the purchase of the machinery business of Brauer and Wagner (30) on the initiative of B & W, after a prior decision on their part to go out of the machinery business and devote themselves to shoe manufacturing.[14] A partial figure for the expenditures involved in all these acquisitions is again small—$182,000 with no figures for 19, and 10 and 27 probably not complete. At least four cases involved going businesses which were clearly competitive with United: Monfils, 1937, $2,000 (6); Hero, 1920, $73,000 (21); Edwards, 1931, $8,000 plus royalties (27); and Advance, 1927, 50,000 (28). The sum of the outlays on these five represents a good part of the total, $133,000 out of $182,000. Of the other cases, only two did not involve potential competition: Lockett (19) and Pope-Rand (23).

The ten acquisitions in addition to Littleway that involved only patents and patent rights include two other examples of acquisitions of some significance, although on a much smaller scale than the Little transaction. The first was the acquisition of the Henne-Preo patents on heel-seat-fitting machinery (17). United first secured a license on the patents in 1923 for $14,000 plus half the royalties received on the machines; in 1930 there was a complete assignment of the patents to United for $125,000. This was a situation in which an outsider and potential competitor had a process which was recognized by United as superior to United's own machine, and United proceeded to acquire the patents moving, as indicated above, in two steps.[15] The second significant patent acquisition was that from the Beacon Folding Machine Company (16). Licenses under Beacon's patents on binding, folding, and skiving machines were taken out in 1925 for $80,000. The license agreement contained a convenant that United could purchase the patents and other assets in the field on the death of Beacon's chief officer, T. C. Rowen. This occurred in

[13] Number 20.   [14] G-1248, III, 161 ff.   [15] G-1146, 7, 8, III, 52–90.

1929, whereupon United made the purchase for a total of $75,000, including the royalties paid between 1925 and 1929. Prior to the licensing agreement in 1925 there had been a history of patent interferences and mutual infringements between Beacon and United; the license agreement (actually a cross-licensing agreement) thus was a justifiable means of settling the patent problems. But was the covenant to acquire the whole business at Rowen's death a necessary part of such an agreement or an effort to forestall possible future competition?[16]

Three acquisitions in this group were the subject of extended discussion in the record: General (1), Reece (2), and Blake (3). Reece again represents an example of United's passive role as the logical market for a seller seeking to get out of the shoe machinery business.[17] The acquisition from Reece made in 1934 consisted entirely of patents and applications, to a total value of $55,000, an unimpressive sum. The problem of the "importance" of the patents considered apart from their value in the transaction—a knotty one—will receive some further examination below in the discussion of the significance of United's patent structure as a source of market power. The Blake acquisition of patents on so-called automatic machinery for $15,000 in 1932 was clearly unimportant. The testimony of Sampson, executor under the will of Hyams, who had financed Blake's experiments, shows clearly that the initiative was on the part of the seller (the Hyams Trust), and the sale was an attempt to salvage whatever was possible from the clearly unsatisfactory investment in the Blake experiment.[18] The point is further strengthened by S-217, a letter to Hyams from Morin, whom Hyams had hired to test the Blake machinery,[19] in which Morin says that the Blake system (an attempt at automatic machinery) was a failure: the machines were too slow, they did not function regularly, and the manufacture of shoes on them was not and could not be a commercial proposition.

There remains the acquisition of General Shoe Machinery Company, initiated in 1923 and consummated in 1927, an acquisition of patents, an experimental line of machinery, and some other assets. The total payments by United were $450,000: $300,000 for the patents paid in 1923, and $150,000 for other assets four years later. While there is some question of the importance of some of the patents

[16] G-1107–1129, III, 10–37.   [17] Tr. 8930–8999; testimony of Reece.
[18] Tr. 7705–45, esp. 7725–37.   [19] Cf. S-216.

acquired, which will be considered in the general discussion of patent acquisitions, the most important aspect of this acquisition turns on the question of intent and oppressive and deceptive practices, which will be discussed below, in the evaluation of United's performance.

The remaining five acquisitions of patents and applications were numbers 15, 18, 22, 24, and 26. Number 15, the acquisition of Gimson Shoe Machinery Corporation, was chiefly a foreign transaction and thus outside the scope of the case: British United acquired the whole Gimson business in a general line of shoe machinery; USMC acquired only the United States patents and applications. The four other items were insignificant: 18 (Union Lockstitch) and 22 (Keighley) together totaled $18,000; 24 (Thum) was the acquisition of several patents on wood heel machines for their "nuisance value"[20] and no information on the price paid is in evidence; 26 (Victor Shoe Machinery Co.) shows an even greater lack of information: the evidence[21] does not make clear what was acquired, when and for how much.

In summary, the record of acquisition is as follows: on major acquisition of patents and inventions, Littleway, of clear competitive significance and substantial size, made in two steps, 1924 and 1927; two minor acquisitions of patents not without importance competitively or insignificant in size, Henne and Beacon, made in 1923 and 1929 respectively; and a number of minor acquisitions which amounted to little either individually or in aggregate. The total contribution of all the acquisitions to the maintenance of United's market position was probably small, and most of that contribution was furnished by the Littleway process. If none of these acquisitions had occurred, the most that would have resulted in the way of change in the competitive situation may be sketched as follows: Little might have become a "major" competitor of the order of magnitude of Compo, but probably much smaller; some of the other acquired processes might have been successfully commercialized, e.g., Henne-Preo, and some of the acquired businesses may have continued, e.g., Hero Mfg. Co. (21) as minor competitors producing a small number of one or two machine types, such as now exist.[22] Thus it can fairly safely be asserted that acquisitions have had some but not a major effect in maintaining United's market power in the period since the original merger and the acquisitions immediately following it.

[20] G-1209, 10; III, 125-30.   [21] III, 141-160.   [22] Cf. above, pp. 52-53.

3. LEASING

Does United's system of marketing machinery by lease rather than by sale provide significant support to United's market power? Evidence bearing on this problem must be analyzed in the light of United's market position so that the initial question might more explicitly be put: does leasing, when carried on by a firm with United's dominant position in the market, contribute to the maintenance of that dominance?[23] Here, as in the previous section, only the effects of leasing on the operation of the market are considered, rather than United's "intent" in operating a leasing system or in including and enforcing (or not enforcing) particular clauses in its leases, all matters which will be examined under the head of United's performance in the market. This discussion of leasing does not take into account the major price terms of the lease—the rental or unit charge—and the effects of the pricing methods and the level of pricing on the market; but it does consider all the other significant aspects of leasing that bear on United's market power.

The first, and perhaps most important, aspect of the lease itself is its term. On its face the lease runs for ten years, subject to termination by United for breach of terms by the lessee. It can also be terminated because the lessee has, in United's judgment, more machinery than he needs in terms of his shoe output over the previous 12 months; and it terminates automatically if the lessee becomes bankrupt.[24] When the lease expires, if neither party calls for termination, it extends indefinitely, subject to cancellation by either party on 60 days' notice.[25] On expiration of the original lease, the lessee and United may sign a renewal lease on the same terms as the original one which, since 1939, has run for five years, and from 1922 to 1939 ran for 10 years.[26] The practice, however, differs considerably from what appears in the language of the lease, and it is the practice rather than the language which is primarily significant.

The actual duration of leases (including renewals) in the past is a disputed fact and one which is not clearly settled by the evidence

---

[23] Here and in the ensuing discussion the minor qualification made necessary by the fact that some machines are sold are omitted. It has already been indicated above, Ch. II, that with a few trivial exceptions only minor machines are sold and that most of these are offered by one department—the General department.

[24] Exhibit F, annex to Answer, Form A Lease, para. 12.

[25] Para. 13.   [26] Answer, para. 64.

in the record. The pertinent items are four; they cannot be said to conflict because they do not all refer to the same experience. First, a general statement by Brown, the president, on cross examination is that the average lease life of a machine is 10 years; the basis of the statement is unspecified studies made by the Corporation. In the context, the statement presumably refers to the current or immediately past situation, but the time reference is not explicit and therefore is open to doubt.[27] Second and third are two corporate documents offered by the Government. A memo. to the Terms Committee by its clerk, dated May 1938, speaks of the average lease life in 1934 as being 7.8 years for major machines and 9 years for all machines.[28] G-1530 [29] shows the number of machines of each department which have been out on lease for 15 years, 20 years, and 25 years as of 1 March 1948. The totals for all the departments are respectively 30 per cent, 16 per cent, and 8 per cent of total number of machines sold. Though the document is not clear on the point, the 30 per cent presumably includes the 16 per cent, which in turn includes the 7 per cent: i.e., the table shows the numbers of machines out 15 years of more, etc. The provenance of this document is not clear: there is no indication of its source on its face; Brown, when asked to identify it on cross examination as showing the results of a study by Lybrand, Ross Bros. and Montgomery, refused to do so and said it was a study prepared by "someone in our organization."[30] The total number of machines shown on it and the subtotals for some departments vary considerably from the total of "lease only" machines outstanding in shoe factories on 1 May 1947 shown in Ex. G, annex to the Answer; but the differences do not seem to be too great to be explicable in terms of: the lapse of time; the difference between "lease only" machines, and all machines out on lease, including optional terms machines; and the difference between machines on lease in shoe factories and all machines on lease, including those used in the outside trades. The final item is S-373, a tabulation showing the number of machines returned in the fiscal years 1930–32, 1934, 1937, and 1941 which had been shipped since the 10th preceding fiscal year and the total number returned in those years, as well as a distribution of the total number of returned machines by the number of years between the fiscal year of shipment and the

[27] Tr. 8545.   [28] G-470, III, 206. The memo. begins on p. 200.
[29] V. 280 ff.   [30] Tr. 8545-7.

fiscal year of return, for the same years. This tabulation shows that from about 40 to 50 per cent of the machines returned in these years had been shipped since the 10th preceding fiscal year, the figure varying unsystematically from year to year. Only a small proportion of the returns were made in the same fiscal year as the shipments; for the other 8 preceding fiscal years, the distribution varied somewhat unevenly but with some tendency for high numbers of returns of machines shipped in the second and fourth preceding fiscal years and low numbers of returns of machines shipped in the eighth preceding fiscal year. These figures in general are fairly consistent; the only explicit contradiction is between Brown's 10-year average of unspecified date and the 9-year average mentioned as current in 1934 in G-470, a small difference. The general picture these figures present is an average lease life of about 10 years, with a fairly substantial dispersion about the average; some 30 per cent of the machines remain out on lease for 15 years or longer; on the other hand, 20 to 25 per cent are returned in five or fewer years after shipment. The Government charge that the leases are in effect perpetual[31] is not supported by the evidence, unless it means no more than that in most cases the termination of one United lease marks the beginning of another, in which case this merely repeats in another form the fact of United's large share of the market.

Machines may be returned before the expiration of the lease for a variety of reasons, some of which have been indicated above. The situation arising in respect to two kinds of returns is of particular interest in the present discussion: the return of a machine for replacement by another United machine, and the return of a machine for replacement by a competitive machine. The first situation may arise because the shoe manufacturer is changing his product, or because he wishes to replace an old United model by a new United model. In either case, it is always United's policy to "accept" the return of the machine, i.e., cancel the lease, on payment of the deferred charges and the costs of replacing broken and missing parts and transporting the machine from the shoe factory to Beverly.[32] In the case of the replacement of a United machine by a competitive machine, the situation is different. United, on the face of the lease, need not "accept" the return of the machine at all, in which case the shoe manufacturer would continue to be liable under the terms of

[31] GTB Part I, p. 258.   [32] Tr. 10504–7, 10522–30. Testimony of Wogan.

the lease. In practice, return of the machine is accepted on payment of termination charges in addition to the charges above, that is, payments in settlement of the shoe manufacturer's liability under the unexpired portion of the lease.[33]

The factors entering into the determination of the settlement are not in the record; what is available is an exhibit showing the amounts actually paid in certain recent instances without, however, any comparison between these payments and the liabilities under the leases in all cases. S-442 shows the payments made in respect of the 299 leased machines returned before their leases had expired during the period 1 June 1948—21 May 1951 (after the commencement of the case) and replaced by competitive machines. In 229 of these cases termination payments to settle the unexpired portion of the lease were waived; no explanation of this waiver and no tabulation of the liabilities waived is shown. On the 70 machines where such payments were charged, they amounted to an average of $148 per machine and were charged as follows: for 34 rental machines, 25 per cent of the rentals for the unexpired period; for 5 unit charge and rental machines, 50 per cent of rentals; for 31 unit charge machines, 50 per cent of the minimums. In addition there were deferred payments due on these machines of some $22,000, of which about half was covered by credits in the right of deduction funds, leaving an average of some $150 per machine due in cash. Thus, exclusive of shipping charges and replacement of broken and missing parts, figures for which were not given in the exhibit, there was an average of some $300 per machine payable in cash on these 70 machines when they were returned. The 229 machines on which no termination charges were made fell into two groups. The first, consisting of 130 machines, had practically all their deferred charges covered by right of deduction fund accumulations, so that, exclusive of shipping and repair charges, unspecified, these were returned without any significant cash payment. The other 99 involved cash payments of about $80 per machine for 87 machines, which was about one-third the total liability for deferred payments on these machines; for the other 12, deferred payments were waived (no explanation given). These 12 had repair charges averaging about $40 per machine; repair charges for the other 87 were not shown, nor were shipping costs for any of them. It is difficult to put these fragmentary figures together, and it is far

[33] Tr. 10538–9. Testimony of Wogan.

from clear that they represent the typical experience of lessees in the period covered by the case. If these difficulties are overlooked, the guess may be hazarded that lessees returning machines to United before the expiry of their leases in order to replace them with competitive machines might, even if the machines are not in the early period of their lease-lives, face cash outlays of $100 to $350 (plus shipping costs) on the average; in particular cases, of course, the figures might be much higher or lower.

Both the length of the lease and the payments due on termination when a United machine is replaced by a competitive machine act as substantial deterrents to the selling prospects of actual and prospective competitors. The length of the lease means that a customer is "tied-up" for a substantial future period, on the average, with respect to any particular machine a competitor would like to offer him: the settlement terms indicate that the cost of "untying" to the customer may be substantial; the possibility that United might refuse the return of the machines, i.e., insist on payment in full of the liabilities under the unexpired portion of the lease, although unlikely in fact to occur, may be an additional deterrent of some force. These deterrents to replacing a United by a competitive machine are real and substantial and operate under the present system in which both United and most of its competitors lease. With these deterrents, a competitive machine can replace a United machine only if it is substantially better or substantially cheaper.

A more speculative attempt can be made to compare (1) the deterrent effects of these features of the leasing system on the ability of competitors to replace United by their own machines, with (2) the deterrent effects of the ownership of machines by the shoe manufacturers on the sale of machines to replace them which would operate under a sales system. A rationally calculating businessman, considering the acquisition of a new machine, should take no account of past payments for existing machinery, whether or not they have been amortized in an accounting sense. His only interest is in the relation between the acquisition cost of the new machine (its sales price minus the second-hand or scrap value of his old machine) and the operating savings (in increased output, higher quality, lower labor or maintenance costs, etc.) realized by replacing the old with the new machine. (He is also concerned with the probability that an even better new machine will appear next year; in the present context this may be ignored.) If this relation is favorable, the businessman will make the acquisition; if not, he will refuse it. If the manufacturer is considering the replacement of a United lease machine with a competitive sales machine, then his acquisition cost is the sales price of the new machine plus the cost of returning the old machine to United. If he is considering replacing a United machine with a competitive lease machine, then he must compare the relation of the lease costs of the new machine to its productivity with the same relation for the United machine, and take into account the costs of returning the old machine to United (in addition to any initial payments, etc., on the new machine) as the acquisition cost of the new lease. Thus the difference made by United's leasing system, as compared with a sales system, is that, under a sales system, payments in respect to old machines, already in the possession of the manufacturer, are bygones while under a lease system payments must be made in order to part company with the old as well as to acquire the new. Of course, everything depends on the actual values of the various charges in the two situations, which cannot easily be discussed in general terms. Something, however, can be said on this point. Since the various deferred payments and termination charges are not primarily for the purpose of producing income and do not in fact produce income,[34] it seems fair to say that the incidence of these payments involves something more than the payment over time under a lease system of the equivalent to what is paid in one lump under a sales system; and that thus the comparisons spoken of above will, other things equal, be in favor of the new machine more frequently under the sales system than under the leasing system.

All this is concerned with rational calculation. It may be argued that businessmen do not calculate rationally and that they are less willing to let bygones be bygones than economists tell them to be.[35] If so, however, the deterrent effect on competition of the leasing system may be even stronger than indicated above, since in an instinctive as opposed to a reasoned comparison, the present payment for the return of the old machine under a lease system in addition to the payment, spread-out or lump-sum, for the new machine, may weigh even more in relation to the cost represented by the present value of

[34] See Wogan's testimony, Tr. 10504–7, 10522–30 and S-246.
[35] See George Terborgh: *Dynamic Equipment Policy,* published for the Machinery and Allied Products Institute by McGraw-Hill, esp. ch. i, xiv, and xv.

services still embodied in the old machine to which no future cash outlay corresponds under a sales system, than reason indicates it should. The most that can safely be said here is that the psychological aspect of the comparison is arguable.

The next characteristic of the lease itself which has an impact on United's market power is the full-capacity clause. This provides, in substance, that each leased machine shall be used to its full capacity upon whatever work it is capable of performing which is being done in the lessee's factory.[36] Thus, this clause forbids on its face the non-use of a United machine and the use of a competitive machine to perform a task, even if the lessee makes the appropriate minimum payments on the United machine. The application of this clause in practice has been subject to challenge by the Government; consideration of the practice with respect to the question of coercive practices and threats will be deferred to a later section where the whole problem of United's "intent" will be examined. One aspect of United's practice should be noted at this point however: the full-capacity clause is waived for a "reasonable time" if a lessee wishes to try out a competitive machine.[37] This means specifically that the tryout as such is not a breach of the lease and that, when the United machine in question is a unit-charge machine, only the actually earned unit-charges (or, if applicable, the charge for use less than the minimum) are paid by the lessee, rather than the charges on work done by the competitive machine which could be claimed under the full-capacity clause.

The mere existence of the full-capacity clause acts as a deterrent to the marketing of machines competing with United machines. It means in effect that the shoe manufacturer must choose finally between the use of United and the use of competitive machines whenever the alternative is presented; he cannot, except during the exempted reasonable trial period, use them both in such as way as to shift the work between them. He can, of course, use United and competitive machines together in the same operation provided that he always allows variations in the load to be absorbed by the competitive machines, using the United machines to full capacity for the work available, an arrangement which makes the use of the competitive machine more expensive than the use of the United machine and thus discourages the manufacturer from using the competitive machine altogether.

[36] Annex to Answer, Ex. F, para. 5.   [37] Tr. 10516–18. Testimony of Wogan.

Certain practices followed by United in operating its leasing system, though not appearing in the lease, are formalized through "management letters" which constitute unilateral modifications of the terms of the lease until further notice.[38] The practices in connection with the administration of the right-of-deduction fund, which do not appear in the lease but only in management letters, operate to some degree to tie the various United machines together in spite of the fact that the leases as such are made on each machine individually. This fund is built up by crediting to each lessee a certain per cent of the total rentals and royalties, including charges for use less than the minimum, he pays to United. The plan was originally established in 1922 with a 2 per cent credit,[39] raised to 3 per cent in 1937,[40] and to 4 per cent in 1949.[41] The credit can be used against deferred payments due when machines are returned and, since fiscal 1940, against charges due on use less than minimum.[42] S-270-1 show the relative importance of the right-of-deduction fund credits and cash payments in meeting deferred payments in the period 1925–1950: the share of the payments made in cash declines from about 50 per cent in the early years of the plan to 25 per cent or less in recent years; in 1950 the cash payments were only 10 per cent of the payments due to which the fund applied. S-334 gives similar information for charges on account of minimums, showing that the credits from the right-of-deduction fund accounted for more than 50 per cent of the charges due in the period 1949–1950 (fiscal years). Credits to the fund are pooled for all machines in any one factory.[43] A factory which is equipped chiefly with United machines will in general be able to cover all or nearly all of its deferred payments arising from "normal" returns by the credits in the fund. An operator with a single United machine might not be in the same position; neither would a factory which suddenly returned all its machines. Further, unit-charge machines probably contribute more, and rental machines less, to the pool than required to cover their own deferred payments.[44] From this it can be concluded that the right-of-deduction fund, as it operates, furnishes an incentive of moderate strength for the shoe manufacturer to use many United machines and to continue as a United customer.

---

[38] S-125, 6, 7, 8, 266, 8 are examples in the record.   [39] S-114.   [40] S-266.
[41] S-128.   [42] S-334.   [43] S-128.
[44] Tr. 8579–82, colloquy between Brown and Court.

An additional feature of the fund's operation is worthy of note: the fact that credits are available only to firms who have not violated their leases in any way and who are not in arrears on any payments. While in the abstract it seems clearly reasonable that United should condition the credits, which are unilateral gifts on its part, not part of the lease contract, on the observance of the contracts, in practice such an arrangement has an additional tying effect in that it tends to chip away at the distinctness of the separate lease contracts, since it conditions the benefits on the lessee's performance under all its contracts to United.

Another practice under the leasing system which is not specified in the lease and indeed which United does not formalize in any writing is the provision of service on leased machinery without separate charge. This system dates back to the early history of the industry,[45] and much testimony in various parts of the record is devoted to discussing its merits. This discussion is not relevant to the inquiry of the present section but will be examined below. However, the provision of service as part of the "bundle" in the lease does have some effect in making the entry of potential competitors somewhat more difficult than it might be under other arrangements. This is germane to the question of the bases of United's market power. The first result of the tie-in of machine and service is that a would-be entrant into the market must be prepared to offer service as well as machines, thus increasing by so much the problems of entry. In particular, the offer of machines for sale might be affected since the shoe manufacturers are in general not accustomed to providing their own service, and the position of United in the market means that independent enterprises for servicing shoe machinery have no worthwhile market in which to operate. United's control over service also contributes to a slight extent to the concentration of machine-building know-how in United's hands. Independent servicing organizations, or service departments within the shoe factories might, if they existed, provide a pool of technical experience and trained personnel on which a would-be entrant into the market, as well as United's existing competitors, could draw and thus provide a conduit for the spread of technical knowledge to other producers than United. There are, of course, other more important bases for United's strong position in technique but the control of service adds something further.

---

[45] Tr. 8511–12, Brown.

Finally, the leasing system initiated by United and followed by its more important competitors[46] means that there is no substantial second-hand market in most types of shoe machinery, especially in major machines. The lack of such a market reinforces United's market power to a substantial degree in two ways. First, second-hand machines themselves represent an important kind of competition to new machines: the existence of a second-hand market would set sharp limits to the price and other policies of producers of new machines. Second, the general availability of second-hand machines would facilitate greatly the copying of such existing United machines as are not protected by patents, or elements of them not so protected, which is at present to a large extent prevented by the difficulties a competitor, actual or potential, has in getting a lease machine into a shop where it can be torn down and its workings studied. Not only is copying of existing machines—where it would be legal to do so—prevented but, more important, modifications and improvements, except such as are sold to United, are also prevented in the same way. This, in connection with the lack of service experience in others than United, mentioned above, contributes to United's technical leadership. These propositions are obvious and need no elaboration.

To be sure, there are important counter-arguments against the existence of competition from second-hand machinery; consideration of these is more appropriate to a discussion of remedies and accordingly will be deferred.[47] What is clear and relevant to the present question is that the absence of a second-hand machinery market, which is a consequence of the leasing system, is a substantial support to United's market dominance and is probably second in importance in its effect on United's market power only to the duration of the lease and the circumstances surrounding terminations of leases among all the aspects of the leasing system which affect that power.

4. UNITED'S FULL LINE OF SHOE MACHINERY

The fact that United markets nearly every kind of machine which falls within the classification of "shoe machinery" established above[48]

---

[46] Tr. 9752–3, Mason, Compo, stating in effect that Compo leases because United does; Tr. 13564, 585, Kamborian on leasing practices of International Shoe.

[47] At the appropriate point it will be argued that the alleged "undesirable" consequences of a second-hand market are not in fact undesirable from a social viewpoint. See below, Ch. VIII.

[48] Pp. 28–30.

has already been commented on at some length, as has the difference between United and its existing competitors in this respect.[49] United's full line supports its market power in two minor ways and one major way. The first minor way has already been noted: the tying effect of certain aspects of the lease system as now administered. The effect of such tying depends, of course, on the fact that there are many machine types which can be tied together. The second is merely the extra selling effectiveness of a full line. This involves both the convenience in dealing with one supplier, one set of service representatives (under the leasing system), and so forth; and the possible extra sales value of the argument that the machines are in some sense specially adjusted to each other (whether or not this is in fact the case).

The major effect of the full line is the opportunity it gives United to compete against single-line or short-line sellers through price discrimination, an opportunity which exists as long as there are important machines in United's own line which face no competition. By pricing machines facing competition at low markups over cost,[50] and machines facing no competition at high markups over cost, United makes the achievement of success by short-line competitors much more difficult than it would be if United could not discriminate in price. The potentiality of this kind of competiton may be as strong a deterrent to the would-be competitor as its existence is a limitation on the ability of actual competitors to thrive and grow. The full details of United's price policy will be examined in a later chapter in connection with the consideration of United's performance in the market; here it suffices to say that a sufficiently wide range of price discrimination exists to justify the inference that it is an important barrier to the development of competition. A Terms Committee memorandum to the President, dated July 26, 1950,[51] shows the varia-

---

[49] Pp. 52–53.

[50] Cost in this discussion is defined as long-run average cost. For United, this is probably equal to long-run marginal cost, since United's operations are such as to suggest strongly that long-run costs are constant with scale over a wide range of output covering the present output. (See discussion below, pp. 92–99.) Long-run average cost includes all costs except profits and permanently sunk costs, such as organizational expenses for the original corporation. The latter are negligible. Given the crudeness of our measures of price-cost relations, and the wide variations shown by these measures among machine types, a more refined discussion of the definition and measurement of price discrimination appears unnecessary.

[51] S-310.

tions in the number of years required to return the ten-year investment on the proposed new terms for 66 machines.[52] Since the number of years required to return the ten-year investment is a measure
of the price-cost margin (the higher the number of years, the smaller
the margin), the spread of these figures shows the extent of price discrimination. The spread for 66 machines is shown in Table 1. The

TABLE 1

Number of Years Required to Return 10-Year Investment. (Based on Expected Revenues from Proposed New Terms)		Number of Machines
0	and less than 2	1
2	4.5	29
4.5	5.5	13
5.5	8	19
8	10	2
10	12	1
12	14	1

same exhibit shows the distribution percentage of gross profits[53] calculated on the balance sheet method. While testimony of the corporation's officers has impeached the usefulness of these computations,[54]
they still are of some service as an indicator of the variations of
margins relative to each other and have the advantage of appearing
in more familiar terms than do the results of the ten-year investment
formula. The distribution of 67 machines (including the previous 66)
by percentage gross profit expected from the new 1950 terms is shown
in Table 2.

Both tables clearly bring out the wide variations in margins between price and cost among various machines, which is all that is
relevant to the present contention. The differences between them do

[52] Ten-year investment, briefly, is the average cost, including research and development, manufacturing, service, and accumulated interest, of putting a machine into the
hands of a lessee and maintaining it for one lease life. The number of years required to
return the ten-year investment, on the basis of expected annual lease-revenue, for any
machine type is a measure of the rate of return on the investment in that type of
machine. A more detailed explanation is given below, pp. 116–122, including a discussion of cost allocation.

[53] Before general overheads but net of Beverly factory overheads.

[54] Tr. 8403–4, 8435–6, testimony of Brown; 10606–10611.

not affect this conclusion, and consideration of such differences in detail can be postponed.

United's ability to discriminate widely in pricing various machine types springs from its general market position rather than directly from the leasing system as such: with the same market power United could, in general, discriminate just as much under a sales system. But one particular aspect of the way in which the leasing system reinforces United's market power is directly related to the practice of price discrimination: the effect of leasing in preventing the copying of machines with no or little important patent protection. In the absence of a leasing system, United's ability to earn high returns in

TABLE 2

% Gross Profit Expected (Balance Sheet Formula) From Proposed New Terms		Number of Machines
less than	− 10%	3
− 10 and less than	0	4
0	10	19
10	20	16
20	30	9
30	50	16

relation to costs of particular machine types would be limited to those types which were relatively well covered by patents. In the absence of such coverage, the high-markup machines would provide an active field for copyists and rebuilders of old machines, thus creating competition which would force down the price terms on those machines. This copying competition would not be limited to "Chinese copies," but would also embrace inferior copies of machines whose general organization was not covered by patents but which incorporated patented special features. The copies, minus the special patented features, would command a lower price than the "originals," but the value of the special feature as such would set an upper limit to the price for the whole United machine which might be far lower than the machine could return in the absence of any copies at all.

That Compo, specifically, and other competitors as well, continue to exist in the face of the potential implicit in United's ability to discriminate in price does not in itself show that the effect of price discrimination on competition is unimportant. In the first place, existence is one thing and growth another: only Compo, among the competitors, has shown significant growth. And even in Compo's case, United's ability to catch up on a new process introduced by a rival has been impressive. Has this ability been entirely independent of the fact that United was able to accept lower returns on the machines it put out to compete with Compo than on other machines in its line? G-1984[55] shows explicit consideration of the competitive advantages accruing to USMC through its power to discriminate; and G-202[56] shows an explicit recognition (dated January 1939) that such discrimination in regard to cement-sole-attaching machines has existed. The same conclusion is supported by direct evidence of Table 3,

TABLE 3

Machine	Years in Which It Is Expected 10-Year Investment* Would Be Returned	
	On Previous Terms	On New 1950 Terms
Cement sole attaching B	8.48	6.0
Sole laying A	7.2	4.0
Sole stitcher C	8.16	5.3
Outsole rapid lockstitch O	6.1	4.66
Welt sewer K	2.21	2.21
Inseam sewer B	3.9	3.9

*The ten-year investment figures make no allowance for development and research costs, thus assumed to have been fully amortized previously.

which shows the number of years in which it was expected that the ten-year investment would be returned for various types of bottoming machines.[57] The first of these machines is the principal sole-attaching machine used in the cement process; the second, an alternative machine of less important use for this purpose, which is also used for sole-laying as well as sole-attaching. The sole-stitcher C is the principal sole-stitching machine in the Littleway process, which is closely competitive with the cement process. The welt sewer K,

[55] VI, 398 ff., esp. p. 401. This is a memorandum to the General Manager, dated 1935, examining the probable effects of reducing the charges on United's sole layer (SLA) and sole attacher (UAB) on Compo's revenues.
[56] VI, 408. This is a Program Committee report which mentions that the UAB, the most important cement-sole-attaching machine, has not been profitable and is unlikely to be so for some time in the future.
[57] S-310.

its new replacement, the inseam sewer B, and the ORL-O are, of course, the principal sole-attaching machines used in the welt process in which there is little competition for United, either directly by other machines, or indirectly through other processes for making similar shoes.

Further, the power to drive out competitors through price discrimination may exist without being used to the full: checking a competitor's growth may, taking all factors into consideration, be a wiser business policy than attempting to exploit to the full every potential weapon in order to drive him out of the market. Finally, the problem of the relative efficiency of United and its competitors must be examined. Price discrimination may enable United to drive out a single-line competitor if the two are equally efficient in producing and marketing the machine in which they compete. With a more efficient rival, United may be able only to maintain a competitive position by discrimination, which in its absence would have to be abandoned to the competitor. For all these reasons the fact that the practice of price discrimination has not resulted in the complete victory of United over all comers and a clear field for the victor does not conflict with the conclusion that the power to engage in extensive and quantitatively large discrimination is an important source of strength to United in maintaining its dominant position in the market.

5. UNITED'S PATENT STRUCTURE

In considering the importance of patents—their number, character, source and use—to United in maintaining its hold on the shoe machinery market, it is best to begin with the conclusion that United is not now, to any important extent, a patent monopoly. (Undoubtedly, patents were more important at the time of the company's birth.) The art of shoe machinery manufacture is old, and all or nearly all the fundamental machine inventions in it are in the public domain. The fundamental organization and mechanisms of most of the machines United markets may be copied by anyone; most of United's many patents cover improvements in one or another detail of a machine. The same is true of the patents of its competitors. Moreover, the shoe machinery art is crowded as well as old, the one being to a great extent a consequence of the other. Therefore any new patents are likely to be of narrow scope, in the sense of protecting very specifically a particular means of achieving a particular result, rather than covering a broad class of means for achieving a broadly defined result, as is the case of "dominant patents" in new fields. These conclusions are expressed, almost in these words, in the testimony of Ashley, the head of United's Patent Department.[58] In the course of the same testimony this witness further asserts that United's improvement and detail patents, while of considerable commercial significance, can be matched by similarly worthwhile results by any firm that puts comparable effort and investment in research and engineering to find other improvements on the basic devices in the art.[59] Further support for this conclusion is given by the testimony of Smith, Compo's patent counsel and research head, that Compo can "invent around" United's patents,[60] and that unpatented improvements on machines were more important in Compo's history than patented improvements.[61] Put another way, this states that improvements falling short of the standard of patentability have been of greater aggregate significance than patentable ones. This conclusion applied to United as well as to Compo, as shown by the tabulation of "blue-bulletin improvements" 1920–1950.[62] This tabulation shows the number of improvements on existing machines (as distinguished from new models) over the period for 31 important machines, and the number which were patented or on which patents read: only some 200 out of the nearly 5800 improvements were the subject matter of patents.

Within the scope thus set forth, the examination of United's patent holdings can proceed. Table 4, taken from S-202, shows the major features of United's patent holdings as of 15 December 1947.[63] Of the total of United's 3500 odd patents (excluding another 350 owned by United's subsidiaries) about 3300 relate to shoe machinery; the rest are on shoes as such, or methods, or devices, such as lasts, which are not machines. Most (about 75 per cent) of the patents on shoe machinery fall in certain subclasses of five patent office classes: nail-

---

[58] Tr. 7649–7666.   [59] Tr. 7651–2.   [60] Tr. 10269–70.   [61] Tr. 10188–89.

[62] S-219 and Tr. 7818–19. See below, pp. 172–176, for further discussion. A blue bulletin is an interdepartmental communication recording any change in machine design not large enough to be called a model change.

[63] S-204 and 205 show similar information for patents issued, 1920–1947; the results are sufficiently similar to require no additional comment. Similar figures as of a different date and in somewhat greater detail, are shown in G-2482 (X, 76). Again the results do not vary enough to deserve separate comment.

ing and stapling; boot and shoe making; sewing machines; cutting and punching sheets and bars; and button, eyelet, and rivet setting. United (together with its subsidiaries) holds about 40 per cent of all United States patents in the specified subclasses of the four classes.

TABLE 4

UNITED'S PATENT HOLDING, 15 DEC. 1947 (S-202)

Patent Office Classes (Number of Subclasses)	U.S. Total Patents	United Patents	Of which Machinery	Lasts, Methods and Devices
1. *United, Excluding Subsidiaries*				
(1) Nailing and stapling (38)				
Boot and shoe making (all) Sewing machines (51)	6,651 (100%)	2,530 (38%)	2,012	518
Cutting and punching sheets and bars (36)				
Button, eyelet and rivet setting (13)				
(2) 83 miscellaneous classes	approx. 235,000	789	623	166
Subtotal		3,319	2,635	684
(3) Boots and shoes (all)	3,120 (100%)	255 (8%)		
Total		3,574		
2. *All Subsidiaries*		*Subsidiaries Alone*		*United Plus Subsidiaries*
Classes as above (1)		95		2,625
(2)		218		1,007
(3)		28		283
Total		341		3,915

These holdings are large in some sense: a question arises as to what, if any, appropriate standard of comparison exists. The record shows only Compo's patent holdings: about 150 as of the beginning of 1951.[64] For what it is worth, the ratio of Compo's to United's patent holdings—150 to 3574—is greater than the ratio of Compo's to United's total assets—$3,250,000 to $104,860,000. A more general comparison can be made by considering the evidence given by the Com-

[64] Tr. 10202–3, Smith.

missioner of Patents to the Temporary National Economic Committee.[65] In Hearings, Part 3, appendix, Exhibit 189[66] there is shown a distribution of patents held in 1938 by size of patent holding. Only five corporations held more than 3000 patents at that time; another 17 held between 1000 and 3000 patents. It is clear from these figures that United's patent holdings are relatively large; indeed, United is one of the largest holders of patents in the United States.

In evaluating the significance of United's 40 per cent relative share of total U. S. patents in the subclasses which might crudely be called "shoe machinery" subclasses,[67] it is important to know who holds the other patents—specifically, how many of the other patents are held by shoe machinery manufacturers or others connected with the shoe trade. This information is shown, in too great detail, in S-203, a listing of patents held by others in the relevant subclasses of the five patent office classes shown in Table 4. The listing comprises 65 pages of patent numbers and names of assignees. On the basis of a sample of 12 pages, the accompanying results were reached.

Class	Total Pages	Sampled Pages	Number of Patents Belonging to:				
			Shoe Machinery Firms*	Sewing Machine Firms†	Shoe Firms	Others	Total
Nailing and Stapling	7	2	6	(others)	3	94	103
Boot and shoe making	22	3	39	(shoe machy.)	34	121	194
Sewing machines	13	3	6	53	1	181	235
Cutting and punching, etc.	21	3	2	(others)	5	180	187
Eyelet, etc., setting	3	1	1	(others)	3	50	54

*All firms which have ever appeared as competitors of United in any part of the evidence or testimony are classified as shoe machinery manufacturers.

†As indicated in column. They have been included with "others" where the arts bore no special relation to the production of sewing machines as such.

These results are of course crude. Particularly, the identification of shoe manufacturers, resting purely on the name of the concern, is poor; and perhaps many of the patents classified as belonging to

[65] 76th Congress, 1st session.
[66] See also Testimony of Commissioner Coe, pp. 845–848.
[67] Table 4, p. 80.

"others" in fact belong to shoe manufacturers. There are undoubtedly errors in the identification of United's competitors, but these are probably small, given the names of competitors in the Government's evidence as a check. Crude as it is, this sample justified the conclusion that the greater part of the patents not held by United in these classifications are held by businesses in no way connected with shoe machinery or shoe manufacture and are therefore of no great importance in judging the competitive effect of United's holdings. Or, put more directly, the competitive significance of United's patent aggregation—in so far as it can be shown at all through mere counting— is probably understated by the 40 per cent statistic which can be computed from Table 4 above.

Nearly all United's machinery patents arise from United's own development. Of the total of 2635 patents shown as machine patents in the table, only 138 (5 per cent) were acquired from others. Acquisitions plays a similarly unimportant role quantitatively in all of United's patent structure: 77 (11 per cent) of the 684 patents on lasts, methods, and devices were acquired; 32 (13 per cent) of 255 shoe patents; making, for all United (excluding affiliates) patents a total of 247 (7 per cent) acquisitions out of 2574 patents.[68] The qualitative importance of acquisitions has already been discussed above in connection with the general discussion of acquisitions;[69] something further on this point will be said below. Discussion of the circumstances surrounding patent acquisitions will be postponed to take its place in the general examination of United's behavior in the market.

It is argued by the Government that an examination of the role of acquisitions in United's patent structure should not be limited to acquisition of patents and applications, but should also go behind the patents and look to the acquisition of inventors, both from competitors and in general.[70] Two things are complained of, the fact of the acquisitions *per se,* especially of the services of inventors formerly working for competitors; and the restrictive covenants contained in the contracts under which United inventors are hired. On the first point, the hiring of inventors from competitors has in general been incident to the acquisition of patents or the whole business of the competitors[71] and can be considered as part of these acquisitions

---

[68] S-202.   [69] Above pp. 57–63.   [70] GTB Part I, pp. 136, 415–18.
[71] See discussion of acquisitions on pp. 57–63 above.

and judged in the general judgment of them. The use of restrictive covenants in inventors' contracts is not peculiar to United; the hiring of such good inventors as are available is certainly not to be condemned *per se*. The evils here, if any, arise from United's position in the market. This position makes United the natural market for those who wish to offer their inventive talent for hire; no special reaching out to engross the supply of inventors is necessary. Here again, the conclusions are similar to those on acquisitions in general, and the ultimate conclusion—that there is a snowballing effect of large market power but its magnitude is not necessarily great—is also the same.

What does a United patent represent? A partial answer to this question, in very broad terms, was given at the beginning of this section. This answer can be somewhat further particularized by examining a classification made by United in 1938 of those of its patents which had commercial use according to "importance."[72] This classification runs in terms of four classes:

(a) Patents regarded as of outstanding importance
(b) Patents of less importance . . . but still of large importance and value
(c) Patents of still less importance but which afford very useful specific protection upon our commercial machines, methods, etc.
(d) Patents of minor importance.

United's own patents are divided as follows:

Class	a	b	c	d	Total
Number	40	151	538	490	1219
Per cent (rounded)	3	12	44	40	100

The affiliates' 290 patents are classified in a roughly similar way; worthy of comment is the large number of (a) and (b) patents of the Littleway Process Company: 5 and 5, respectively, out of 35 patents. Fewer than half the 40 very important patents read on major machines, based on the description of these patents given in G-2494 (X 104). These include:

5 patents on Eyeletting machines, covering methods and devices for invisible eyeletting and an eyelet.
4   on Staple side lasting machines (2 Reed, acquired from Little,

[72] G-2490. X, 95. See also G-2491-3 on following pages indicating method of classification and care used in making it. From these documents it would appear that the classification represents the opinion of competent persons in both United and United's outside patent counsel, given after some consideration, and therefore deserves the weight to be attributed to an informed expert judgment. It is of course a judgment and in no sense a "fact."

2 Goddu, developed by United), covering methods, general organization of a machine and machine parts.

2   on Clicking machines, covering the aluminum beam (Hogan) and a pattern die and method of using it.

1   on Consolidated hand method lasting machine-L, covering parts for power shift of gages, raceway, and stop.

1   on Pre-welt lasting machine A, covering the method.

1   on Goodyear Universal Channeling machine B, covering the general organization.

1   on Paper peg, which is used in the Fiber fastening machine.

In addition, three patents cover a strip-feeding mechanism for use in nail-making machines: these have to do with supply rather than machine business. The remaining patents in the group relate to 11 minor machines. Of the 13 class (a) patents held by United's affiliates, six relate to shoe manufacture. These are the B.B. Chemical's patent on an insole reinforcing method (Ellis), and the five Littleway Process Co. patents referred to above.[73]

Another aspect of the relation between United's patents and its major machines is brought out by considering the time distribution of the patents commercialized in United major machines.[74] The tabulation of 34 major machines (or selected machines) and the patents commercialized by them by date of machine commercialization and date of patent is given in detail in Table 5. The main points of the table are shown here in summary.

Period	Number of Machines Commercialized	Average Number of Patents per Mach.	Per cent of Which		
			Pre 1920	1920–30	Post '30
Before 1910	4	16.1	80	15	5
1910–19	13	41.9	60	17	23
1920–29	7	25.6	22	26	52
1930–39	8	21.0	5	21	74
1940	2	4.0	0	0	100
Before 1920	17	36.5	62	17	21
1920 and after	17	20.9	14	22	64
Entire period	34	28.4	44	19	37

[73] Note that two of these are Reed, acquired from Little, and three Goddu, developed by United.

[74] See Admission of Defendant in response to Order of Court of 13 June 1950. Also G-2907, Table 1, XI, 261–2.

In short, these 34 important machines fall into two equal groups: 17 old machines on which the major (quantitative) share of patent protection has expired and which have relatively few "new" patents covering them; and 17 new machines, a major part (quantitative) of the patent coverage on which is still in "new patents. (This, of course, says nothing about the scope or strength of the patents involved.) All the 12 largest revenue earners—the machines earning $500,000 or more in 1947—are included in the 34 selected machines. Their place in the time periods of the table is as follows:

Before 1910	none	Earnings Rank Order*
1910–19	6	1, 2, 3, 4, 6 and 7
1920–29	4	5, 8, 9, 12
1930–39	2	10, 11
1940–	none	

* See Table 2, above.

Thus, as shown by the machines producing the major fraction of its machine revenues, United does not rely heavily on the protection of recent patents.[75]

The use of United's patents in relation to major machines can be viewed in the broader perspective of the general use pattern of United's patents. S-202, already cited above, shows the various uses of United's 3319 patents in Groups (1) and (2) of Table 4 above—all the patents except those on boots and shoes. This information is summarized in Table 6.

Commercial use, in a wide sense, includes all the 1744 patents shown in categories 1 through 8, 53 per cent of the total. Other totals, corresponding to other definitions, are of interest, including:

(a) Sum of 1, 2, 5, 6, 7, 8: "Commercial use" (above except limited adopted machines)   —   1647   50

*(b) 1, 2, 3, 4, 5, 6: "Commercial use" except inventions not adopted, used only in trials, etc., classes 7, 8   —   1155   35

(c) 1, 2, 5, 6: Combination of above two exclusions   —   1058   32

* This is the definition United adopts in Ashley's testimony, Tr. 7537–44, and in the summary of S-202.

[75] This point is brought out in somewhat more detail by examining the revenue rank listings of the machines shown in Table 5.

TABLE 5

TIME DISTRIBUTION OF PATENTS COMMERCIALIZED IN 34 SELECTED MACHINES
(Admission of Defendant in Response to Court Order of 13 June 1950)
(Cf. GTB Patent I, App. 11; cf. also G-2907, XI, 261)

Machine	Yr. Adopted	Revenue Rank 1947 (Table p. 36)	Pre-1920 Patents No.	Pre-1920 Patents Per Cent	Post-1920 Patents No.	Post-1920 Patents Per Cent	Post-1930 Patents No.	Post-1930 Patents Per Cent	Total No.
(1) Machines commercialized before 1910									
CHM Laster	1899	15	35	85	6	15	2	5	41
Gearless Sole cutter	1898	—	0	0	2	100	0	0	2
Universal slugger	1899	24	11	85	2	15	1	8	13
McKay sewer B	1908	—	6	67	3	33	0	0	9
Sum 4 (16 pat/mach)			52	aggregate 80	13	aggregate 20	3	aggregate 5	65
(2) Machines commercialized 1910–1919									
McKay automatic heeler B	1910	7	31	51	30	49	20	33	61
Univ. rounding and channeling E	1910	6	21	81	5	19	2	8	26
Goodyear welt sewer K	1911	2	47	67	23	33	14	20	70
Rex pulling over C	1911	⎱ 3 ⎰	37	57	28	43	13	20	65
Rex pulling over D	1913		37	64	21	36	8	14	58
Loose nailing No. 2	1913	16	23	72	9	28	2	6	32
Bed laster No. 6	1913	4*	27	66	21	51	14	34	48
Clicker C	1914	17	18	51	17	49	11	31	35
ORL–O	1914	1	34	51	33	49	25	37	67
Bed laster No. 7	1915	4*	36	82	8	18	3	7	44
Inseam trimming C	1916	14	8	73	3	27	0	0	11
McKay sewing R	1917	—	0	0	7	100	5	71	7
Eyeletter C	1919	—	6	29	15	71	7	33	21
Sum 13 (42 pat/mach)			325	60	220	40	124	23	545

TABLE 5—Continued

Machine	Yr. Adopted	Revenue Rank 1947 (Table p. 36)	Pre-1920 Patents		Post-1920 Patents		Post-1930 Patents		Total
			No.	Per Cent	No.	Per Cent	No.	Per Cent	No.
(3) Machines commercialized 1920–1929									
Wood heel attacher	1922	21	2	12	14	88	6	38	16
Autom. sole leveler D	1922	9	7	33	14	67	8	38	21
USMC sole stitching C	1926	—	3	9	32	91	24	68	35
Staple side laster B	1926	5	10	40	15	60	10	40	25
Staple side laster C	1926	10	3	10	27	90	20	67	30
Heel seat laster D	1928	8	9	37	22	63	11	31	31
Wood heel nailer	1929	12	6	29	15	71	14	67	21
Sum 7 (26 pat/mach)			40	22	139	78	93	52	179
(4) Machines commercialized 1930–1939									
Fiber fastening B	1931	25	6	26	17	74	12	52	23
Cement sole attacher B	1931	11	0	0	43	100	40	93	43
Stitchdown thread laster B	1932	23	0	0	13	100	11	85	13
USMC sole laying A	1933	22	0	0	18	100	15	83	18
Duplex eyeletter B	1934	—	3	27	8	13	4	36	11
Heel seat laster E	1935	10	0	0	28	100	19	68	28
Goodyear sole laying F	1938	13	0	0	12	100	8	67	12
Toe laster C	1939	20	0	0	20	100	16	80	20
Sum 8 (21 pat/mach)			9	5	159	95	125	74	168
(5) Machines commercialized 1940–									
Pre-welt laster B	1941	—	0	0	7	100	7	100	7
Platform cover laster C	1944	—	0	0	1	100	1	100	1
Sum 2 (4 pat/mach)			0	0	8	100	8	100	8

*Grouped together in Table 2, p. 34.

(d)   1, 2, 5:   Use by United as in (c) above, excluding
                   licensing (6)   —   999   30

(e)   1, 3, 5, 6, 7:   "Recent use," broadly defined
                                            —   1026   38

The definition of "commercial use" implicit in the Government charge that only 30 per cent of defendant's patents are commercial[76] is not quite clear. It corresponds to some definition of the defendant's,

TABLE 6

Use	Number of Patents	Per Cent of Total
1. Adopted for machines introduced *since* 15 Dec. 1930	545	16
2. Adopted for machines introduced *before* 15 Dec. 1930	404	12
3. Limited adopted *since*	87	3
4. Limited adopted *before*	10	—
5. Shop machines, methods, devices, used commercially but not the subject matter for adoption	50	2
6. Licenses granted, not included above	59	2
7. Not adopted, but developed *since* 15 Dec. 1930 and used in commercial manufacture of shoes, in trials, or otherwise	285	9
8. Not adopted, but developed *before* 15 Dec. 1930	304	9
9. Remainder	1,575	47
Total	3,319	100

since it is based on G-2488,[77] a memorandum from Cobb to Donham in 1938, which states that as of July 1938 31 per cent of all the patents then owned by United were or had been in commercial use.[78] Table 6 above refers only to 3319 patents, rather than United's total holdings of 3574. The difference is accounted for by the 285 patents on boots and shoes.[79] If it is assumed that none of these is commercial in the relevant sense, then the implicit definition of United's other documents comes close to both (b) and (c) of the totals shown on page 85 above.

[76] GTB Part I, 434.   [77] X, 89 ff.
[78] Also, cf. Answer p. 52, cited in GTB Part I, for a figure of the same magnitude.
[79] Group (3) in Table 4.

Whatever the appropriate definition of commercial use, the proportion of United's patents having commercial use does not in itself indicate anything. Some comparative standard is needed before any judgment on the significance of the degree of commercial use can be formed. It is clear, both from general observation on the nature of the patent grant and the operation of the patent system and from the testimony of Ashley that 100 per cent is not the appropriate standard. Some patents turn out to require a long development period before they can be commercialized; some represent inferior alternatives which have been supplanted by better ones; some represent subject matter which looked promising at the time the patent was issued but since has been abandoned, etc. The record is not rich in evidence which would provide a specific standard. Compo uses commercially some 25–30 per cent of its 150 patents.[80] On their chief competitive machines United and Compo show the following: United has 61 patents pertaining to cement sole attaching presses, of these 41 are commercialized by either the USMC Cement Sole Attacher A or B; Compo has 51 patents relating to this subject matter, of which 28 are commercially used.[81] Ashley offered a general opinion that United's used proportion was high and indicated his basis for so believing— testimony of Patent Commissioner Coe before a House Committee in 1935 that fewer than 5 per cent of all patents were of commercial value, and general familiarity with the experience of other large corporations.[82]

On the basis of these salient aspects of United's patent structure summarized in the preceding pages, what conclusions—subsidiary to the conclusion initially stated—can be drawn about the importance of United's patents in maintaining its market position? Only one seems to follow from the facts: United's large number of patents, both absolutely and relatively in the art, makes it harder for a rival, actual or potential, to create a device that does not infringe a United patent and that can be successfully used in the manufacture of shoes without access to patents owned by United, than would be the case if United's patent holdings were smaller. This theorem assumes that United does not license readily to competitors (absent Government compulsion or pressure or some sort) or would-be competitors, a conclusion

[80] Tr. 10202–3, Smith.   [81] Tr. 12689–90, Ashley, referring to C-26.
[82] Tr. 7569–76.

borne out by the evidence.[83] From this theorem a corollary of slightly greater power can be drawn: United's large patent holdings tend to have a snowball effect, making it natural for inventors not associated with rivals who make shoe machinery inventions to sell them to United, since it is almost certain to be able to use them—if anyone can—and since the inventor as well as other potential buyers are likely to be blocked from such use by United's patents. Neither of these results is without some effect in making United stronger and rivals weaker than they might be were United to hold fewer patents or license freely. But given the fundamental limits on the qualitative significance of patents in the field,[84] these conclusions based entirely on statistical effects and referring to "typical" patents, in some sense, are of very limited force.

The proportion of United's patents which are not in commercial use, whether it is high or low, does not bear on these conclusions one way or the other. The rationale of the Government's contention that patents not in commercial use somehow lie secretly in wait for the unwary would-be rival, springing out of ambush to attack him when he develops a shoe machinery invention, is obscure.[85] The patents are patents, and the would-be rival has precisely the same opportunity to search the existing patents and discover a United patent which reads on his own invention whether it is commercialized in a machine and listed in a Red Book or lies sleeping in United's Patent Register. The extent of commercial use, if it is relevant to any conclusion, may be relevant to one on the extent to which United's research is fruitful and its results made useful in the manufacture of shoes; it does not bear on the contribution of patents to United's market power at all.

It is not impossible that appropriate information on the qualitative significance of particular patents might lead to much stronger conclusions on the effects of United's patent holdings on its market position. In particular, the significance of particular acquisitions and

[83] Tr. 7523, would not license to Compo, Ashley; Tr. 8840 ff., indicating United in general licenses only to inventors from whom patents have been acquired or as a result of interference proceedings at application stage, Ashley; S-210, 14 instances of licenses to shoe manufacturers under post-1930 patents, each resulting from an interference, a United acquisition or a mutual infringement situation; Tr. 8851 ff. in regard to licensing to Landis and G-1464, V 245, there cited; G-2874, XI 134 ff., Memo by Edmands, dated July 1941, indicating reasons for United to license and intention of licensing primarily to non-competitors.

[84] Above, pp. 78–79.   [85] See GTB Part I, p. 433.

the non-use of particular patents can only be judged in relation to the specific content of these patents. Thus, for example, the importance of the Littleway acquisition[86] may in part depend on the content of the Reed patents in relation to the Goddu developments which were, according to United, the basis of the Littleway process as commercialized. It is precisely on a point of this sort that the kind of evidence available in the record falls short of what is necessary for a well-supported finding. Interpretation of the content of two similar patents, comparison of the relative merits of the inventions disclosed in them, assessment of the extent to which they block one another, and other similar judgments are worthwhile only when made by an expert specifically qualified in the patent art of shoe machinery. The only such expert testimony available in the record is that of the officers and employees of United. The difficulty of relying entirely on such testimony is not merely that it may be "interested" in the narrow sense of the word. It is more that the particular evaluations of exactly these questions made by United in the past in the course of dealing with the patents concerned were made by these same officials and their predecessors, and it is natural that these evaluations should be (quite honestly) defended as correct by those who made them. Absent some disinterested expert testimony, or cross examination of United's expert witnesses by equally expert counsel, it appears impossible to come to worthwhile conclusions on the qualitative aspects of particular patents, whenever the questions involved are controversial and have some bearing on practices condemned by the Government.

6. THE CONTRIBUTION OF UNITED'S MERCHANDISE ACTIVITIES TO ITS POWER IN THE MACHINERY MARKET

This topic is inserted for the sake of formal completeness, rather than because there are any significant conclusions to be drawn on it or, indeed, evidence on which such conclusions could rest. Evidence on the relation of the two kinds of activity suggests that whatever contribution is made runs the other way; this is considered below in connection with the discussion of United's supply business. It can be argued that there is some pure sales advantage which accrues to United because it markets the supplies "to go with its machines" as

[86] Cf. above, pp. 59–60.

well as the machines, of a sort similar to the pure sales advantages of a long line of machinery.[87] But there is no specific evidence to show the magnitude of this effect; general considerations suggest it is not significant.

7. UNITED AS A "NATURAL MONOPOLY"—ECONOMIES OF SCALE AND THE SIZE OF THE MARKET

Just under the surface of United's presentation of its case is the contention that United is, in effect, a natural monopoly. Its dominance in the shoe machinery market is the expression of this situation: it reflects a position "thrust upon" United by the technological realities underlying the market and thus escapes the ban of the Sherman Act. The "naturalness" of United's virtual monopoly arises from the interaction of two factors: the smallness or thinness of the shoe machinery market on the one hand, and large size necessary for efficient operation on the other.

The possibility that United is a natural monopoly will be examined in the light of the evidence in the record. Since the size of the market has already been considered,[88] the examination will focus on the existence or non-existence of economies of scale sufficient to explain United's present position. In this connection, two prefatory comments are in order. First, scale is not one dimensional in a firm with as varied an output as United: there may be some economies that arise from producing and distributing large numbers of one machine, others which arise from the production and distribution of many varieties of machines, and still others which depend on both. Second, and more important, a judgment that economies of scale of one or another kind exist is in itself not very useful without a fairly close indication as to what part of the size range they apply. Thus, the conclusion that a certain function is performed more efficiently by a company the size of United than, say, by a company the size of Compo, tells nothing about whether or not United's performance could be expected to be more efficient than that of a company half the size of United.

The most general evidence on the question of United as a natural monopoly is negative, though by no means conclusive—the existence of Compo. That Compo, a company about 3 or 4 per cent of the size of United, as measured in total assets, not only exists but

[87] Cf. above, p. 74.   [88] Above, pp. 27–39.

has grown considerably since its founding[89] and has earned a higher
rate of return than United[90] suggests strongely that it is not necessary
to achieve United's size to operate efficiently in the shoe machinery
industry. The significance of the comparison is increased when it is
made in the context of the fact that Compo arose as a major innovator in the field and that its success cannot be attributed in any sense
to its ability to get into various corners of the market which cannot
efficiently be reached by a big concern, e.g., poor credit risks or firms
in areas distant from United's branch offices. The inconclusiveness of
the comparison arises, of course, from the fact that Compo manufactures a much smaller variety of machines than does United and, in
particular, it manufactures machines which are, by and large, less
complicated from the design, production, and service points of
view than some of United's major machines. If the complexity
is necessary, then the United-Compo comparison cannot tell the
whole story. Whether the complexity is necessary is an issue which
is not clearly settled, although there is much testimony on the
point by United witnesses which indicates that it is. On the other
side are the innovations of Compo and Kamborian, which may
mean that another path is possible.[91]

In addition to the overall evidence above, there is some evidence
on the basis of which a few comments can be made on scale economies in some of the separate activities of United—manufacturing, distribution, service, and research. These comments can be eked out
with the aid of certain general arguments, but the total result is sug-
gestive rather than conclusive. More evidence is available on manufacturing than on any of the other activities, much of it in the testimony of Wilson Palmer, vice-president and general superintendent
of manufacturing. He indicates that Beverly is essentially a large
"job shop" with a wide variety of products and small orders.[92] The
typical lot size for a machine order is 75 pieces, which is very small
relative to the scale of the whole shop. Each lot involves only a small
number of repetitive parts, very complicated machining operations,
and a great deal of setting-up time.[93] There are some 107,000 different
parts in stock of which 80,000 are "active," in the sense of being con-

---

[89] C-34.   [90] C-33, 34, 38, and S-412.
[91] This point will receive further discussion in connection with the evaluation of
United's progressiveness below, pp. 147–202.
[92] Tr. 6622-24.   [93] Tr. 9296-98.

tinuously manufactured and bought. In any year 40,000 different parts are manufactured.[94] Assembly is relatively unimportant cost-wise; it is parts manufacture which is Beverly's major activity.[95] Each machine uses parts which are also used in other machines, "borrowed parts" in USMC terminology, as well as "standardized parts" such as cotter pins, screws, springs, etc., which are found in a great many products of the metal-fabricating industries. In addition each machine has "machine parts" which are peculiar to it. Some of all kinds of parts are purchased but more borrowed and standardized parts than machine parts.[96] The economies of manufacturing many different machines are realized, as far as parts manufacture goes, chiefly in the use of borrowed parts manufactured by USMC; but these form a relatively small portion of the total number of parts, ranging from 2 per cent in the Rex puller C to 6 per cent in the Toe Laster C and nearly 8 per cent in the Orl-O.[97] Since the machine parts are manufactured in small lots anyway and the standardized parts could be fairly readily purchased, no significant economies could arise in respect to their manufacture, no matter what the overall scale of manufacture was. All this evidence indicates that there are no significant economies of scale in Beverly manufacturing operations compared to even a fairly small shop, given the small lot size and the relatively small importance of specially made parts (as opposed to parts which can readily be purchased) common to a large number of machines.

With respect to distribution (as distinct from service), there is practically no evidence in the record pointing one way or the other on the existence of scale economies. Distribution activities, carried on by the branch offices, includes sales contacts, order taking, stocking and distributing parts, and in general serving as a channel between the shoe manufacturer and United. The personnel involved are salesmen, clerks, branch managers, and assistant managers. A general consideration of their functions suggests no reason to believe that there are significant economies of scale in a large distribution organization, either in having more rather than fewer branches, or in having larger rather than smaller branches, after some minimum size is reached. This conclusion rests on several facts: the work involved

---

[94] Tr. 6626, 6729, 6744.   [95] Tr. 6916.   [96] Tr. 6124–39, testimony of Bigelow.
[97] Testimony of Bigelow, Tr. 6124–39, also Palmer, Tr. 9267 and, more generally, Tr. 6754 and 6859–60.

is not highly specialized or skilled; there are no great opportunities for the division of labor; no great amount of equipment is required; personnel, office space, etc., can be varied more or less proportionately with the work load. The one relevant fact in evidence bears on the distribution and stocking of parts, the greater part of which is carried out by the branches.[98] This suggests that there are no great economies in parts distribution to be achieved by central storage in a single large depot.

The most economical scale for the provision of services was the subject of considerable testimony in the record. Evidence on this point was contained in the testimony of Wogan,[99] Walker, an assistant General Manager,[100] and Bartschi, a shoe manufacturer.[101] Wogan testified that machines were divided into ten groups for service purposes, and that ten "carefully selected men" could form a complete team for servicing all United machines. Walker's evidence stressed several points, including the importance of continued training, especially actual experience under varying conditions in varying factories in keeping roadmen efficient; the significance of United's general pool of know-how in the provision of service; the importance of specialized services provided by the Boston office, such as that of the Shoe Ex department, which solved difficult shoe-making problems; and the impossibility of forming 82 teams of "carefully selected men" from the 820 roadmen in view of the requirements of balance and flexibility, the variations in individual skill, the necessity of shifting men about to cope with sudden emergencies or to fill vacancies caused by accidents, illness, etc. His testimony further brought out that roadmen were recruited chiefly from operatives, assistant foremen, and sometimes foremen in shoe factories; average salary was about $3500 per year, with a maximum of $4500 in the branches and $7200 for roadmen operating from the Boston office. The highest paid men, with 21 years' experience, earned $7500. S-323 A and B shows the number of roadmen attached to the various branch offices: the maximum number was 121 (Haverhill), the minimum 5 (in Los Angeles), the next smallest number was 27 (in Rochester); the average number per branch office was 57. S-321 shows the number and experience of men providing service from the Boston office. Including 9 in Shoe Ex, 10 in the Goodyear department, and 8 in the

[98] Tr. 10987, Palmer; also 6284-6287, Waelter, assistant superintendent of agencies.
[99] Tr. 10421-3.   [100] Tr. 10970-11115, 11178-81.   [101] Tr. 4883-5, 4924-5.

Cement-shoe department, the total was 60. The Planning department also falls in this classification. Walker, on cross examination,[102] indicated that the 5 roadmen in Los Angeles provided adequate service because most of the factories in the area were small ones making slip lasted shoes, in which little machinery was used. There were, however, some welt and cement shoe factories in the district, and machinery from at least six other department was also in use there. S-376 shows expenditures on service classified into road service, planning department, and Shoe Ex, and divided between branches and Boston. In 1950, the last year covered, branch office road service accounted for $3,069,000 out of total expenditures, of $3,453,000; a similar picture is shown in the other years, going back to 1940.

These figures suggest, but fall very short of confirming, the following conclusions. First, branch office road service could be performed at the same, or only slightly less, efficiency by a much smaller organization than United: with fewer branches, with Rochester-rather than Haverhill-size (27 as against 121) staffs of roadmen, there could be a road service force one quarter the size of United's; there is nothing inconsistent with the evidence in the assumption that such a force would function as efficiently as the present size one, with the slight reservation that its total accumulated pool of know-how might in some way be less.[103] There may be economies associated with the specialized expert service provided by the Boston office, especially the Shoe Ex and Planning Departments. Even here, smaller firms might efficiently run somewhat smaller departments of a similar sort, but limits to subdivision are suggested by the small size of the Shoe Ex department with only 9 men. These Boston activities were quantitatively unimportant, however, accounting for little more than 10 per cent of total service expenditures. Thus, even substantial economies in the performance of these functions would lead to overall savings of very small proportions.

Bartschi, the manager of J. Edwards shoe factories, testified in some colorful passages that he estimated United was providing service to his factory far more cheaply than he could provide it himself by hiring mechanics.[104] This testimony may indicate that a small

[102] Tr. 11178–81.

[103] Note that Compo employs about 100 servicemen (Tr. 9721, Mason) compared with United's 820.

[104] Tr. 4883–5, 4924–5.

service unit—one set up for a 5000-pair-per-day factory—is at a substantial disadvantage relative to United in the cost of providing service. It may also be interpreted to show that United gives service away at "prices" below cost, at least with respect to some customers, in the sense that the costs of service exceeded the allowance made for them in figuring lease terms. Indeed in the context, and in light of later testimony by Walker,[105] this may be the more likely explanation. But even if the first interpretation is the correct one, it tells nothing about the comparison in service efficiency of United and a company one-half, one-quarter, or one-tenth United's size.

In sum, then, the evidences on scale and efficiency in the provision of service, such as it is, suggests that a company of United's size may have advantages over smaller companies, but that these advantages are likely to be small and with respect to companies of, say, half United's size, non-existent.

Although United's research activities were perhaps the most discussed subject in the whole record,[106] little of the testimony bears directly on the relation of research to the scale of the firm. The general tenor is to emphasize the expense, complexity, and riskiness of United's research, and the necessity of arrangements in the market which will pay for it. Explicitly the necessary arrangements include leasing; implicitly, they include price discrimination, and by inference, monopoly. From this, the further inference may be drawn that a smaller enterprise than United would not be able to finance research on the appropriate scale; i.e., the scale on which it is now carried on by United. But the leap, in this line of argument, from the undisputed facts on the expense, complexity, and number of "dry holes" involved in shoe machinery research to the conclusions indicated is not successfully sustained on the level of general argument.

Considering certain aspects of the matter on a more detailed level, something more can be said. It is clear that there are advantages in research to a company which produces a large variety of machines and deals with a great many shoemaking methods that arise from the application of the fund of shoemaking technique to as many problems as possible on the one hand, and to the building up of that fund from experience in many fields on the other. Further, to the extent that research and development problems in different processes present similar elements, skills and experience created in one area

---

[105] Tr. 13223–33.   [106] Roberts, Tr. *passim.*

can be applied in another. To the extent that continuity of activity and training through activity is important to a research division, operations in many fields and operations on a large scale are both important in a situation where the volume of output in any one field —with some exceptions—may be too small to support a large continuous research program. Given the inevitability of "dry holes," a research program large enough to permit the successes to pay for the failures is a necessity. But all these truths throw no light on the question of whether United's scale is the minimum scale at which the advantages can be secured, or whether they would be available to the same degree, or to almost the same degree, in an enterprise half its size.

Some light on one aspect of the question of scale and efficiency in research is provided by an examination of S-246, which shows the distribution of research personnel by departments and activities as of 1 July 1949. This shows no section with so few "productive personnel" as to lead readily to the conclusion that the minimum division of labor necessary to reasonably efficient functioning could not be achieved in a section of half the size, except perhaps the handbooks and catalogs section (9 men), materials research section (7 men), and tanning department (13 men). This is of course essentially speculation, but it does not seem unreasonable speculation in the light of the evidence. A broader, and perhaps a firmer, basis for the same conclusion is provided by S-401, showing the growth in the number of research-department personnel over time. This shows that the present size of the department is about twice what it was in the mid-thirties; yet there is no indication in the testimony that USMC research was carried out on an inefficiently small scale at that time. The tables shown on pp. 86–87 above (showing patents commercialized on 34 selected major machines by date of machine introduction) and examination of S-147, a, b, and c (correlations of patents and blue bulletin improvements) for the dates of patented improvements embodied in blue bulletins likewise show no special lagging in research results, as indicated by these measures, in that period. It is true that a substantial part of the research work on "fundamental" subjects—lasts, leather, and leather substitutes—has been done in the last ten years,[107] but since the fruits of this work are in large part not yet ripe, the work cannot really enter into the judgment.

[107] S-383.

All in all, it seems fair to say that the testimony of the corporation's expert witness—Roberts—gives grounds for believing that economies of scale in research do exist, and may even be of substantial importance. The magnitude of the economies and the part of the size range to which they are relevant are, however, not shown, and at least suggestions in the evidence tend toward a finding that United's present size is not necessary to achieve the economies discussed. On this state of the record a conclusion that economies of scale in research require United to be its present size or to carry on research activities to its present extent hardly is warranted.

As it is with research, so it is with all the above argument on economies of scale as a justification of United's market position. The evidence is meager, and what there is does not point unequivocally in one direction. The deficiencies of the evidence in providing a basis for judging at what scale of operations such advantages as appear likely to exist in service and research are available to their fullest extent are especially important. Altogether this evidence would not support a finding that United was a "natural monopoly," even in the absence of any other evidence as to the sources of United's market power. As a rebuttal in the face of the variety of substantial evidence discussed above, which shows the important roles of the original acquisitions, leasing, and the long line of machinery in creating and maintaining United's market power, and the minor but not insignificant assistance lent by later acquisitions and United's patent structure, the evidence has no force in supporting the contention that United's monopoly was "thrust upon it"—the result only of striving for excellence and efficiency in the narrow shoe machinery market.

IV. United's Performance in the Market

United's position in the machinery market has been examined, and the conclusion reached that United has substantial power in that market, based chiefly on acquisitions, leasing, and full-line selling. This and the following chapter will examine United's behavior in the market with a view to an evaluation of its performance, both to check the conclusion on the existence of power, and to see how the power is used. The discussion will encompass two somewhat diverse topics. The first is the exploration of United's conduct for evidence of "specific intent" to monopolize the shoe-machinery market in the shape of coercive, exploitative, or exclusive practices aimed at particular rivals and not comprehended in the previous discussion of the sources of United's power. The second topic is the examination of United's performance in the economic sense, to see how it has operated irrespective of any "intent" on the part of the corporation and its officers. This chapter will deal with "specific intent" and with price-cost aspects of economic performance. Chapter 5 will deal with research and progressiveness, the effects of United's performance on shoe manufacturing, and some general conclusions on United's performance and its liability under the complaint.

1. COERCIVE PRACTICES

An inquiry into coercive practices seeks to discover whether United has a "specific intent" to monopolize which has been expressed in its conduct in relation to competitors, actual or potential. Conventionally, coercive practices have been treated as distinct from the exercise of market power in general; indeed, earlier anti-trust cases often contained discussions of the distinction between the lawful use and the abuse of market power; e.g., U. S. *v.* U. S. Steel, 215 US 417; U. S. *v* Swift and Co., 286 US 106. Further, this line of analysis has often run from illegal practices as a cause to market power as a consequence, Standard Oil of N. J. *v.* U. S., 221 US 1.

This view of the problem is essentially misleading. If a firm engages in "coercion" in its dealings with its rivals, there must be some reservoir of force available to the firm which makes this coercion possible and accounts for the acquiescence of the rivals in situations which, by definition, are not the result of mutually free bargains. In general, only three possible kinds of "force" exist which a firm can use in this way: physical force—violence or the threat of violence, fraud, or market power. The use of the first two is tortious in itself, without reference to the statutory standards of the Sherman Act. Violence, threats of violence, and fraud of all sorts are not unknown in Sherman Act cases, but they do not play any large part in the present record. The only important basis of the coercive practices which the Government has charged, to the extent that they exist, is thus United's market power. It is the fact that the other party to a bargain with United, whether he is the seller of a business, the assigner of a patent, or the lessee of shoe machinery, has no real alternative to dealing with United in most of these situations that makes possible the turning to United's advantage of the normal instruments of bargaining in business relations: delays, refusals to deal, representations which fall short of complete candor, and so forth. United's market power is, so to speak, focused on the particular transaction to the disadvantage of the other party involved.

If this conclusion is correct, what is the use of examining the alleged coercive practices in detail? It might fairly be answered: none, since market power and its bases are alone significant. But there are two reasons not to rest with such an answer, at least in the particular context of the present suit. First, coercive practices are given a very prominent position in the Government's picture of the case as presented in its Trial Brief.[1] Second, under current legal doctrine, it may

---

[1] See GTB Part I *passim.* For example, pp. 137–49, acquisition of General; pp. 166–70, acquisition of Kamborian; pp. 264–80, "enforcement" of lease clauses; pp. 282–96, attempted elimination of Compo through terms changes; pp. 454–73, illegal use of patents.

be necessary to show intent to exercise market power, as well as its mere existence, to justify a finding of liability under Section 2 of the Sherman Act. See, for example, American Tobacco Co. *v.* U. S., 328 US 781. The examination of specific examples which follows thus has a double purpose: to indicate what the Government considers "coercion" and to show the extent to which United's market power was indeed utilized in specific transactions. Only a sample of all the instances the Government cites are examined, containing what appear to be the strongest cases in the most important areas of such practices.

The first important area in which coercive practices are charged is in connection with acquisitions by United of assets, patents, and businesses. The example most worth examination is the acquisition of General Shoe Machinery Corporation. The undisputed facts about this acquisition are these. The company was a successor to the Boylston Shoe Machinery Company, an early competitor of United's. International Shoe Machinery Company had an interest in it, represented by substantial stock ownership by Rand, International's president. International's motive in assisting General was to try to create an alternative source of supply to United, because of United's leasing policy.[2] With the change in United's leases which came about after the Clayton Act suit, International was satisfied and no longer was interested in General.[3] The initiative in the transaction came from Rand, speaking for International.[4] At the time of the transaction, General was developing a full line of shoe machinery, based chiefly on the work of its inventor, Ballard. A set of such machines had been manufactured and were on trial at Groate Shoe Company, in Spencer, Massachusetts. These machines were capable of successful operation in producing welt shoes.[5] The dealings between United and General were begun in March 1923.[6] The first transaction took place in August 1923, when United acquired the Ballard patents and applications and certain other patents and inventions for $400,000. At the same time Ballard entered the employ of United.[7] General was clearly in bad financial condition when the transactions began and had been for some years previous.[8] Five years later, International having acquired the remaining assets of General, United acquired these assets from International in a series of transactions involving

[2] G-653, IV 14.   [3] G-653.   [4] Tr. 3002–15, testimony of King.
[5] G-657, IV 29 ff.   [6] G-653.
[7] G-676–82, IV 71–83; the figure of $400,000 is given in G-653 on IV 21.
[8] S-274 a–k.

British United as well as United. BUSMC, through a subsidiary, acquired certain assets formerly belonging to General which were in England for $75,000.[9] At the same time United acquired patents and jigs, tools fixtures and spare parts from International, also formerly the property of General, for $75,000.[10] Shortly thereafter, International paid General the same total sum as was involved in the International-United transactions, $150,000, in full payment for International's acquisitions of General's assets and patent rights.[11]

The Government's contention in respect to this transaction is that, essentially, it involved an agreement between United on the one hand and Rand and Gladney (counsel for General) on the other by which General would be removed as a competitive threat in exchange for a higher price than was finally paid and that the whole transaction would be somehow disguised so that its true nature was not apparent; in this connection International was in some sense to act as a cover. This in itself is bad; worse, United did not fulfill the agreement, delaying over the final acquisitions of assets for five years as a device for worsening the already bad financial condition of General and concluding the bargain at a lower price than originally agreed. United, through the testimony of Winslow, denies this, maintaining that the two transactions were entirely separate. The first was simply a matter of acquiring certain useful inventions which might have raised infringement problems in relation to United patents anyway. The second was merely a favor to International, to help them in the liquidation of General and to look after the servicing of certain machines in shoe factories which International had acquired from General.[12]

The evidence does not go so far as to establish the Government's contentions, but it does raise considerable doubt as to the completeness of the Winslow explanation. There are several items which are hard to explain on Winslow's view of the transactions and are consistent with Government view. These are, briefly:[13]

G-651 (1, 2) Letter, Gladney to Rand, June 22, 1923. Especially the phrase "my investigation convinces me that if we obtain money from any outsider, it will mean that the company has already been placed within the reach of United." But, of course, this is only Gladney's view of United's motives; it cannot bind United.

[9] G-770, 771, IV 155–6.   [10] G-772, 3, 4, IV 156–7.   [11] G-777, IV 161.
[12] Tr. 6492, 6559.   [13] All the G exhibits listed are in IV.

G-653 (14–21) Winslow memo on the Rand-Gladney-King-Winslow-
Todd conversations of 9, 10, 12 March 1922. This clearly indicates
International's motives.

G-655 (27–8) Letter from Winslow to Copeland, president of General,
dated 9 March, informing him of possibility that General is infringing United patents. Is the coincidence in date of this letter
and the conversations recorded above merely chance? Or does it
indicate the use of infringement notices as a bargaining technique
and also, perhaps, as a cover in the acquisition of competitive
businesses? Also, in this connection G-659 (44), letter from Fish
(outside patent counsel) to Howard (general manager), 26 March
1923, minimizing the importance of infringement, after examination of the General machines at Spencer. But also G-665, memo
from Howard to Winslow, 30 March 1923, which summarizes
importance of Ballard inventions and raises some questions about
patents which might block USMC developments.

G-683–4 (82–84) Letters, Gladney to Rand, 25 November 1923, 27 Feb.
1924, complaining about non-closure of transaction with United
Mention is made of the "original agreement."

G-714, 717–24, 727–30, 732 (108–119) Various memos and letters, from
July to December 1927, showing selection of Booth as appraiser of
General's assets by Winslow in response to request from Rand,
Winslow's interest in appraisal as shown by Booth's consultation
with him, and transmittal of appraisal to Rand. Appraisal $50,000
for General machinery, drawings, jigs, etc.

G-734 (120) Letter, Winslow to Rand, 31 December 1927, expressing
sympathy with fact that low appraisal will come as a disappointment to Rand. (Consistent with Rand's position as a stockholder
in General, not with Rand's position as president of International.)

G-740, 41, 42, 43 (122–125) Correspondence, Rand and Gladney, January 1928, on final transaction. 740 speaks of the "delays of the
last two or three years" (Rand); 741 (Gladney) covers the trans-
mission of a "purely formal letter" which "purports to keep within
the ceremony we have observed in connection with this transaction," the purely formal letter being 742, 743 (Gladney) repeats
the comments on the delay, and observes that the pertinent question was the fair value of business and assets of General in June
1923.

The picture presented by these documents is not substantially
altered by the oral testimony of Winslow on cross examination[14] and

---

[14] Tr. 6804–23.

the testimony of Rand and Gladney.[15] Although all deny that any subterfuge was involved in the transactions, the testimony is characterized by bad memory and lack of knowledge on many important points.

While the existence of an agreement to conceal the nature of the General transaction between United and International is not proved, the points cited above, especially the repeated references to an "understanding" between Rand and Gladney and the coincidences of the payments by United's British subsidiary and United to International on the one hand, and International's payments to General on the other, do suggest strongly that the 1923 and 1928 transactions were part of one whole and that United used to the full its bargaining advantages through delay and apparently succeeded in completing the transaction at a lower price than at least Gladney and Rand originally expected to get when the 1923 deal was made.

The acquisition of General has been treated in such detail in order to illustrate the character of the evidence on which the Government's charges of coercive practices rest. Suppose that the conclusions which are described above as "strongly suggested" by the evidence are correct. They show nothing more than the ability of United to exercise pressure on International once International had decided to liquidate General because it was unprofitable, and because the original reason for putting money into it no longer existed. International had no real alternative to dealing with United, and this made possible United's delay, etc.

It might further be argued that along the lines of Judge Hand's opinion in the Aluminum case, 148 F. 2d 416, acquisition in itself can be evidence of intent, absent both coercive practices of the sort considered above and significant effects on market power since it indicates the embracing of every opportunity. In this connection S-168 and S-343 are relevant. The first is a list of companies which were offered to USMC for purchase and rejected; the second a list of patents owned by these firms which were likewise offered and rejected. The first list includes such relatively significant competitors as Landis and Moenus. Thus, there were some opportunities United rejected. This evidence, plus the consideration of the character of oppressive practices charged by the Government as revealed in the General case, leads to the conclusion that a finding of "specific intent"

[15] See esp. Tr. 595–613.

to monopolize, aside from the intent to drive a hard bargain and to take advantage of every power which it possessed, is not justified on the basis of United's acquisitions alone.

The second area in which coercive practices are used by United, according to the contentions of the Government, is in the "enforcement" of its lease clauses.[16] Logically, the charge as stated is meaningless. If the leases themselves are valid, then "enforcement" of their provisions in the sense of requiring the lessees to abide by their contracts is only normal business practice. If the leases are in themselves illegal, then "enforcement" of their terms can hardly be a separate offense but its illegality simply reflects the vice of the leases. But the examples the Government offers to support the charge suggest a more meaningful interpretation—namely, that there is differential enforcement of the lease terms among customers in different situations. Specifically, whenever a customer has a competitive machine, all applicable lease terms are "enforced" to the full; in a situation in which a lease clause might be applicable but no competition is involved, there is no enforcement. Thus, for example, the return of a United machine in order to replace it by a competitive machine involves the payment by the lessee of minimum royalties or rentals adjusted to lease expiration, but the return of a similar machine in order to perform the same process by hand labor does not, although on the face of the lease the liability is the same in either case.[17] This differential enforcement does represent "coercion" in the sense defined above, the focusing of United's power on specific bargaining relationships. Again its use depends entirely on United's market power which makes it inevitable, by and large, that the customers will sign the leases and put themselves in the position where the "enforcement" of the lease clauses against them is possible.

The Government evidence contains a number of instances of such "enforcement" in connection with competitive machinery, a sample of which is listed below.

Billing of customers under full capacity clause when competitive machines were used and refunding the amount by credits when competitive machines were removed:

Unity Shoe Mfg.	VI 265–71	G-1910–17	(1936–7)
Barr and Bloomfield	VI 245–47	G-1894–97	(1936)

---

[16] GTB Part I, pp. 264 ff.   [17] See G-1641, V 396–7 for example of this.

Shapero Bros.   VI 272–76   G-1918–23   (1936–7)
Mayer-Herman Co.   VI 76–81   G-1729–32   (1937)

Indication that returned machines would not be "accepted" at Beverly until settlement of payments under excess capacity clause was made, followed by shoe manufacturer's discontinuance of use of competitive machines.

Dunn and McCarthy   VI 124–6   G-1773–4   (1931)

General indication that full capacity clause, other lease terms are enforced when manufacturer uses competitive machines and are not in other circumstances in which they might be applicable.

Mishawaka Rubber Co.   VI 211–213 G-1858–8   (1932)

This is of special interest because Mishawaka is apparently a subsidiary of U. S. Rubber, and correspondence is between Winslow and president of U. S. Rubber.

A full list of all examples of use of the full-capacity clause between 1935 and 1945 is given in GTB, part I, app. 3, where 44 examples are cited.

In addition to practices related to competition, two examples of coercion in connection with the signing of renewal leases are offered. These appear to be the only examples of this practice shown. In both cases the lessees were holding machines after the expiry of the lease in accordance with paragraph 13 of the lease.[18] United indicated that shipments of further machines would be held up until renewal leases were signed.

Florsheim Shoe Co.   V 289–90   G-1538   (1933)
L. V. Marks & Sons   V 290–94   G-1539–44   (1941)

Again the coercion here, as in the case of the "enforcement" of the full-capacity clause, reflects primarily United's market power. Had there been serious question of the customer's ability to turn to another supplier when United refused to ship new machines, the tactic could hardly have been applied. But these examples show, which the earlier ones do not, an attempt to prevent customers from using privileges specifically written into the lease and in this respect may lie nearer to the kind of coercion based on essentially tortious action discussed above.

---

[18] Cf. Answer, Exhibit F (p. 343, Annex).

The third area in which charges of coercive practices are pressed by the Government is in the use of patents. One aspect at least of the Government's charge can be dismissed without discussion: namely, that there is something coercive about serving notice of infringement on the sellers of machines which United believed infringed United's patents.[19] Another, the charge that the use of method and article patents is illegally tied to the use of machines by the lease in a manner similar to the practice condemned in B. B. Chemical Co. *v.* Ellis[20] deserves similarly brief treatment. The documents assembled in XI, 313–464, show chiefly that after the outcome of that suit was known United strove to rearrange its business methods in conformity with the findings in the case. The documents cited in GTB Part I to indicate that United proposed to continue the interdicted practices[21] do not support this conclusion. Nor is it clear that the removal of explicit licenses from the leases falls under the ban of the B. B. Chemical Co. *v.* Ellis decision, as argued by the Government; absent such a conclusion, there is no support for the Government view that a continuing illegal practice is involved.

The Government also objected to the acquisition of patents by United to prevent their commercialization by others, to the patenting of United developments aimed at "neutralizing" the advances of rivals, fencing-in, in short, and to the use of United patents to "compel" the assignment of patents on improvements held by others to United.[22] Documents showing examples of the first practice are offered in XI, 280–89. These documents show in general the acquisition of patents for their "hedging" value, or possible "hedging" value, e.g., as second best devices to those used by United. None of the eight examples shows a clear prospect of commercial use by others, some of them indicate that use of the acquired patents would involve infringement of United's patents and that the acquired patent is of doubtful value. No evidence of "coercion" appears in any of the documents; any illegality, if it exists, must arise from a determination that it is either per se illegal to acquire a patent for "hedging" purposes, or that it is illegal for a patentee to hold more than X patents or more than Y per cent of the patents in any classification, or for a patentee to supply more than Z per cent of the market. Argument to support this proposition, or the underlying view that anti-trust litiga-

[19] GTB Part I, appendix 13.   [20] GTB Part I, 465–9.   [21] G-2966–8, pp. 400–3.
[22] GTB Part I, pp. 455–65.

tion is an appropriate vehicle for amending the patent laws in any "desirable" direction is lacking.

The "illegality" of fencing-in raises similar questions. It is clear enough from the examples offered, though they are only three in number, that United engaged in this practice to at least some extent. Thus G-2266, 2918, 2919[23] show a clear instance of this practice. United acquired, in 1933, a patent on a clamping apparatus on wood heels from Koeppe, not then in use or applicable to techniques then in use, because of the possibility of future developments which might make the patent useful to United or to Compo, and thus United should get it rather than allow Compo to do so. There is no indication that Compo in fact tried to get the patent.

A good example of United's use of patents in bargaining, and the relation of this use to the acquisition of inventions, is provided by the history of the Henne-Preo transaction.[24] The Government classified this under the heading "Compelling the assignment of related patents"; the documents are shown in XI, 294–303 and comprise G-1147, 2922, 1145, and 1146. The more complete set of documents presented in S-282 a-q show the same picture, nor is anything of significance added by the testimony of Ashley, Tr. 8813–20; 9388. Together with the information previously presented on the actual acquisition of the patents, these documents show clearly a policy which might fairly be summarized: If you can't lick 'em, join 'em, but first make sure you can't lick 'em. After careful consideration of the possibility of preventing the marketing of the Henne-Preo machine by claiming infringement of patents owned by United, or provoking and winning interferences on applications on file, United decided its chances were not good enough—"Summed up, we have probably four 50-50 chances to prevent the Henne machine going on to the market—"[25] and made the agreement with Henne which finally resulted in United's acquisition of the patents. Note, incidentally, the conservatism of United's decision: the four chances were independent, not compounded; the risk of failing on all four was thus one in sixteen, yet United chose to buy rather than run that much risk of competition. Clearly nothing here is illegal in itself, neither license agreements, infringement suits, interferences. Nor are these, in the absence of fraud or deliberate bad faith, which is nowhere shown, "oppressive" in themselves. Whatever character this

[23] XI 289–90.   [24] Cf. above, pp. 61–62.   [25] G-1148, XI 303.

transaction had making it other than a normal patent-licensing trans-action arises derivatively from United's market position, and the effect of the transaction in contributing to the maintenance of that position.

In addition to the patent practices analyzed above, the Government charges United with the deliberate infringement of the patents of competitors[26] and with bringing infringement suits in bad faith.[27] If these charges are true, then they are examples of coercive practices based on tortious conduct, not merely on the utilization of United's market power in specific transactions.

Three instances of deliberate infringement are cited: one involving the Hamlin Machine Co.; one, the International Shoe Machinery Corporation (Kamborian); one, the Peerless Machinery Company. The last of these refers to events too far in the past to merit examina-tion in any detail—1914–22. In the other two cases United put out machines which its respective competitors charged were infringing their patents, both sued, and both suits were decided against United.[28] In neither case do the United documents offered in evidence by the Government support the charge that infringement was deliberate and in bad faith.[29] In the Hamlin case there are several letters from Salinger, outside patent counsel, which give varying views on the question whether United's machine infringed Hamlin's.[30] None of them indicates an absence of substantial doubt on the point. Here the allegation of bad faith rests entirely on the question of the conduct of the appeal from the District Court's decision in the infringement suit; a matter (presumably) completely outside the scope of the present case. Thus the evidence in the record does not sustain charges of coercive patent practices based on tortious actions by United.

In its Answer to paragraph 3 of the Court Order, the Government lists seven instances of infringement suits initiated in bad faith. Pre-sumably this means suits initiated in circumstances in which the corporation did not believe there was infringement of its patents, though this is not explicitly stated in the answer. Of the seven in-stances, four refer to supplies—the second, third, and sixth to wood

[26] GTB Part I, pp. 375–405.
[27] Govt. Answer to para. 3 of Court Order of 8 May 1950.
[28] Cf. GTB Part I for citations.
[29] The documents are in IX, 173–200 for Hamlin; 200–234 for International.
[30] G-2313, 2315, 2316.

heels, and the seventh to eyelets—and consideration of them is more appropriate to the later discussion of United's activities in the supply markets. Examination of the evidence cited by the Government in the remaining three instances in no case shows bad faith in the sense indicated above. In each case, the opinions of outside patent counsel[31] indicate a belief that United had some chance to win the suit. The fact that counsel in some places advised that the chance was less than even, or that certain claims which United hoped to rely on were weak, or raised other similar cautionary points, and the fact that United lost a suit, or lost an appeal, certainly do not sustain the conclusion that the suit was brought in bad faith.

The specific documents in each instance are as follows:

Instance (1) IX, 130–50. Alleged infringer, Hamlin Machine Co., date 1932. G-2283[32] indicates that Salinger thought there was "some chance" of some of the claims at issue being sustained. The Government presumably relies on G-2293[33] in which Holmes characterizes the judgment for United in the District Court on one of the claims as "unexpected"; and G-2297[34] which indicates that as part of the settlement following the decision for United on some claims and for Hamlin on others, Hamlin proposed a deal about German patent rights by which United waived infringement claims, and Hamlin agreed not to sue to have the patent annulled on the ground that the invention had been disclosed to Boulton, United's inventor, by Mathey, Hamlin's inventor. Neither of these seems to justify the Government's conclusion of bad faith.

Instance (4) XIII, 99–110. Alleged infringer, Gordon, date 1928. G-3457[35] shows Salinger's judgment that the chances of success in a suit were less than even. United in fact lost[36] and lost on appeal as well.[37] After the suit, Gordon tried to sell his patents and machines to United. His asking price, which started at $125,000, went down to $65,000; United was willing to pay no more than $30,000–$50,000.[38] None of this indicates bad faith; the Government, if it relies on anything, must rely on Salinger's estimate of the chances and the fact that infringement was not found by the court, but these hardly amount to conclusive evidence of bad faith.

Instance (5) XIII, 119–157. Alleged infringer, Freeman, distributor

[31] Holmes or Salinger of Fish, Richardson and Neave.   [32] 130 ff.   [33] 140.
[34] 150.   [35] 99.   [36] G-3465, 110.   [37] G-3472, 116.   [38] G-3466–70, 111-17.

of machine manufactured by Abbot-Wilson, date 1930–31. The documents here indicate no question about the wisdom of bringing the suit. The Government presumably relies on G-3495 and the following documents, which raise questions about the propriety of the manner of United's giving notice of infringement, and at most show that Holmes was urging caution on United lest their behavior, even if well within their rights, become the basis of testimony in the suit which might prejudice the outcome, even if irrelevant to the issue. Reliance is perhaps also placed on G-3501 [39] in which Holmes indicates that United lost the suit, the outcome of which was "virtually" determined by the decision in the previous Gordon case. But this of course was wisdom after the event, at least as far as the documents in evidence show.

Summing up, this evidence may show a willingness on the part of United to undertake infringement suits even with low chances of success. Given the large number of United's patents and its size and strength relative to the typical opponent in such a suit, this litigiousness may well have added somewhat to the value of United's patents as a barrier to the entry of competitors. Even so, this was not the result of illegal behavior but rather the result of defects in the functioning of the patent system. That such defects can appropriately be corrected through anti-trust suits is by no means a self-evident proposition.

Two other areas in which the Government charges United with coercive practices are the alteration of lease terms in order to drive out competitors[40] and the development and marketing of machines with the specific purpose of driving out competitors.[41] Both these practices form a part of the more general picture of discrimination in United's price policy and are best considered below in the context of the general discussion of United's price policy.

One practice of United's which may more appropriately be described as "exclusionary" than "coercive" can also be discussed as part of the examination of United's specific intent to monopolize— the purchase and scrapping of second-hand machinery. The existence and extent of the practice is amply documented in XIV, 1–131. The documents are chiefly annual reports of the Fitting Room and General Departments which list purchases of second-hand machinery.

[39] 154 ff.   [40] GTB Part I, pp. 280–323.   [41] GTB Part I, pp. 345–9.

both United sales machines and sales machines put out by competitors, in considerable detail. Typical examples are G-42 (p. 18), G-43 (p. 23), G-49 (p. 35), G-62 (p. 95), G-65 (p. 97). G-61 (p. 95) indicates that the purchases and trade-ins attained a volume of $70,000 to $80,000 per year and involved some 2000 machines in the fiscal years 1937 and 1938; other documents indicate that these were probably the years of maximum activity. Many of the annual reports contain clear expressions of United's purpose in buying such machines at auctions and accepting them in trade-ins: namely, to keep them out of the hands of second-hand dealers because of the undesirable competition such dealers furnished to the lease and sale of new machines by United. Implicit in some of the expressions is a desire, if not an intent, to hasten the end of the second-hand market altogether. Typical examples are shown in G-55 (p. 1), G-2308, a memo from the clerk of the Terms Committee (p. 67), G-44 (p. 67), G-55, 56, 58, 60 (pp. 67–8) and G-64 (p. 69). G-3712 (p. 116) indicates clearly that every part of the machines purchased was to be destroyed.

The testimony of Wogan on this practice[42] admits that purchases were made and indicates that in 1942 a change in policy was instituted, and instructions were issued to stop the practice. No real explanation is given either of the previous practice or the change. This testimony appears to be contradicted by some of the documents in evidence. G-51 and 52 (pp. 37, 38) both show purchases of second-hand machinery after 1942, totaling 73 machines. Perhaps these are the over-enthusiastic acquisitions of scrap metal by subordinates to which Wogan refers.

The significance of these attempts to end the trade in second-hand machinery is different from that of the practices discussed above as coercive. They are examples of engrossment pure and simple, activity which has no useful result other than the enhancement of United's market power. No profit to United could result from these purchases in any other way; moreover, the expression of purpose in the documents is sufficiently clear without the buttress of argument. The magnitude of the purchases was trivial, but their interest lies in the fact that they offer the only example of "monopolization" pure and simple which the evidence sustains. These purchases are not readily explained as "normal business practices" which incidentally serve to

[42] Tr. 10554–60.

support or increase United's market power, but were not primarily directed to this end.

A final word on specific intent on a more general level than the preceding analysis of coercive and exclusive practices is in order. Through the vast collection of documents from United's files that have been offered in evidence, dealing with all aspects of its business over thirty years, concern with the existence and activity of competitors, actual and potential, runs like a red thread. No detailed count is needed to demonstrate this proposition; the most cursory turning of the pages of sixteen volumes of exhibits reveals its truth. No competitor is too small, no machine too trivial, to deserve mention. The movement in and out of a shoe factory of each competitive machine is followed with all the attention a doting mother devotes to an only child. The OMIR's, a high achievement in commercial intelligence, despite the defendant's disclaimers,[43] the annual reports of the operating departments, the occasional surveys of a new field or reviews of an old one by the research division, the memoranda set before the terms committee when lease terms are to be fixed, all reveal the same concern. It may be said that all this shows only diligent attention to the details of United's business which constitutes the substance of excellence and accounts for United's superiority in the market. In the light of United's actual position in the market during the whole period in question, and of the substantial barriers to the growth of competitors already analyzed, however, there is something almost obsessive in this preoccupation with competitive activity. Fear of competition may not in law be relevant to intent to monopolize; but for whatever relevance it may have, the conclusion that United feared a competitor above all things is one which jumps out from the evidence.

2. PRICES AND COSTS

One of the major economic benefits competitive markets provide is the price-cost relationships which they enforce. Under competition, continuous pressure is exerted on prices, forcing them toward costs, and resulting in low margins of profit. Ideally, these margins are pushed down to a size just sufficient to reward entrepreneurs and capitalists for continuing in business; in actual competition this

---

[43] See above, pp. 48–50.

result is achieved to a more or less crude approximation. Under competition, prices correspond closely to costs not only in the aggregate, but for each individual good produced under competitive conditions. Indeed this correspondence, product by product, of prices to costs is one of the important economic advantages which decentralized, private enterprise economies can claim over other forms of social-economic organization. It is the means by which the result of production in accordance with the demands of consumers with maximum efficiency—the greatest output from the existing stock of resources—is achieved. Conversely, one of the important economic disadvantages of monopoly is that it results in wide differences between prices and costs, which may appear in the form of "monopoly profits," but need not necessarily do so.

For the single product firm, with accounting profits used as a sufficiently close approximation to price-cost margins, the existence or non-existence of relatively high rates of return is an adequate test of cost-price relations. For the multi-product firm, such as United, the problem is more complicated. Both the overall relations between costs and prices, as shown in the rate of return in the whole business, and the relations between costs and prices on each individual product must be examined. Unusually high profit rates, in relation to all the relevant circumstances, can in themselves be sufficient indication of poor performance in respect to price-cost margins, even for the multi-product firm, but their absence is not necessarily an indication of good performance. A low rate of profit in the aggregate may be the result of "too high" profits on some products and "too low" profits on others, indicating that the firm is producing too much of some products and too little of others in relation to demand. Thus after evidence on United's aggregate profit rate is examined, the relations of costs to prices on individual machines will also be considered.

The only evidence which compares United's profits with those of a group of similarly situated manufacturers is S-412, the Dean study which compares United's book earnings, 1925–1949, with those of 72 other manufacturers of durable equipment. This shows that United's earnings were just about the same as the average of the group—namely, about 10.0 per cent net earnings, after taxes, on invested capital. United's rate of return was more stable over time than that average of the 72 companies: fluctuating between 13.8 per cent (1936) and 7.7 per cent (1932), while the average of the 72 companies reached nearly 18 per cent in 1928 and fell to minus 2.6 per cent in 1932. United's earnings rates are not so large either absolutely, considered in the light of general knowledge of corporate returns, or in terms of the comparisons presented in the evidence to support any finding of overall monopoly profit. Nor, indeed, is this charge pressed by the Government, although it appears in the Complaint.[44, 45]

Before presentation of the analysis of cost-price relationships in detail, it is appropriate to indicate the general character of United's costs in the machinery business, as a way of showing the relative importance of the various kinds of activities constituting the "product" which United provides when it leases a machine. The basic information is contained in exhibit S-335 which shows a division of United's costs between machinery and other business, and a breakdown of the costs by various classes. The document shows the relevant figures for the fiscal years ending 1947, 1948, 1949, and 1950. The division of United's expenses between machinery and other business required a cost allocation which United does not ordinarily perform, dividing certain overhead expenses between machinery and other business. S-335 shows figures based on three different methods of allocation leading to somewhat different results, but not significantly so. The three allocation methods are explained in the testimony of Kemp, Treasurer of United.[46] The essential points are as follows: Most of the accounts permitted direct segregation of machinery and other business; e.g., roadmen's salaries were chargeable to machinery business; salesmen's salaries were separately accounted for and chargeable to merchandise business. Three accounts[47] were not so separable: branch office operations, Boston office administration, and general

[44] See Tr. p. 11910; Complaint, p. 48.

[45] It is worth noting that the evidence cited pertains only to United's total business. Strictly speaking, what is relevant to the discussion of United's position and performance in the shoe machinery market is material on United's profit rates in the machinery business. This information is not available in the record. Although a separation of income and expenses between machinery and other business, and computations of net profit in the two branches are offered (S-335), no figures on the apportionment of capital between machinery and other activities are given. Failing these, meaningful profit rates cannot be calculated; profits in relation to sales are not useful for the purposes of the present investigation, either in themselves or in comparison with profits-to-sales ratios of other sellers.

[46] Tr. 11238–251.

[47] Totaling some $5,900,000 out of total expenses of $18,000,000 in 1947.

expenses; these had to be divided according to some method. The three methods which were used[48] were:

I. Allocation was based on the judgment of various department heads and other knowledgeable officials of United on the proportion of time the employees of the three departments spent on machinery business and other business.[49]

II. Two factors were involved in the second allocation method:

(a) Branch office administrative expense was allocated to machinery business in the proportion that salaries and expenses of personnel in branches directly assignable to machinery business formed of the total salaries and expenses of personnel in the branches directly assignable to machinery or other activities.

(b) General expenses and Boston office administration were allocated to machinery business in the proportion that Boston and branch office personnel assigned directly to machinery business formed of total Boston and branch office personnel directly assigned to machinery or to other business.[50]

III. Allocation of all the overhead accounts to machinery business in the proportion that all directly identifiable machinery costs of operation and service formed of total directly identifiable machinery costs plus merchandise sales costs.[51]

Of the three methods of allocation, Kemp offered his judgment that the second is the best.[52]

The percentage distribution of machinery expenses on the three allocation formulae, as well as gross earnings and net revenues, are shown in the table following for the fiscal year ending 1947. The other years show sufficiently similar figures so that these may be discussed as representative. The differences among the results of the three methods of cost allocation are not great enough to make worthwhile separate consideration of each, and on the strength of Kemp's testimony and its middle position with respect to the actual figures, II is used as the basis for the following discussion and any later discussions of costs to which these figures are relevant.

Some grouping of the categories in Table 1,[53] together with a change in titles, summarizes more clearly the picture of United's

---

[48] Marked I, II, III in S-355.   [49] Tr. 11246–7.   [50] Tr. 11247–8.   [51] Tr. 11248.
[52] Tr. 11250.   [53] P. 119.

machinery business revealed by the cost figures. This is shown by the following table:

Activity		Expense Categories of Table I	Per Cent of Total Expense
Machinery manufacture	(8)	depreciation of leased mach'y	17.5
Machinery distribution	(6)	operating supervision and (11) branch office operations	15.6
Service	(7)	machine services	20.1
Research	(9)	research	20.1
Total of above			71.9
Overhead		(12) Salaries and expenses of administrative depts., plus (13) general expenses	20.1
Total			92.0

A word on the identification of "manufacturing" with depreciation of leased machinery is in order. If the stock of leased machines outstanding were constant, and the inventory of machines and machine parts in the hands of United likewise constant, and there were no changes in price levels, then the depreciation of the stock in any year would be equal to the manufacturing costs of that year, since manufacture would be carried on at just the rate required to replace machines as they depreciated. Although none of these conditions holds strictly, and the departure from constancy in the case of price levels has been large, depreciation may serve as an approximate representation of manufacturing costs. To the extent that the stock of machines is growing in value, either through increase in numbers or through rising unit value per machine, the annual depreciation figure understates the relative importance of manufacturing activities in United's machinery business.

Speaking broadly, therefore, United's machinery business can be divided into four kinds of activity: manufacturing, distribution, service, and research, each of which is more or less equal in importance in terms of resource use; with the general management of all these activities about as important as any one of them individually.

The first aspect of machine-by-machine price-cost relationships which will be examined is a general one: the degree to which United's pricing system and marketing method facilitate or hinder comparisons of prices and costs on particular machine types. The

TABLE 1

UNITED SHOE MACHINERY CORPORATION
Fiscal Year Ending 28 February 1947
Percentage Distribution of Machinery Business Income and Expenses
(Computed from S-335)

	I		II		III	
	Income	Expenses	Income	Expenses	Income	Expenses
1. Gross Earnings	100.0		100.0		100.0	
2. Unit charges and rentals	96.3		96.3		96.3	
3. Initial and deferred payments	1.1		1.1		1.1	
4. Merch. profits (gross)	2.6		2.6		2.6	
5. Expenses:	61.5	100.0	64.6	100.0	66.9	100.0
6. Operating supervision		5.5		5.3		5.1
7. Mach. service		21.2		20.1		19.5
8. Depreciation of leased machinery		18.4		17.5		17.0
9. Research		19.6		18.7		18.0
10. Other direct costs		4.7		4.5		4.3
11. Branch office operations		8.4		10.3		9.7
12. Salaries and expenses of adm. depts.		10.0		11.8		14.3
13. General expenses		8.5		8.3		8.8
14. Discounts allowed		3.5		3.1		3.3
15. Bad debts		—		—		—
16. Other charges		—		—		—
17. Earning before Federal Income taxes	38.5		35.4		33.1	

significance of an easy or difficult comparison of prices and costs for a multi-product firm is clear: the internal efficiency of the firm in the sense of its ability to maximize its profits by choosing the appropriate combination of outputs clearly depends on its ability to know price-cost relations for each product. This criterion of internal efficiency applies without respect to the market situation of the firm, and the extent to which its individual efficiency does or does not contribute to social efficiency. (It should be noted that a firm operating in a perfectly competitive market would have internal efficiency—in the sense defined—forced upon it by the operation of the competitive market which would "choose" the appropriate output combinations for the firm. But no real firm is in precisely this situation; and United, of course, operates in a situation in which the pressure of market forces on internal policy is very weak indeed.)

The very nature of United's marketing methods, as well as examination of the formulae which are used as "guides" in setting prices, provides a strong argument for the difficulties of price-cost comparisons, and this conclusion is confirmed by testimony in the record. The leasing system means that the prices under existing lease contracts are inflexible upwards for the long duration of the lease. The existence of outstanding leases with long periods to run probably acts as a deterrent upward changes in terms on new contracts: the history of prices and costs and the character of the postwar increases support this argument.[54] The possibilities of downward price adjustments are not necessarily similarly inhibited by the long duration of the leases. S-248 shows that there were 43 machines on which reduction in lease terms were made in the period 1922–1946. This indicates a moderate degree of price flexibility; it also means that for the great majority of machine types there were no changes in prices in this 25-year period. This was a period in which costs in general were rising,[55] and it was a priori unlikely that the rises were such as to make appropriate all through the period exactly those price relations among various machine types which were fixed at the outset. By contrast with the lease method of distribution, a sales system would allow price changes in response to increases in costs much more promptly; and it would probably create a smaller drag on downward price adjustments as well, simply because of the greater

[54] See Tr. 8368–73, 8425, 8452–3 (Brown), 10579–605 (Wogan).
[55] S-413, Chart 3 and Tr. 8368–9, 8452 Brown.

frequency with which prices would necessarily be reviewed by management.

The testimony of Messrs. Brown and Wogan[56] shows clearly that the Corporation uses the "10-year investment formula" as the basis of cost information on which pricing decisions are made. This formula purports to show the average outlay per year involved in leasing a particular machine for ten years. Examples of its computation are numerous in the documents printed in GTB, I; G-337 (I, 140 ff.) may be cited as a specific example. The formula is explained in the testimony at length by Branch,[57] and its application to particular machines is illustrated by Brown.[58] The elements of the computation are these: an estimate of the field or ultimate number of machines which the Corporation can expect to distribute is made by the appropriate operating department; actual research and development expenditures applicable to the machine type already incurred are divided by the estimated field to give a development cost per machine; to this is added the Beverly factory cost of manufacture[59] to get total machine cost. To this total is added 60 per cent, representing 6 per cent interest for ten years on the total machine cost; an estimate of probable service cost furnished by the operating department; interest at 6 per cent per year on the accumulating service expenditure, not counting the first year's outlay; estimated installation costs and 6 per cent interest for ten years on the installation costs. The result is taken as a "guide" to pricing; according to Brown[60] it represents the "out-of-pocket expense" involved in developing and supplying a particular machine. The expense shows by the formula is indeed out-of-pocket in the sense that general "Boston office" overheads are not included, but overheads of manufacturing and Beverly research are included in the machine cost estimates.

The shortcomings of a formula such as this in providing cost information on which pricing decisions can be based are many and for the most part obvious. Some of them arise from the bundle of different elements provided under the leasing system—for example the problem of accurately estimating service costs. Others are inherent simply in the problems of marketing machines which will be

---

[56] Tr. 8329–31, 8403–4, 8435–6; 10403, 10606–11.   [57] Tr. 8279–85.
[58] E.g., to Universal Heat Activator, 8345–56.
[59] Based on experience of manufacturing machines used for trials, etc., usually done before terms are set.
[60] Tr. 8330–3.

made and marketed over long periods of time: the estimate of the field over which research and development expenses are apportioned would be equally necessary if machines were sold rather than leased, although in that case there might well be greater flexibility of prices in response to revisions of the data underlying cost estimates. The importance of the so-called "interest" elements in the formula is great, and the unreality of the calculations in this respect is obvious. In particular no account is taken of the time distribution of research and manufacturing expense on the one hand, and the time distribution of actual machine leasings on the other. Thus, the accumulation of machine and service costs at 6 per cent interest for ten years starting from the time of the calculation is obviously arbitrary. These arbitrary elements, and the necessity of basing many of the estimates on average experience of one sort or another—e.g., estimates of service expense[61] —result in a blurring of cost computations and an inability to analyze cost on particular machine types, the result of which is to make difficult a close adjustment of prices to costs, even should such an adjustment be desired by United.

The problem of estimation involved in the application of the ten-year investment formula and the variability of the magnitudes which must be estimated are illustrated in various documents in evidence. Thus S-256, S-258, and S-271 show annual average earnings per machine over varying periods for the Clicker-C, the Rex-Puller C and D, and the Heel Seat Fitter-A, respectively. The range of variation of average annual earnings shown was:

Machine	Period	High	Low
Clicker	1941-50	$72.52	$61.11
Puller	1934-50	$448.88	$281.26
Heel seat fitter	1936-41	$278.00	$221.00

S-438 a and b show the results of a comparison between actual revenue for the fiscal year ending February 1937 with the standard expected revenue computed according to the formula used in price setting for new machines.[62] The standard revenue is computed as 250 days × capacity in pairs per day × royalty per pair. The 48 machine types for which the comparison was made showed the following distribution of the ratio of actual to expected earnings, in percentage terms:

---

61 Tr. 8149, Brown, on Universal Heat Activator.   62 See Tr. 14440.

30%	to	50%	2 machines
50		70	7
70		90	11
90		110	13
110		130	8
130		150	4

Table 2 is based on S-440 which shows average annual earnings for each year of the period 1936–1948 for 21 new unit-charge machines put out in the period 1937–1950 and also standard expected revenue used in computing terms for each of the machines. The table shows "standard" revenue and the high and low values of actual average revenue for each of the machines which were out five years or more during the period.

TABLE 2

Machine Type	"Standard" Earnings UC only	Annual Average Earnings High	Low	Total Number of Years Covered
1. Unishank assembling A	$375	$422	$228	14
2. U. molding A	562	491	239	14
3. Cement lasting A	875	571	257	14
4. Edging B	584	356	216	14
5. Pre-welt lasting A	250	303	217	14
6. Lacing A	563	539	308*	11*
7. Sole laying F, Goodyear	450	454	307	11
8. Goodyear sole laying and tacking C	500	521	236	11
9. Lasted bottom ironing	1,563	880	541	11
10. Pre-welt lasting B	313	277	225	8
11. Platform cover lasting C	360	307	201	5

*Excludes first year in which average earnings were $29.

The precise significance of each of the three tabulations shown above is not the same; none the less, they all support the same conclusion: the variation of actual machine earnings per year, both in year-to-year terms for any one machine and among machines in relations to "predicted" earnings, is sufficiently great to introduce a substantial element of error into any pricing formula which involves the prediction of income for ten years into the future. It should be emphasized, however, that the necessity for similar predictions—in an implicit sense, at least—would not be entirely removed merely by the subsitution of a sales for the lease system of marketing. Should substantial market power remain with the seller under a sales system, permitting extensive and significant price discrimination among machines, then the "correct" pricing for maximum profit would require —at least implicity—similar predictions of the yield of services of the machine over a long future period. But under the sales system, errors in pricing would be more clearly revealed and more quickly correctible when detected than under the present arrangement. O course, should the change from leasing to selling be accompained by other changes which would reduce the market power of the seller considerably, then his power to practice price discrimination would be considerably restricted, and the whole prediction problem minimized, as prices moved closer to costs and demand considerations played a smaller role in pricing. The result of the inability to ascertain the costs of particular machine types with accuracy is necessarily the reliance on some averaging out of costs over many types of machines, blunting considerably the edge of managerial control in the enterprise.

The general point is particularly well illustrated by the last of the foregoing tables.[63] Actual average annual earnings failed to reach the standard on the basis of which terms were set in every year of the period for seven of the eleven machines there shown (nos. 2, 3, 4, 6, 9, 10, 11). While this may show that United's earnings are modest and that the pricing formulae exaggerate them considerably, it also shows, what is more to the point, that United may be persistently mis-anticipating returns in relation to costs on particular machines for periods as long as 14 years.

Examples of difficulties of estimation and prediction on the cost as well as the revenue side are also available. Thus G-310,[64] a research department memorandum to the Clerk of the Terms Committee dated December 1946, a comparison of experience with the Clicker C from 1935 to 1939 with the "predicted" service-cost figures based on departmental averages, showed average annual service costs per machine as $4.07, compared with the formula value of $14.18. Another memorandum of the same character and date referring to the Welter K is shown in G-349.[65] This indicates an even larger discrepancy of service cost experience and "expected" costs based on the average of 6 per cent of cost, but in the other direction: actual costs averaged

---

[63] Table 2, p. 123.   [64] I, 46 ff.   [65] I, 168 ff.

$56.73 per year, compared with scheduled value of $24.72. These computations are based on the balance sheet rather than the ten-year investment formula. This is essentially the application to an individual machine type of the allocation procedure II described above.[66] The arbitrary character of overhead allocations which limits the usefulness of this formula is not in point in the consideration of service costs which are direct expenses or very nearly entirely so.

Direct testimony by the chief officers of United repeats the conclusions of the foregoing argument. Thus Brown, in answer to a question by the Court,[67] indicates that he has never known "exactly" what it cost to put out a particular machine. At another point[68] he indicates specific inability to determine what profits were being earned on the Clicker C, and even to produce figures showing that it did in fact earn any profit. Wogan endorses the view of Brown[69] and adds the comment—significant in the light of the argument above—that it is easier to compute the net profit on parts than on machines because "the leases are for a long period of time, and the parts are sold immediately."

It is appropriate to add here that these same officers disclaimed any intention of choosing profit maximization as a goal of corporation policy.[70] Rather their view was that the Corporation should aim at the widest possible distribution of machinery consistent with "fair" or "reasonable" profits.[71] Whether this can be interpreted as showing a preference of market control to higher profits, as an obscure and imprecise expression of a policy of long-run profit maximization based on the rule that competition had best be avoided, or taken at its face is debatable. In any event, whatever its basis, such a policy is a dubious one as a guide to that efficiency of resource use which is one of the important results of a regime of competition.

The second aspect of cost-price relationships to be considered also relates to comparisons among machine types—the question of price discrimination among machine types. The basic facts on the extent of discrimination in United's prices (lease terms) and the range of price differences involved have already been presented above.[72] Tables 1 and 2, pages 75, 76, show respectively the spread of years required to return the ten-year investment and calculated profit rates on the balance sheet formula for 66 lease machines on the

[66] Pp. 116–117.   [67] Tr. 8412.   [68] Tr. 8646–49.   [69] Tr. 10845.
[70] Tr. 8325-6, Brown.   [71] Tr. 8325-6, Brown.   [72] Ch. III, pp. 74–78.

basis of the new terms put into effect July 1950. While neither the ten-year-investment formula nor the balance-sheet formula can be taken as anything more than a very crude approximation to costs, the differences between these approximations and more accurate computations cannot be shown to be correlated with the terms differences in such a way that the apparently discriminatory price structure is not in fact so. Such an arrangement of errors is too improbable to deserve consideration. Thus these tables can be taken as indicative of United's intent to discriminate in price among the various machine types, although only crudely corresponding to the actual degree of achieved discrimination. To this evidence can be added the testimony of chief officers of United that the Corporation's price policy is indeed discriminatory. Thus Brown[73] says "our terms are really based primarily, and, in fact, on the important machines entirely upon the benefit of the machine to the shoe manufacturers." And the same point, that prices are fixed largely on "the value of the machine to the user of the machine" is made by Wogan;[74] in fact, the relation of discrimination to competition, and pricing as a method of "splitting the benefits" of the machine between the shoe manufacturer and United are all described clearly by Wogan in this part of his testimony.[75] This parole evidence is not cited to "support" the statistical evidence, which needs no such support, but rather to show that the Corporation's chief officers understand the character of its machine pricing policy.

This strong evidence of widespread and quantitatively large discrimination in prices among various machines is of great significance in the evaluation of United's market performance. Wide differences in the margins between costs and prices among the various machines which constitute United's line mean that the shoe manufacturers are not offered a choice among the various techniques of shoe manufacture on terms that correspond to the real social costs of providing the machinery for the alternative techniques. This, in turn, means that shoe manufacturers do not offer the consuming public a choice among shoes of various constructions on terms corresponding to their real social costs—that is, the use of resources they involve. Thus for example, the table on p. 77 above indicates clearly that the relative terms on which a women's shoe manufacturer can make welts and cements do not correspond at all to the relative real costs of the two

---

[73] Tr. 8388–89.   [74] Tr. 10465.   [75] Tr. 10464–72.

processes. In the particular case, the competition of Compo makes the cement process relatively "too cheap" and the welt process consequently relatively "to dear."

It might be argued that the differences in relative prices of different machines are so small in an absolute sense as not to affect either the choice of manufacturers as to processes or the ultimate choice of consumers as to shoe constructions; i.e., that the demand of shoe manufacturers for machines, and of consumers for shoes are insensitive to the magnitude of price differences which could arise out of the existence of price discrimination in machine terms. Even if this were true, the price policy of United would represent a "taxing," so to speak, of the wearers of one kind of shoes for the benefit of the wearers of another. But this argument of the lack of price-response is not supported by the evidence. On the contrary, many of United's documents show consideration of widely differing alternative prices for new machines, in connection with the influence of these prices on the potential field of the machines.[76] In the face of these documents, it is hard to give much weight to Brown's testimony to the contrary.[77] Moreover, the general situation of the shoe manufacturer, with his wide choice of partly competing and partly complementary techniques, suggests the force of the effect of terms differences on the choice of technique. Once this effect is granted, then it is clear that the price terms on which the consumer chooses between various types of shoes do not correspond to the relative real resource costs of these alternatives.

The significance of widespread and quantitatively large price discrimination as an indicator of United's unsatisfactory market performance is greatly dependent on the temporal aspects of the pattern of discrimination observed. In general, it can be said that discrimination of the kind discussed here is never entirely absent in any actual market, especially one in which the typical seller produces many products under conditions of common overhead costs of various types. Only in the abstract perfectly competitive market of economic analysis would the price structure of the multi-product firm be free from any inter-product price discrimination. But in any real market in which a substantial degree of competition existed, the pattern of price dis-

---

[76] See, e.g., G-2119, 58-9; G-337, I, 145; G-4566, I, 220; G-2090, I, 325; G-470, II, 200; G-618, II, 526.
[77] Tr. 8573-75.

crimination would be a continually changing one over time, and, indeed, the force of competition would show itself to a substantial degree through the character of the change in price-cost relations among particular products. Typically, when one producer in the market introduced a new product, he would be able to realize a relatively high margin over costs on that product. As his rivals copied the product, either directly, or by producing functionally similar products if the original innovation was protected by patents, competition would force down the margin of the innovator; another innovation would set off another cycle of price-cost changes.[78]

United's price structure shows no such pattern. In general differential margins are frozen and remain unchanged for periods of 20 years and more.[79] Only the occasional appearance of a competitive threat causes a change;[80] and it is of course the infrequency of such competition which leads to the rigidity of the structure. The rigidity, the result of the lack of competition, is an excellent indicator of the degree of United's long-run market dominance. The existence of a large price-cost margin for a long period of time, as shown for example by the Welt Sewer K or the ORL-O, is a clear sign of United's market power and the lack of potential competition; had potential competition existed, it would have either become actual or forced margins down.

Thus United's cost-price relations have been such as to indicate poor market performance, in the sense of wide departure over long periods of time from the kind of results which would exisit in a competitive market, in two respects: (a) the shoe manufacturer's and ultimately the shoe-wearer's choice among different shoe constructions is not made on terms which correspond to the real social costs of the alternatives; and (b) United's own knowledge of its costs in respect to individual machine types is so imprecise as to raise serious doubts as to the purely internal efficiency of its operations. These two effects are different, but ultimately they issue in the same result—a less efficient use of resources than could be achieved with a market functioning in a more nearly competitive fashion.

This judgment is purely in terms of the overall results of United's price policy in respect to various machine types. It takes no account

---

[78] Essentials of this process are described in Dean, *Managerial Economics,* ch. 3 and 8.
[79] See discussion on pp. 120–121 above and evidence cited there.
[80] See below, pp. 130–134.

of the impact of particular price decisions on particular competitors, what might be termed the specifically exclusionary aspects of price discrimination. It is to this side of United's pricing policy that the Government has directed its attention:[81] For this, if for no other reason, this aspect of the matter requires some discussion. All that has been said above on the relation of results to "intent," and the significance of "coercive" practices as indications of a specific intent to exclude could be repeated here.[82] In brief, what of the foregoing discussion is relevant to price discrimination can be put as follows. In order that United be able to practice price discrimination, some amount of market power on its part is necessary. Given the market power, the practice of price discrimination will, in general, allow United to achieve higher profits than it could achieve in the absence of discrimination. The essence of such discrimination for profit will consist in the charging of higher margins (over costs) on machines in which there is little competition—either from other machines or from hand labor, and lower margins on machines in which there is much competition. Now this is also precisely the pattern which would be shown if the "intent" behind the discrimination was driving out competitors, rather than increasing profits. In general, a distinction between the two kinds of "intent" cannot be made merely by looking at the actual price structure, if it can be made at all. Nor will a judgment of "intent" rest validly on the distinction between just meeting and undercutting the prices of competitors. The market position of the discriminating seller will do much to determine the results, whatever the "intent." If he, as does United, controls nearly 90 per cent of the market, and the obstacles to entry are considerable, a discriminatory price policy will exclude or sharply limit the competition of single-line sellers whatever the underlying "intent." On the other hand, if a seller faces rivals of equal or roughly equal strength, so that the result of any program of discriminatory price cutting initiated by him is as likely to favor his rivals as himself, the effect of exclusion will be absent, whatever the "intent."

Only in the extreme case, where the discriminating seller, though having higher out-of-pocket costs than his rivals (or the same costs), sells below these costs, can the inference of "intent to exclude" be

---

[81] See GTB I, pp. 280–323.

[82] See above, pp. 57–59 for discussion of acquisitions from this point of view, and pp. 100–102 for discussion of coercive practices in general.

unambiguously drawn from the discriminatory price policy. Note that even a price cut, followed by the demise of a rival and then by a price rise, does not point unequivocally to an "intent to exclude," as distinguished from an intent to make high profits, in the absence of the cost situation described in the previous sentence. And also note particularly that the relevant cost comparison is one of out-of-pocket or variable costs of the particular machine in question, not "full costs" based on an arbitrary assignment of overheads, since it is precisely the scope for varying contributions to overhead, including profits, by different machine types which makes it possible for discrimination to arise.

Specific examples of discrimination which the Government points to as showing an intent to drive out competition can now be considered in the light of the foregoing discussion. The Government, in its answer to Paragraph I of the Court's Order of May 8, 1950, lists 57 instances of machine pricing which show discrimination in order to secure a monopoly or restrain competition. Not all of these instances are distinct: some are separate steps of a series of terms changes on a single machine, made with reference to a continuing competitive situation; some are steps in series of terms changes involving different models of the same machine, again in reference to a continuing competitive situation. It is not quite clear just what a "distinct" example of discrimination is, but eliminating the types of duplication mentioned above leaves some 43 examples. Nine of these have been examined in detail: the six which the Government selected as "most flagrant" in response to the Order, and three further instances involving Compo, United's most important competitor.[83]

In all nine of the instances the existence of discrimination is clear. It manifests itself in various ways. One is the reduction of previously set terms in the face of growing competition—instances 12 and 13, the mocassin-seam attachment on the ORL-O in the face of competition from Union Lockstitch machines; instance 18, the cement-sole attacher B to compete with Compo; instance 16, the staple side-laster C, previously used on Littleway shoes, to prevent the increasing substitution of cheaper and supposedly inferior tack-lasting in the growing cement shoe field. Another is the offer of a new model machine at the same or lower terms as the previous model which it is

---

[83] The Government's Answer gives the documentary references for each instance and its connection with competition.

designed to replace, even though the cost of the new machine is higher than that of the old one—instance 1, heel-seat fitter A, a machine higher in cost than the model which it replaced but offered at lower terms because of competition from hand labor, Compo, and other machine manufacturers; instance 8, expedite heel finisher D offered at same terms as previous BB model although its manufacturing costs were substantially higher, $275 as compared with $185, in order to meet competition of rebuilt second-hand sale machines. A third is the failure to increase sale price (and lease terms) on a machine in the face of rapidly rising bulletin costs because of the presence of competition, combined with the appearance of the long-since "justified" increase when "competitive conditions" had changed, shown in the case of the perforating machine-A which faced competition from Peerless machines. Finally, there is the somewhat extreme example provided by the wood-heeling machine model B. This shows not only the development of a new machine—the model B— to meet the competition of German machines with the Alpha and USMC wood heeler in the slipper trade, and the setting of low terms on the machine in comparison with the Alpha, which had about the same manufacturing cost; but also an attempt to segregate the market in the slipper trade from the rest of the market and prevent the use of the B, with its lower terms, in place of the Alpha in the shoe trade in general. This was done both by setting high minimum levels of use for the B, appropriate to slipper manufacturers but not to shoe manufacturers, and by furnishing the model B on an individual basis to slipper manufacturers in New York among whom competition from German machines existed, without announcing it to the trade at large. The intent to limit the use of the model B is indicated by the expression of concern lest the movement of some slipper factories from the metropolitan area spread the use of the machine among shoe manufacturers and so reduce the use of the Alpha.

All nine instances offer indications of awareness by United's officials that terms changes were connected with the existence of competitively offered machines, over and above the objective facts of the terms changes, their discriminatory character in the price-cost sense, and the presence in the market of machines competing with those which showed changes in terms. But whether this shows an intent to "drive out" competitors or merely to compete with them on equal terms is much less clear. No expression which unambiguously indicates the aim of driving United's competitors out of the market can be found in the printed part of the Government offers relating to instances 12 and 13, the ORL-O moccasin seam attachment; instance 15, wood-heeling machine B; instance 10, USMC perforating machine A; instances 21 and 22, cement-spraying unit C and D; instance 4, wood-heel attaching machine A; instance 1, heel seat fitting machine A; instance 8, USMC expediting and finishing machine D. In the case of the staple side laster C, instance 16, the problem does not arise, since it is essentially a question of competition between two United machines.

Only in one of the nine cases, therefore, are there expressions which can fairly be construed as showing specific intent to exclude a competitor from the market. These appear in connection with the cement-sole attacher B, the second machine developed to meet the competition of Compo's new process. G-2, an annual report of the Cement Shoe Department for 1933[84] speaks as follows, "The writer had confidently expected that after we came out in January 1932 with our USMC Cement Sole attaching Machine—Model B, and auxiliaries, and the mechanical difficulties had been ironed out, we would enjoy a gradual elimination of our competitors in the cement shoe field." He goes on to indicate the disappointment of these confident expectations and says, "Just what to offer for the present emergency is a serious problem." Somewhat more subtly expressed thoughts along the same lines are revealed in G-1984, a memorandum to the General Manager from E. R. Noyes dated July 1935.[85] Here a computation is presented to show the effect of a reduction in royalty rates from 1 cent a pair to $\frac{1}{2}$ a pair on Compo's revenues, and an indication that this might absorb the greater part of Compo's net profits. But this document must be interpreted in the light of the fact that United actually reduced its royalty rate from 1 cent to $\frac{3}{4}$ cents, NOT $\frac{1}{2}$ cent.[86]

If intent is judged in terms of results, only a moderately stronger conclusion emerges. The failure to drive out Compo's sole-attaching machines needs no comment. In the case of the moccasin-seam attachment to the ORL-O, the documents indicate no reduction in outstanding competitive machines up to 1943 when wartime material restrictions limited the use of the attachment; no evidence on the

[84] VI, 360–3.   [85] VI, 398–402.   [86] G-1986, VI, 402–3.

present situation appears in the record. The cast of the heel-seat fitting machine A, shows a small decrease in outstanding competitive machines relative to the large increase in United machines over a fifteen-year period. This, and the general context of the situation, suggests that the important "competition" against which terms reductions on this machine were effective was the competition of hand labor. In the instance of the USMC Xpedite heel finishing machine D, some gain in the use of USMC machines relative to competitive machines is shown. At the end of the period covered by the documents, 1938, there remained 300 competitive machines out in comparison with 562 USMC; in 1930, there were 698 USMC and 660 competitive machines. In the case of the USMC perforating machine A, the documents indicate that competition had decreased in a situation where United's terms remained the same but no explanation of the decrease is given. The wood-heel attaching machine A triumphed over its Compo rival but the results appear to be due at least as much to the technical deficiencies of the Compo machine as to United's price policy.[87] The new model D Cement-Spraying Unit showed a gain over its Compo competitor which the previous model C had been unable to achieve. Here discrimination played an important role in that the more expensive and efficient D was offered on the same terms as the cheaper C. Likewise, the discrimination inherent in the development and offer of the wood heeling machine B for the slipper trade only seemed to have achieved its goal; G-90, an annual report of the Heeling Department for 1935,[88] speaks of the model B as having served its purpose. Finally, the change in the royalty rates and process charges for the use of staple side-laster C on fore-part and side-lasting of cement shoes also appears to have achieved its aim of reducing the use of the cheaper CHM lasting method in this field.

The examples here examined include the two cases in which the Government charges that the Corporation priced at terms below costs in the sense of out-of-pocket plus development costs, and anticipated a loss when terms were set: instances 8 and 18. In instance 8, USMC Xpedite heel finishing machine D, it is not clear from the evidence that a loss in this sense was anticipated or sustained. In the second case, that of the cement sole attacher B, it is reasonably clear that

[87] G-90, VII, 201–2.   [88] VII, 445–50.

development costs were not covered.[89] But the logic which classifies this as an "intended" loss is faulty: bygones must always be bygones, and once the development costs have been incurred any producer would market the machine if it covered its manufacturing costs. Only if it could be shown that United expected to be unable to cover its development costs in advance of designing the machine would this constitute evidence of intent to exclude; no such showing is made.

This examination of a sample of the Government's instances of pricing tactics allegedly exhibiting an intent to exclude competition is inconclusive. If "intent to exclude" means a specific intent to drive competitors completely out of the market by the adoption of price policies which are explicable only in terms of exclusionary policy— e.g., selling below out-of-pocket costs, no evidentiary basis appears to support a finding of such intent. On the other hand, if the intent in question is displayed by the conscious adoption of price policies which will, in given competitive situations, be relatively advantageous to United and relatively disadvantageous to United's competitors offering machines of one or a few types, and which contribute to a change in the competitive balance in the market in United's favor, it is clear that these examples support the allegation of intent. But, on this definition, it is not clear what a finding of intent adds to the previous conclusions on the existence and consequences of widespread discrimination in terms among machine types except the already obvious result that United was aware of the existence and significance of the pricing pattern.

The preceding section of the discussion of price-cost relationships in the machinery market focused on the comparison of price-cost margins among the various machine types. The aim of the analysis was to elucidate the amount and significance of inter-machine price discrimination as one aspect of United's performance in the machinery market. The present section turns from inter-machine discrimination to inter-customer discrimination, setting forth its extent and significance as another part of United's performance in terms of cost-price relations.

United's lease terms are the same to all customers. Discrimination among customers arises therefore only in so far as they do not receive the same things in return for their uniform payments. Of all the

---

[89] G-1973, VI, 364 and G-202, VI, 408. The latter is a two-sentence extract from a program committee report of 1939, entirely without context.

elements in the lease "bundle," it is clear that service, provided without separate charge, might be expected to vary most as between individual shoe manufacturers. Since service, in the broad sense in which United usually defines that term including installation of machines, instruction of operators, and repair of machines, accounts for 20 per cent of the cost of the "bundle,"[90] variations in the amount of service provided to different shoe manufacturers could well account for quantitatively significant discriminations among them.

The existence and magnitude of such variations was the subject of considerable evidence, both parole and documentary. The important testimony is provided by L. B. Walker, an assistant general manager, in Tr. 11027–58, 11065–69, 11078–96, 11209–16, and 13223–49. The relevant exhibits are S-329, S-330 and S-330A, S-418 which is a tabulation based on S-402, and G-4797. Both the exhibits and the testimony are primarily concerned with the variations in service provided to a group of factories in the Milwaukee district in recent years. The representativeness of this experience for the Corporation as a whole is attested by Walker.[91] Also relevant is the testimony of Bartschi, general manager of G. Edwards Shoe Company[92] which was summarized previously,[93] and Walker's comments on the situation at the Edwards plant which appear in the last section of his testimony cited immediately above.

The data presented in S-329, 330, and 330A show the service hours furnished to 39 shoe manufacturers in the Milwaukee district for the fiscal year ending February 1948, as well as the number of United machines on lease, shoe production, and process used. Some of the information contained in these exhibits is summarized in Tables 3 and 4 following.

The material shows clearly that the service United actually provides in one year, whether measured in relation to shoe production or in relation to the number of United machines on lease, varies widely among a group of similarly situated and competing factories. Thus, the highest amount of service provided to a welt factory was more than 13 times the lowest amount, measured per unit of output, or more than 415 times the lowest amount, measured per machine. Variations in the corresponding figures among the smaller samples of cement and stitchdown factories were less, but even here the high

---

[90] See above, pp. 117–118.   [91] Tr. 11095.   [92] Tr. 4883–5, 4924–5.
[93] Pp. 96–97.

figures were 2 to 5 times the low ones. That this large range of variation is not the result merely of a few extreme situations is shown by
the spread between the third and first quartile values of service/1000
pairs and service/machine figures in the case of the welts (the only
group large enough to provide a basis for a meaningful computation
of quartiles). The third quartile values of these two measures were
respectively 1.8 and 1.6 times the first quartile values; and it must be
remembered that, by definition, half the firms showed measures outside this range—either smaller than the first or larger than the third
quartile.

TABLE 3

	Welts 22 factories[a]			Cements 7 factories[b]			Stitchdowns 5 factories[c]		
	(1) 1,000 pair shoes per mach.	(2) service per 1,000 pair shoes	(3) hrs. mach-ine	(1) 1,000 pair shoes per mach.	(2) service per 1,000 pair shoes	(3) hrs. mach-ine	(1) 1,000 pair shoes per mach.	(2) service per 1,000 pair shoes	(3) hrs. mach-ine
High	4.9	24.2	27.9	6.1	5.2	31.4	6.2	6.4	20.5
Third quartile	2.9	7.4	14.3						
Median	2.4	4.6	12.8	4.8	3.8	16.9	5.4	3.8	17.4
First quartile	1.8	4.1	8.9						
Low	1.2	1.8	6.1	3.3	2.0	6.7	1.8	2.7	11.4

[a]Excludes Nunn-Bush, Whitewater which showed 6.3 serivice hours per thousand
pair of shoes, an unusually high figure.

[b]Excludes Cross Country, which had no production in fiscal 1948.

[c]Excludes Bauer and Stein Slipper, with 1 USMC machine and Peninsula with 2
USMC machines.

Table 4 brings out some of the details of the figures for the 22
welt factories; in cements and stitchdowns, the samples were too
small to provide a reliable basis for similar tables. In the previous
table, the medians, etc., shown refer to the respective arrays for each
measure: 100 pair/machine, service/1000 pairs, and service/machine.
In the three parts of Table 4 the figures for two of the measures corresponding to the median, etc., factory in terms of the third measure
are shown. Thus in part (1), the entry corresponding to L under
service hours/machine shows the service hours per machine for the

factory which had the lowest value of service hours per 1000 pair. As is clear from comparison with the corresponding entries under "welts" in Table 3, this is not the same as the lowest value of service hours per machine. (In some cases the median factory is hypothetical, in the sense that the value is an average of the values relating to two factories. In those cases the "corresponding" value is a similar average of the measure in question for the same two factories.) A comparison of the three parts of Table 4 leads to the following important conclusions: (a) There is a fairly high degree of association between the value of service hours/1000 pairs of shoes and service/hours per machine. This appears from the comparison of parts (1) and (2), as well as the comparison of both these with the appropriate entries in Table 3. (b) There is an even stronger relation between service hours/1000 pair and productivity as indicated by 1000 pair/machine, but one which is inverse: the higher productivity, the lower service hours/1000 pairs. This is shown by parts (1) and (3). (c) There is no significant association between service hours/machine and 1000 pair/machine. This is clear both from (2) and (3).

The first conclusion, on the positive association between the values for each factory of total service hours per machine and per 1000 pairs of shoes, respectively, is important because it settles what might otherwise be an open question on the present state of the record. What is really under scrutiny in this section is the degree to which United gives varying amounts of service to customers who make the same payments; assuming that the part of any manufacturer's payments to United under machine leases which is chargeable to the use of the machine alone, the pure lease element, is the same, either per machine or per unit for rentals and unit charges respectively. The best evidence on this, of course, would be a set of tabulations of service hours per dollar of payments under leases, excluding such payments as initial license fees and payments on termination of leases, but including rentals, unit charges, and payments for use less than the minimum. Figures of this sort are not in evidence. In their absence the figures in terms of service per 1000 pairs and service per machine can be used as good indexes of service per dollar of unit charge revenue, and services per dollar of monthly rental revenue. Then the fact that both these indexes vary together forecloses the possibility— otherwise open—that in the actual figure for service per dollar of

TABLE 4
22 Welt Factories

(1) Values of service hours/machine and 1,000 pr./machine corresponding to H, 3Q, M, 1Q, and L of service hours/1,000 pair

	svce. hours per 1,000 pair	corresponding svce. hours per machine	corresponding 1,000 pair per machine
H	24.2	27.9	1.2
3Q	7.4	14.3	1.9
M	4.6	13.4	2.9
1Q	4.1	13.2	3.2
L	1.8	8.6	4.9

(2) Values of service hours/1,000 pair and 1,000 pair/machine corresponding to H, 3Q, M, 1Q, and L of service hours/machine

	svce. hours per machine	corresponding svce. hours per 1,000 pair	corresponding 1,000 pair per machine
H	27.9	24.2	1.2
3Q	14.3	7.4	1.9
M	12.8	4.2	3.0
1Q	8.9	4.8	1.8
L	6.1	4.5	1.4

(3) Values of service hours/1,000 pair and service hours/machine corresponding to H, 3Q, M, 1Q, and L of 1,000 pair/machine

	1,000 pair per machine	corresponding svce. hours per 1,000 pair	corresponding svce. hours per machine
H	4.9	1.8	8.6
3Q	2.9	5.8 to 3.6[a]	16.8 to 10.5[a]
M	2.4	4.7 to 3.4[b]	11.1 to 8.0[b]
1Q	1.8	8.9	4.8
L	1.2	24.2 or 9.1[c]	27.9 or 11.0[c]

[a]There were five factories with productivity figures of 2.9.

[b]There were three factories involved in the computation of the median, one with a figure of 2.6, and two with figures of 2.2, either of which could be used for averaging.

[c]There were two factories with productivities of 1.2.

income from machines leased the movements of the two elements of unit charges and monthly rentals might compensate in such a way as to produce uniformity in the final service per dollar figures.

Unit charges, of course, provide the bulk of revenue from machines under lease. As of fiscal 1948, unit charges plus charges for use less than the minimum provided more than 80 per cent of total of unit charge and monthly rental revenue.[94] As a further check on the use of the per 1000 pair and per machine figures in the absence of money figures for unit charges and rentals, an index combining service per 1000 pairs and service per machine with weights 80 and 20 respectively[95] was computed, for the sample of the full 23 welt factories. In order to do this, it was necessary to express both service per 1000 pairs and service per machine as multiples of the respective figures for one factory—and the one with the lowest value of service per 1000 pair[96] was chosen as the base. Table 5 shows the usual H,

TABLE 5

	(1) Index Weighted Average of Service/1,000 Pairs and Service/Machine	(2) Index Service/1,000 Pairs
H	45.9	54.6
3Q	3.8	4.3
M	2.4	2.7
1Q	2.2	2.4
L	1.0	1.0

3Q, M, 1Q, L values for the weighted average index, and the index of service hours per 1000 pairs.

This shows a quite good approximation of (2) to (1), and demonstrates strongly that the use of service per dollar figures would not change the conclusions of this analysis in any significant way. The fact that (1) is consistently below (2) for every entry means that the relative variation among the factories in service hours/machine was

[94] See S-245, for dollar figures for the years 1924–1950.
[95] Cf. S-245 cited above.   [96] Number 20, S-330.

smaller than that in service hours/1000 pairs, as was pointed out above.

The second conclusion, that the more productive a factory is, the less service it requires per 1000 pair of shoes, is obviously important and takes on greater significance in the light of Walker's testimony on the character of the differences between shoe factories' service requirements.[97] This point will be developed immediately below in relation to the problem of the persistence over time of differences in service requirements among factories. It might be noted here, however, that the relation of service per 1000 pairs and productivity, considered in the light of the conclusions of the previous paragraph, supports the inference that a more productive factory paid more for service relative to what it received from United, than a less productive factory: benevolence, but hardly efficiency.

The relation between productivity and service per 1000 pair, as well as the lack of relation between productivity and service per machine are the more striking in that they hold for repair hours alone, as well as for total service hours. In broad terms, a more intense use of machines does not in itself necessarily lead to high demands for repair service or for total service of all kinds. In fact, the two different relations between productivity and service relative to production and relative to number of machines, respectively, is somewhat puzzling. One explanation—but not necessarily the only possible one—is that the frequency of breakdown and difficulty of repair of different types of machines show a loose inverse relationship to the "importance" of the machine types in shoe production. If this were the case—which could be determined only by an examination of figures for each machine type—the inference of the dis-incentive effects on efficiency of existing service arrangements could be strengthened.

A further aspect of the variation of service requirements among the 22 welt factories in the Milwaukee district is brought out by Table 6: the fact that variations in productivity do not account for all the variation in demand for service, as measured in terms of service/1000 pairs of shoes. The table shows the welt plants subdivided into five groups, such that all the plants within each group have closely similar productivity as measured by 1000 pairs/machine. High, median, and low values for service/1000 pair and also for service/machine are shown for these groups, and the ratio of the

[97] Tr. 13223–49.

high to the low values. These ratios ranging from 1.8 to 5.4 show clearly that there are substantial variations in service requirements among plants which are related to causes other than differences in productivity.

It is the contention of United that what are in effect uniform charges for provision of widely varying amounts of service are justi-

TABLE 6

22 WELT FACTORIES, GROUPED ACCORDING TO PRODUCTIVITY
DISTRIBUTION OF SERVICE/1,000 PAIRS AND SERVICE/MACHINE

Group, 1,000 Pair/Machine	High	Median	Low	Ratio: High Low
(1) 1.2–1.4 (3 plants service/1,000 pairs	24.2	9.1	4.5	5.4
service/machine	27.9	11.0	6.1	4.6
(2) 1.6–1.9 (5 plants) service/1,000 pairs	8.9	7.6	4.8	1.9
service/machine	16.4	14.3	8.9	1.8
(3) 2/1–2.2 (3 plants) service/1,000 pairs	5.9	4.8	3.3	1.8
service/machine	13.2	10.2	7.1	1.9
(4) 2.6–3.2 (9 plants) service/1,000 pairs	5.8	4.3	2.7	2.1
service/machine	16.8	12.3	7.5	2.2
(5) 4.8–4.9 (2 plants) service/1,000 pairs	4.5		1.8	2.5
service/machine	21.5		8.6	2.5

fied on an insurance principle. Service demands are unpredictably variable; therefore the manufacturer prefers a system of known charges under which all service requirements will be met to a system of specific charges for work performed which would face him with fluctuating and unpredictable service costs. This argument is implicit in the testimony of Walker[98] and is brought out clearly in the statement of the Court.[99]

The substance of this argument is the assertion that over the years the average amount of service provided to different shoe factories tends to be the same. If this is not so, if some plants have persistently

[98] Tr. 11078–96.   [99] Tr. 11209–12.

high service requirements and other plants have persistently low service requirements, then the insurance argument falls to the ground. To be sure, there would still be "insurance" in the sense of pooling of risks. But it would be the kind of insurance in which firms with predictably greater risks would pay no more than firms with predictably smaller risks; or, in other words, it would involve price discrimination among the insured.

The facts on which the insurance argument can be tested are presented in S-402 and S-417. S-402 shows the service hours in total and by types, output according to unit charge records, and United machines on lease for the fiscal years 1946 through 1950 for four factories in the Milwaukee district, three welt and one lockstitch process. S-417 contains certain computations based on these figures, including computations of service hours per 1000 pairs of shoes and per machine for each of the factories in each year. The figures for service per 1000 pairs and per machine converted into index numbers are shown in Table 7. For each index, the median value for all the factories and all the years was used as the base: These median figures were 9.6 service hours per machine and 4.9 service hours per 1000 pair.

A weighted index of service, combining the two indices shown in Table 7 with weights of 0.8 for service/1000 pair and 0.2 for service/machine[100] was also computed; this index is shown under the heading "weighted index" in the table. The information in the table appears inconsistent with the fundamental premise of the insurance argument, that on the average service requirements tend to be the same for all companies or at least that there are no predictable differences among them. Plants 3 and 4 have quite different service requirements, with that of the former consistently about 3.5 times that of the latter. Plants 1 and 2 (both owned by the same company) do have closely similar service requirements, but there are substantial differences between the figures for this pair and those for either plant 3 or plant 4. Inspection of the separate indices for service per machine and service per 1000 pairs leads to similar conclusions.

A statistical analysis of the consistency of differences among the companies was made to check the conclusions based simply on inspection of the data. The analysis was directed to answering the question: how likely is it that the differences among the four companies

[100] Cf. above, p. 139.

TABLE 7
INDICES OF SERVICE, FOUR MILWAUKEE FACTORIES
Fiscal 1946-1952

Year	1 Midstates Ideal (Welt)			2 Midstates Watertown (Welt)			3 Riedell (Lockstitch)			4 Weyenburg (Welt)		
	Service 1,000 Pr.	Service Machine	Weighted Index	Service 1,000 Pr.	Service Machine	Weighted Index	Service 1,000 Pr.	Service Machine	Weighted Index	Service 1,000 Pr.	Service Machine	Weighted Index
1946	71	101	77	84	82	84	—	73	—	88	99	90
1947	106	148	114	108	82	106	600	207	521	84	101	89
1948	86	127	94	98	93	97	245	118	220	55	74	59
1949	174	168	173	108	99	106	245	145	225	61	59	61
1950	151	180	157	100	93	99	227	121	206	62	68	63

in the values of the service requirements indices over time arose simply by chance fluctuations in a situation where the average value for every company tends to the same. Or, the question might be put: how likely is it that the values of the indices which were calculated arise from random drawings, each year, from a population of index values in which each company is as likely to get a high value as a low value? If the answer to the question is that such a result is likely, purely on the basis of chance drawings from the same population of index values, then the impressionistic conclusions of the previous paragraph are wrong, and the insurance argument is justified, at least as far as the data go.[101] The test was on six different sets of observations: the service per machine, service per 1000 pairs, and weighted average indices for all four plants, and for the three welt manufacturing plants (excluding Riedell) only. The results are shown in the accompanying table, in terms of the probability that the actually observed pattern would arise by chance if the average values for all the companies tended to be the same.

INDEX TESTED

Group	Service/1,000 Pair	Service/Machine	Weighted Average
All 4 plants	$0.025 < P < 0.05$	$P < 0.01$	$0.025 < P < 0.05$
3 welt plants	$0.02 \ < P < 0.05$	$P < 0.01$	$P < 0.01$

This table shows that in every case the probability that the actually observed results could arise by chance in a situation in which there were no consistent differences in service requirements among the various factories was small. All the probabilities are less than 0.05, and three of them are less than 0.01. In general, statistical practice leads to the rejection of hypotheses with probabilities less than some critical value as inconsistent with observation. The selection of a critical value is not a theoretical problem; it is essentially a matter of practical judgment. It may fairly be said that 0.05 is the critical value generally used in the applications of statistics to the social sciences. On this basis then, the null hypothesis—that there are no

---

[101] The test used was a distribution-free test for one-factor experiments, analogous to a variance analysis. It is described in Mood's *Introduction to the Theory of Statistics*, McGraw-Hill, 1950, pp. 398 ff. It consists of a test of the null-hypothesis that the observed pattern of values for each company for each year arises from random samplings from the same unknown population, by comparing the frequency for each company of values above and below the median of the whole set with what would be expected on the null-hypothesis.

consistent differences among the companies in service requirements, as measured in the various ways set forth in the table—can clearly be rejected. The insurance argument is not consistent with the evidence. It is noteworthy that this inconsistency appears even within the group of three companies, all using the welt process, as well as in the total sample in which one lockstitch firm appears.

A word of caution on the character of the evidence is in order here. The sample analyzed was indeed small—the experience of only four companies over a period of five years. It may well be unrepresentative of the larger experience of the company. But since it is the Corporation's offer, in support of the Corporation's argument—essentially a rebuttal argument—the burden of providing adequate evidence rests with it, and the skimpiness of the evidence cannot stand as an argument against accepting the results of the foregoing analysis.

The conclusions of the statistical analysis are reinforced by the final testimony of Walker on the question of service variation among manufacturers.[102] In this passage Walker explains some of the reasons for variations in service needs. Among the factors he stresses are differences in the quality of management and in labor-management relations among different firms, differences in location in so far as these affect the stability of the labor force and the character of management-worker relations, differences in the quality of shoes made, differences in the type of market served which affect lengths of runs, number of types of shoes made in the plant, and differences between new and experienced producers. All of these are essentially systematic in character rather than random; that is, they are characteristics which attach to particular factories over fairly long periods of time, and thus condition service demands in the same way from year to year. This testimony thus interprets in concrete terms the consistent difference among firms in service requirements which was brought out by the statistical analysis above, and goes far to assuage any doubts arising from the small number of firms and relatively short span of time covered in the sample. Taken together, Walker's testimony and the analysis of S-402 and related items dispose of the insurance argument as a justification of United's present method of charging for service.

Another consequence of the provision of service in the lease bundle without specific charge is the existence of interlocal discrimination. This appears in two ways. First, plants located far from centers of

[102] Tr. 13223-249.

service pay no more for service than plants located near it. The quantitative significance of this appears in the variations in the relative amounts of travel time to total service hours among the factories of the Milwaukee district shown in S-329: the average proportion of travel time was about 20 per cent, but some firms showed as much as 40 per cent and others as little as 15 per cent. Second, and probably more important, service is provided in distant shoe production centers such as outstate Missouri or Tennessee on the same terms as it is given in Boston or Brockton, although it is clear that the costs of providing this service are not the same in all these places. There is no evidence in the record from which the magnitude of this second effect can be determined. It is probably small, but together with the first it is just another way in which United's pricing system operates to discourage the most economical use of resources.

In summary, United's economic performance score in respect to price-cost relations is poor. Its pricing formulae and marketing methods are such as to make difficult an accurate knowledge of the costs of any particular machine type. Widespread discrimination in terms among machine types showing persistent patterns over time exists. This pricing pattern indicates an inefficient use of resources, inasmuch as alternative methods of shoe production are not offered to manufacturers on terms corresponding even roughly to the relative real social costs of developing and producing the machinery involved. Intercustomer and interlocal price discrimination arising from the offer of service as part of the lease bundle without separate charge leads to further inefficiencies in resource use. In particular, efficient shoe producers in the best locations pay more, relative to what they get, for service than less efficient or less well-located rivals. The mutually reinforcing effects of United's market dominance and the leasing system lead to price-cost relations which depart widely from the competitive ideal in ways which are clearly indicative of substantial inefficiences in resource use.

V. United's Performance in the Market, *Continued*

1. RESEARCH AND PROGRESSIVENESS

United's research activities and the results they have produced in the form of new and improved shoe machinery are the most discussed topics in the case. Roberts, United's vice-president in charge of research and development, testified for the Corporation for fifteen days, nearly all of which he gave to this topic. In addition, various subordinates of his were on the stand for thirteen days, in which their testimony was devoted to one or another aspect of the topic, and there were four days of views at Beverly, in which Roberts demonstrated the development history of several machines. Together, this represents nearly 30 per cent of the parole evidence, not counting testimony on research and progressiveness by other Corporation officers and a few expert witnesses, the latter rather brief. The volume of the testimony (and other evidence) contrasts sharply with the paucity of the conclusions analysis of it supports, as will appear in what follows. The paucity of conclusions indicates the importance of the problems presented no more than it does the volume of evidence. Rather it arises from the inherent difficulties of making adequately supported generalizations in the field on the basis of the kind of evidence which is available.

An evaluation of United's research and development work occupies quite a different position in the Government's case than it does in the Corporation's defense. The Government views United activities in this sphere chiefly as one more instrument of monopolization: the market for new and improved shoe machinery is "pre-empted" and competitors are thus excluded from it. United is indeed charged with "shelving" new developments and "suppressing" patents, but this result is incidental to the purpose of forestalling competition.[1] When necessary, United, in the Government's view, uses its research combined with deliberate infringement of adversely held patents to catch up with and outdistance the rare competitor who introduces an improvement that United has failed to anticipate.[2] The Corporation is, of course, concerned with refuting these charges, which it denies completely. But the more important part of its offer with respect to research and development has a positive aim: to show, first, that it is largely by excellence in this sphere that it has achieved and maintained its market position; second, that the present marketing arrangements—explicitly the leasing system, and by inference United's market position—are necessary to the maintenance of any substantial and worthwhile research effort in the shoe-machinery field. This position is developed in various parts of the testimony of Roberts, as well as that of Brown, Wogan, and Winslow. It appears most clearly and explicitly in Roberts' testimony of June 4—Tr. 12799–916, especially 12815–19, 12824–6, 12827–91.

Judgment on the major contention of United in respect to research and development is clearly far more important to the ultimate disposition of the case than judgment on the Government's charges. Unfortunately, the difficulties in the way of reaching such a judgment are even greater than its importance. These difficulties are twofold. First, the judgment involved is essentially speculative: would or could matters in this area be better or worse done if they were done otherwise than under the arrangements which in fact prevailed, and by how much? Speculations here lack an analytic model which relates research results and market structure to serve as a bench mark, in the way that the model of a competitive market serves as a bench mark for the preceding discussion of price discrimination. Second, the subject matter involved is one of great technical difficulty; and those most trained in its mysteries are precisely the research employees of United whose decisions are under scrutiny. The natural bias of these —to defend their own previous judgments and conclusions, rather than merely to represent their employer's interests—limits severely

---

[1] See GTB I, 350–357; and Complaint, paras. 73–80.
[2] GTB I, 357–73.

the value of any general conclusions which they may draw, invaluable as is their testimony on particular concrete events. The attempt to get independent testimony of comparable expertise through Compo will be discussed below; it is enough to say here that it did not solve the general problem. Nor did other disinterested expert testimony on the high technical capacity and excellent war work of United's research department,[3] likewise discussed further below, deal directly with the problem at hand, which is as much one of economic incentive as it is of technical capacity.

None the less, something can be done. In particular, at least the magnitude and character of United's efforts in research can be set down and various partial measures of the achieved results examined. These facts on what did occur, together with some logical analysis of possible variations in incentives to do research under different market conditions, will provide at least a basis for a critical reading of the arguments of United's major witnesses, even if in themselves they sustain no definitive judgment.

United's witnesses have emphasized the special difficulties of machine design in shoe manufacture repeatedly. In rude summary these difficulties—which set the problems of shoe machinery design and development apart from all or nearly all other research and development problems of industry—are three. First, the variety of styles, lasts, constructions, and sizes of shoes mean that runs of identical products are very short. Therefore machine flexibility and versatility are important. The temporal instability of the first three of the variables aggravates the problem. Second, the wide variety and temporal instability of shoe constructions, in an essentially narrow market, make the problem of securing a field of use large enough to pay for a new machine difficult. Finally, the fundamentally variable character of the chief raw material—leather—both from piece to piece and even from moment to moment creates great problems in designing machinery to handle it. These problems are further complicated by the complex space curves presented by last and shoe surfaces, necessitating in many machines motions in more than one plane or a pair of perpendicular planes. In short, nearly every problem in shoe-machinery development is a problem in shoemaking and, since shoe-making is an art dealing with variable materials on essentially handicraft principles, rather than a scientific technique operating on stand-

[3] Rowe, Tr. 12410–423, 12745–81.

ardized materials in mechanically repetitive fashion, problems in shoemaking create machine design problems of great complexity.

The most striking fact about United's research activity is its large scale. Total United research and development expenditures in fiscal 1950 were some $4,300,000; total employment in research activity involved nearly 600 people. Table 0, computed from S-401, shows

TABLE 0

TOTAL RESEARCH EXPENDITURES AND PERSONNEL, 1930–1950 (FISCAL)

Year	Expenditures $1000			Personnel		
	Beverly	Boston	Total	Beverly	Boston	Total
1930	1399	453	1852	243	28	271
1931	1286	370	1657	242	31	273
1932	1254	594	1848	240	31	271
1933	931	163	1099	215	30	245
1934	952	201	1154	218	32	250
1935	1018	243	1261	227	35	262
1936	1127	276	1403	245	48	293
1937	1342	313	1655	260	65	325
1938	1520	360	1880	300	72	372
1939	1657	386	2043	350	73	423
1940	1907	394	2301	362	82	444
1941	2004	387	2391	360	79	439
1942	1367 (538)	315	1682	190 (123)	34 (18)	224
1943	520 (2434)	59 (227)	579	103 (245)	18 (36)	121
1944	537 (2827)	45 (236)	582	141 (226)	28 (28)	169
1945	1186 (2140)	117 (150)	1302	130 (240)	22 (21)	152
1946	1655 (2238)	219 (62)	1874	402 (10)	58	460
1947	3174	368	3542	470	66	536
1948	3588	574	4162	546	109	655
1949	3991	692	4683	526	119	645
1950	3691	652	4342	481	91	572

total research expenditures and research personnel, divided between Beverly and Boston, for the fiscal years 1930–1950. For the years 1942–1946, a substantial part of United's research resources were devoted to war work; figures for this work are shown in parentheses for those years, but not added into the totals. The Boston figures represent research administration, planning, and similar activities; the Beverly figures, actual design and development expenditures.

United is large not only in an absolute sense, but relatively. Roberts[4] cited various Government sources to show the relatively large size of

4 Tr. 12806–812.

TABLE 1

UNITED SHOE MACHINERY CORPORATION DISTRIBUTION OF RESEARCH
DIVISION EXPENDITURES, FISCAL YEAR ENDING 2/28/50
(S-425)

1. Research		$ 719,932	
2. Shoe machinery development including trials and checking*		1,859,974	
3. Development of parts, devices, and attachments for commercial machines, engineering testing, some checking, assistance to factory in setting up first commercial machines of new design*		257,680	
4. Miscellaneous expense		3,515	
5. Work for USMC done by B.B. Chemical Co.		144,441	
			$2,985,542
6. Operating department service (development of parts, devices, and attachments —Section 25; and shoemaking service, $2,162†			
7. Handbooks and Catalogs	$ 14,696		
			254,784
			$3,240,326
8. Tanning research & development		275,780	
9. Work for affiliates other than B.B. Chemical Company		85,038	
10. Work (not research or development) for Beverly Factory and other departments of USMC and Industrial Trades ($10,130.)		89,502	
			450,320
			$3,690,646

*Each includes part of a total of $159,099 expended on development work on parts, devices, and attachments for commercial machines, similar to but more extensive than Operating Department service work separately identified. This does not include an additional $26,656, development on commercial orders for machines or parts identified as funds expended by other departments.

†Does not include $4543 additional development on commercial orders for machines or parts identified as funds expended by other departments.

United's research efforts in its pioneering days. United was the 11th industrial company to start a research department, which dates back to its founding in 1899. As early as 1920, when the National Research Council made its first survey of United States industrial research laboratories, United's was five times the average laboratory in personnel and eight times it in expenditure. In 1938 United had one of the 45 largest laboratories devoted to industrial research owned by businesses in the country. A similar study for 1946 shows that United had the 75th largest laboratory, measured by number of technical personnel, in American industry.[5] The only machinery manufacturer with a larger laboratory was General Motors; the other larger firms were in petroleum, chemicals, electronics, and electrical engineering. About this time, according to a Federal Trade Commission study, United was the 134th largest manufacturing corporation in the United States.[6]

The distribution of United's research efforts among various activi-

TABLE 2
UNITED SHOE MACHINERY CORPORATION DISTRIBUTION OF TOTAL
RESEARCH EXPENDITURES FROM ANALYSIS OF ORDERS
PERIOD 3/1/30–2/28/50
(S-422)

Total Research Expenditures from order analysis 3/1/30–2/28/50—	$26,258,000
Broken down into—	
Development of shoe machinery and improvements and commercial shoe processes	$25,243,105
Development of new shoemaking methods and processes	838,900
Expenditures not directed to specific shoe machinery, shoe processes, or shoemaking methods (research on leather, leather substitutes, tanning machinery, improved gears, lasts, last materials, plastic heel covers, plastic upper materials, plastic heels, high frequency box toe and linings, miscellaneous Shoe Laboratory work, Engineering Department orders, sundry miscellaneous orders, etc.)	10,175,995
	$36,258,000

[5] National Research Council, *Industrial Research Laboratories in the United States,* 1946.

[6] A list of 1000 large manufacturing corporations and their subsidiaries and affiliates, 1948. FTC, June 1951.

ties appears in Tables 1, 2 and 3. The first table shows the distribution of Beverly research expense for fiscal 1950. The second divides all research expenditures from fiscal 1931 to fiscal 1950 into three classes: development of shoe machinery and improvements and commercial shoe process, development of new shoemaking methods and process, (not commercial), and expenditures directed to general objects rather than specific machines. The first of these categories corresponds to the first subtotal of the previous table and might be called shoe-machinery development and improvement proper. In 1950, this accounted for about 80 per cent of Beverly expenditure; over the whole period, it represented about 70 per cent of total research expenditures.

The information presented in Table 1 can be combined as shown in Table 3 to show the relative importance of different types of activities in United's research program.

TABLE 3

Activity	Items of Table 2	Expenditure $1,000	% of Total
Research	1	720	20
Development of new shoe machinery and methods (inc. trials)	2*	1780	48
Improvements on commercial machines	3* and 6†	578	16
B.B. Chemical Work for USMC	5	144	4
Affiliates	8 and 9	366	10
Service jobs	7 and 10	95	3

*The $159,000 partly included in 2 and 3 of Table 2 (q.v.) was divided evenly between them.

†For the explanation of this classification see testimony of Roberts, Tr. 13268–71, and Bigelow, Tr. 6191–6212.

Table 3 brings out several important points: the substantial relative importance of general research, the results of which are applicable to many design problems rather than being special to some particular machine; the major position occupied by the development of specific new machines and commercial shoemaking processes; and the much smaller importance relative to this activity of the improvement of existing commercial machines. This last point is especially important, in that, to the extent that fiscal 1950 can be taken as a representative

TABLE 4

UNITED AVERAGE ANNUAL EXPENDITURES ON SHOE MACHINERY, RESEARCH, AND DEVELOPMENT 1929 (FISCAL) TO 1950 (FISCAL), BY PERIODS AND DEPARTMENT
(Dollar Figures in $1000)

Department	(7 Yrs.) 1929–35 Expend. ($)	(7 Yrs.) Dept. (%)	(6 Yrs.) 1936–41 Total Expend. ($)	(6 Yrs.) Dept. (%)	(5 Yrs.) 1942–46 Total Expend. ($)	(5 Yrs.) Dept. (%)	(4 Yrs.) 1947–50 Total Expend. ($)	(4 Yrs.) Dept. (%)	(22 Yrs.) 1929–50 Total Expend. ($)	(22 Yrs.) Dept. (%)	(22 Yrs.) Total (%)
Cement shoe	110	13	125	12	83	15	199	13	124	13	9
Cutting die	—	—	19	2	7	1	31	2	12	1	1
Eyeletting	13	2	24	2	11	2	24	2	17	2	1
Fitting room	69	8	87	9	24	4	42	3	58	6	4
General	120	14	106	10	22	4	101	7	90	9	6
Goodyear	134	16	187	18	114	21	377	25	192	20	13
Heeling	75	9	114	11	36	7	88	6	79	8	5
Lasting	178	21	244	24	189	35	540	35	268	28	19
Littleway	—	—	43	4	17	3	67	4	28	3	2
Metallic	20	2	16	2	3	1	21	1	15	2	1
Pulling over	32	4	42	4	39	7	43	3	38	4	3
Rubber shoe	86	10	27	3	3	1	2	—	36	4	2
Total above	837	73	1015	77	548	65	1534	53	955	100	66
"Standard Shoe"	154	13	11	1	—	—	—	—	52	—	4
Non Dept.	149	13	282	21	290	35	1338	46	434	—	30
Grand Total	1143	100	1316	100	841	100	2900	100	1441	100	100

Computed from S-241.

year, this gives quantitative limits to Roberts' parole evidence on the importance of continuing to improve existing machines as a research objective. In various portions of his testimony Roberts has emphasized the fact that new machines cannot be developed each year, and the research staff can only be employed properly in a continuous manner by trying to improve the existing machines.[7]

Table 4 shows the distribution of Beverly research expenditure for shoe machinery proper divided by machine departments in terms of annual average expenditures for four periods covering 1920–1950 (fiscal).[8] The major points brought out by the table are the increasing importance of research expenditures not allocable to specific departments, which grew from 13 per cent of the total in the early period 1929–1935) to 46 per cent in the last period (1947–1950); and the relative constancy of the shares of the individual machinery departments in the total expenditures among departments. The extent of stability, and of departures from it, is brought out in Table 5, which shows the departments listed in order of the magnitude of research expenditures over the whole period, and their ranks in average annual expenditures during each sub-period.

TABLE 5

Department	Ranks, by Periods			
	1929–35	1936–41	1942–46	1947–50
1. Lasting	1	1	1	1
2. Goodyear	2	2	2	2
3. Cement shoe	4	3	3	3
4. General	3	5	7	4
5. Heeling	6	4	5	5
6. Fitting room	7	6	6	8
7. Pulling over	8	8	4	7
8. Rubber shoe	5	9	11	12
9. Littleway	12	7	8	6
10. Eyeletting	10	10	9	10
11. Metallic	9	12	12	11
12. Cutting die	11	11	10	9

[7] See, for example, Tr. 12823–4.
[8] The total expenditures covered are $31,698,000 compared with $36,258,000 in Table 3. This table refers only to Beverly expenditures, while the previous one includes all research expenditures. It also includes two more years than the other.

The stability of the three leading departments, which received over 60 per cent of the departmentally allocated funds over the whole period, is striking. Equally notable are the sharp decline of Rubber shoe and the rise of Littleway. The general impression of stability is further increased if the war period 1942–1946 is omitted—making more stable through time the positions of General and Pulling-over, which were unusually small and unusually large respectively during this period.

The division of departmentally allocated funds among the operating departments roughly follows their relative contributions to revenue from leased machinery, as appears from Table 6. The correlation

TABLE 6

Department	% Share of Average Annual Research Expenditure 1947–50f*	% Contribution to Lease Revenue Fiscal 1947
Lasting	35	20
Goodyear	25	36
Cement shoe	13	5
General	7	5
Heeling	6	7
Littleway	4	2
Pulling over	3	8
Fitting room	3	5
Cutting die	2	7
Eyeletting	2	1
Metallic	1	3
Rubber shoe	—	—
Total	100	100

*"f" stands for fiscal year.

is, of course, not close but justifies the statement that, broadly, machine types which are important revenue producers receive most of the research funds and unimportant ones conversely.

Further evidence on the relation between the allocation of expenditures on shoe machinery development over the period 1931–1950f among various objectives, and the relative importance of these objectives in the shoe industry, is shown in Tables 7 and 8. These compare the relative distribution of development expenditures on machinery used for different shoe constructions with the proportion of total shoe production made according to each construction for the whole period 1931–1950. In order to make this comparison, some allocation among processes must be made for expenditures on machines used in more than one process. The first table shows the results when such expendi-

TABLE 7
UNITED SHOE MACHINERY CORPORATION DISTRIBUTION BY SOLE ATTACHING PROCESSES OF RESEARCH EXPENDITURES ON DEVELOPMENT OF SHOE MACHINERY AND IMPROVEMENTS FROM ANALYSIS OF ORDERS
Period 3/1/30–2/28/50*
(S-423)

	Production		Research Expense	
	Thousands of Pairs†	%	$	%
Goodyear welt	2,434,935	31.0	5,559,589	22.1
Cement exc. sliplasted	1,892,850	24.2	4,838,610	19.2
McKay	1,081,892	13.8	2,936,300	11.6
Stitchdown	1,033,381	13.2	1,764,819	7.0
Nailed, etc	463,747	5.9	1,472,841	5.8
Lockstitch	328,483	4.2	3,410,225	13.5
Sliplasted	317,134	4.0	2,448,149	9.7
Prewelt	153,857	2.0	1,389,555	5.5
Turn	129,658	1.7	1,423,017	5.6
	7,835,937	100.%	$25,243,105	100.%

*In this tabulation expenditure for work on development of shoe machinery for use in more than one process is equally divided between the processes.

†USMC statistics, Government figures, not susceptible of breakdown by processes.

tures are allocated equally to all processes involved; the second, when the allocation is in proportion to the number of shoes produced by the several processes. The resulting divisions of research expenditure among shoe constructions are broadly similar; where they differ, the second is based on the more logical allocation procedure and therefore presents a more appropriate basis for comparison with figures of shoe production. The comparison in Table 8 shows a very close relation between the division of expenditures and the division of shoe pro-

duction; in Table 7 the relationship is less close but still fairly good.
These tables reinforce the broad conclusion, above, that the division
of research effort has paralleled the relative importance in manufacturing terms of the research objectives. The evidence summarized

TABLE 8

UNITED SHOE MACHINERY CORPORATION DISTRIBUTION BY SOLE
ATTACHING PROCESSES OF RESEARCH EXPENDITURES ON
DEVELOPMENT OF SHOE MACHINERY AND IMPROVEMENTS
FROM ANALYSIS OF ORDERS
Period 3/1/30–2/28/50*
(S-424)

	Production		Research Expense	
	Thousands of Pairs†	%	$	%
Goodyear welt	2,434,935	31.0	8,630,001	34.2
Cement exc. sliplasted	1,892,850	24.2	7,393,432	29.2
McKay	1,081,892	13.8	2,914,861	11.5
Stitchdown	1,033,381	13.2	1,862,351	7.5
Nailed, etc.	463,747	5.9	630,621	2.5
Lockstitch	328,483	4.2	1,289,220	5.1
Sliplasted	317,134	4.0	1,607,757	7.4
Prewelt	153,857	2.0	409,341	1.6
Turn	129,658	1.7	504,536	2.0
Total	7,835,937	100.%	$25,242,120	100.%

*In this tabulation expenditure for work on development of shoe machinery for use
in more than one process is divided between the processes in the ratio of the shoe production of each process to the total production of the processes for which the machine
could be used.
†USMC statistics, Government figures, not susceptible of breakdown by processes.

in the last few pages goes far to refute the Government contention
that United's research was aimed primarily at "competition." Further
evidence contrary to this view is presented in Table 9, which orders
the 12 departments in two ways: the departments are divided into
three groups according to market share, high, medium, and (relatively) low; and within each group they are ordered according to
"revenue potential." This is the share of total machine-lease revenue

each department would produce if United's market share in every department were 100 per cent; it is computed by dividing the actual per cent contribution of each department to total revenue by its actual market share and scaling down the results so that they sum to 100 per cent. The market-share and revenue-potential figures of the table refer to 1947 and following years; the shares in departmentally

TABLE 9

Department	1947 Market Share %	1947 Revenue Potential* %	% Share of Research Expenses Allocated to Departments 1947–50
Goodyear	94	33	25
Lasting	94	18	35
Pulling over	98	7	3
Heeling	91	7	6
Cutting die	91	6	2
Metallic	93	3	1
Littleway	92	2	4
General	73	6	7
Eyeletting	87	1	2
Cement shoe	50	9	13
Fitting room	45	8	3
Rubber shoe	48	0.5	—

*Revenue potential—% share of 1947 lease revenues/market share, normalized to add up to 100%. It shows the per cent of total machine lease revenue each department would contribute if United's market share in each were 100%.

allocated research expenditures to the period 1947–1950. In general, it is to be expected that high revenue potentials would be correlated positively with high research outlays, since high revenue potential indicates either important markets, markets in which United has room to expand, or both. If "beating competition" as such were an important goal of United's research policy, it might be expected that two fields with the same revenue potentials would show research expenditures inversely related to market shares: the more of the field not in United's hands, the greater the need for research outlays in the field. The figures of Table 9 do not show such a relation. A comparison of research expenditures among the pulling over, heeling, cutting-die, general, cement-shoe, and fitting-room departments, which have roughly the same revenue potential and represent the three market share groups, fails to reveal any consistent relation between research expenditures and market share.

An analysis of the use of the $10,000,000 not expended on the development of shoe machinery and commercial shoe processes, or

TABLE 10

RESEARCH EXPENDITURES ON LASTS (FIT., ETC.), LAST MATERIALS, LEATHER SUBSTITUTES FOR SHOE PARTS AND LEATHER

Total Expenditures and Expenditures in Last Ten Years

(S-383)

	Last Ten Years	Total
*Lasts		
C-3 lasts	$ —	$ 273,000
Fit	183,200	203,200
Foot Comfort	140,000	140,000
Shoe fitting studies	75,000	75,000
Pilot plant for two part Geometric Grade Last manufacture and application of two part lasts to shoemaking	388,000	388,000
Total	$ 786,200	$1,079,200
*Last Materials		
Wood impregnates	3,600	33,600
New materials for lasts	77,000	77,000
New materials for last heel ends	11,000	27,000
New materials—related to machinery development	16,000	36,000
Aluminum furnace for lasts	—	62,000
Total	$ 107,600	$ 235,600
*Leather		
Research on leather	122,000	122,000
Research on collagen	505,000	505,000
Total	$ 627,000	$ 627,000

*"Fundamental research"—see text.

TABLE 10—Continued

	Last Ten Years	Total
Leather Substitutes		
*Kent—remaking of scrap leather	$ 14,000	$ 28,232
*Porous plastic insole	157,800	157,800
*Substitue sole material	24,643	24,643
Celastic Box Toes	5,999	27,866
Plyrubber heels	—	92,303
B.B. duck	—	15,000
Ridgeflex insoles	—	11,776
*Union Carbide-cements and shoemaking problems on vinylite	50,000	50,000
Unshakoff heel cover	—	81,300
Plastic upper material	41,036	41,036
Plastic heels	66,595	90,732
Pilot plant for above	15,200	15,200
Heel tests	1,462	1,462
Flocking—B.B. Co.	203,000	203,000
High frequency box toes and counters	653,600	653,600
Plastic eyelets	42,900	42,900
Plastic shoe linings	26,227	26,227
Plastic welt	30,100	30,100
Clark insole	324,527	352,527
Griswold insole	416,291	416,291
Total	$2,073,380	$2,361,995
Grand Total	$3,594,180	$4,303,795

*"Fundamental research"—see text.

on non-commercial shoe processes,[9] is not available in detail comparable to that of the departmentally allocable expenditures discussed above. Some indications of the object of these expenditures are provided by S-241 which covers Beverly expenditures only and S-383 which refers to all research expenditures. First, attention should be directed again to Table 4 which shows the increasing importance of research on shoe machinery not specifically connected with existing operating departments, although this is not part of the $10,000,000 aggregate expenditure, 1931–1950 (fiscal) referred to. Second, S-421

[9] See Table 2 above, p. 152.

also shows the expenditure, in this same period, of $5,752,000 of Beverly (not total) research funds on other than shoe machinery development. Of this, some $1,167,000 was spent on B.B. Chemical work; $750,000 on work for other affiliates, making a total of $3,833,000 on work for affiliates. Another $1,104,000 was spent for the development of parts, devices, and attachments for commercial machines as experience indicates difficulties or problems created by existing designs.[10]

Table 10 shows the allocation among various purposes of some $4,300,000 of the total of $10,000,000 referred to above which was spent on lasts, last materials, and leather substitutes. As the table shows, more than 80 per cent of these expenditures were made in the last ten years. Some of the items in the table are starred. This represents an attempt by the writer (resting on the general testimony as to the character of shoemaking processes and techniques and the problems of research in shoe machinery) to separate those objects of expenditure which are at least potentially fundamental in character, in the sense that they contain the promise, if successful, of fairly radical changes in technique in shoe manufacture, from those which are more in the nature of improvements in detail of existing techniques. This distinction is of course crude, since one class shades into the other, but even in rough terms it may be helpful. The starred items are those which were classified as more "fundamental"; they involved a total expenditure of $2,350,000, of which $1,890,000 were expended in the last ten years. This is about half the expenditure in this period shown in the table, and about 9 per cent of all the Beverly research expenditure over the same period.[11]

A particular aspect of United's research effort which received extended treatment in the record was the problem of testing, especially the question of the length of testing periods in relation to the speed of development of new machines.[12] Evidence on United's resource inputs in testing was offered in S-350–53, summarizing the experience in connection with four machines selected by United as illustrating the range of testing problems United faces; and also in S-420, an affidavit in lieu of parole testimony by Booma, assistant director of research in charge of shoe machinery development. Two

[10] See Table 1 above, and Tr. 6191–6212, testimony of Bigelow.
[11] Cf. S-421.
[12] See testimony of Roberts, Tr. 12645–65 and Booma, Tr. 11480–585.

of the machine developments covered were typical of simple testing problems, where variable shoemaking conditions had relatively little effect on the performance of the machines. These were the tack detector[13] and the lacing machine A.[14] For the former, tests were complete in 15 months, one of which was used in testing the research model, three in building the first of the six commercial models shipped out for testing, and eleven for testing the commercial models. The total development period, counting from the first idea on the successful method, and ignoring earlier failures, was 22 months. In this period some $36,000 was spent, and on the average the equivalent of 2.5 men were working full time on the problem in terms of man-hours spent. The lacing machine A had a longer development history: the first good idea appeared in 1931; in December 1933 tests on the first operating model began. By July 1934 a second model was designed as a result of the first tests, and put on test. Tests lasted three months; in September the process of checking drawings for the commercial model began, testing continued during this period, and the first machine was produced from drawing nineteen months later. After another three months' testing, the machine was adopted in July 1936, a total development period of some six years. In this period $67,000 was expended concentrated in the period in which the first model was built and the period during which drawings for the commercial model were being prepared and altered to incorporate changes based on the continuing tests. The time equivalent of three full-time men per year was used on the project on the average over the six-year period.

The two difficult machines were the Goodyear automatic inseam sewer[15] and the cement toe laster with toe trimming means,[16] neither of which are yet commercial. The development history of the automatic inseamer stretches back to 1917, since it was part of the projected C-3 automatic line. Over the whole period, an average equivalent of 2.5 full-time men were working on the project, with a high of six and a low period extending for over seven years in which fewer than one-half equivalent full-time men were at work on the problem. Monetary outlays total some $500,000 for the period. The whole history was complicated by the incapacitation of the designer in 1943, two years after a model was adopted for experimental use ("limited-adopted"). The first limited-adopted models manufactured

[13] S-350.   [14] S-351.   [15] S-352.   [16] S-353.

commercially did not appear until 1950, and current tests show the need for further changes. The cement-toe laster shows a briefer history but not a dissimilar one. Development first started in December 1938; the model was built a year later. After 13 months of trials, a redesigned machine was built and put on trial. Two years later, a second redesign was built, and various trials and modifications occurred over the next three years. In 1947 a decision was made to build three further machines for testing purposes, and these were built and put out for testing in 1949 and 1950. The tests are still in process and reveal serious problems of standardization of the preceding operations. Over the whole period of 13 years, some $770,000 was expended, with individual annual figures running as high as $180,000 in 1948f and as low as $35,000 in 1941f (excluding the war years). Over the whole period an average of nearly 13 equivalent full-time men worked on the development, excluding the war years, with annual figures as high as 25 and as low as 8 equivalent full-time men.

By and large, these documents leave an impression that in the difficult cases matters often proceed rather slowly with a small investment in machines under test, and at times with a small number of men working on a given project. But that this procedure is less wise, less economical, or less generally desirable than an alternative which would involve large expenditures, or more concentrated effort, in no way follows from the evidence. In other words the documents show only United's practice but offer no standard at all for evaluating it, except perhaps the standard of the variation in practice in different cases, which must then be correlated with the variations in the "objective difficulty" of the problem to be solved. Whether any standards are available for this latter comparison will be discussed further below in connection with the evidence on the practices of Compo.

The technical competence of United's research staff was never seriously questioned by the Government. None the less, United offered various testimony on this point[17] of which that of Rowe, Tr. 12410–24, is most interesting. Rowe is himself an engineer and has an active interest in several companies manufacturing knitting

[17] See Tr. 12425–77, Prof. Schmitt of M.I.T., on quality of United's research on collagen; S-361, 2 on research on shoe fit; S-294, various letters from Service departments on United's war work.

machinery and machine tools, among other things. During World War II Rowe served for some time as head of Section 12 of OSRD, in which capacity he dealt with United's research department, as well as the research departments of many other firms and with research efforts in universities and technical institutes as well. He testified to United's great technical ability, asserting that they had no equals in the field of machine development involving the control and coördination of complex motions in small spaces and similar problems. Further he gave United high marks for speed as well as capacity, and said, in a colloquy worth noting:[18]

> Court: It is sometimes said, as you perhaps know, Mr. Rowe, that a laboratory of an industry which is in a relatively sheltered position shows in the research workers the characteristics of perfectionism, seeking to make sure that the product which they are working on is more perfect than is necessarily desirable in the competitive situation, (that) they who work in the research laboratories of a protected industry come to demand perfection the way they wouldn't in a more competitive situation.
> Witness: I had that theory when I went to United . . . I was greatly surprised at the speed with which they took up the problem, worked out the fundamental details, made the models and mockups, and had the solution.
> Court: In other words, you found that their speed of performance was as great as that in other laboratories where perhaps the companies concerned had a larger number of competitors?
> Witness: Yes, sir.

This, in the absence of any evidence in the other direction, can be taken as dispositive of the question of United's technical competence. But, of course, referring as it does to United's wartime performance, it offers no guide to the incentive or lack of incentive to the use of that competence in any particular direction created by the peculiar conditions of the shoe machinery market. Nor does Rowe's further testimony[19] add anything on this point.

The foregoing discussion of United's research efforts must be compared in some way with the results of those efforts. As previously mentioned, no satisfactory overall measure of these "results" is available; instead various partial measures must be scrutinized, and

[18] Tr. 12422–3.   [19] Tr. 12745–93.

some overall judgment based on these fragments, if they warrant one. The first aspect of United's performance with respect to progressiveness which can be examined is the "age" of machine models —the time which elapses from the first appearance of a new machine model until its replacement by another model, if it is so replaced, or to the present, if not. The significance of the change from an old to a new model usually represents a sufficient change in the organization of the machine so that a new head casting is required.[20] Even so, this may mean anything from a fundamentally new machine, to the adaptation of an existing machine to work on a smaller or larger size-range of shoes than it was originally designed for, without any changes of principle in its operations. The basic information on the age of models is contained in S-111, which lists all United machine models offered to shoe manufacturers since 1899, by departments, showing for each model the date of commercialization and, where the model is not still (1950) commercial, the date on which it ceased to be offered (i.e., terms were withdrawn). This document lists some 600 models and is somewhat unwieldy for use in raw form. Various tabulations based on it are presented in the four accompanying tables.

Table 11 shows the distribution, by departments, of currently outstanding machines by the period of commercialization. It also shows for each department, and for all combined, the median year of commercialization, and the median age of the machine models in 1950 and for comparative purposes, the relative contribution of each department to United's revenue from leased machinery.[21] The median age of all United current (1950) machine models was 28 years: half had been developed in 1922 or before, half later. Two departments, Metallic and Cutting die, yielding nearly 10 per cent of total machine revenue, each had a median model age over 40 years. The "youngest" (liveliest?) departments were: Littleway, median model age, 13 years; Cement shoe and Eyelet, 17 years; and Lasting, 18 years. Together they produced nearly 30 per cent of the total revenue, Lasting alone yielding over 20 per cent.

The next table, Table 12, shows a somewhat similar distribution for machines no longer commercial. In this case the time period shown is the number of years elapsing between commercialization of the new model and withdraw of terms on it. The median figures

[20] See Tr. 3585, Roberts.   [21] G-4725.

TABLE 11

MACHINES CURRENTLY OFFERED, BY DEPARTMENT AND YEAR OF COMMERCIALIZATION
(Computed from S-111)

Year Commercialized	Fitting Room	General	Good-Year	Heeling	Lasting	Rubber Shoe	Metallic	Pulling Over	Cement Shoe	Little-way	Cutting Die	Eyelet	Total All Depts.
Before 1900	—	11	4	2	2	—	4	—	—	—	—	—	24
1900–1909	4	37	6	4	—	—	2	2	—	1	4	—	60
1910–1919	7	20	15	4	4	1	—	3	—	—	—	1	55
1920–1929	12	21	4	3	7	4	1	1	—	2	3	—	58
1930–1934	5	17	7	6	4	4	1	1	8	—	1	1	55
1935–1939	4	9	1	3	7	—	2	1	1	8	—	—	37
1940–1947	3	5	6	1	6	—	—	—	1	1	—	—	23
1948–1950	4	7	1	3	—	—	—	—	1	2	—	—	18
Total	39	127	44	26	30	9	10	8	11	15	8	3	330
% share of total machine revenue, $£47$, by depts. (G-4725)	4.5	4.8	36.6	7.4	20.3	0.3	3.0	8.4	5.2	1.8	6.9	0.9	100
Median year of commercialization	1923	1919	1917	1929	1932	1929	1905	1914	1933	1937	1909	1933	1922
Median Age, 1950	27	31	33	21	18	21	45	36	17	13	41	17	28

TABLE 12

MACHINES NO LONGER OFFERED. DISTRIBUTION BY TIME IN YEARS BETWEEN COMMERCIALIZATION AND TERMS WITHDRAWAL AND BY DEPARTMENTS

(Computed from S-111)

Years	Department												Total All Depts.
	Fitting Room	General	Good-Year	Heeling	Lasting	Rubber Shoe	Metallic	Pulling Over	Cement Shoe	Little-way	Cutting Die	Eyelet	
0–4	5	17	8	1	4	2	1	1	7	—	—	—	46
5–9	3	29	6	—	1	3	2	—	2	—	—	1	47
10–14	3	32	10	2	4	1	6	2	1	1	2	1	64
15–19	12	32	15	5	—	—	2	1	2	—	1	3	74
20–24	8	21	20	1	4	—	3	2	—	1	1	2	63
25–29	2	43	7	4	1	—	9	3	—	—	—	1	70
30 or more	2	77	16	3	3	—	9	5	—	2	—	5	122
Total number of machines	35	251	82	16	17	6	32	14	12	4	4	13	486
Median age at withdrawal, years	17	23	20	20	14	6	25	25	4	27	15	24	21

for each department and for the whole distribution are also shown. In general, these median figures are smaller than the corresponding figures of Table 11: the median of the whole distribution is 21 years, compared with 28 years for machines still commercial. This difference is not surprising, since the second table includes not only machines which were withdrawn when new and better models were built, but also machines which were withdrawn when the demand for their services vanished with changes in shoemaking processes, as well as machines which were failures initially.

TABLE 13

Twenty-five Most Important Revenue Producing Machines in 1947f and Years in Which They Were Commercialized
(Computed from G-294 and S-111)

Machine Model	% Share of Machine Revenue	Year of Commercialization
1. ORL-O	13.4	1914
2. Welter-K	10.2	1910
3. Rex puller (C and D)	6.3	1910, 13
4. Bed laster	5.5	1914, 15
5. Staple side laster B	3.8	1927
6. Universal rounding and channeling	3.3	1910
7. McKay heel loading	2.9	1910
8. Heel seat lasting D	2.7	1930
9. Goodyear automatic sole leveling	2.7	1923
10. Heel seat lasting E	2.7	1936
11. Cement sole attaching	2.6	1932
12. Wood heel nailing	2.4	1930
13. Goodyear improved sole laying	1.9	1939
14. Goodyear inseam trimming	1.3	1916
15. CHM McKay side lasting	1.2	1925
16. Loose nailing	1.2	1909
17. Clicker C	1.2	1908
18. Staple side lasting C	1.2	1927
19. USMC Sole stitching	1.0	1927
20. Toe lasting	0.9	1945
21. Wood heel attaching	0.8	1923
22. USMC Sole laying	0.7	1934
23. Stitchdown thread lasting	0.5	1925
24. Universal slugging	0.5	1899
25. Fiber fastening	0.5	1932

The two tables discussed above treat a machine model as a unit and do not distinguish between major and minor machines, or large and small revenue producers. Given the wide differences in the importance of different machines, in both shoemaking and revenue terms, a more refined treatment is desirable. Table 13 shows the twenty-five most important machine models in terms of revenue production (1947f) and shows the year in which each one was commercialized. Together, these 25 machine models accounted for a little more than 70 per cent of revenue from leased machines in fiscal 1947. The weighted average age of these models, using the revenue shares as weights,[22] is 32 years. This is somewhat higher than the median (unweighted) age for all commercial machines, 28 years. Ten machines—numbers 1, 2, 3, 4, 6, 7, 14, 16, 17, and 24 on the list—were commercialized before World War I. Together, they accounted for nearly 46 per cent of the total machine-lease revenue, or more than two-thirds of the revenue produced by the twenty-five machines listed. At the other extreme, two machines—numbers 13 and 20—were first commercialized in the ten years prior to the filing of the complaint in the present suit; together they brought in 2.8 per cent of total leased-machine revenue in 1947f.

TABLE 14

DISTRIBUTION OF 25 MOST IMPORTANT MACHINES MEASURED BY EARNINGS IN FISCAL 47 BY YEAR OF COMMERCIALIZATION

Period	Number of Machines Commercialized	Share of 47f Machine Revenue Accounted for by These Machines
Before 1900	1	0.5
1900–1909	2	2.4
1910–1919	7	42.9
1920–1929	7	11.2
1930–1934	5	8.9
1935–1939	2	4.6
1940–1944	—	—
1945–1947	1	0.9
Total	25	71.4

[22] E.g., counting the age of the ORL-O into the average 13 times, and the USMC sole stitcher (number 19) once.

Tables 14 and 15 bring out some further points on the age of the 25 most important machines. Table 14 shows the distribution of the 25 machines by period of commercialization and the share of total lease revenue produced by machines commercialized in each period; it is self-explanatory. Table 15 compares the relative distribution of

TABLE 15

PERCENTAGE DISTRIBUTION OF MACHINES COMMERCIALIZED BY YEAR OF COMMERCIALIZATION, ALL COMMERCIAL MACHINES, AND 25 MOST IMPORTANT COMMERCIAL MACHINES

	%	All Cumulative %	%	25 Most Important Cumulative %
Before 1900	4	4	8	8
1900–1909	8	12	19	27
1910–1919	28	40	18	45
1920–1929	28	68	19	64
1930–1934	88	88	18	82
1935–1939	8	96	12	94
1940–1947	4	100	7	101

the twenty-five important machines by the time periods of commercialization with that of all machines now commercial, as computed from Table 11. The comparison of the two cumulative percentage distributions shows clearly that a fairly substantial difference in the time pattern is manifested, with 27 per cent of the important machines first introduced before 1910, compared with 12 per cent of all machines.

In addition to designing new machine models, the Research division directs its efforts to the continuing improvement of existing models. Indeed much of the early testimony of Roberts, especially that given at Beverly,[23] is devoted to a discussion of this effort and the importance of its results to the shoe industry. This theme is also sounded frequently later, especially in connection with expositions of the advantages to the shoe manufacturer of the partnership between himself and United which is the effective result of the leasing system.[24] Thus, the results of United's research cannot be judged only in terms of new models; improvements to commercial machines must also be reckoned into the balance.

[23] Tr. 3653–4111.   [24] See, for example, Tr. 12824–860.

The problem of defining a "unit improvement" on which a measure of improvement can be based is the same as that of using the model as a unit.[25] The unit improvement used here is the kind of change recorded in a blue bulletin, a vehicle of interdepartmental communication normally used to record changes in any part of a commercial machine which originate in the Research Department.[26] Any such change of any part of a commercial machine which does not reach the magnitude of a model change[27] is recorded in a blue bulletin.

The specific content of blue-bulletin changes and the possible range of variation in the character of such changes is detailed in two places in the record: the transcript of the Beverly hearings referred to on the preceding pages and S-147a, b, c, the three volumes of blue-bulletin patent correlations. The meaning and significance of these changes, however, can be evaluated only on the basis of appropriate expertise, thus raising once again the problems connected with the appraisal of United's research achievements discussed on pages 147–165 above. Fortunately, a way out of the dilemma exists, although it is but a rough path. Some blue-bulletin improvements are the subject of patents, others are not. The record as a whole reveals clearly the competence, diligence, and thoroughness of United's patent department; and thus it can safely be presumed that every blue-bulletin improvement which meets the standard of invention required for patentability is indeed patented.[28] This enables all recorded blue-bulletin changes[29] to be divided into two classes: those which meet the patentability standard and those which do not.

Table 16 represents a tabulation of blue-bulletin changes for a sample of 30 machines, based on S-219, a list of such changes for the same 30 machines. The selection of this sample and other features of the exhibit are explained by Ashley and Proctor.[30] The sample

[25] See above, pp. 166, 170.

[26] There are other changes which may originate in the Manufacturing Department rather than in the Research Department. These are not the subject of blue bulletins, but are recorded in other ways. See Tr. 3591–4, 3657–62, Roberts.

[27] See above, p. 166.

[28] The nature of the improvement activity in general means that the subject matter standards of patentability will always or almost always be met by the blue-bulletin changes.

[29] All changes since 1920 of the appropriate sort have been recorded.

[30] Tr. 7818–22.

TABLE 16
BLUE-BULLETIN IMPROVEMENTS, 30 SELECTED MACHINES FROM 1920 OR
DATE OF COMMERCIALIZATION TO FEBRUARY 1951
(Computed from S-219)

	Years	Number of Changes	Of Which Patented*	Total Changes Yr. (Approx.)	Patented Changes Yr. (Approx.)
1. ORL–O	31	330	13	11	0.4
2. Welt sewer K	31	104	4	3	0.1
3. Rex puller, C, D, E	31	377	22	12	0.7
4. Bedlaster, 6 & 7	31	340	5	11	.02
5. Staple side laster (B & C?)	24	248	10	10	0.4
6. McKay Heel loading	31	358	14	12	0.5
7. Heel seat lasting D	21	458	18	22	0.9
8. Goodyear auto, sole leveling	31	284	14	9	0.5
9. Cement sole attaching A & B	21	401	27	19	1.3
10. Wood heel nailing	21	231	5	11	0.2
11. Goodyear improved sole laying	31	151	9	5	0.3
12. Loose nailing	31	307	5	10	0.2
13. Clicking C	31	538	20	17	0.7
14. Toe laster C	6	56	—	9	—
15. Wood heel attaching	28	145	5	5	0.2
16. Stitchdown thread lasting	26	124	5	5	0.2
17. Universal slugging	31	114	2	4	0.1
18. Fiber fastening	24	190	7	8	0.3
Averages, 18 machines	27	264	10	10	0.4
19. CHM lasting	31	71	2	2	0.1
20. Platform cover lasting	6	33	1	6	0.2
21. Pre-welt lasting	9	38	3	4	0.3
22. Cement toe lasting	15	182	5	12	0.3
23. Goodyear welt & turn sewer	31	274	11	9	0.3
24. American lightning nailing	31	96	2	3	0.1
25. Wood heel nailing C	1	11	—	11	—
26. Duplex eyeletter	31	91	1	3	0.0
27. USMC eyeletter C	31	82	2	3	0.1
Averages, 9 machines	21	98	3	5	0.1
28. Heel seat fitting	19	112	10	6	0.5
29. Ensign lacing	31	120	2	4	0.1
30. Lacing A	13	83	4	6	0.3
Averages, 3 machines	21	105	5	5	0.2
Averages, 30 machines	24	192	7	8	0.3

*Includes improvements on which there exist patents reading on the subject matter thereof, although they were not granted on the improvements (cf. Tr. 7817).

included some of the machines on display at Beverly and others not
then displayed. In the tabulation, the machines are presented in three
groups. The first contains the 18 of the 25 most important revenue-
producing machines previously discussed which were included in
S-219, listed in order of importance. The omitted 7 machines stand
numbers 6, 10, 14, 15, 18(?), 19, and 22 on that list.[31] The 18
included machines accounted for 60 per cent of United's leased-
machine revenue in 1947f; all are major machines in the Government's classification. The next group of nine machines are also major
machines, but one of less earnings significance than the first group.
The final group of three machines are minor machines. For each
listed machine, the table shows the number of years from the date of
commercialization, or from 1920 to the date of the information,
20 Feb. 1951; the number of blue-bulletin changes recorded on that
machine; the number of these which were patented; and the average
number of blue-bulletin changes and patented blue-bulletin changes
per year over the period. The table also shows average information
of the same sort for each of the three groups of machines described
above, and for the whole sample. In counting changes which were
the subjects of patents, two kinds of situations were counted: both
changes the inventions embodied in which were the basis for patents,
and changes, which though not themselves the basis for patents, were
covered by United patents in the sense that the patents read on the
subject matter of the changes.[32]

The table shows that the total number of blue-bulletin changes
over the life history of a commercial machine is large, but the number of these which achieve the standard of patentability is very small.
For the "average machine," there were 192 blue-bulletin changes
recorded over its 24-year life to date, of which only eight were the
subject matter of patents. This shows an average of eight blue-
bulletin changes per year, of which 0.3 per year, or one every three
years, achieved the measure of invention signified by a patent. These
figures varied among the several groups. The 18 high revenue producers of the first group show an average of ten blue-bulletin improvements per year, of which 0.4[33] were patented (speaking

[31] The question mark after 18 indicates doubt as to whether the 5th machine listed
in Table 16 includes both models, in which case 18 is covered, or includes only the
Model C, in which case it is not.
[32] See Tr. 7817.   [33] One every 2½ years.

loosely), over their average life to date of 27 years. The nine less lucrative major machines of the next group and the three minor machines of the third showed improvement rates closely similar to each other, and about half the level of the first 18. Over the 21-year average life (both groups) all blue-bulletin changes averaged five per year for both groups; patented ones 0.1 per year for the majors, 0.2 per year for the minors, or 1 every 10 and every 5 years respectively. The difference in the rate of patented changes between the two groups is not significant in view of the variability of the figures within each group. Clearly improvement efforts are concentrated on the important machines;[34] but even among these, the rate of appearance of changes which reach the level of patentability is low.

Within the group of important major machines, there is considerable variation in improvement rates among the individual machines. This variation is broadly correlated with the revenue importance of the machines; for both total and patented changes per year, the figures for the first nine machines run higher than those for the second nine. None the less, individual exceptions stand out: the welt sewer K, the second most important machine in revenue terms, shows the lowest improvement rate of the 18 in total changes and one of the lowest in terms of patented changes. On the other hand, the Clicker C, in the middle of the second division in revenue terms, shows the third highest rate of improvements both total and patented; both machines are pre-1920 developments. It is perhaps worth noting that the first and second machines in terms of improvement rates—the heel seat laster D (no. 7) and the cement sole attacher (no. 9)—are both machines in the development of which the Government charges that competition played an important role. The clicker is not a machine which has been seriously threatened by competition. The rates for all three machines are separated from those of the rest by a considerable margin in terms of all changes; in terms of patented changes the gap is a little less striking. Some differentiating factor appears to be at work; that on the basis of two out of only three instances this can be marked out as the threat of competition in any conclusive fashion is dubious, but at least the suggestion appears.

Another interesting difference between the 18 important machines and the 12 unimportant ones appears when the relation between

[34] See Roberts, Tr. 12837, for a statement to this effect.

improvement rates and model age is examined. Within the first group the distribution of improvement rates among the ten old machines, developed before 1920, does not differ significantly from the distribution among the eight newer machines developed since 1920. Within the second group, however, the six pre-1920 machines show a fairly consistently lower rate of improvement than the six machines developed since 1930. Thus machines which are both old and unimportant tend to remain relatively unchanged through time.

The third partial measure of the results of United's efforts in research and development is provided by the study of the course of productivity per unit of labor input in shoe manufacturing. These figures have the advantage over those used above of pointing to the ultimate result: the gain in the efficiency of shoemaking. They have two important limitations. First, not all the gains in productivity shown arise because of changes in United's machinery; some are attributable to changes in the efficiency of management, some to changes in the character and work habits of the labor force, some to machinery originating outside United, e.g., fitting-room sewing machines, or Compo machines; some changes as shown by available indices are illusory, arising from shifts in style or process of shoe manufacture within the rather broad classifications used in constructing the indices. This last difficulty is most important in the use of crude total-pairs-produced figures as a measure of shoe output, since shifts from heavier to lighter constructions, and from men's to women's shoes have important effects on the labor inputs per pair of shoes. Second, the gains in efficiency shown are measured only in terms of labor inputs; changes of output in relation to raw-material inputs and capital requirements are also significant, but no data on them are available (either in the record of the case, or in general). But again, despite these limitations, the use of labor-productivity figures has some value as another contribution toward a description of the results of United's research.

The important items of evidence on labor-input reductions in shoe manufacturing are three: S-355, a tabulation showing output, labor inputs, and input per unit of output for the shoe industry in 1899, 1939, and 1947; G-4808 for identification, a Bureau of Labor Statistics study on productivity dated 1939, of which the Court will take judicial notice; and S-356, an examination of labor savings achieved in particular shoemaking operations by the introduction of new machines.

The substances of S-355 is reproduced in Table 17. The BLS study which the Government asks the Court to notice makes several important points, in addition to what is shown by the table. First, it calls attention to the importance of the original mechanization process: between 1863 and 1895, labor input per unit was reduced by 80 to 90 per cent, the exact figures varying among the several shoe constructions. Second, it asserts on the basis of an engineering analysis there cited that about 38 per cent of the increase in output

TABLE 17

	1899	1939	1947
Shoe production (1,000 prs.)	217,965	424,136	484,964
Productive workers	141,830	218,010	220,654
Average work-week (hrs.)	55	35.7	38.3
Man-hour input (1,000)	405,000	405,000	419,652
Man-hours per pair	1.86	0.955	0.865
Pairs per man per 8 hours	4.3	8.4	9.25
Index, productivity	100	195	215
		100	110
Index, labor input*	100	51	47
		100	92

*Not in original exhibit, calculated from line 5.

per man-hour from 1900 to 1923 was accounted for by machinery changes; but only about 12 per cent of the increase in output per man-hour from 1923 to 1936 was accounted for by machinery changes. This, if true, is indeed interesting; it suggests that the man-hour figures of S-355 have little significance. But it seems dubious that the statement can be accepted at its face value without a thorough account of the exact character of the engineering analysis, which is not available. None the less, it at least suggests a problem. Third, the BLS study draws the following conclusion (inter alia): "It is not too much to say that machinery as such has played a small role in the last 10 or 15 years in decreasing the labor time required to make a pair of shoes, but it has played a considerable role in making possible basic style changes without substantially affecting the labor time requirements in manufacturing shoes." (By which, presumably, is meant, "without style changes affecting the labor time requirements.") This is at best the testimony of an absent expert witness, disinterested, but not subject to cross-examination. Still it deserves some weight.

S-356 shows the savings in man-hours made in a selection of 27 operations by the introduction of new machines from various early periods to the present. For 18 operations, the time span is 1915–1949, and the frequency distribution of the per cent reductions in labor-input requirements per unit for these 18 is:

less than 10%	1	40 to 50%	2
10 to 20%	2	50 to 60%	1
20 to 30%	7	60 to 70%	2
30 to 40%	2	70 to 80%	1

The greatest reduction was on an upper-cementing operation on rubber shoes performed by hand in 1915, and on the upper-cementing machine, rotary, model Rb in 1949.[35] The smallest labor-input saving was that in the assembling operation achieved when the Rex Model H was substituted for the Model C. It is not clear how these eighteen operations were selected for inclusion in the sample.

The other nine operations analyzed in S-356 were treated in more detail. For eight of them, each model change in machines used is dated, and reductions in unit labor requirements are correlated with the model changes. In addition, in most cases changes in labor requirements in years intermediate between model changes were also recorded. All eight operations were of substantial shoemaking importance, involving major machines.[36] Two different aspects of

[35] S-11 shows that the machine was commercialized in 1927. An analysis with the aid of S-111 of the commercialization dates of the improved machines shown in this tabulation reveals that the average date of commercialization of all 18 was 1922. Two machines had been commercialized within the two previous years; 3 between 9 and 15 years before 1949; 9 between 16 and 20 years before 1949; 3 between 22 and 30 years; and 1—the Rex assembling machine H—was first commercialized at the end of 1915. Thus the figures really show that *some time* during the period there was a reduction of unit labor requirements of the magnitude shown by the distribution, but at least most of the reduction was in the mid-twenties in general, with only such further reductions since as might arise from blue-bulletin improvements.

[36] The one operation not so treated, tip finishing (No. 1 in the exhibit), showed only one process change, which occurred in 1932. This operation was not included in the tabulations and analysis which follow.

the results of parts of the life histories of these processes appears. This time distribution is as follows:

Process and number in S-356	Period covered	Distribution of total labor-saving through time		
McKay side lasting (2)	before 1915 to 1950	80% before 1915		
Goodyear welt side lasting (3)	1910–1950	1910–15 30%	1915–26 50%	1926–50 20%
Goodyear welt heel and toe lasting (4)	1907–1950	1907–24 41%	1924–35 10%	1935–50 49%
Toe and heel lasting flat-lasted work (5)	1907–1950	1907–24 65%	1924–35 8%	1935–50 7%
Goodyear welt sewing (6)	1902–1949	85% before 1912		
Goodyear outsole sewing (7)	1902–1951	70% before 1914		
Moccasin seam attach (8)	1931–1940	1931–33 55%	1934–40 45%	
Wood heel fitting and attaching (9)	19?–1950	up to 1922 20%	1922–31 65%	1931–50 15%

Only one of the eight processes—Goodyear welt heel and toe lasting —shows a large deviation from the general pattern of great productivity gains in the early part of the relevant period and small ones in recent years.

The second aspect of research results on which the figures of S-356 shed some light is the content in terms of productivity increases of model changes and also of the constant improvements that take place on commercial models—the blue-bulletin improvements. The relative labor saving consequent on a model change can be divided by the number of years between the first appearance of the previous model and the appearance of the successor to yield an average per cent per year of labor saving "attributable" to the model change. Similarly, where the exhibit shows changes in labor requirements between two years in which there have been no model changes, the average per cent labor saving per year, derived in the same fashion, can be "attributed" to the blue-bulletin improvements which have been made on the machine over the interval. The "attribution" of these average annual per cent labor savings to model changes and blue-bulletin improvements, respectively, is, of course, very crude. Other changes may account for the observed labor savings[37] to a

[37] See above, pp. 177–178.

varying extent. None the less, the figures so computed can be taken as crude estimates of the upper limits of the productivity results of model changes and blue-bulletin improvements respectively, for the appropriate machines. The average annual per cent changes attributable to each type of machine change is shown in Table 19 below, for each machine for which the data of the exhibit permitted computations to be made.

The table contains 14 entries for each measure. The distributions of the two measures are shown in Table 18.

TABLE 18

Annual Average % Labor Saving Model Changes	Annual Average % Labor Saving Blue-Bulletin Improvements
12.7	9.5
8.5	4.0
6.0	2.7
4.0	2.7
3.4	2.2
3.0	1.5
2.3	0.9
1.7	0.4
1.7	0.3
1.7	0
1.5	0
0.6	0
0.4	0
0.4	0
Q3 4.0	2.7
Median 2.0	0.65
Q1 1.5	0

It is interesting that the level of the two distributions is as little different as it is. The blue-bulletin distribution is much less regular, and of course, sharply skewed. What the distributions show (accepting the significance of the figures for the moment) could be summarized in words as follows: The average effect of a series of blue-bulletin improvements per year is not unlikely to be nothing, measured in terms of labor-saving. But where it is greater than nothing—two-thirds of the cases tested—its magnitude may run something like one-third to one-half the average annual effect of a model change over the life of the model. Given the large degree of doubt as to the exact meaning of these measures of labor-saving in relation to model changes and blue-bulletin improvements, the foregoing inferences from the frequency distributions can be taken as suggesting problems, rather than pointing to conclusions.

Some standard of comparison by which the changes in labor-input requirements in shoe manufacturing which have been considered in the preceding pages can be evaluated as "high" or "low" or "average" are needed; without a standard the figures for shoe manufacturing are meaningless. Neither party has advanced such a standard, and the record is barren on this point. If it is appropriately subject to judicial notice, perhaps the performance in labor-saving of other American manufacturing industries can be taken as a standard. Measures of changes in labor-inputs from 1899 to 1939, generally considered authoritative by students of the subject, are contained in *Employment in Manufacturing, 1899–1939: an Analysis of Its Relation to the Volume of Production*.[38] The figures of the large volume are summarized in a paper by the same author, *Labor Savings in American Industry, 1899–1939*.[39] These studies show that unit labor requirements (wage-earner hours per unit of output) in all manufacturing industries declined 64 per cent in the period 1899–1937 (an average rate of decline of 1.7 per cent per year over the period). Leather shoes, as shown in this study, had a decline of 46 per cent in unit labor requirements in the same period.[40] Of the 58 industries for which wage-earner-hour figures were available for the period 1909–1937, 18 showed smaller labor-savings than shoe manufacturing, among which were flour-milling, meat-packing, linen goods, felt hats, cottonseed products, and lumber-mill products. For the whole period 1899–1939, only data on wage earners, rather than wage-earner-hours, were available for most industries. Of the 55

[38] Solomon Fabricant, published by the National Bureau of Economic Research, New York, 1942.

[39] National Bureau of Economic Research, Occasional Paper 23, New York, 1945.

[40] This is roughly consistent with the decline of 49 per cent in the longer period 1899–1939 shown on p. 177 above. However, Fabricant's index is a better one than that computed above, since it divides shoe production into men's, women's, and infant's, and thus eliminates apparent changes in labor requirements arising from shifts in output among these three classes. Some problems of this sort still remain in the index, however.

TABLE 19
Labor Savings: Model Changes and "Blue-Bulletin Improvements"
(From S-356)

Number of Example and Machines	Model Changes		"Blue-Bulletin Improvements"	
	Years	% Savings in Labor Input per Year	Years	% Savings in Labor Input per Year
(2) CHM McKay side laster to CHM Improved McKay Side CHM Improved McKay side	5	3.4		
laster			35	0.3
(3) CHM Welt side to CHM Improved Welt side	4	6.		
Goodyear upper stapling B			11	0
Goodyear upper tack pulling			11	0
Staple side lasting B			24	0.9
(4) Heel seat lasting B to D	6	3.		
Heel seat lasting D to E	5	4.		
Heel seat lasting E			15	2.2
Bed lasting No. 7			11	0
Toe lasting C			5	4.0
(5) Heel seat lasting D			21	1.5
Bed lasting No. 6			27	0
(6) Goodyear welt shoe machine to Goodyear Universal welt & turn sewing G	7	2.3		
Goodyear Universal etc., to Goodyear welt sewer K	3	12.7		
Goodyear welt sewer K to Goodyear Inseam Sewing B	25	0.6		
Goodyear Welt sewer K			27	0.4
(7) ORL to ORL–K, L	8	1.5		
ORL–K, L to ORL–M, O	2	8.5		
ORL–O to OSA	37	0.4		
(8) ORL–O Moccasin seam attachment			20	2.7
(9) Wood heel attaching to wood heel attaching model B	28	1.7		
Screw removing to Screw removing model B	28	0.4		
Wood heel nailing to Wood heel nailing model C	21	1.7		
L wood heel nailing to wood heel nailing	22	1.7		
Screw removing			9	0
Wood heel attaching			9	2.7
Wood heel nailing			2	9.5

industries for which such figures were available, only 10 showed smaller labor-savings, so measured, over the period than shoe manufacturing. Leather manufacture—tanning—itself showed a labor-saving, in terms of wage-earner-hours, some 25 per cent greater than that of shoe manufacture in the period 1909–1937.

What emerges from a comparison of United's research efforts with such objective analysis of the fruits of these efforts as the record permits? On the effort side, it is clear that United does engage actively, continuously, and on a large scale in a well-organized and technically efficient research program. Further, the objective evidence on the division of expenditure among specific machine types, and among various broad classes of research, does not sustain the charge that United's research is in any specific sense aimed at "eliminating competition"; in fact, this evidence points in the other direction.[41] The major objective of research expenditures has always been the development of specific new shoe machines. The improvement of existing commercial machines occupies a relatively small, but not insubstantial position as an object of research expenditure. Spending on fundamental research and on projects not specific to particular machines has been of increasing importance in recent years, but still is relatively small.

On the results side, there is no record of spectacular achievement. Man-hour requirements of shoe manufacture have declined substantially over the years, but the decline has been less than that shown by manufacturing industry as a whole; and the shoe industry ranks near the bottom of individual manufacturing industries in terms of long-term productivity gains. Nor is it clear what part of such productivity gains as have been achieved are assignable to better United machines; that this part is less than 100 per cent and is probably changing seems certain. New models appear only infrequently; the median age of currently commercial models is 28 years, and the important machines in terms of revenue production are even older. The weighted average age, with contributions to machine-lease revenue as weights, of the 25 most lucrative machine models is 32 years. Many of the most important of these, in which United has a

---

[41] Of course, in the general sense that the achievement of technical superiority over its rivals with respect to any particular machine results in the improvement of United's competitive position in respect to that machine, all of United's, as all of any business's, research aims at "beating competitors," but the Government is not condemning United on such grounds.

market share of nearly 100 per cent, are even older. Blue-bulletin improvements, to be sure, flow along fairly steadily at the rate of 10 or so a year for the more important machines. But only 1 in 25 of these improvements achieves the measure of invention represented by a patent. Nor do other figures on blue-bulletin improvements, showing the research expenditures in this direction or the upper bounds on the productivity results on individual operations, suggest a different estimate of their significance. In short, progress in shoe machinery has not been made by leaps and bounds; rather it is glacial in its character.

This conclusion still begs the central question: is progress relative to United's efforts *and* to the difficulty of the problem of improving shoe machinery great or little? If the problems are indeed as difficult as they appear to the Corporation's witnesses, the results may be good or even spectacular. But, in the absence of competent independent testimony on the difficulty of the problem, the "objective" comparisons of results with efforts can yield one significant conclusion: United has not met the burden of bringing forth positive acceptable evidence to support its view of the excellence of its own research as being such as both to explain United's position in the market, and to justify whatever practices may be necessary to insure its continuance at its present level.

An attempt was made by the Court to get expert testimony from a disinterested source on (among other things) the problems of shoe-machinery research and development by testimony from the officers of the Compo Corporation, United's most important competitor. Such of this evidence as bears on the problems discussed in this section falls into two parts: the objective record of Compo's achievements, set against its efforts; and the opinion testimony of Smith, Compo's research director, designer, and patent counsel.

The evidence of Compo's activities is restricted essentially to one field, cement-sole-attaching and certain preparatory and auxiliary operations. This field corresponds to the activity of the cement-shoe department of United, plus part of the work of the B.B. Chemical Company. The major facts are simply: Compo Corporation was formed in 1928 to develop and exploit the inventions of Bresnahan, a shoe manufacturer, in cement-sole-attaching processes and machinery. Bresnahan was one of the founders of the company; other shoe manufacturers assisted in financing it. Previous to the formation of Compo, Bresnahan had offered his inventions to United, but United thought his price too high and turned him down. Compo thrived after its formation; United entered into the cement field commercially soon after Compo, and today the two corporations divide the market about equally.[42] This division of the market may be taken as a fair indication that the choice between United's and Compo's machines in terms of functional efficiency is a narrow one. The testimony of Smith on the development of the cement process[43] and C-3, Compo's research expenditures for 1929, 34, 39, 44, and 49, permit an estimate of the total research expenditures of Compo from the end of 1927 to the end of 1949, based essentially on linear interpolation between the figures given in C-3. The total expenditure for the 22-year period was about $1,600,000; most, but not all, of this went into cement-sole-attaching and auxiliary machinery. It should be noted that Compo did not develop its own cements until after the first half of the period, but worked under an exclusive purchase arrangement with Du Pont.[44] In about the same period, 1930–1950 fiscal, United and B.B. Chemical together spent some $3,660,000 in the development of cement-sole-attaching and auxiliary machinery, cements and chemicals. Of the total, $2,770,000 was spent on machinery.[45] Thus, it can be said that in this particular instance it required 60 per cent more expenditure by United to achieve over the same period of time the same results as a competitor. This discrepancy occurred in a situation in which the competitor took the initiative, so that both the stimulus and the problems differed from the typical situation in which new machine were carried on by United in a "favorable" way; the stimulus was more intense,[46] and Compo had demonstrated the possibility of a workable solution and a path along which it could be found.

Further, if it is considered that Compo found it possible to do the original development job successfully on the basis of research by an independent supplier on one essential component (although it later changed to producing its own cements),[47] the appropriate comparison might be $3,660,000 to $1,600,000 or a 130 per cent greater expenditure by United, since integrated development of supplies is not necessary if outside suppliers stand ready to do the job on the basis of the profits they expect to achieve if successful.

In addition to the venturesomeness of the Compo development,

[42] See above, pp. 48–49.   [43] Tr. 10086–114.   [44] Tr. 10134–6, Smith.   [45] S-389.
[46] See G documents cited on p. 132 above.   [47] Tr. 10178, Smith.

and the relatively small resources it required, its speed was impressive. Work on the presses started in November 1927, and on the conveyors in which the presses were ultimately incorporated in February 1928. By 1929, 50 conveyors had been produced, but of a sort which Smith characterized as quasi-experimental; the first commercial machines of the present types appeared in 1931.[48] And all this was done by a small development staff. At present, the technical and research staff of Compo includes only 27 people—14 engineers and draftsmen, 4 chemists, 3 laboratory assistants, and 6 shoemaking experts.[49]

The force of this example is very great. It is, however, limited because of the simplicity of the machinery used in the cement-shoe process, relative to such other important types of shoe machinery as pulling-over machines, welters, outsole stitchers, and some lasting machines. This simplicity goes to testing as well as to design problems. The comparison is made by Smith himself,[50] as well as repeatedly by United's witnesses. Thus, to the extent that complex machinery of these types is essential to shoe manufacture, and United excels in the development of such machinery, the Compo experience is dumb on the achievements of United's research in relation to the possible. None the less, this instance speaks convincingly on two important points. It shows that United does not necessarily excel in developing simple machinery, and what is more important, it shows that complex machinery may not always be necessary in shoe manufacture. The Compo experience, including the rejection by United, at an earlier stage, of Bresnahan's inventions because of skepticism on the possibilities of developing suitable cements, on which the whole process turns, at least suggests, if it cannot prove, that United may not always be able to see the possibilities of a simple method, perhaps because of its own dedication to complexity.

The suggestion that United may be slow in developing simple machinery is reinforced by the history of the lasting machinery used for the slip-lasting process. This new process in women's inexpensive casual and play shoes has grown rapidly in importance recently.[51] The first machine used in the lasting operations for this process was

[48] Tr. 10080–90, 10103–14, Smith.

[49] Tr. 9721–24, Mason, President of Compo.   [50] Tr. 10237–245.

[51] S-93 shows an increase in the number of factories using the slip-lasted process from 4 in 1937 to 267 in 1947.

the cement side lasting machine developed by Kamborian;[52] though this machine was not originally developed for the particular construction, it was adaptable to it and was used instead of hand labor as the construction grew in importance.[53] Smith of Compo listed the process and the lasting machinery used in it as the sixth of the six most important developments in shoe machinery in the last 25 years, with the qualification noted above.[54] The machine was first invented in early 1938, and an experimental model was produced in a month. The first commercial model was made in 12 to 14 months, and quantity production was achieved in 1941, all manufacture being undertaken by outside producers, not by Kamborian's International Shoe Machinery Corporation.[55] One United view of this development is expressed in G-264,[56] a program committee report on lasting dated March 1944. The report mentions the slip-lasting field (described as hand cement-lasted slippers and moccasins) as one in which United has no suitable equipment, but the Kamborian machine is "reasonably satisfactory." United's machine in this field, the platform cover laster C, was commercialized early in 1945.[57]

Smith's account of the Reece experience in the development of a high-speed inseamer, and his general opinion testimony on the problems of developing complex machines form the second part of the Compo material that bears on the evaluation of United's research and development efforts. Smith discussed the difficulties he experienced when working at Reece on a high-speed inseam stitcher. The development started in 1926 and in 1937, when it was abandoned, it was some 10–12 years from completion, by Smith's estimate. The development staff included Smith, two other designers, and a draftsman. About $1,000,000 was spent on development in this period on the inseamer, a bed laster and, to a lesser extent, an outsole stitcher. Smith estimated that any manufacturer would have required comparable development time;[58] but it is not entirely clear from the context whether this implies that no manufacturer could usefully have employed a larger research staff on the project, or that the same time would have been required with the same resources. The following testimony, generalizing the experience to cover other complicated machines, suggests the first interpretation. [59, 60]

[52] Tr. 13550–563.   [53] Tr. 10215–16, Smith, examination by Proctor.
[54] Tr. 10005–7, for the original listing, examination by Rowley.
[55] Tr. 13530–63.   [56] I, 115.   [57] S-111.   [58] Tr. 10248–9.   [59] Tr. 10249.
[60] The Reece discussion appears in Tr. 10008–12–53.

Compo examined the problems of making an inseam sewing machine between 1936 and 1938 and decided the resources required to deal successfully with the problems were so great as to preclude any attempt by it. Smith estimated at the time it would cost several hundred thousand dollars to copy a foreign welter and add improvements, of which about $100,000 would go for tools, jigs, and fixtures. Even without United's competition, the problem would have been impossible for Compo, simply because of Compo's small size.[61]

As mentioned above, Smith listed what in his view were the six most important developments in shoe machinery since about 1925. These were, in order of their importance: the cement-sole-attaching press and conveyor (Compo), the high-speed welter (United), the automatic toe laster (United), the automatic heel seat laster (United), cement extruder (United), cement side laster for slip-lasting (International).[62] Four of the six were, as indicated, United developments; the two non-United developments have been commented on above.

Smith also offered views on the difficulties of designing and testing automatic shoe machinery,[63] on the deterrent effect of trade-in second-hand machinery on research,[64] and on the difficulties of doing research in a sales as opposed to a lease market[65] which were substantially those presented by Roberts in various parts of the record already cited, or to be discussed below.

Finally, Smith made some interesting comments with respect to the relative quality of United and foreign shoe machinery; his knowledge on this was confined to the period before World War II.[66] In general, he found foreign machinery to be merely copies of old United models on which patent protection had expired, and thus inferior to United machines. But this was not always the case. Smith mentioned the Moenus outsole stitcher, which in 1939 was capable of 1000 stitches per minute, compared with United's then current figure of 650, but which was not commercialized. Moenus also produced an inverted pulling over machine and a micro-tack laster, which were commercial, and were offered for sale, rather than on lease.

In general, this part of the evidence in part confirms the testimony of Roberts and other United witnesses; in part it varies from it. United's views of the magnitude of the problems involved in develop-

---

[61] Tr. 10252–57.   [62] Tr. 10005–07, 10212–16.   [63] Tr. 10266–7.
[64] Tr. 10278–9.   [65] Tr. 10283–5.   [66] Tr. 10289–92, 10326–35.

ing the more complex types of shoe machinery were repeated by
Smith. The list of important machine developments in recent years
gives much credit to United, but whether, in view of United's position in the industry, the 2 out of 6 score of "outsiders" shows United
is lagging relative to its opportunities is not clear. And finally the
existence of at least some foreign machinery of high quality not
copied from United models and produced for a sale market raises
questions about the validity in fact of United's arguments on the
relation of leasing to the quality of research, the logic of which will
be discussed below. But the evidence on this point is meager and
does not in itself sustain any conclusion, one way or the other. The
Compo evidence taken as a whole, including both Compo's experience in the development of cement sole attaching machinery, and
the opinion testimony of Smith, weakens, rather than strengthens
United's case. It certainly raises more new questions than it answers
old ones, but it reinforces the previous conclusion[67] that United has
failed to meet the burden of proving positively the excellence of its
research in the way required by the role that United has assigned
to research excellence in its argument of the case.

    In addition to the factual evidence on the character and results of
United's research activities broadly viewed, examination of which
has formed the bulk of this section, and the detailed testimony on
the development history of particular machines, which occupied a
large part of Roberts' testimony, and which will receive some brief
mention at the end of this section in connection with an examination
of the Government's charges on suppression of patents and with-
holding the results of research, the material offered by United included a substantial amount of argument on the relations between
the quality and quantity of research in the shoe machinery field and
United's position in the market, the leasing and unit charge systems,
the provision of service in the lease bundle, and other general aspects
of the functioning of the shoe machinery market. These arguments
appear repeatedly throughout the record and are voiced by various
witnesses. Indeed, whenever certain subjects are approached, counsel's questions and the witnesses' answers thereto fall into a pattern
and make a single argument, repeated with minor variations.[68] The

[67] Above, pp. 183–184.
[68] The most explicit, systematic, and continuous exposition of them appears in the
testimony of Roberts. See esp. Tr. 12814-52, 12862-91, and 12907-13.

main points of the argument can be summarized fairly briefly. Leasing generally, the unit-charge system, and the provision of service as part of the lease bundle are all requisite to a successful program of research in shoe machinery. Coverage of the whole shoe machinery field and provision of a full line of supplies are also important to successful research. What all these features of the market structure explain is United's excellence in research. Excellence in research, in turn, explains United's position in the market: United supplies such a large part of all the shoe machinery needed because it offers the best machines, as well as the service that keeps them running efficiently, and it offers these things more cheaply than they could be offered under other market arrangements.

The virtues of the leasing system itself in relation to research are chiefly that it provides a steady stream of income, from which a steady level of research outlays can be financed. An efficiently operating research organization must function on a continuous basis, since training is slow, and the continuous acquisition of knowledge and experience by its staff is one of the most important aspects of successful functioning for a research organization.[69] Moreover, a sales market would provide less income in total than does leasing.

The leasing system, together with a unit-charge basis of payment, results in a partnership arrangement between the shoe manufacturer and the shoe machinery producer which is beneficial to both. Since United is paid on performance, including high rate of output and dependability of production, the design of rugged, high-performance machines is stimulated. Every improvement in an existing machine which increases its production rate, or decreases the repair time it needs on the average, benefits the manufacturer; through the unit-charge system it benefits United as well, and thus United has a continuing stimulus to improve existing machines, as well as to develop new ones. By contrast, in a sales market, United would profit only once, on the initial sale transaction, and thus it would have no stimulus to continue improvements of existing machines. In the effort to promote sales, energy would be directed toward cheapening rather than improving machines, and thus machinery designed for a sales market would be inferior to machinery designed for a lease

---

[69] Note that the greatest drop in leased-machinery income, fiscal 1930 to fiscal 1932, was 15 per cent (S-242), while the greatest drop in research outlays in this period was 32 per cent, from fiscal 1930 to fiscal 1933 (S-241).

market. Further, unit-charge payments under a lease make more predictable the probable returns from machine improvements and new designs than they would be in a sales market. This further facilitates development in machinery, since the outcome of expenditures on research is less chancy.

The provision of service in the lease bundle reinforces the desirable incentives to research provided by the unit charge. Since any reduction in service costs benefits United, ruggedness and simplicity of machine design are stimulated. Also, the service force is an important source of information on machine performance, and thus on suggestions for improvements, modifications, and the design of new machines. Service also includes training, and the lease system thus operates to produce a higher level of skill and productivity of the operatives at the shoe factory, again to the benefit of United and the manufacturer.

The fact that United offers a wide line of shoe machinery is also important to its success in research and development. First of all, the interrelatedness of the whole range of shoemaking problems makes it desirable to have an organization which can deal with the whole range. Then, the provision of a long line of machinery means that United can see that there is the appropriate coördination among the machines used in manufacturing a shoe by any given process. This advantage extends also to the provision of supplies; the coördinated development of machines, and the supplies used with them, produces better results than the separation of the two functions. Moreover, from a financial side, the long line means that revenue accruing from production of shoe machinery as a whole goes to finance development in shoe machinery as a whole. This is especially important in relation to auxiliary machines, the development of which by themselves might not be attractive.

In sum, the leasing system as it now operates serves to maintain a delicate balance in the complicated interrelationships among the various shoe construction processes, the machines needed in making them, the service and training requirements involved in continuous functioning of the factory, the stimuli and rewards of the shoe manufacturer and the shoe machinery manufacturer. Any modification of or interference with this system will upset this balance; with results that are unforeseeable in detail but certainly unfavorable in the large.

The final stage of the argument is the proposition that United's market position simply reflects its superiority in developing and producing the best machines, the result of the beneficial operation of its marketing arrangements as discussed above. This proposition is asserted, rather than argued.[70] At this point in the analysis, no space need be spent in commenting on it. Rather, it is the propositions leading up to the assertion which deserve examination.

One way to show at least part of the content of the argument summarized above is to compare it with a somewhat different, but not entirely dissimilar, argument on the benefits of monopoly in promoting successful research in the shoe machinery field. Since the monopolist faces no rivals, a substantial part of the risk involved in research outlays disappears—the risk that the improvements or new machines forthcoming will be inferior to those developed by a competitor. This means that any improvement developed by the monopolist, provided it is larger than some minimum, can be sold to the customers, since no other improvements are forthcoming to compete with it. The absence of competition also makes research less risky in another way: it permits the concentration of research effort on problems which are fairly sure to yield to time and effort, and diminishes the costs involved in trying less certain paths toward vaguer goals, though pursuit of these might possibly result in large leaps forward in the unlikely event of success. Further, the monoply, especially if it covers all or nearly all the broad field of shoe machinery, can practice price discrimination in various ways, including quantity discrimination through unit-charge leases, and inter-machine discrimination, and thus get a larger total revenue from its machine business than a number of competitors similarly situated could achieve in the aggregate. Then the monopolist would have the advantage that all ideas, all suggestions, the work of independent inventors, the inventors interested in the art themselves, would naturally flow to him. Thus any gains from the mating of ideas arising in different parts of the industry, or the joining of talents of different men would accrue to the monopolist. In an otherwise similar situation in which there was competition, some losses on account of failure to achieve this matching would be probable. Similarly, economies in design arising from the absence of a necessity to "design around" patents held by rivals, and from the ability to combine all best techniques and methods without the delay arising

[70] See Tr. 12877–83.

from cross-licensing negotiations and the losses when licensing is impossible, would all accrue to the research department of the monopolist. And, of course, the monopolist is able to coördinate all the machines needed in the various shoe manufacturing processes, without worrying about the problems of flexibility that might arise if his machines had to be designed to function with a variety of machines made by other producers. If to his monopoly of machines, there were added a monopoly of service, some of the advantages to the monopolist mentioned above might be increased, especially those connected with the flow of information and ideas from all parts of the shoe manufacturing industry to the producer of shoe machinery.

Together, these arguments are substantial. Do they justify for the monopolist an exemption from the Sherman Act, especially if his monopoly has been achieved by methods which would not entirely escape its ban? Whatever the answer to this question as a matter of law, as a matter of economic policy a positive answer would appear in order only if two conditions were met by the monopolist. First he would have to make a very strong showing that the actual results flowing from these advantages were important, in the sense that he could point to a record of achievement in research and development which would be unambiguously excellent. Second, he would have to show that the advantages were important to the results; that absent the monopoly, no such record of achievement would be at all likely; and that the difference between what was done and what would have been done under other circumstances would probably be substantial.

Now the arguments in favor of leasing, unit charges, and service in the lease bundle, in so far as they have substance, are to a large extent arguments in favor of discriminating monopoly because of its advantages in financing and performing research. The important extent to which leasing and the lease bundle contribute to United's market power have been discussed in detail above,[71] as have the prevalence and significance of price discrimination.[72] The arguments on the importance of income stability, and on the coördination of performance of different machines (as well as of machines and supplies, which will be discussed further below) are without any substantial merit. The actual fluctuations in United's research expenditures, plus the capacity of any profitable corporation so

[71] Pp. 64–73.   [72] Pp. 73–78, 125–134.

desiring to budget fairly stable sums for research in spite of income fluctuations, especially when research expenditures are of the order of 10 per cent of total gross income, suggest that United's witnesses have exaggerated the importance of income stability arising from leasing. Further, it is the combination of leasing with a very large market share that makes for income stability; if substantial competition existed in many fields, United's income would probably fluctuate much more than it now does even if leasing were universal. The ability of Compo to design successful machines for a few processes suggests that the importance of coördination has also been exaggerated, and that no substantial losses would arise if there were less "coördination" in the sense of the foregoing argument. The contention that a machine supplier who sold, rather than leased, machinery to shoe manufacturers would cease to have any interest in improving his machines hardly bears examination. While he would indeed cease to have any financial interest in a particular machine which he had once sold, he would continue to have the greatest interest in his ability to make another sale, either of the same machine model to another customer, or another model to the same customer. In either event, his ability to make more than one sale would depend on the excellence of his machines, and their continued performance, to just as great a degree as does United's lease income, even though the mechanism of connection would be less rigid and less visible. Moreover, under a sales system, the shoe manufacturer who owned machines would be stimulated, and able, to make improvements on them himself.

It is indeed true that the operation of a service department by United is an important source of information on machine performance, and of suggestions as to improvements and even new designs. These virtues need not depart from the service department if it is operated on a system of separate charges, possibly in competition with independent providers of service or with the shoe manufacturers' own service staff. Only if United's service on an independent-charge basis proved to be so expensive that few or no manufacturers bought it would United's research department be deprived of the benefits of contact with a service organization—an outcome which seems unlikely, in view of the testimony offered on the efficiency of United's service.

To the extent that United's full line is important not only because of "coördination," but because the full line enables income from the whole process to pay for research from the whole process, the result is an undesirable allocation of research resources. This proposition can only mean that United now spends money on developing some machines which it could not expect to recover by leasing (or selling) the machines which result from the development effort.[73]

Under a system in which developments were expected to stand on their own feet, in the sense that no expenditure on machine development would be undertaken if the results were not, *in advance,* expected to pay for the development costs (though, of course, such expectations would sometimes, perhaps frequently, be disappointed), no such expenditures would be made. And it is clear that a development expenditure not expected to result in an improvement of sufficient value to the shoe manufacturers to enable the newly developed machine to pay for itself should not be undertaken. (Note that this argument applies only to development of specific machines, not to general research which might be useful in many different ways.)

There is a small residue of valid advantage, or possible advantage to research in the leasing system which does not depend only on the efficacy of the leasing system in maintaining United's position in the market. This is the fact that, under a leasing system, even with competition, it might be expected that the degree of customer-supplier loyalty would be higher than under a sales system. To the extent that this was true, the competitive risks for the individual leasing firm might be cut down, and his lessees would continue to prefer his improvements over his rivals' improvements, unless the margin of difference in favor of the rivals was clear and substantial.

The discussion of the relation between United's research efforts and its marketing system so far has tried to show that United's contentions on this point amount to a plea for monopoly, on the argument that monopoly is necessary to support research in the peculiar circumstances of the shoe machinery market. Even if the propriety of the argument were admitted, and the evaluation of the past results of United's research more favorable, the argument as made would not support the conclusion that United's monopoly and the marketing methods that support it are, on balance, socially desirable in view

---

[73] Perhaps this proposition is only another expression of the fact of intermachine price discrimination. If so, it has no relevance to the research problem. Only if it has the meaning ascribed to it above, does it deserve analysis.

of the progress they yield. The argument is incomplete, looking only to the advantages arising from the more generous provision of funds for research possible under existing as compared to alternative arrangements. There is also the problem of the difference in incentive to do research and to embody its results in machinery which appears in the market as between a situation of monopoly supported by leasing, and an alternative situation in which leasing was absent and greater competition existed. The combination of monopoly and leasing operates to centralize all decisions on machine development from the decision to try to build a new machine to the decision to replace an existing model by a new model in United. United's monopoly (speaking somewhat loosely, and ignoring the existence of some competition in certain areas) means, of course, that United is the sole source of decisions to initiate development on a new machine, and United determines in detail what form the development takes, among a possibly large number of alternative forms it might take. This in itself involves some losses, in that the ideas of United, or any other single organization, tend to get fixed in certain ways: some techniques or devices become "favorites"; blind spots may develop with respect to others. General observation of many types of creative intellectual activity suggests that several independent centers of effort produce a greater variety of ideas and outlooks than can develop in any single center.

Moreover, United's monopoly position may tend to promote caution rather than boldness in exploiting new developments. "Premature" commercialization or "premature" freezing of a development, may result in losses arising from unforeseen failures in performance, *vide* the experience of the OSA.[74] Caution can at worst lead to a delay in the time when receipts begin to flow in; thus the commercial forces tend to push in the direction of caution. In a situation where there is significant competition, including competition in the development of machinery, the pressures are somewhat different. There, delay may mean a relatively long-run rather than a temporary loss of revenue, in that it may permit a rival to capture the market for a new development if his is the first to appear. This is of course a speculative argument, but it does receive some support from the instances of the heel seat laster E and toe lacing machine A discussed below, in which the possible threat of competition arising from the

[74] Tr. 4014–37, Roberts.

expiry of patents led to a quickening of the completion of developmental efforts on these two machines.[75]

Leasing operates to put a further range of decisions in the hands of United which under a sales system would rest with the shoe manufacturers. As the owner of the machines, it is United which bears the risks of obsolescence. Thus it is United which evaluates the relative risks of supplanting an old machine with a given improved model, and waiting a while for further improvements, which, if they appear, would have shown the investment in the first new model to have been unwise. This, of course, is the other side of the decision to bring out a particular new model spoken of in the preceding two paragraphs. But under a sales system, even without competition, at least part of the risks of obsolescence involved in decisions of this type would be borne by the shoe manufacturers who decided whether to buy the present new model or continue to use the old one until further improvement appeared. With competition in shoe machinery production, as well as a sales system of marketing, the shoe manufacturer's scope for choice would be further broadened, since his comparison would involve not only the current new model of one manufacturer as against the possible advantages of waiting for that manufacturer's next new model, but also the possible advantages of waiting for the next new models of all the manufacturers. Given the inevitable spread of opinion among shoe manufacturers on the actual advantages of the current new model over the old model, and the even wider spread of opinion on the probabilities of further improvements that would make profitable waiting rather than buying the current new model, the absence of centralization of this aspect of the decision to replace an old by a new model would lead to a situation in which the making of such decisions would become an element of competition among shoe manufacturers, and the choice by shoe manufacturers among improvements of different magnitudes offered with different frequencies an element of competition among shoe machinery manufacturers.

Two advantages would arise from the change in the incidence of the risk of obsolescence consequent on the replacement of a leasing by a sales method of marketing. The first is clear, the second somewhat speculative. To the extent that the end of leasing would shift some of this risk from the shoe machinery manufacturer to the shoe

[75] See below, pp. 199–201, United denies that this was the case.

manufacturer, the machinery manufacturer would be encouraged to a bolder policy in developing and offering new machines. This effect would be reinforced by the existence of competition in the machinery industry, because of the further incentive offered to the machinery seller by the opportunity to replace, by his own new machines, the existing machines of a rival, and thus break down existing customer attachments to a rival and build up new ones to himself. In this case, part of the obsolescence risks involved in putting out a new machine are borne in effect by the rival machinery sellers, as well as by the shoe manufacturers.

The second advantage is the greater likelihood that a closer approximation to the "right" decisions on which developments to commercialize and which new models to buy, viewed ex-post, will be achieved through the processes of competition in offering new developments and competition in selecting them—in other words through a process of trial and error—than through the processes of centralized planning by one machinery maker. The right decisions, viewed ex-post, are those that machinery makers and shoe manufacturers would have made had they been in possession of certain knowledge of the future course of development of machines over whatever period of change is under consideration. The whole problem, of course, turns on the actual and inevitable ignorance of the future course of developments when any decision is made, either by a shoe manufacturer or by a machinery manufacturer. If it can be shown that United will always possess a better combination of information and judgment in this respect than any one of the shoe manufacturers (not, of course, any particular one in respect to all decisions, but the best one in respect to any particular decision, whoever he may be), not to speak of possible rival machinery manufacturers, then it can be argued that the centralized decision will lead to better results—in the sense of a better approximation to the ex-post correct decisions—than the results of the process of competition. But this proposition is not easily to be believed: the general attitude of pragmatism and empiricism toward the facts of life which underlies the whole of modern technology and business hardly is consonant with the ready acceptance of human infallibility, either in Rome or on Federal Street; and the available history fails to support the proposition that United always knows best.

Another aspect of the alternative distributions of the risks of obsolescence under various marketing arrangements worth comment is that the present arrangement, under which United bears the whole burden, represents one more example of the position of benevolent protector and compulsory insurer which United maintains in relation to the shoe manufacturers. Any costs involved in this risk burden are of course part of the costs of shoe manufacture. By assuming these costs, and by preventing any competition among shoe manufacturers in respect to the decisions involved, United once again protects the inefficient from themselves, and shifts part of the differential costs to the efficient firms.

This summary and critique of the purely argumentative part of United's testimony on the relation between its marketing methods, its research results, and its market position only reinforces the conclusions based on the analysis of the objective record of United's research activities, and the comparative examination of United and Compo. United has failed to make its case that its size in the market, being the consequence of its excellence, is not open to attack under the Sherman Act as such; and further, that its marketing arrangements arise naturally out of the demands for the achievement of excellence through the continuous large-scale research which that achievement requires in the face of the special problems of design and development in the field of shoe machinery.

The Government's view of United's research activity as merely another instrument of monopolization is such as to require litttle discussion. Clearly the performing of research, the hiring of inventors, the achieving of superior results do not all become illegal activities because they contribute in some degree to the maintenance of United's market position. Aside from contentions which seem to be essentially of this sort (although not explicitly so), and matters of patent infringement dealt with above in the discussion of coercive practices,[76] the Government's case in this area involves two points. The first is the "holding in reserve" of inventions, which are brought out only in the face of competition or possible competition. The instances which the Government relies on are cited in schedule C of the Government's answer to the order of the Court of May 8, 1950. They include the heel seat laster E, developed because of the threat of Moenius competition (1935); the OSA, limited adoption of which was undertaken when the competitive threat of the Landis

[76] See above, pp. 108–112.

stitcher was felt (1946); and the lacing machine A, adopted in response to foreign competition (1938). In all three cases United, through the testimony of Roberts, denies that inventions or developments were in any way kept in reserve. He goes through the developmental history of the three machines, and in each case shows some work on the problem before the appearance of the competitive machine.[77] In at least one of the three cases, that of the OSA, the testimony here, as well as in other parts of the record, on the magnitude and duration of the development effort and the paucity of Government evidence,[78] none of which does more than suggest the usual concern with the appearance of a few Landis stitchers, in the period 1939–1947, clearly shows the failure of the Government contention. In the other two cases the testimony of Roberts fails to meet squarely the Government's point that the timing of commercialization was strongly influenced by the presence of competition. In the case of the heel-seat laster, at least one document suggests strongly that there was such an influence.[79] In the case of the lacing machine A, a weaker suggestion of the same sort appears in two documents.[80]

[77] Tr. 12490–515.   [78] G-85, I, 229; G-86, 229; G-78, 231; G-77, 233.

[79] G-1968, I, 84, a memo. from the Terms Committee clerk to Wogan, dated March 7, 1940. The memo. lists examples of cases in which cost information was not complete when terms were set. One example where "cost was not a prime factor" was that of the heel-seat laster. "The only case since Form-A leases that I recall where terms were made without knowledge of manufacturing cost is the USMC Heel Seat Lasting Machine—Model E. Enough was known of its merits to warrant increasing the 4/10¢ royalty of the previous Models B and D to ½¢ for the E. Terms had to be made in a hurry due to the entrance of German competition and to obviate the difficulty of collecting back royalty on five outstanding machines. Our only very rough guess as to costs proved to have been far from accurate and it was nearly three years before more accurate costs enabled us to check terms against investment."

[80] G-470, 471, II, 200–8. Two memoranda from the Terms Committee clerk, one dated 26 May 1938 to the Committee, the other dated 16 November 1938 to the general manager. They talk in terms of "creating a patentable machine that was superior to all others (so that) we could be able to meet serious competition and protect our market." The discussion indicates that terms cannot be made "in the usual way," either on the value of the operation or to recover the investment in a reasonable period and insure a profit. Rather, terms must be made so as to "insure against failure to dispose of at least the 100 made so that on the one hand we may recover as much as possible of the money already spent, and on the other hand that the unrecovered balance, which we will have to consider as a contribution to the object (see quotation above) will be as small as possible."

Both the examples reflect an untypically hasty decision to proceed with manufacture and to worry about costs, prices, and profits later. In the case of the lacer, the competitive stimulus was provided by foreign copies of the Ensign lacer-B, on which patent protection had expired.

Even assuming that Roberts' failure to meet the Government's contention squarely shows its validity, is there anything other than might be expected of either United or any patentee similarly placed? During the life of patent protection on a machine, a new model might not be brought out by the patentee, unless there was a clear advantage in so doing. The expiration of patent protection, however, or the appearance of some other threat of competition might lead to commercialization of the new development to avoid disadvantages which would otherwise result. Given United's market position, this event is rarer than it otherwise might be; but its occurrence shows no special evil intent. It is the infrequent occurrence of similar events that should be the cause of complaint.

The second contention of the Government is on the suppression of patents, Schedule D of the Government's Answer to the Order. Here the Government relies essentially on a listing of patents in the defendant's Red Books which are allegedly not used, and on the argument that any patent is *ipso facto* commercially practicable and its non-use represents "suppression" to the disadvantage of the public. The actual examples cited involved three USBMC machines, the Ballard clicker, and the Goodyear inseam sewer B. The United view of these situations is given by Roberts.[81] In brief, his answers with respect to the first four of these cases—the British pulling over machine, the British toe laster, the British outsole stitcher, and the Ballard clicker—is that in general these patented developments were not embodied in commercial machines because they were inferior to other developments which were so used, and in certain instances where they were not inferior they were used in other machines than the ones for which they were originally developed. With respect to the GIS-B, Roberts simply asserted that when the machine was fully adopted in 1949, the patents covered were commercialized, and this was the earliest practicable date of commercialization, in view of the problems of the machine's development. It is clear that these answers stand against the Government's bare assertions, resting on an empty definition of what is a "commercially practicable" invention, and therefore this part of the Government's case can be given no weight.

In sum, the Government's contentions which are relevant to the subject matter of this section either lack support in evidence, or assert

[81] Tr. 11801–905.

nothing that is not essentially the consequence of United's market position, rather than a cause or explanation of it, and therefore add nothing to the Government's case.

2. UNITED AND THE SHOE MANUFACTURER

As seen by the shoe manufacturer, United's activities are clearly benevolent. The testimony of 15 shoe manufacturers, representing a wide variety of firms in terms of size, location, type and price of shoe manufactured, and general history, leaves no doubt of this. The testimony occupied some 900 pages of the transcript,[82] and nearly the whole of it shows that the shoe manufacturers consider themselves well and cheaply served by United. The testimony emphasizes low costs, with machine royalties and parts running to some 7 to 10 cents per pair of shoes; prompt and efficient service, the self-supply of which would be extremely expensive; the general helpfulness of United in training operators, planning layouts, and solving difficult shoemaking problems; the friendliness and fair-play which characterize dealings with United, including one conspicuous example of United's fair dealing on patent matters and generous help in starting a new business;[83] and the importance of the leasing system in facilitating the entry into shoe manufacturing of those testifying. No concern with the OMIR's was manifested and no testimony was brought out to show that these were in any way objectionable to the manufacturers.

The one exception to these characterizations is provided by the testimony of Wolff, of Wolff-Tober Shoe Company in St. Louis. Under cross examination by Rowley,[84] Wolff was unable to recollect definitely earlier statements made to Rowley, indicating dissatisfaction with the level of United's charges, with United's technical progress, with United's use of the full-capacity clause in connection with Compo heel-attaching machinery in the Wolff-Tober plants, and with certain patent dealings with United. This testimony certainly discredits Wolff as a witness; it also raises the question (which might be raised in the abstract) of whether a shoe manufacturer might be expected to testify adversely to United, given the nature of their relations. But the question remains abstract; in the concrete, no other manufacturer who testified gave any hint of concealing

---

[82] Tr. 4573–4612, 4823–5081, 5103–5254, 5278–5377, 5401–5692, and 5733–5830.
[83] Vaisey, Tr. 5007-81.   [84] Tr. 5590–5620.

adverse views of United, whether in consciousness of favors received or to come, or for what other reason. In any event, it is clear that United does not oppress shoe manufacturers in any way that makes them generally conscious of such oppression.

The major conclusion to be drawn from the testimony of the shoe manufacturers is perhaps its lack of usefulness in helping to decide the outcome of the case. The type of testimony they offered would have been relevant and important if coercive practices by United actually occupied a major role in the case. Allegations of such practices did indeed play an important part in the Government's presentation, but, as has already been argued above,[85] this emphasis of the Government was misplaced. Given the Government's pleadings, the Corporation may well have been forced to provide the kind of response it did. But, to the extent that the major issues turn on the existence of United's market power and its impact on the industry, the shoe manufacturers could only be expected to contribute usefully to an understanding of the subject, if at all, under well-prepared and skillful cross examination by the Government, which was lacking.

One specific aspect of United's relations with shoe manufacturers, much discussed in the testimony, also received some illumination from the documentary evidence: the relation of United's leasing system and its policy thereunder to ease of entry into the shoe manufacturing industry. The manufacturers in the testimony cited emphasized the role of the leasing system in facilitating their own start in the industry with little capital, and contrasted (either explicitly or by implication) this situation with that which would exist under a sales system in which the would-be shoe manufacturer would need enough capital to purchase all his machinery.

The impressions conveyed by this testimony can be tested against certain documentary evidence, and elucidations of it by Ross Briggs, manager of United's credit department.[86] United frequently requires of a new manufacturer a deposit on machines leased. Where the lease terms on a machine specify an initial payment, no deposit is required; but where there is a termination charge (deferred license fee or return charge), deposits are usually required.[87] Over the period

---

[85] Pp. 100–114.   [86] Tr. 13435–7.

[87] Of the 66 machines for which terms are shown in S-310, 63 bore termination charges and only 3 initial payments.

1945–1951f about 60 per cent of the 767 new entrants into shoe manufacturing who leased at least one unit-charge machine were required to make deposits, the figure varying from 75 per cent to 53 per cent in individual years.[88] The size of the typical deposit is not clear from the record. S-443 shows a distribution by size of 462 deposits held at the end of 1951f; but only 257 were deposits of shoe manufacturers leasing at least one unit-charge machine, and an unspecified number of non-shoe-manufacturing lessees were included. For this sample, the average size deposit was about $1500, but the distribution was considerably skewed: the median deposit was $750; one-quarter of the deposits were less than $200; one-quarter, greater than $2000. But, failing the identification of which of the accounts were those of new shoe manufacturers leasing one or more unit-charge machines, the utility of these figures is doubtful.

Briggs testified that the required deposit was customarily twice the amount of the deferred payment for the machine, sometimes less, and rarely more.[89] An analysis of the size of termination payments (as shown in the cases of 38 machines, terms for which were shown in I of the GTB) shows that on the average the aggregate termination charges for a group of major machines would run about one-third their insurance value, which in turn is a little greater than their manufacturing and development costs. For individual machines, the ratio of termination charges to insurance value varied from 15 per cent to 70 per cent, with about five-sixths of the values lying between 20 per cent and 50 per cent. Assuming that under a sales system the sale price of a machine would be roughly twice its manufacturing and development cost,[90] the figures above suggest that the typical deposit United requires of a newly entering shoe manufacturer is equivalent to one-third the cost of his machines to him, were he buying them. This figure may vary widely. For a substantial minority of new entrants it may be zero; for a few the required deposit might run as high as 75 to 100 per cent of the sales price of their machines, were they to buy them.

These computations suggest that the deposit requirements of United create barriers to entry of roughly similar size to those which would exist under a sales system, provided some system of install-

<hr>

[88] S-447.   [89] Tr. 13436–7.
[90] Cf. the General department formula, Tr. 8360, Brown.

ment financing, say under chattel mortgages, were available to the purchaser. Such installment financing of purchased equipment would require down payments, and one-third of the purchase price might easily be a typical down-payment magnitude. Thus, in respect to the capital requirements for the acquisition of shoe machinery, the lease system of United probably operates to make it no easier, and no harder, for would-be entrants to set up a business than would a sales system combined with some form of installment financing.[91]

This conclusion on the magnitude of capital requirements does not dispose of the problem of ease of entry. Even though the capital needed for entry to meet United's requirement of deposits is much the same as that which might be needed under a sales system with installment financing, there remains an important difference between the two situations. At present, with the leasing system and its dominant position in the market, United combines the functions of banker and machine supplier in such a way as to make its own judgments on credit worthiness, the size of deposits required, etc., final. There is no other credit source to which a would-be entrant can turn, in the event that he is rejected by United.[92] It is the essence of competition that the customer have genuine alternatives open to him: in this case alternative sources of credit, so that a market test of his credit worthiness, rather than the judgment of a single lending agency, would determine the necessity for and the size of deposit required of particular customers. In this respect, the present arrangements depart widely from the competitive standards. Given a sales system and the existence of more than one supplier for most machines, the tie-up of credit and machine which now exists would be broken.

The Government charges that United has the power "arbitrarily to determine who may engage in the manufacture of shoes in the United States";[93] if "arbitrarily" be interpreted in a procedural sense —meaning that United has this power subject to no appeal and no accounting for its use—the charge is substantially correct. (It is not

[91] The evidence related to this point proffered by United through Emerson, vice-president of the First National Bank of Boston, does nothing to support a different conclusion. Tr. 11936–71.

[92] Briggs's testimony does not indicate on what basis the size of the deposit, or its complete waiver, is determined; presumably it is on United's estimate of the applicant's credit standing.

[93] Complaint, para. 97b, p. 47.

entirely so, since it may be possible for certain kinds of shoes to be manufactured without United machinery; however, there is no showing that this potentiality has materialized into any substantial reality.)

There is, however, no evidence to show that this power has been used in an "oppressive" fashion, in that would-be manufacturers possessed of experience and an appropriate degree of financial responsibility have been refused access to shoe machinery by United. In fact, if anything, the great bulk of evidence on relations between United and the shoe manufacturers points in the opposite direction. United does make available machinery on fairly easy terms. It provides planning services to design factories; it trains workers; it solves any kind of technical shoemaking problems; its service arrangements keep machines running in the face of special difficulties without extra charges. By doing all this, United assumes a great deal of the managerial burden which under other marketing arrangements would fall on the new shoe manufacturer. This benevolent paternalism is likely to permit and even encourage the entry into the industry of firms with managements of a low degree of competence. The fairly high turnover in the industry, with annual exit and entry together amounting to some 20 per cent of the total number of firms,[94] tends to bear out this speculation. Moreover, the averaging features of the leasing system with respect to service costs, including planning and training, results in the well-managed firms' bearing part of the costs of the poorly managed ones.[95] In short, United's methods of using its market power certainly do something to promote easy entry into shoe manufacturing, and thus to maintain large numbers of firms there, but at the expense of that stimulation of efficiency that it is one of the goals of competition to achieve.[96]

[94] See S-445, showing entrants, exits, and number of firms for the years 1946–1951f.

[95] See above, pp. 134–146.

[96] If shoe manufacturing was an industry which would be one of small numbers of large firms, in the absence of United's leasing policies, this conclusion would have to be qualified. Under such circumstances, the increase in numbers might stimulate competition sufficiently to outweigh the disincentive effects of subsidizing the inefficient at the expense of the efficient. In fact, the characteristics of shoe manufacturing are such that it can be expected to be an industry of large numbers and relatively easy entry even in the absence of the push in this direction provided by United's marketing arrangements and lease terms. Thus the qualification is of no practical importance.

3. SUMMARY OF UNITED'S PERFORMANCE AND CONCLUSIONS ON LIABILITY

United's performance in the market has been examined under four heads: coercive practices, price-cost relations, research and progressiveness, and effects on shoe manufacturing. In none of these respects did United's performance receive outstandingly high marks; in one it was difficult to assign any grade with confidence.

While most of the coercive practices that the Government charged were seen to be the result rather than a contributing cause of United's market power, at least one activity appeared which can only be interpreted as an attempt to exclude competition: the policy of purchase and scrapping of second-hand machinery. In addition, the continuous and almost obsessive concern with the minute details of the activity of all competitors, no matter how small and weak, which appears in nearly all the documents from United's files offered by the Government, was noted.

In respect to the relation of prices to costs, United's behavior showed very wide departures from efficiency in several important respects, First, United's internal accounting system and its method of marketing made cost control difficult, so that United's actual knowledge of the costs of furnishing particular machines was meager. Second, United's pricing formulae showed widespread and persistent price discrimination of substantial magnitude between different machine models. This indicated a departure from efficient resource use in shoe manufacture, and the offer to consumers of choice among various types of shoes on terms which did not correspond to the relative casts of producing them. Third, United's manner of providing service in the lease-bundle without separate charge resulted in substantial discrimination among shoe manufacturers, and the penalizing of efficient manufacturers for the benefit of inefficient ones.

While United's score on research and progressiveness was not found to be so low as the Government has charged, it was not found to be so high as United claimed, or clearly so high as to outweigh deficiencies in other respects. Nor did critical analysis sustain United's double argument, on the one hand, that the existing organization of the market is the only one which would guarantee an adequate research and development program, on the other, that United's dominant position in the market results only from its peculiar excellence in research and development. In sum, the results of United's research efforts might be no worse than what would have been achieved under an alternative arrangement; nor, on the evidence offered, can it be said that they are clearly better. Thus, research and development, important as they are, do not weigh heavily in the scale on either side of the case.

Finally, United's relations with shoe manufacturers are those of benevolent paternalism, promoting equality, perhaps, but clearly not promoting efficiency.

If there is any showing of benevolent use of market power which places a monopolist outside the ban of Section 2 of the Sherman Act, when that monopolist has neither had his monopoly thrust upon him nor acquired it solely as the result of excellence and the preference of all customers for him over his actual and potential rivals, the showing summarized above is not it. It is clear that the Government is entitled to a finding of liability against United, under Section 2, with respect to the machinery market, in accordance with the law as expressed in the *Aluminum* (148 F. 2d 416), *Griffith* (334 U. S. 100), and *Schine* (334 U. S. 110) cases. It will be argued below that practicable remedies exist[97] which give content to the finding of liability, inasmuch as alterations in the market are feasible which will lead to results more in conformity with the standard of competition which the Sherman Act prescribes.

[97] See below, Ch. VIII.

Part Two

The Supplies Markets

VI. United's Position in the Supplies Markets

1. CHARACTER OF THE MARKET

Shoe factory supplies, like shoe machines, comprise a wide range of individual items of greatly different types. But, unlike shoe machines, the supply items are not so intimately bound together either by technical production relations or by substitution and complementarity in use as to constitute in any meaningful sense the commodity traded in a single unified market. Nor, as will appear, does United's position on the selling side of the market in itself justify the treatment of the several submarkets involved as a single one.[1] Instead of a single market, then, there is a variety of submarkets, with quite varying degrees of connection among them. All of these submarkets have in common, of course, the feature that the items dealt in are used by shoe factories in the process of making shoes, although for at least some items shoe factories are neither the only nor even the most important users. But differences among the various classes of products, both in respect to their character and application to shoe manufacture, and in respect to the materials and methods of production used in manufacturing them, are wide.

The Government contention[2] that United is "engaged in a program designed to enable it to provide all shoe factories in the United States with all shoe-factory supplies required by them" is denied by United,[3] and there is no positive evidence in the record to support the Government's view. Indeed, there is no evidence of any sort which shows what supplies others sell which United does not sell, except for the mention in the testimony of the shoe manufacturers

---

[1] See p. 30.   [2] Complaint, para. 90.   [3] Answer, para. 90.

of welting for welt shoes, which United does not sell.[4] Thus, there is
no basis for determining what proportion of the total value of all
shoe-factory supplies and findings, excluding leather, is formed by
the classes of supplies and findings which United and its subsidiaries
sell.

Viewed functionally, the supplies handled by United and its subsidiaries can be classified in four groups: (A) expendable machine
parts, (B) materials driven, set, or applied by machine, (C) shoe
parts not included in (B), and (D) shoemaking accessories and
miscellaneous factory supplies.[5] The merchandise classes shown in
G-3962,[6] a summary of United and competitive sales by classes of
merchandise for the fiscal years 1938–1948 based on the sales record
system,[7] plus the merchandise distributed by United subsidiaries
distributing directly,[8] can be divided among the four groups as
follows:

A. *Expendable machine parts*

cutters and irons	rolls and wheels
machine knives	Sharpening stones and wheels
needles and awls	abrasives
brushes	finishing roll covers
machine awls and drivers	

B. *Materials driven, set, or applied by machine*

nails and tacks	fiber fastening
eyelets, hooks, etc.	waxes
wire	adhesives
lacing thread	insole reinforcing (IRR)

C. *Shoe Parts (not included in B)*

tapes	box toes
wood heels	liquids (finishes, etc.)
shanks	shoe laces

D. *Shoemaking accessories and miscellaneous factory supplies*

equipment (racks, carriers, etc.)	lasts
shoe forms	dies (cutting)
hand tools and knives	paper
cutting blocks and boards	marking ink
shoe boxes	belting

---

[4] Tr. 5185, MacBride.

[5] See memorandum to the Court on behalf of United by Joel Dean, "Supply Activities of United Shoe Machinery Corporation."   [6] XV, 109–19.

[7] See further below, pp. 221–225.

[8] See below, Table 1, p. 215; Table 2, pp. 216–217.

Note: This classification shows 33 merchandise classes: 30 based on G-3962, plus three items distributed directly by subsidiaries and not shown there. The classes presented in the Dean memorandum are slightly finer in certain cases, with the result that 37 classes are shown. Thus, for instance, the Dean memo separates hand from machine brushes, and other waxes from stitching wax, while the above classification does not. The finest classification appearing in the record refers to 75 classes of merchandise (Tr. 6982, Howard). Such differences are insubstantial, and in no way influence the conclusions of this analysis or the Dean memo.

This tabulation gives some indication of the wide range of items sold in the various supplies markets.

If the merchandise classes sold by United and its subsidiaries represented all the kinds of supplies falling within the four classes which were sold in the whole group of supplies markets, then United's weighted average market shares in the four classes and United's sales figure could be used to estimate the relative importance of the four types of supplies in the whole market. An estimate made on this basis shows:

Functional Class	Relative Importance in Whole Supplies Market. %
A	4
B	15
C	46
D	35

These figures almost certainly are biased, overstating the relative importance of the first class of supplies, and understating that of the third and fourth classes, and probably the second as well. That this is most probably the case follows from the nature of the items included in the first class, as well as United's high market share in items of these types; by contrast in the third and fourth classes it is quite likely that there are types of items which United does not produce at all. The probable bias of the estimates thus reinforces the point made by the table as it stands; items of the machine—accessories type are relatively unimportant in terms of dollar volume in the whole market, while shoe parts and various accessory tools and equipment, as well as supplies other than shoe parts and machine supplies are relatively important.

The distribution problems involved in dealing with various types of merchandise also vary widely. Some items, like insole reinforcing (IRR) or shoe boxes are relatively uniform and are sold in bulk terms. Others, such as the machine accessories come in a very wide range of sizes, shapes, and other specifications, and distribution of them involves large inventories. Thus S-342 shows that United handles some 5500 varieties of machine knives, of which the most frequently ordered item accounted for only 5 per cent of the total sales, and 64 items made up 75 per cent of the total. Similarly, some 9000 types of cutters were handled in one year, of which the largest selling types accounted for 2 per cent of the sales units, and the 517 items making up the standard stock list accounted for only 43 per cent of the total unit sales.[9] Some items, such as lasts,[10] presented very special problems of speedy distribution.[11] Others, such as cans and receptacles, United carried merely as a convenience item for the shoe manufacturer.

All these elements of variation among the many supply items limit meaningful generalizations about the supply market or group of markets as a whole. In the discussion that follows, the applicability of specific conclusions to particular types of merchandise activity will be indicated and broader generalizations will be few.

2. UNITED'S ACTIVITY IN THE SUPPLIES MARKETS

United's distribution activities are carried on in two major ways. United's own sales department is the major distributor for most products. In 1947 this department had some 200 employees, 60 in Boston, and 140 in the branches. Of the latter, 88 were salesmen.[12] In addition, certain of United's subsidiaries distribute their product directly. These include F. W. Mears and Co., wood heels; United Last Co., lasts; Hoague-Sprague Co., shoe boxes and box forming machines;[13] B.B. Chemical Co., insole reinforcing (IRR);[14] and Shoe Form Co., shoe forms.[15] Not all of the sales of either United or its subsidiaries were to the shoe trade; outside trades were a significant outlet for sales. The subsidiaries which distributed directly sold products of their own manufacture. The items distributed by

---

[9] S-342 shows similar information for 4 other kinds of machine accessories and for eyelets. The topic is further developed in Tr. 6982–3, 11379–83, 11406–7, Howard.
[10] Distributed directly by United's subsidiary, see below, Table 2, pp. 216–217.
[11] Tr. 11427–34, 11435–8, Holmes. [12] Tr. 6981, Howard.
[13] S-197. [14] Tr. 8658, 8660–1.
[15] S-187. This subsidiary used the assistance of United's sales department.

United's sales department were in part supplied by United itself
including both Beverly and the branch factories,[16] in part by the
subsidiaries, and in part by outside manufacturers. Table 1 below
gives an analysis of the dollar volume of sales of United and sub-

TABLE 1
ANALYSIS OF SALES OPERATIONS, 1948 AND LATER
$1,000
(S-340a)

Channel, Source and Customer	Sales $1000	% Total
Sales Department Sales		
To shoe trade	17,708	46
of which, made by United and subs	13,204	34
made by outside suppliers	4,504	12
To allied trades	346	1
To repair and outside trades	3,569	9
Miscellaneous sales*	1,034	3
of which, to shoe and allied trades	489	1
to outside trades†	544	2
Total sales department sales	22,656	59
Subsidiary Company Sales		
To shoe and allied trades	11,293	29
To repair and outside trades	4,829	12
Total subsidiary company sales	16,122	41
Grand total all sales	38,778	100

*Includes sales of O. A. Miller (trees), Hughes Eyelet (eyelets), miscellaneous branch
sales direct to trade, plus electric motor sales by electrical department.
†Eyelets are the largest item in this (Tr. 7295, 7323).

sidiaries for 1948f[17] which shows the relative importance of various
channels, sources, and outlets. In general, the discussion which follows will deal only with sales to the shoe and allied trades, since
nothing in the case is related to United's supply activities in the out-

[16] See Complaint and Answer, para. 24.   [17] S-340a.

side trades. This means that the total sales figure for 1948f with which this section is concerned is some $30,000,000 or 75 per cent of the total figure shown in the table.

The relative importance of United's sales activities to United is shown by their contributions to United's net and gross income. S-335 shows that in 1947f the United sales department's gross profits and income from dividends (including dividends from subsidiaries), interests, and real estate contributed about the same share to United's total gross income: 17 per cent for the former and 14 per cent for

TABLE 2
Sales Merchandise Classes by 1947f Sales Volume
(Shoe Trade Only)
(From G-3962 and S-197)

Merchandise Class	Sales $1,000	Functional Class	Supply Source
1. Wood heels	3,747	C	Sub (direct)
2. Shoe boxes	3,612	D	Sub (direct)
3. Lasts	2,165	D	Sub (direct)
4. Nails and tacks	2,162	B	Sub. & outside
5. Eyelets and hooks	2,081	B	Branch and outside
6. Shanks	1,734	C	Branch
7. Box toes	1,678	C	Sub
8. Adhesives	1,666	C	Sub
9. Insole reinforcing	1,009	B	Sub (direct)
subtotal 1–9	19,854		
10. Dies	989	D	Sub
11. Liquids	974	C	Sub
12. Cutters and irons	828	A	Beverly
13. Wire	531	B	Outside
14. Cutting blocks and boards	413	D	Outside
15. Machine knives	411	A	Beverly
16. Equipment	405	D	Outside
17. Needles and awls	388	A	Outside
18. Brushes	334	A (some D)	Sub
19. Abrasives	327	A	Outside (some Beverly)
20. Tapes	316	C	Outside
subtotal 10–20	5,916		

TABLE 2—Continued
SALES MERCHANDISE CLASSES BY 1947f SALES VOLUME
(Shoe Trade Only)
(From G-3962 and S-197)

Merchandise Class	Sales $1,000	Functional Class	Supply Source
21. Waxes	250	B (some C)	Sub
22. Shoe forms	212	D	Sub (direct)
23. Lacing thread	202	B	Outside
24. Fiber fastening	198	B	Branch
25. Hand tools and knives	173	D	Outside
26. Shoe laces	144	C	Sub
27. Machine awls and drivers	143	A	Branch
28. Rolls and wheels	135	A	Beverly
29. Sharpening wheels & stones	108	A	Outside
30. Paper	77	D	Outside
31. Finishing roll covers	43	A	Outside
32. Belting	33	D	Outside
33. Marking ink	30	D	Outside
subtotal 21–33	1,748		
Total	27,518		

the latter; the gross machinery earnings contributed the remaining 69 per cent of total gross income. The relative contributions to net earnings are more difficult to determine because of a lack of analysis of the account, "dividends, interest and real estate" in S-335, and the complete absence from the record of a consolidated income statement and balance sheet of United and all its subsidiaries. S-355 itself, on the basis of cost allocation II[18] shows that in 1947f machinery contributed 56 per cent, and United sales plus dividends, interest, and real estate, 44 per cent of net income after Federal income taxes. S-340c, with the same allocation basis, shows total net profit after taxes from sales activities of United and its subsidiaries as $2,550,000 for 1948f. This compares with $4,905,000 for the previous year for the machinery business, as shown by S-335, with the same cost allo-

[18] Cf. above, pp. 116–117, for a discussion of the choice of II as the "best" allocation.

cation basis. This suggests that sales activities are somewhat more than half as important as the machinery business in generating net income for United.

United sales department and subsidiary sales to the shoe trade in 1947f are shown in Table 2 below in 33 merchandise classes ranked in order of sales volume. The table also shows the functional group of each supply class: A, expendable machine parts; B, materials set, driven, or applied by machine; C, shoe parts not in B; D, shoe-making accessories and miscellaneous shoe factory supplies. Finally it shows whether each item was manufactured by United (Beverly or branches), subsidiaries, or outside manufacturers. The total sales of $27,500,000 for 1947f checks closely with the figure for United sales to shoe trades only plus subsidiary sales to shoe and allied trades of $29,500,000 for 1948f shown in Table 1 above. The 9 mer-

TABLE 3
Distribution of Sales Merchandise by Supply Source and Functional Class (Shoe Trade Only)

Supply Source		A	B	C	D	Total
			Functional Class			
Beverly—number of merchandise classes		3	—	—	—	3
1947f sales $1000		1,374	—	—	—	1,374
% of total sales		5.0	—	—	—	5.0
Branches	No.	1	2	1	—	4
	$	143	2,279	1,734	—	4,156
	%	0.5	8.3	6.3	—	15.1
Subsidiaries (USMC Sales)	No.	1	3	3	1	8
	$	334	4,078	2,796	989	8,197
	%	1.2	14.8	10.2	3.6	29.7
Subsidiaries (Direct Sales)	No.	—	1	1	3	5
	$	—	1,009	3,747	5,989	10,745
	%	—	3.7	13.6	21.8	39.1
Outside Suppliers	No.	4	2	1	6	13
	$	866	733	316	1,131	3,046
	%	3.2	2.7	1.1	4.1	11.1
All sources	No.	9	8	6	10	33
	$	2,717	8,099	8,593	8,109	27,518
	%	9.9	29.5	31.2	29.5	100

chandise classes for which annual sales were more than $1,000,000 accounted for nearly three-quarters of total sales shown. The next 11 classes, with annual sales of $300,000 to $1,000,000, added another 22 per cent, leaving only 6 per cent to the 13 minor classes for which annual sales were less than $300,000. The nine important classes included 4 C, 3 B, and 2 D classification items; almost all of them were supplied from United-owned sources. The 13 minor classes included 5 D, 4 A, 3 B, and 1 C classification items, as many of which were supplied from outside sources as from United sources.

Table 3 below represents a rearrangement of some of the information shown in the previous table. It shows merchandise classes, sales volume, and relative share in total sales for each combination of functional class and source of supply. The main points shown by this table are the relative importance of outside sources of supply for items in both A and D classifications, as opposed to B and C, and the great importance of United subsidiaries, both as direct sellers and as suppliers to United's sales department for items of B, C, and D classifications. It also repeats the earlier point of the minor importance of A classification supplies in total sales: the A class amounted to about 10 per cent of the total, and each of B, C, and D to about 30 per cent.[19]

The character of United reliance on outside suppliers is further indicated by S-191 and S-193, which show, respectively, merchandise items made by outside suppliers to United specifications for United sale, and manufacturers for whose products United acted as exclusive distributor to the shoe trade. Together these two types of supply relations accounted for $3,500,000 of $4,500,000 of merchandise made by outside manufacturers which United distributed to the shoe trade in 1948f.[20] The other $1,000,000 presumably represents merchandise of outside manufacture for which United neither served as exclusive agent nor provided specifications. The two tabulations below show the items, suppliers, and 1948f volume of exclusive agency and United-specified merchandise.

[19] Note that the importance of outside suppliers is somewhat understated in this tabulation, since it classes items 4 and 5 (Table 2) as subsidiary and branch supplied respectively and omits consideration of certain minor items in other classes which were made by outside suppliers. The outside supplied items in these classes probably accounted for about $500,000 of sales (cf. S-193, S-187) which would raise the outside share to about 13 per cent. This compares with 15 per cent for a similar figure in 1948f shown in Table I. [20] Table 1.

Items for Which United Was Exclusive Distributor in the Shoe Trade

Merchandise Class	Supplier	1948f Sales $1,000
Synthetic insole and midsole materials*	Du Pont	521
Abrasives	Carborundum	327
Tapes	Minn. Mining	316
Cutting blocks	Endicott Johnson	248
Hooks (eyelets and hooks)	Tubular Rivet & Stud†	247
Paste (adhesives)	Union Paste Co.	158
Repairing crayons (liquids)	Mullen Brothers	53
Wood heel glue (adhesives)	Marstin Adhesive Co.	24
Straps (misc. ?)	Tie Co.	15
Buttons (misc. ?)	Morely Button Co.	4
Total		1,913

*United no longer distributes this material (Answer, para. 91). For this reason and because of the inadequate market definition reflected in the estimates of competition of S-341, this item has been omitted from all succeeding tabulations and also from Tables 2 and 3 above. Without it, the total above is 1392.

†This company is 20 per cent owned by United (Answer, para. 24).

Items Made to United Specifications by Outside Suppliers

Merchandise Class	Supplier	1948f Sales $1,000
Shoe wire	Am. Steel & Wire Am. Brass	530
Needles and awls	Torrington Co.	388
Lacing thread	Linen Thread Co.	202
Wire nails	C. F. Baker Co. Industrial Nail & Packing	186
Racks (equipment)	Beaver Dam Rack Co.	166
Sharpening stones & wheels	Norton, Lombard, Carborundum, Waltham Grinding Wheel, Behr-Manning	97
Total		1,569

The items of outside manufacture distributed by United for which it neither provided specifications nor acted as exclusive channel included abrasives, belting, cutting boards and blocks, finishing roll covers, marking ink, hand tools and knives, paper, and some adhesives.[21]

3. UNITED'S MARKET POSITION IN THE SUPPLIES MARKETS

United's relative share of sales in the various classes of supply items is a disputed question, on which conflicting evidence appears in the record. The Government relies chiefly on G-3962,[22] which shows a summary of figures from salesmen's reports under the sales record system for the years 1937–1948f. The sales record system was initiated in 1937 in an attempt to improve the efficiency of United's sales efforts; each salesman in the branches makes an estimate of competitive sales twice each year, in August and in February. The figures for each branch are then summarized and totaled in the Boston office to show overall figures of United v. competitive sales.[23] This document covers only sales department sales; there is no serious disagreement about the market share figures for the subsidiary products which are distributed directly, and United's offer provides the only worthwhile evidence on this point. United decries the accuracy of the sales record system figures. Howard, for example, testified that the salesmen always overestimated their own sales and underestimated competition.[24] Instead, United has based its own estimate of its market share for various classes of supplies partly on the results of a survey made especially for the trial,[25] and partly on Howard's judgment as applied to the sales record system estimates.[26] The results of this process are presented in S-341, where the market share for each product class is shown in terms of a quadripartite classification: greater than 80 per cent; between 60 and 80 per cent; between 40 and 60 per cent; and less than 40 per cent.

Table 4 presents market-share data for 33 merchandise classes[27] based chiefly on G-3962, the sales record system summaries, and other sources indicated in the footnotes, together with the United market-

---

[21] S-187 compared with S-191, 3 shown above.   [22] XV, 109–19.

[23] See Tr. 7040–3, Howard, manager of Sales Dept., and G-3965, XV, 121 ff., an example of the instructions to salesmen for preparing their reports.   [24] Tr. 7079–82.

[25] S-196 and Tr. 11390, Howard.   [26] Tr. 11345.   [27] Cf. Tables 2 and 3 above.

TABLE 4

UNITED SALES MERCHANDISE (SHOE TRADE ONLY)
MERCHANDISE CLASSES, BY MARKET POSITION
(From G-3962 and Other Sources, see Notes)

Merchandise Class	Source[a]	Sales $1,000 1947[f]	Market Shares % 1947[f]		Change in Market Share 1937–47 % Points	Functional Classification Dean[b]
1. *Merchandise classes with 1947 market shares greater than 80%*						
1. Nails and tacks	subsid. & outside	2,162		82	+7	B
2. Eyelets, hooks, etc.	branches & part. subsidiary	2,081	(60–80)	87[d]	0	B
3. Cutters & irons	Beverly	828		100	0	A
4. Wire	outside	531		96	+5	B
5. Machine knives	Beverly	411	(60–80)	99[d]	0	A
6. Equipment	outside	405	(60–80)	100[d]	+5	D
7. Needles & awls	outside	388		100	0	A
8. Brushes	subsidiary	334	(60–80)	90[d]	+10	A[e]
9. Shoe forms	subsidiary*	212		93	+20	D
10. Lacing thread	outside	202		93	+25	B
11. Fiber fastening	branch	198		100	0	B
12. Hand tools & knives	outside	173		82	0	D
13. Machine awls & drivers	branch	143		100	0	A
14. Rolls & wheels	Beverly	135		100	0	A
15. Sharpening stones & wheels	outside	108		90	0?	A
Subtotals (average)		8,311		90	+4	
2. *Merchandise classes with 1947 market shares of 50 to 80%*						
1. Blocks & boards	outside	413		70	+8	D
2. Abrasives	Beverly outside	327	(40)	52[d]	0?	A
3. Tapes	outside	316		67[e]	+30[e]	C
4. Waxes	subsidiary	250		68	+10	B & C
5. Finishing roll covers	outside	43		54	−40	A
6. Marking ink	outside	30		61	+20	D
Subtotals (averages)		1,379		65	+10	
3. *Merchandise classes with 1947 market shares less than 50%*						
1. Wood heels[f]	subsidiary*	3,747		27	0	C
2. Shoe boxes[f]	subsidiary*	3,612		15	?	D
3. Lasts[f]	subsidiary*	2,165		30	−?	D

TABLE 4—Continued
UNITED SALES MERCHANDISE (SHOE TRADE ONLY)
MERCHANDISE CLASSES, BY MARKET POSITION
(From G-3962 and Other Sources, see Notes)

Merchandise Class	Source[a]	Sales $1,000 1947[f]	Market Shares % 1947[f]	Change in Market Share 1937–47 % Points	Functional Classification Dean[b]
4. Shanks	branch	1,734	(<40) 49[d]	15	C
5. Box toes	subsidiary	1,678	25	7	C
6. Adhesives[g]	subsidiary	1,666	37	−7	B
7. Insole reinforcing[h]	subsidiary*	1,009	49	?	B
8. Dies (cutting)	subsidiary	989	29	+10	D
9. Liquids	subsidiary	974	41	−27	C
10. Shoe laces	subsidiary	144	6	−4	C
11. Paper	outside	77	28	+15	D
12. Belting	outside	33	22	0	D
Subtotals		17,828	30	0	
Totals		27,518	50	2	

[a]Sources of supply are given in S-187. There are four classes: Beverly; the branch factories—United Awl and Needle, J. C. Rhodes and S. O. & C. Co., United Shank and Findings, and O. A. Miller Treeing Machine Co.; the subsidiaries—Celastic Corporation, S. A. Felton and Son, B.B. Chemical Co., The Shoe Lace Co., W. W. Cross Co., The Shoe Form Co., F. W. Mears Co., United Last Co., and the Hoague-Sprague Corp.; and outside suppliers. The last four subsidiaries distribute their major products directly, and products made by them and distributed directly are starred in the table: "subsidiary*"; some B.B. Chemical products are also distributed directly and similarly marked.

[b]For the definition of the four functional classes see pp. 212–213 above.

[c]Some of the brushes were hand brushes, which belong in category D; the major part were machine brushes in A.

[d]In each of these cases the market share estimate here shown differs from the market share estimate made by United in S-341, which is shown in brackets. As explained in the text, these differing estimates were rejected.

[e]The variability of the year-to-year figures shown in C-3962 casts some doubt on the validity of these percentages.

[f]The sales and market share estimate for these items are shown in S-197, S-370, and S-347, not in G-3962. As explained above in the text, there is no dispute about these figures.

[g]The figures shown in G-3962 for adhesives are corrected to show United's share of the total market, not merely the market represented by cement shoes attached on United machines. (See G-3965, XV, 121 ff., esp. p. 124 for the definition of the figures originally entered.) The corrections are based on various figures in the record showing United's share of total cement shoe production.

[h]The figure for this item is based on the testimony in Tr. 8034–36, 8660–1, and includes process royalties as well as sales of merchandise. The market share figure shows IRR sales as a proportion of *all* reinforced insole sales, not as a proportion of tape reinforced insole sales; the latter are 60 per cent of the former.

share classification shown in S-341 whenever it does not correspond to the figure based on the sales record system. In general, the agreement is good: in only 6 of the 33 classes is there disagreement, and even in these, though the absolute magnitude of difference is substantial, the general picture of United's position shown by the two estimates is the same.

When there is a difference, the sales record system estimates appear to be the more reliable. Howard's "exercise of judgment" in respect to those sales-record-system figures which were not checked by the market-potential survey[28] seems to have taken the form of substituting a range of 20 percentage points for the actual per cent figure shown by salesmen's estimates, but always a range consistent with that figure. This suggests that Howard does not take very seriously his own comment that the salesmen always underestimate their competition and overestimate their own sales. Moreover, the continued collection and analysis by the Corporation of the estimates over a period of at least 12 years[29] suggests both that some reliance was placed on them, and that no *consistent* bias was detected in them, or else it would have been remarked and an effort made to correct it. Thus the choice between United's and the Government's figures—where there is a choice—boils down to an assessment of the reliability of the market-potential estimates. These estimates were made by applying to the number of pairs of shoes of various types made in one year estimated average material requirements per pair, to get estimates of total U.S. consumption of the materials in question. The United sales figures were then compared with these totals to give figures for United's market shares.[30] This method was not applicable to certain types of materials and supplies, hence the limited coverage of S-196. The average material-requirements-per-pair figures estimated by United were checked by Loudon, a consulting engineer, through a survey of several shoe factories: some A. S. Beck plants making women's welts, cements, and sliplasted shoes, and J. F. McElwain Company's Nashua, N. H. plant making men's welts. The results of this survey showed considerable variance between the sample figures and United's overall averages, but no systematic deviation in one direction for all supplies, either to the high or low sides. In 25 instances the sample figures were higher

---

[28] See below.   [29] XV and XVII, *passim*.   [30] Tr. 7080–83, S-196.

than the averages used in computing the totals shown in S-196; in
17 instances, lower; and in 13 the same.[31] This great variance, the
smallness of the check sample, and the absence from it of some types
of shoe constructions all cast doubt on the reliability of the market-
potential estimates. Further problems are raised by the fact that no
attempt is made, either in the exhibit itself or in the discussion of it
in the transcript, to consider the impact of fluctuations of inventories
of supplies in the hands of shoe manufacturers for the particular
year on the comparison between the sales record system estimates
and the market potential estimates. Such fluctuations might well
account for 10 percentage points spread in either direction between
estimates of the two kinds computed for any one year. The cross
examination of Howard on the reliability of S-196 gives further support to a skeptical view on this point.[32]

Thus, the figures of the table above[33] can be taken as the best
available estimate of United's current market share for each of the
33 merchandise classes there shown. These fall into three groups: 15
merchandise classes in which United's market share is greater than
80 per cent; 6 classes in which the share lies between 50 and 80 per
cent; and 12 classes in which it is less than 50 per cent. The first
group includes 30 per cent of the aggregate value of sales merchandise; the second, 5 per cent; and the third, 65 per cent. The low
market share group is not only the greatest in aggregate dollar
volume, but it also contains 7 of the 9 most important merchandise
classes—those with sales volume of $1,000,000 or more annually.[34]
Broadly speaking, therefore, United's position in the several submarkets of the supplies field can be summarized in terms of two
groups of items: one involving a larger number of types of merchandise, each of rather small dollar volume of annual sales in which
United supplies nearly the whole market; the other involving a
smaller number of types of merchandise, each with large annual dollar sales, in which United's market position is substantial but far
from dominant. Merchandise in the first group accounted for 35 per
cent of United's sales volume in 1947f (including all subsidiaries,
sales to shoe trade only); United's weighted average market share

[31] Tr. 7197–8, G-4759.
[32] Tr. 11389–405; esp. 11394–401, discussion of the eyelets estimate; and 11402–4,
discussion of knowledge of United's salesmen of shoe production in the factories which
they visit.   [33] Table 3, p. 218.   [34] Table 4 above.

for merchandise in this group was 87 per cent.[35] Merchandise in the second group accounted for 65 per cent of United's sales in the same period; and the weighted average United market share for classes in this group was 30 per cent.

TABLE 5
NUMBER OF MERCHANDISE CLASSES AND PER CENT OF TOTAL SALES, DISTRIBUTED BY MARKET SHARE GROUPS, FUNCTIONAL CLASSIFICATION AND SUPPLY SOURCE
(From Table 4, pp. 222–223 Above)

Market Share Group	Func- tional Class	No.	Total %	Beverly N	Beverly %	Branch N	Branch %	Subsid. N	Subsid. %	Outside N	Outside %
1. 80% or more	A	7	28	3	16	1	2	1	4	2	6
	B	5	62	—	—	1	2	2	51	2	9
30% total sales or	C	—	—	—	—	—	—	—	—	—	—
$8,311th	D	3	10	—	—	—	—	1	3	2	7
Total		15	100	3	16	2	4	4	58	6	22
2. 50–80%	A	2	27	—	—	—	—	—	—	2	27
	B	1	18	—	—	—	—	1	18	—	—
5% total sales or	C	1	23	—	—	—	—	—	—	1	23
$1,379th	D	2	32	—	—	—	—	—	—	2	32
Total		6	100	—	—	—	—	1	18	5	82
3. sum of above	A	9	28	3	14	1	2	1	3	4	9
50% or more	B	6	56	—	—	1	2	3	47	2	7
35% total sales or	C	1	1	—	—	—	—	—	—	—	3
$9,690th	D	5	13	—	—	—	—	1	2	4	11
Total		21	100	3	14	2	4	5	52	11	30
4. less than 50%	A	—	—	—	—	—	—	—	—	—	—
	B	2	15	—	—	—	—	2	15	—	—
65% total sales or	C	5	46	—	—	1	10	4	36	—	—
$17,828th	D	5	39	—	—	—	—	3	38	2	1
Total		12	100	—	—	1	10	9	89	2	1

Table 5 brings out the differences in the kinds of merchandise which make up the two groups: the first, in which United has a dominant market share; the second, in which United's market share

[35] This figure represents the weighted average market share for the 21 merchandise classes in the first two market share groups of Table 4 above. As the table shows, the two groups separately showed average market shares for United of 90 per cent and 65 per cent respectively.

is relatively small. The single most important group of merchandise classes in the first group are materials driven, set, or applied by machine, nearly all of which were supplied by United's subsidiaries. These included eyelets, nails and tacks, and waxes. Also important were expendable machine parts, supplied both by Beverly and by outside sources and shoemaking accessories supplied by outside sources. In the first group were cutters, irons, and needles; in the second, shoe racks, and blocks and boards for cutting. By contrast, the low market share group included no expendable machine parts and little supplied by outside suppliers. The most important items were shoe parts made by branches or subsidiaries (distributed directly in the latter case) and shoemaking accessories, also made by subsidiaries and distributed directly. The shoe parts included insole reinforcing (a class B item, since it is applied by machine), wood heels, and shanks; the accessories, lasts, and shoe boxes.

Table 4 provides some information about the stability of United's market shares over time for the period 1937–47f. In general, the table shows little change: the weighted average change in market share over the whole period is so near zero (2 percentage points increase) as to be insignificant. Of the 33 individual merchandise classes, 14 showed no change, 8 showed small increases and 3 small decreases in market share, while 6 showed large (15 percentage points or more) increases and 2 large decreases in market share. There was no other significant common feature of any of these groups; although 4 of the 5 decreases did fall into the third market-share class of the table, in which United's market share was relatively small.

Information on the kind of competitors United faces in the several supply markets appears in scattered fashion in various parts of the record. The only general survey is provided in S-195, a list of competitive sellers of supplies, compiled from two trade directories, *Shoe Factory Buyer's Guide* and the "Annual" of the *Shoe and Leather Reporter,* both for 1948, and from the lists of W. S. Ponton Co., a commercial mailing list house. None of these sources can be considered particularly reliable as to current activity or exact business of a firm; recognizing this, United marked specially firms which could be sworn to as active by United employees, and further distinguished firms which were "important" competitors.[36] The exhibit is a document of about 100 pages, and an average of about 15 names

[36] Tr. 7036–7.

of competitive suppliers appears on each page. A ten-page sample in the center of the document[37] showed 30 firms which were known to be active, of which 18 were important competitors. Of the 30, only 3 were listed as offering more than one kind of supply; none of these was among the 18 important competitors. If this sample is representative, it suggests that United's competition consists of perhaps 300 firms, of which as many as two-thirds are considered significant by United. In general, these firms are single-line sellers; perhaps as many as 50 offered more than one line. None even distantly matched United in terms of variety of offering.

More detailed information on the relative importance of United and its competitors for particular markets in recent years is scattered through the documents of the Sales Department offered in evidence and printed in GTB, XV, XVI, and XVII, and some is also available in the oral testimony. Thus the testimony of Ross, president of Torrington Co., United's supplier of machine needles and awls, indicates that the Kimball Co., the only competitor mentioned in the evidence, was a very small organization.[38] This is a field, of course, in which United's market share is nearly 100 per cent. In eyelets, another field in which United had a large market share, the principal competitor was the Atlas Tack Company, which was also the most important supplier of competitive eyeletting machines.[39] Atlas was also active as a competitive supplier of nails and tacks, again a market dominated by United.[40] Another competitive supplier in the field of nails and tacks was J. W. Young Co.,[41] which was also a competitive machinery supplier, selling nailing machines.[42]

More revealing is the relative importance of United and its largest competitors in markets which United does not dominate. In shoe tapes, United accounted for some two-thirds of the total sales; the next largest competitor, Excell, had 12 per cent of total sales; followed by Boston Machine Works with 7 per cent, Lynn Specialty Co. with 3 per cent, and 12 other suppliers.[43] In shanks, United sold about half the total volume. The next largest seller was Campello, with about 20 per cent, followed by Eastern Tool and U.S. Pegwood with 8 per cent each, and 30 other known suppliers.[44] In cutting dies, United's sales were a little less than 30 per cent of total sales. West-

[37] Pp. 34–43.   [38] Tr. 7008–11.   [39] G-293, I, 1 ff., p. 4.   [40] G-257, XV, 82.
[41] G-257, XV, 82.   [42] G-293, I, 1 ff.   [43] G-4425, XVII, 136.
[44] G-4389, XVII, 88 ff.

ern Supply Co., United's most important rival, accounted for 9 per cent of total sales; there were five other sellers with 5 to 8 per cent of the market, and 20 smaller suppliers.[45] Box toes provided an example of a market in which United was not the largest seller. Beckwith Box Toe Co. sold 53 per cent of all types of box toes; United 25 per cent; two other sellers 8 per cent each. Sixteen other known sellers plus some "unknown" are listed as accounting for the remaining 25 per cent of sales volume.[46] The market for adhesives, solvents, softeners, etc., used in the cement-shoe process is also one which United does not dominate. Compo, of course, is United's most important rival, although United considered the work done on Compo machines as foreclosed to it, and therefore not part of the market in which it competed.[47] This accounts for about half the total market;[48] in the other half, United supplies about 75 per cent of the total consumption, and the largest competitor, Pierce and Stevens, about 16 per cent of the total.[49]

In general, the evidence cited above points in the direction of two conclusions: (1) United is a long-line seller, large in absolute size, most of whose competitors in specific supply markets sell only one or a few lines, and are small in size relative to United; (2) even in markets that United falls short of dominating in a percentage share sense, United is usually the largest seller, and is frequently three or four times as important in terms of market share as its largest rival. The amount of evidence, and its coverage of specific markets, falls short of what would be required to establish these conclusions firmly.

The combined evidence of United's market share and the character of competition in many instances suggests that in some of the supplies sub-markets, United occupies a position of considerable market power. This suggestion received further reinforcement from consideration of the selling advantages United gains from its full line, and its ability to link supplies and machines. United's long product line gives it economies in adding a small-volume item which can be handled by an already existing organization. Some of this economy is a real social gain, in the sense that a given volume of supplies can be distributed with less cost by a long-line seller than by a number of single-item sellers. But some are more in the nature of inertial

---

[45] G-4028, XV, 244.   [46] G-4009, XV, 211.
[47] G-3965, XV, 121 ff. "Instructions" for filling out Sales Record System Reports, para. 6, p. 124.   [48] Cf. pp. 48–50.   [49] G-3977, XV, 150.

advantages, which increase the advantage of an existing seller as against would-be new entrants, but result in no long-run net social economies. This is particularly the case for the greater ability of the existing long-line producer to venture into the distribution of an item of doubtful profitability, carrying it on the profits of its established lines, as compared with the situation of would-be single-line entrant, or an existing single-line seller. If the item eventually proves worthwhile, the cost of distributing it may well be the same for either the old or new seller. This advantage, while not in itself illegal, since it accrues to any profitable established seller irrespective of his market share or market conduct, will help a seller with a dominant position to maintain that position, and therefore is appropriately subject to consideration. In addition, the seller of a full supply line achieves certain pure salesmanship advantages, the appeal of getting it all in one package, which further adds to his advantage over otherwise equally efficient single-line sellers. This effect, and the previous one, accrue to all items in the line. To the extent that the long-line seller dominates the field in several submarkets, he can prevent his existing rivals from achieving the same benefits to the same degree, as well as gaining from them at the expense of would-be entrants. United's ability to tie supplies and machines together operates in several ways to preserve United's market position. In the first place, a selling point of considerable importance is provided by the appeal of "standard" items. Secondly, the same kind of one-package advantage which was indicated above in relation to supplies arises from the offer of both machines and supplies by a single seller. Thirdly, pricing policies which induce the use of United machines with the aim of facilitating the sale of United supplies can be followed; evidence on this point will be discussed below.

The closeness of the tie between machines and supplies may be technological in nature, and, indeed, much of the argument of the Dean memorandum on supplies rests on the premise that this is indeed the case. That document emphasizes the relationship of high market share to "machine intimacy",[50] and in general, machine intimacy appears as the most important explanation of high market share. The substance of this view is the necessity of correlating closely the technical characteristics of supply items to those of the machines through which they are fed or in which they are used as

[50] See pp. 212–213 above.

parts, and the consequent natural advantage that the major machine manufacturer has over other would-be suppliers in producing and marketing supplies of this category. This argument is given some further support by the fact that in two of the B class merchandise items where there was competition, the most important competitors were themselves suppliers of machines—eyelets and heel nails.[51] There is, however, important evidence which tends to weaken the argument and suggest that non-integrated sellers, offering supplies only, can do as good a job technically as the machine producer. First is the fact that a not insignificant share of the merchandise in the A and B classes in which United showed very high market shares was manufactured by outside suppliers and sold by United. This was true of needles and awls and sharpening stones and wheels in the A category, and stapling wire, lacing thread, and some tacks and nails in the B category.[52] These items were made to United specifications,[53] but the testimony of Howard on the difference between items so made and closely similar commercial times[54] fails to support a conclusion that United's specification is crucial in the production of the items. Further, in the particular case of Goodyear needles and awls, a very small independent supplier, Kimball, was apparently able to offer products higher in quality and lower in price than those supplied to United by Torrington.[55] Scattered evidence suggests that independent suppliers of some other items in these classes were also able at least to match United's quality: nails;[56] cements;[57] lacing thread.[58] These individual exceptions to the proposition that technical needs require production of machines and intimately associated supplies to be in the same hands weaken the force of the proposition considerably; while it might be true for particular individual items, although no positive detailed evidence is offered to show it for any such item, it can no longer stand as a valid explanation of the high market share of United in supply items of this class.

For some items in which United does not have a very high market share, analysis of price behavior and of ties between machine and supplies, which will be examined below in the general context of United's performance in the supply market, suggests that United possesses significant market power. This applies to cements, pastes,

[51] Cf. above, p. 228.   [52] Table 4.   [53] See p. 220 above.   [54] Tr. 7116–28.
[55] G-4362, 3, 4, 7, 70, 1, 2, 3, 9, XVII, 60–80.   [56] G-150, XV, 53.
[57] G-3, XV, 142.   [58] Tr. 7872–4.

dies, waxes, shanks, and insole reinforcing. However, for many of the major items manufactured and distributed by United's subsidiaries, and for some supplied by subsidiaries and distributed by United, there is no evidence, either in terms of market share alone, the character of competition, or performance in the market, to support a finding of significant market power on the part of United. This conclusion applies to wood heels, lasts, shoe boxes, box toes, and shoe laces.

4. UNITED'S ACHIEVEMENT OF MARKET POSITION— ACQUISITIONS AND INTENT

·Virtually all of United's supply manufacturing activity is the result of acquisitions. As appears in Table 3 above, only some 5 per cent of the dollar value of supplies United sold to the shoe trade in 1947f was manufactured in Beverly; the rest of the 74 per cent produced in the United organization was manufactured in branches and subsidiaries, nearly all of which were acquired by United as going businesses. These acquisitions stretch over a long period of time, and none of them is recent. Below, the acquisitions are listed chronologically by fields, that is, the earliest acquisition in any particular supply field determines the order of listing of all acquisitions in that field, together with whatever information is relevant on the history of the acquisition, and an indication of the present status of the business so acquired.

1. J. C. Rhodes—eyelet manufacture. Acquired *1899*. Hughes Eyelet Co., acquired by J. C. Rhodes in *1918*. JCR now operated as a branch factory.[59]
2. B.B. Chemical Co.—chemicals, etc. United acquired half interest in predecessor, Boston Blacking Co., in *1900*. Majority interest acquired by United in *1927*, 100 per cent in *1930*. Later recreated in present corporate form. A subsidiary.[60]
3. W. W. Cross—tacks }
4. S. A. Felton—brushes } presumably before *1920*, since not mentioned in G-3754, which purports to list post-1920 acquisitions. Both now subsidiaries.[61]
5. United Last Co.—lasts. Acquired in *1916;* the initiative came from U.L., and a promoter, Harris.[62] At the time, U.L. had about 25 per

[59] G-2339, IX, 234 ff., letter from Choate, Hall and Stewart to Justice Dept.
[60] G-3754, XIV, 157 ff., letter, Choate, Hall and Stewart to Justice Dept.
[61] See S-187.   [62] See Tr. 11413–15, testimony of Holmes, President of U.L.

cent of the market or somewhat less than its present 30 per cent share.[63] Framingham Last Co., acquired in *1925* by United Last; at initiative of Framingham, which was in financial difficulties. At the time F. was not a direct competitor of U.L., since it made metal lasts for rubber shoes, while U.L. made lasts for leather shoes only.[64] United Last is now a subsidiary.[65]

6. American Shank and Finding⎫
   Union Shank   ⎬ acquired in *1919*, united and reorganized into United Shank and Finding in 1920, now a branch, making shanks.[66] H. F. Crawford Mfg. Co., acquired in *1925*. From 1915 to 1925 United had acted as selling agent for Crawford's shanks.[67]

7. United Awl and Needle Co., acquired in *1920* from Torrington and others.[68] Now a branch, manufacturing machine awls and drivers and fiber fastening.[69]

8. F. W. Mears, and two subsidiaries, Maple Wood Heel Co., Slipper City Wood Heel Co., acquired in *1922*. Mears sought a partnership with United, and was steered by Baxter Whitney (see below) to seek out United; Whitney wished to leave the wood heel business.[70] Baxter D. Whitney. This wood heel machinery business was acquired in *1922* at the same time as the Mears acquisitions, at Mears' insistence, because it "had the best turning machines on the market," acquiring it was better than "buying out other heel companies . . . (and having) machines not up to the minute."[71] This transaction included restrictive covenants on Whitney, which precluded him from competing, and required his giving United first claim on any inventions in heel-turning machinery he made for a period of ten years.[72] Star Wood Heel Company, acquired from Mears in *1925*. Mears himself did not own this company until 1923, after his sale to United.[73] Merrimack Wood Heel Co., acquired in *1927*; along with this company went several important patents and the service of Harley Russ, who had made the inventions embodied therein.[74] Fellows Wood Heel Co., acquired in *1928*.[75] The separate companies other than F. W. Mears Heel Co. have been dissolved, and F. W. Mears operates as a subsidiary of United making and distributing wood heels.[76] Note: S-168, a list of some companies offered to United

[63] Tr., and Table 4 above.   [64] Tr. 11417–26, Holmes.   [65] S-187.
[66] G-2339, S-187.   [67] G-3756, XIV, 174 ff.   [68] G-3760–2, XIV, 180.
[69] S-187.   [70] Tr. 11980–12018, testimony of Hubbell, retired v.p. of United.
[71] G-4271, XVI, 177 ff.   [72] G-4282, XVI, 181 ff.   [73] Tr. 12050–2.
[74] G-4286–90, XVI, 186–92.   [75] G-4291, XVI, 192–3.
[76] Answer, para. 90 and S-187.

for purchase and refused includes the Williamsburg Wood Heel Co., which acquisition was refused sometime before 1932, because of a "policy of no further expansion in wood heels."

9. Hoague Sprague Corporation—shoe boxes and shoe-box forming machinery, majority of stock acquired by United in 1925.[77]

10. Celastic Corporation—box toes and box-toe material. Not really an acquisition in the strict sense. The company was formed in 1925, 50 per cent owned by United and 50 per cent owned by Du Pont. United transferred its assets and good will from its previous box-toe business (no indication of when or how acquired or developed) to the new corporation in exchange for the stock; Du Pont's contribution was the Celastic process.[78]

11. Shoe Lace Co.—shoe laces. In 1927 United acquired stock of Shoe Lace Ltd. (of R. I.); in 1932 a new corporation, Shoe Lace Co., was organized which traded its stock for the assets of Ltd., which has since been dissolved.[79] Shoe Lace is now a subsidiary.[80]

12. Shoe Form Co.—shoe forms. United acquired a majority of its stock in 1934;[81] it is now a subsidiary.[82]

Of this list of acquisitions, three groups are in fields in which United is dominant: Rhodes and Hughes in eyelets where United's market share is about 87 per cent; United Awl and Needle, in machine awls and drivers, in which United's share is 100 per cent; and American Shank and Finding and Union Shank in shank manufacturing, in which United's share was just under 50 per cent, but United was very large in relation to its competitors.[83] United Awl and Needle is the most recent of these acquisitions, and it dates back to 1920. No information is available in the record that shows the market share of the acquired companies before their acquisition; Table 4 above shows no change in the market share of eyelets and machine awls and drivers in the ten years 1937–1947, and a fairly substantial increase in that of shanks, some 15 percentage points over the period. But this provides no basis for a conclusion on whether or not United bought in order to secure market control in these fields.

It is worth noting that the acquisition of majority, and finally complete, control of B. B. Chemical's predecessor by United coincided with United's initial activity in the cement-shoe field. It could well be concluded, on the basis of Compo's experience[84] that if Boston

[77] G-3754, supra.   [78] G-3754.   [79] G-3754.   [80] S-187.   [81] S-187.
[82] Answer, para. 90.   [83] See Table 4, above, pp. 222–223.   [84] See above, p. 185.

Blacking Company did not exist, United would have had to create it, in so far as the supply of cements, solvents, and other chemicals necessary to the cement shoe process went. But this conclusion does not, of course, extend to B. B. Chemical's activities in the field of shoe finishes, thread waxes, and various other products not as intimately related to shoe construction as cements.

One set of acquisitions, viewed together with some of the methods involved in making them, goes far to support an inference of an intent to monopolize on the part of United, existing at some time in the past—the acquisitions in respect to wood heels. The acquisitions themselves are larger in number than those in any field—involving seven wood heel companies and a heel turning machinery company in period of six years, 1922–1928. United's officers of course deny all intent to monopolize; they point rather to the possibilities of improving the quality of wood heels offered by some new Whitney machinery, the initiative of Baxter D. Whitney in bringing together Mears and United, and the general interest of United in doing whatever could be done to improve shoe manufacture.[85] Again, with respect to the acquisition of Merrimack, in 1927, Hubbell testified that the purpose was to acquire the services of Russ, to succeed Mears in the management of United's heel subsidiary when he died.[86] Nothing is said in the testimony about the acquisition of Fellows in 1929.

The evidence which supports an inference of intent to monopolize, through its indication of coercive and dubious practices in the acquisition of wood heel patents and in other dealings in this field in the period 1922–1928, is contained in the documents which fill Vol. XVI of part III of the Government Trial Brief. The first set of documents, G-4065–79,[87] show a 1932 correspondence with Meadow River Lumber Company by Houghton, a subordinate of Hubbell's in F. W. Mears Heel Co. Meadow River was a big lumber company which wished to enter into the making of wood heels (blocks only). The letters, in fairly strong language, paint the difficulties which Meadow River may expect to find in entering the business and recount the number of former money-makers who have failed in competition with United because of United's superior machines and techniques which were not generally available. One of the letters by Houghton

[85] Tr. 11980–93, 12019–12025, testimony of Hubbell.   [86] Tr. 12025–12041.
[87] Pp. 1–12.

characterizes the correspondence as "warning" but not "threatening." Meadow River entered the industry anyway.[88] Hubbell disowned these letters as having been written without authority and suggested that the whole correspondence was initiated by Meadow River in an effort to induce or coerce United into signing a long-term contract for the purchase of lumber from Meadow River.[89] At the same time he indicated that their basic "warning" content was appropriate to the situation and reflected a frank effort to be helpful. It is difficult to accept this interpretation completely or to deny utterly the somewhat threatening tone of the Houghton letters.

Somewhat more tangible evidence of practices which were coercive or which bordered on the predatory appears in connection with the patent transactions in the wood-heel business. The first group of patent transactions involves the alleged infringement of the Russ patent on an automatic wood-heel shaper by New England Wood Heel Co.[90, 91] The documents show United pressing a suit, later settled by consent, on a patent, the validity of which United doubted.[92] The proceedings involved a fairly clear use of United roadmen for espionage,[93] and a faint suggestion of influencing potential witnesses.[94] On the other side, from United's viewpoint, the activities of New England Wood Heel appeared to be directed more toward getting a favorable price from United for its business than toward defending New England's right to continue to use certain machines;[95] the fact of the final consent settlement[96] may reflect this, or may equally well reflect New England's lack of resources to fight the suit.[97] In the nature of the case, it is difficult to find clear-cut evidence of oppressive tactics, especially when the incidents are 28 years old, and oral testimony from only one party is available; but within these limits the foregoing material at least suggests such a conclusion.

A more clear-cut example of the use of roadmen for espionage in connection with the alleged infringement of the Russ patent is provided by the cause of the Vulcan Last Co.[98] The documents make

---

[88] G-4076.   [89] Tr. 12027–34.

[90] Note, the Russ patent was acquired in the Whitney purchase, not in the later transaction with Merrimack. See Tr. 12020.

[91] The transactions are shown in G-4085–90, 4099–4110, XVI, 17–41.

[92] See esp. G-4105, letter from Salinger to United; G-4107, letter from Salinger to United.   [93] See G-4085, 86, 87.   [94] G-4101.   [95] G-4103, 4104, 4106.

[96] G-4110.   [97] G-4099.   [98] G-4119–23, pp. 152–4.

clear that the roadmen's inspection of Vulcan's heel-trimming machines was covert, and clearly against the wishes of Vulcan's management. Another equally strong example appears in connection with alleged infringements on the Monoplane Groover for Cuban heels by the Philadelphia Wood Heel Co. Again the documents make clear the use of covert methods for gathering evidence.[99]

The second group of wood-heel patent practices worth some mention centers around the Sharpneck patent, 1,259,917. A miscellany of internal memos and correspondence[100] show a suit pressed against Day Wood Heel Co. for infringement of the above patent; the documents cover the period 1929–1930. United acquired the Sharpneck patent in 1927, believing that its claims covered certain processes claimed in a patent application by one Naltner. This in turn was expected to be in interference with an application by Nutt, a United employee. Naltner had licensed Day Wood Heel Co. to make heels covered by his claims.[101] Salinger, of Fish, Richardson, and Neave, United's outside patent counsel, expressed strong doubts as to the validity of the patent.[102] None the less, suits were pressed against Day and also against Vulcan, another alleged infringer. Day settled; part of the consideration involved was United's waiver of claims for damages under two Russ patents which had previously been infringed by Day and on which United had sued and won.[103] Vulcan fought the suit, and won both in the District Court and on appeal in the 6th Circuit.[104] This incident shows at least the aim of the corporation to push as far as possible every opportunity afforded it by the patent system, including its superior capacity compared with that of its smaller and poorer competitors to exploit the opportunities offered by the costs and trouble of litigation. All this is set forth quite explicitly in a letter from Packard, of the law department, to Hubbel, dated May 1922.[105] It may perhaps be argued that this reflects merely the weakness of the patent system and that the large dominant concern is under no obligation created by the anti-trust laws to refrain from operating within the framework of the system to its own advantage as it sees fit. Only Congress, by changing the

[99] G-4211, 12, 13, 14; pp. 119–21.
[100] G-4164–70, 4172, 4176–80, 83, 85, 86–92; pp. 83–105.
[101] G-4161, 75–6. [102] G-4185, 6.
[103] G-4189 shows the agreement on Sharpneck; the previous moves on the two Russ patents (1,528,345 and 1,536,691) are shown in G-4196 and 4204, pp. 107–14.
[104] G-4184, 4193, 4194. [105] G-4263, p. 167.

patent laws, can reform this situation. This argument has much merit; but independently of its merit the conduct of United in respect to patents shown in the instances selected above may fairly be construed as evidence of "intent to monopolize" in the sense of excluding competitors by all possible means. Only if the actual commission of specifically illegal acts is necessary for such an inference of "intent" can this conclusion be avoided.

Not all United's actions in the area of wood-heel patents reflected a determination to fight competition in every possible way. United's dealings with the Pope Machinery Company, a supplier of wood-heel-making machinery to United's competitors, in respect to the Vinton reissue patent 16,408, show an instance of "fair" treatment and abstention from exploiting every advantage to the full. Further, they show a division of opinion within the corporation on just what was fair, and how far the competitive struggle should be pushed (with Hubbell, the operating man concerned, wishing to use every possible advantage of United's position, and Packard of the law department, and Donham, the general manager, pressing for more restrained behavior even at the expense of some loss of advantage over competitors). The outcome, as indicated, was the fair treatment of Pope in respect to waiving claims on past infringement and making no claims unless suit was filed against other and financially stronger infringers.[106]

The foregoing samples of United's behavior, together with the string of acquisitions in the field in the early and mid-twenties, can be taken as evidence that United at that time intended to monopolize the wood-heel field, either in the sense of engrossing the major share of the market, or in the weaker sense of establishing a strong position by driving out competitors through predatory and coercive practices. If the evidence is interpreted as showing an intent in the stronger sense, it is clear that this intent has since been abandoned. The record shows no recent examples of similar practices; United refused, about 1932, to acquire another wood-heel company which was offered to it because it had a policy of no further expansion;[107] its present market share (that is, that of its subsidiary, F. W. Mears Wood Heel Co.) in wood heels is too low to support any inference of dominance. If the intent is interpreted in the narrow sense, then

[106] G-4157-60, pp. 70-75.   [107] See above, p. 234.

it may be that the goal was achieved, and thus the intent was no longer relevant after 1930 or some such time. If so, the question remains, does this ancient history of intent or coercive practice in the acquisition of a non-monopolistic position in the market justify any remedial action in the present? It will be argued below, in the discussion of remedy, that, standing alone, it does not.

There are some other practices that may be construed as evincing United's intent to monopolize, or at least to exclude competitors, not in any way connected with acquisitions. One is the practice of creating, or trying to create, a technical bond between supply and machine which will make it impossible to use other than United supplies on United machines. Examples of such ties, or attempts to create them, appear in several places in the Government's documentary evidence.[108] Three memos from Harrington to Homan, both of the research division, dated November and December 1937, discuss the possibility of designing a new plastic eyelet and eyelet-forming machine. These documents stress the desirability of designing the product so that only United machines can be used for it, and in one of them, G-3905, speak of the benefits of "monopolizing the field." In late 1939 and early 1940, several heeling-department documents raise the problem of tying wire to the upper-stapling machine through the use of a special reel carrying the wire and designed to fit the machine. The device is patented, and the memoranda discuss the legality and economic feasibility of requiring the users to return the empty reels, so that they may not be rewound with competitively sold wire.[109] A research department report on abrasives in the shoe industry[110] dated May 1938 speaks of an ideal condition in the market which would be achieved by a linking of abrasive and machine by an exclusive United development. Similarly an Experimental Advisory Committee report of March 1923 speaks against putting out an improved new rubber heel which could be attached on non-United machines instead of the then current model which could not be so attached.[111] The report goes on to suggest that it is better to wait till it is necessary to meet competition, rather than do anything which could make a path for competitors to follow. A recent memorandum on a meeting of research department men in Roberts' office,

[108] G-3904–06 (XV, pp. 41–3).   [109] G-3939, XV, 87; G-94, XV, 93.
[110] G-3994, XV, 172.   [111] G-4306, XVI, 214.

June 1946, strikes the same note again: in a discussion of lasts, and future research on lasts, the tie-in of lasts and machines appears again as a goal.[112]

In all the examples cited, there is nothing that in itself is coercive, predatory, or illegal. Rather the evil in the tying arrangements lies in United's position in the machinery market. Each successful tying arrangement has the effect of barring a competitor from offering the same or a similar supply unless he is also prepared to offer a machine with which it can coöperate. Given United's position in the machinery market, and the great barriers to entry which that position and the practices on which it rests create, this amounts to an effective exclusion of competition from every field in which a successful tie is made. Thus the "intent" to make such a tie, irrespective of its success (which is by no means clear in the examples cited), is clearly an intent to exclude competition. Nor can a different conclusion be drawn by trying to distinguish between United's "desire" to see a certain result occur, when that desire is coupled with a consideration of methods by which the result may be brought about, on the one hand, and United's "intent" to bring about the result, on the other. The two are clearly the same.

An instance of a related tying effect, of a somewhat weaker character, is provided by the testimony of Nash, president of B. B. Chemical,[113] and a sales department memorandum on the finishing liquids program[114] dated 1941. The memorandum urges the importance of selling the full line of finishes known as the B. B. system, and cautions salesmen against using, or permitting to be used, competitive materials in conjunction with B. B. products. Nash, in explaining the virtues of the system, mentions the "possibility" of technical incompatibility between different finishes. This is an attempt to tie together a string of products, rather than tying a product to a machine. There is nothing to indicate that United's position in some of these products is stronger than in others, and therefore that the tying is a method of achieving leverage against successful single-line sellers, as is the case with the machine-product ties discussed above. Still the tying, to the extent that it is successful, operates to make more difficult the entry of single-line or narrow-line sellers; and Nash's testimony leaves room for considerable doubt as to whether there is any

[112] G-4435, XVII, 7–11, esp. last para. on p. 10 headed "Conventional lasts —."
[113] Tr. 8014.   [114] G-4360, XVII, 56–8.

corresponding social benefit which might justify the creation of an additional barrier to entry.

Another practice which may show intent to monopolize is the embracing of opportunities for exclusive distribution rights to the shoe trade for products not manufactured by it. Howard testified that, in general, United's exclusive distributorships came to it as a result of the supplier's initiative.[115] A specific example, the approach to United by Mullen Bros., a manufacturer of repairer crayons, is shown in G-3641[116] dated October 1946. The document recites the history of B. B.'s unsuccessful attempts to manufacture; as S-187 shows, the offer was taken up. Another similar example is shown by United's acquisition of exclusive shoe-trade distribution rights to the Stronghold nail, a patented product manufactured by the Independent Nail and Tacking Co. in 1940.[117] Similar to such exclusive agreements are agreements to divide the market between different types of products. Thus G-3781, 2[118] shows some arrangement between United and F. E. Hudson Co. on clicker blocks, by which United sold straight-sided, and Hudson tapered blocks, and referred to each other orders for the other products. The later of the two documents is dated 1937.

In all the above cases, a better understanding of the results can be achieved by considering that United's generally dominant position in the supply market, in the sense that is by far the largest single seller as well as the seller with the longest line, makes it the natural outlet to which any manufacturer seeking a distributor would turn. Similarly, with respect to some of the acquisitions of supply manufacturers discussed above, in which the sales were made at the initiative of the manufacturer rather than at United's, United was the natural buyer for the would-be seller to seek out. This position, as much as any "intent" on the part of United, contributes to the maintenance and even the increase of the dominant position of United in the supply market. In this respect, the cumulative forces at work are similar to those discussed above with respect to the machinery market.[119] There it was concluded that the acquisitions, after the original acquisitions out of which the Corporation was created, flowed from United's market power, rather than the reverse. If the power were innocent, so were the acquisitions; likewise if the power

[115] Tr. 7027–30.   [116] XVII, 59–9.   [117] G-3783, 4, XIV, 216–7.
[118] XIV, 215–6.   [119] See above, pp. 57–58.

were tainted. While this conclusion applies broadly here, its application raises some problems. In particular, given a long line of supplies, with widely varying market power in United with respect to each individual line, the whole bound up with a machinery business in which United's position is overwhelmingly dominant, does condemnation attach to any particular acquisition, including those in fields in which United is not dominant? No answer to this question in the abstract will be attempted, on the theory that none is necessary. Instead United's use of its power in the supplies market will be examined to provide a basis for a presumption as to the desirability of acquisitions which increase power in old lines, or extend United's activity into new supply fields. Further, the examination of such remedy measures as recommend themselves on other than these grounds may help to dispose of the problem without a general answer to the question previously posed.

While the argument of the foregoing paragraphs suggests that there is a certain "natural" cumulative growth to be expected in United's supply business relative to that of the "market" as a whole, this is by no means the equivalent of suggesting that United's position in the various supply markets is the result of economies of scale. In general, the variety of different sources of supply, and the existence of multi-plant operations in some of United's subsidiaries and branches,[120] suggest strongly that manufacturing economies of scale are not significant in explaining United's market position; and there is no positive evidence, and no argument advanced, to support this view. This refers only to manufacturing economies of scale in the narrow sense; technological gains which arise from integration of supply and machine, or from broad lines of supplies have already been discussed,[121] and will be further considered below in the discussion of research in the supply field. Economies of distribution undoubtedly exist; and it is highly likely that, in general, the addition of another line or another $100 thousand worth of sales can be done more cheaply by United than by a very small single-line seller. But, again, there is no evidence to show that the same economies would not accrue to much smaller sellers than United.[122] On the contrary, the scattered relevant material suggests the opposite. There are 202

---

[120] Heels, Tr. 12088, Russ; lasts, Tr. 11411–15, Holmes; eyelets, Complaint and Answer, para. 24.   [121] Above, pp. 229–231.

[122] Cf. the similar argument in respect to the machinery business, pp. 92–99.

employees of the sales department; 62 in Boston, including 17 field technicians; 140 in the branches, including 88 salesmen.[123] A smaller volume of business could be handled by a smaller force, and sales expense reduced accordingly. Similarly, the fact that substantial inventories are held in the branches, as well as centrally,[124] suggests that volumes of sales much smaller than that United now enjoys could be handled without substantially increased costs arising from the problems of inventory turnover. It is true that there would be some increase in the cost of dealing in such items as cutters and irons, in which there are very many varieties with small sales,[125] but the relative importance of these items in total sales is so small that even a large increase in the cost of handling them would make a negligible difference in total sales expense.[126] Relatively little is spent on advertising,[127] so that any savings in distributing advertising-created good will over a larger rather than a smaller volume of business are negligible. In short, there is nothing in the record to support the view that a seller doing $10 million or even $5 million worth of business with the shoe trade would not achieve substantially all the economies of scale which United achieves with the nearly $20-million-volume of business which the sales department does with the shoe and allied trades.

The foregoing remarks are directed to United's sales activity viewed as a whole. With respect to a few of the individual supply items, there is some more direct, though fragmentary, evidence of the ability of small sellers to compete with United pricewise, which suggests that they suffer no great relative diseconomies in comparison with their large rival. Thus in Goodyear needles and awls, documents covering a period of seven years (1935–1942) refer to the competition of the Kimball Company, a very small firm in Lynn, in respect to both price and quality.[128] In toe-lasting wire, Wilson Steel and Wire Company (not a major producer in steel) was selling wire for less than United was buying it from a U. S. Steel subsidiary.[129] Further instances of the same sort are mentioned below in the discussion of price competition as part of United's performance in the supplies market.

---

[123] Tr. 6981, Howard.   [124] See Tr. 6283–86, Waelter and Bigelow.
[125] See S-342.   [126] Cf. Table 3 above and S-342.   [127] S-340c.
[128] G-3462, 63, 64, 67, 70, 73, 79, 80–85, 86, XVII, pp. 60–82.
[129] G-3947, XV, 93.

VII. United's Performance
in the Supplies Markets

The preceding chapter has shown that United has positions of substantial market power in many, though by no means all, of the supply fields, including some markets in which it has an overwhelmingly large share, and some in which it is the dominant seller, even though it does not supply all or nearly all the demand. The present one will show to what extent United's performance bears out the existence of market power, and how in general this power has been used. Performance will be examined in respect to four items: price and non-price competition in those markets where United meets competition; quantity discounts in relation to price discrimination; the tying together of machines and supplies; and research in supplies. The volume and detail of the available evidence on all these points is insufficient to sustain any precise conclusions in respect to the whole range of supplies markets; rather, what there is can furnish examples of behavior in individual markets, and suggest generalizations as to what United's policy is, without indicating their precise scope in respect to particular classes of supply items.

It is worth noting that the available evidence on pricing of supplies is inadequate to permit the kind of examination of price policy which appeared above in respect to the machinery market. Gross margins[1] are insufficient, taken alone without figures on inventory turnover and selling expenses by individual items, as a basis for testing the absence or presence of price discrimination. Only one clue is provided—the presence in the supplies as in the machinery business of great price rigidity, as shown by S 341, which indicates that most

[1] Given in S-341.

of the gross margins on the supply items were set over twenty years ago. Since the gross margins are the "prices" of United's distributive services, the rigidity of gross margins does suggest a general absence of strong competition, and the dominance of United in most of the field. This tabulation includes only items distributed by United's sales department, and thus any inferences drawn from it do not apply to products sold directly by subsidiaries: lasts, wood heels, shoe boxes, and shoe forms.

1. PRICE AND NON-PRICE COMPETITION IN THE SUPPLIES MARKETS

A variety of examples in the record indicates that when there is competition between United and rival sellers of supply items, United prefers to stress quality and service, and compete on a non-price rather than a price basis. Thus, with respect to toe-lasting wire, several memoranda dated 1936–8 show that United was worried about the success of competition, which it attributed mostly to lower prices, and that price reductions by United were considered as a means of combating competition, especially since the quality of cheaper competitive wire appeared adequate.[2] Exhibits printed on preceding pages of the same volume[3] and testimony of Howard[4] show that United originally introduced a high-grade wire at $24 per 100 lbs., and a year later followed it with a B grade wire at $16; by 1936 (seven years later), 78 per cent of the sales were B grade.[5] Yet competitive prices continued still lower, with one seller selling below United's acquisition cost.[6] Competitive quality was adequate,[7] and in 1938 a memorandum[8] indicates that United itself wonders whether its own quality is not perhaps unnecessarily high.

Similarly, documents in XV, 47–83, on nails covering the period 1936–1941, indicate that competitive business is done at lower prices, and occasionally that competitive goods are even better than United's in quality.[9] This latter indicates that United possesses "good-will" advantages based on reputation, or some other factor than functional differences in product quality, at least in this item.

Again, G-3976–81[10] show summaries of competitive sales in cements, softeners, and solvents, with most competition explained by

---

[2] G-3959, 61, 62; XV, 103–8.   [3] G-3945–58.   [4] Tr. 11318–20, 11353–4.
[5] G-3959.   [6] G-3947.   [7] G-3959, XV, 59.   [8] G-3960.   [9] G-150, XV, 53.
[10] XV, 149–56.

lower price; the documents refer to the period 1940–1949. G-3, an annual report of the cement shoe department for 1934,[11] speaks of United's failure to convince manufacturers that cheaper competitive cements were in fact inferior to United products; and it goes on to speak of the necessity of producing cheaper products, even if competitor's items had to be copied to succeed.

Clicking and pattern dies likewise show competition largely assigned to price, in the period 1938–1943.[12] G 239,[13] a program committee report of 1941, recommends an attempt to develop new dies tied in with machines, as a response to the price competition in the existing types of dies. In the field of Goodyear needles and awls, the competition of Kimball needles, lower in price and superior in quality, is described as presenting a situation not remediable by "superior salesmanship or extraordinary service."[14] This note is sounded again in other memoranda,[15] all in the period 1938–1942. In shanks, G-4407, a memorandum dated June 1940 reporting a discussion on shanks,[16] accounts for the success of competition by 5–10 per cent lower prices, and reports the view of the group that more sales effort, and not price-cutting, was the cure for the problem. A similar document arising from a meeting the following year repeats both diagnosis and recommendation—no lowering of United's prices in order.[17] Shoe forms[18] and shoe tapes[19] also are items for which competitive prices are lower than United's, and competitive success is accounted for by the price differential. In the first case the documents cover 1940–1941; in the second, 1939–1940. Stitching wax is another item in which competitors show lower prices.[20] United's response is to concentrate its efforts on pushing wax-tite, a superior-quality, high-priced item, which does not require heating, but not to compete in price on the standard waxes.[21]

Finally, Howard testified that 70 per cent of competitive sales reported by branches for 1950f were due to lower prices by competitors. He went on to testify that United did not rely on price to build volume, but rather on quality, service, and superior salesmanship.[22]

---

[11] XV, 142.   [12] G-198, 4028, XV, 238, 42.   [13] XV, 245–6.
[14] G-4367, XVII, 65–6.   [15] G-4371–86, XVII, 70–82.   [16] XVII, 104–6.
[17] G-4410, XV, 113–17.   [18] G-4413, 14, XVII, 120–2.
[19] G-4419, 20, XVII, 129–31.
[20] G-4439 (1937), 4440 (1937), 4442 (1945), XVII, 175–9.   [21] G-4440.
[22] Tr. 11327–9.

This testimony and the examples cited serve to establish United practice. What is the significance of the resort to non-price rather than price competition? First, it is clear that, per se, the avoidance of price competition is not illegal. While it is indicative of market power in the narrow technical sense of departure from the behavior which would be expected in the economist's model of perfect competition, the public policy of the Sherman law has never been read to condemn the kind of market power that arises merely from successful non-price competition—advertising, salesmanship, and the like. In the present context, however, the use of non-price competition is relevant not to a judgment of the extent or legality of United's power in the various supplies markets, but rather to an evaluation of what use United makes of such power as it has. In general, the widespread appearance of non-price competition instead of price competition indicates the use of resources to produce "good will" instead of tangible products. Only where the good will rests on functionally significant, qualitative superiority is there no waste involved. It is the contention of the Dean memorandum that this is indeed the explanation of United's ability to command higher prices than its rivals.[23] But the evidence cited above, in respect to toe wire, needles and awls, cements, and shanks, does not support this explanation. Rather, it suggests that the superior reputation of United rests at least in part on non-functional quality differences (wire), superior salesmanship (shanks and needles), pure assertion of superiority (cements), and superior "service" which may or may not be functionally significant (needles). To the extent that these and not functional quality are significant sources of shoe manufacturers' preference for United products, there is an expenditure of resources on salesmanship which is in itself wasteful, and which further increases the difficulty of entry by new suppliers, who must be prepared to compete with United in selling expenditures or accept lower prices for their products.

2. QUANTITY DISCOUNTS IN SUPPLIES

United maintains a quantity-discount system, which applies to celastic box toes, cut nails and tacks, eyelets, and shanks. On shanks the discounts range from 2 to 5 per cent; on the other items they range from 2 to 7 per cent.[24] These discounts are really volume and

[23] Dean, LII–14.   [24] Tr. 11330–31, Howard.

not quantity discounts, since they are based on the annual volume
of purchases by a single buyer, no matter how distributed through
the year, or among various plants owned by that buyer.[25] For cut
nails and tacks, the discount brackets are:[26]

Annual Purchases (1000 lb.)	Discount (%)
25– 100	2
100– 250	3
250– 500	4
500–1000	5
1000–1500	6
1500 and over	7

In addition, there is a 90-day blanket-order plan, with discounts up
to 5 per cent calculated on cumulative orders taken within a 90-day
period on which deliveries are taken within the same period.[27] The
items covered by this plan are not shown in Howard's testimony,
but may be the same as those referred to in G 147,[28] an undated
sales department annual report.[29] These are Be Be Tex cement,
rubber cement, hub paste, stitching wax, lacing thread, and finishing-roll covers.

These discounts are explained by Howard in the following terms:

they are part of an effort to pass along savings that are realized in distribution and manufacturing costs and also, last but not least, our
competition is concentrated among those (shoe) manufacturers where
the volume of sales is the largest, and in order to meet that competition,
in part, as I say, we have established these quantity discounts and the
blanket order arrangements.[30]

Further, Howard's testimony under cross examination on the nature
of the cost savings[31] suggests that they are certainly the less important part of the explanation quoted. Deliveries are made at intervals
to individual plants of large buyers, although Howard thinks there
may be cases in which there is delivery to a central warehouse, without being able to name any; salesmen do make visits to individual
plants as well as dealing with the central purchasing department of
such companies as International Shoe, though less frequently than

25 Tr. 11356–7.   26 Tr. 11355–6.   27 Tr. 11330–1.   28 XVII, 163 ff.
29 Probably referring to 1933, from its place in the sequence of exhibit numbers
assigned by the Government, see Tr. 12.   30 Tr. 11331.   31 Tr. 11356–9.

they would to similar separately owned plants. During this explanation Howard emphasized that savings to United explain the discounts only in part, and competition is also important.

This testimony shows clearly that United's discount system is a vehicle for price discrimination, in order to meet competition in selling supplies to the large buyers. It is reasonable to conjecture that the greater importance of competition among large than among smaller buyers arises because of their superior ability to utilize other sources of supply, including their facilities for self-supply, when they find United's prices too high, as well as their greater imperviousness to United's reputation and salesmanship. This conjecture receives support from scattered evidence showing self-supply or the use of products other than those available through conventional distributional channels to the shoe trade as a whole. Thus G 4389–4390[32] indicate that Brown, International, and Endicott-Johnson make their own shanks; G 172[33] shows that the four largest shoe manufacturers used their own tape-attaching methods for making economy insoles, rather than BB's Bostik and Gold Top methods; Rowen, a Beverly designer, testified that International Shoe used ordinary stitching thread, supplied by American Thread Co., for lacing thread with the Ensign lacing machine;[34] G 4370[35] shows that McElwain was an important customer of the Kimball Company for Goodyear needles and awls; G 3921[36] shows that Brown Shoe purchased rubber-heel nails from United only in an "emergency" when other suppliers did not have required sizes in stock.

That systematic price discrimination related to competition is both an evidence of market power and an indication of poor performance has been argued at sufficient length above[37] so that it needs no repetition here. It is worth commenting on two particular aspects of price discrimination in supplies, however. First, of the four items to which the discount plan applies, three are ones in which United is dominant: in nails and tacks and eyelets United's market share is over 80 per cent;[38] in shanks it is about 50 per cent, but United is more than twice as important as its next largest competitor;[39] only in box toes, in which United has only 25 per cent of the market, and faces a rival with 50 per cent,[40] can the price discrimination involved

---

[32] XVIII, 88–90.   [33] XVII, 144–7.   [34] Tr. 7860–66.   [35] XVII, 69–70.
[36] XV, 71–4.   [37] See above, pp. 73–78, pp. 125–128.   [38] Table 4, pp. 222–223.
[39] See above, p. 228.   [40] P. 229.

in the discount plan be viewed as essentially "defensive," and in response to the activity of stronger competitors. The items to which the blanket-order plan presumably applies show a similar situation. With respect to cements (Be Be Tex and rubber), United's largest rival is Compo, accounting for about half the market. But in the submarket of those using United equipment, United is about five times as large as its nearest rival.[41] The other items are sold in markets in which United is either completely dominant (lacing thread), or several times as large as its nearest rivals (stitching wax, finishing-roll covers). Thus it is clear that the discount schemes are not United's defense against competition in general, but reflect United's use of its power to limit competition to a segment of the market, and to maintain prices in those parts of the market where the problems presented by large buyers are absent. Further, this method of price differentiation operates directly in contravention of United's much-repeated principle of equal treatment for all shoe manufacturers: its chief beneficiaries are large manufacturers. All the information required to determine the extent and effect of discrimination is not available. For this purpose, the distribution of sales among firms in different discount brackets, and knowledge of the stability over time of the position of particular firms in particular brackets is needed. But what evidence there is suffices to support the judgment that the existence of the quantity-discount system shows undesirable performance in the supply field.[42]

3. TYING MACHINES AND SUPPLIES

The Government, in Para 92 e and f of the Complaint, has charged United with establishing such terms on machines used with supplies as will induce shoe manufacturers to install United machines and thus, ultimately, to use United supplies. This complaint is one of several which can be described as involving the tying of machines and supplies.[43] There is evidence in the record that shows that United terms on certain supply-consuming machines were established in anticipation of low rates of return, in terms of the ten-year

[41] Above, p. 229.
[42] See the discount table for cut nails and tacks, above, p. 248. The firms which receive the maximum discount, 7 per cent, must purchase 15 to 60 times as much annually as those which receive the 2 per cent discount.
[43] Complaint, Para 92, GTB Part One, 526–40.

investment formula, and that these low rates were considered desirable in order to promote the sale of United supplies.

Thus in the case of celastic box-toe-conditioning machine, introduced in 1928, various terms committee memoranda and other management communications indicate that terms on the machine were set very low, with expected ten-year profit of $16.70 on a ten-year investment of $440.50, without allowing for service costs. This decision was taken in order to promote the sale of celastic box toes.[44] A similar situation with respect to the fiber-fastening machine B is indicated in G 412 and 270,[45] although less explicitly. Again, one of the documents speaks of the return disregarding service costs, which for this more complicated machine are much more important than for the box-toe conditioner. A memorandum from Gilbert to Wogan[46] dated 1940 mentions, as examples of machines in which terms were set that did not yield a satisfactory return on investment because of the contributions made to the sale of supplies, the duplex eyeletter B and the pasting machine. Other documents show explicitly the situation in the two cases: for the eyeletter, a 1935 terms-committee memorandum shows terms which will return the 10-year investment in 9.5 years, and cites the promotion of eyelet sales as a factor.[47] An earlier terms-committee memorandum (October 1927) shows the change from sale to optional status of the pasting machines A and B in order to stimulate paste sales, even though it was considered undesirable as a general rule to lease low-cost machines of this type.[48] Again, a memorandum from the terms-committee clerk to the general manager in 1929 recommends terms for the insole-lip-cementing machine-C, which would return the 10-year investment in 8 years, noting that the machine is designed to assist in the sale of latex.

The significance of this kind of machine-supply price relationship is much less clear than its existence. Dean argues[49] that it is of no significance. His first point is that, in general, if United is dominant in the machine market, it can make all the monopoly profit possible out of the combination of machine and supply for that machine by charging high prices on its machines, even if the prices on the supply are at competitive levels. Thus, given control of machines, there would be no additional incentive in terms of profit to acquire control

[44] G-3846, 639, 4013, 3847-9, 3854, XIV, 277-90.   [45] XIV, 293.
[46] G-1968, XIV, 295.   [47] G-2119, XIV, 299.   [48] G-2149, XIV, 302.
[49] Memorandum on Supplies, VI 12-18.

of supplies, since it is the demand for the two in combination which sets the limit to the total monopoly profit which can be extracted. Thus, in the light of this analysis, United's price policy, if directed at monopolization of the supplies market as the Government asserts, would be irrational. Second, since entry into supplies is relatively easier than entry into machines, a price policy of low profits on machines and high profits on supplies will encourage entry into the supply markets, rather than bringing about a United monopoly in them. Further, this policy may make it possible for entrants into the machinery industry to survive, by financing losses in the machine field, suffered because of United's discriminatory prices, out of profits on supplies arising from the ability of the new entrant to operate under the "umbrella" of United's profitable supply prices. In other words, Dean argues that if United aimed at monopolizing the supply markets, and maintaining dominance over the machine markets, it would have a pricing policy quite the opposite of that which the Government charges; namely, United would have low prices on supplies fed through United machines, and high prices on the machines.

These arguments are certainly logically correct as far as they go. However, they involve assumptions about ease of entry into the supply field, and about the ability of a non-machine-offering supplier to compete on equal terms with a seller offering both machines and supplies which may not in fact be correct, especially when the integrated seller occupies a position as important as does United. In particular, if the integrated seller, offering both machine and supply, possesses great selling advantages over competitors offering only supplies, and if there is no great difference in the relative ease of entry into machine field and supply field, then United's price policy is consistent with the aims which the Government imputes to it, and will tend to make entry into the particular supplies markets which are affected much more difficult, whatever United's motives were in adopting the policies. The tone of all the documents cited above suggests that the commercial officials and employees of United believe strongly in the first of these propositions: that the offer of machine and supply together provides a great competitive advantage over rivals selling only supplies. In two of the cases listed above, the machines involved are quite simple, judging by the machine costs, and entry into the machine as well as the supply field would not be impossibly difficult for rival suppliers—paste appliers, and insole lip cementers—and some competition in terms of hand application always existed. In the case of eye-letting machines and eyelets, United's principal competitor, Peerless, was also a machine supplier, and therefore the entry into the machine business had already been made. The fourth case presents a some-what different situation, since in the box-toe field United, by offering a machine at little profit, was only copying or modifying the prac-tices of its bigger competitors, who installed machinery for condi-tioning their own products without charge.[50] Thus in three cases, the kind of machine-supply price policy which United followed could be expected to have the effect of frustrating the expansion or entry of rival suppliers, by preventing them from profitable operation in the machine part of the business, which was necessary to competitive success in the supply markets.

The case of the fiber-fastening machine B cannot be explained in these terms, since this was a complicated machine which could not be easily produced by suppliers who might wish to sell fiber, and which had in fact no competitive suppliers. But the evidence that the discriminatory price policy was pursued to the same extent with respect to this machine as with the others is weak,[51] and perhaps other factors than the desire to promote the sale of fiber, not men-tioned in the particular document the Government offers, played a role in the terms decision in this case.

Another type of linkage between supply and machine than that provided by pricing policy is shown as a possible goal of United effort in several instances—the technical connection of supplies to machines in such a way that the use of supplies furnished by other than United is impossible. Such evidence appears with respect to plastic eyelets, wire, and abrasives. In eyelets, the evidence is in three documents,[52] memoranda from Harrington to Homan, dated Decem-ber 1937. They recommend the development of a plastic eyelet and a forming machine which would produce the eyelet as well as set it, in such a way that eyelet and machine would be technically linked together. The memoranda stress the desirability of tying supply to machine, and hold out the possibility of monopolizing the field. There is no evidence to show that the development was ever under-taken. The second instance is documented in G 94 and 3939.[53] The first, an annual report of the heeling and metallic department dated

---

[50] G-4013, XIV, 279 ff.   [51] Cf. above, p. 251.   [52] G-3904-6, XV, 41–43.
[53] XV, 87, 93.

December 1939, raises the question of whether customers using United-provided reels for feeding stapling wire into machines should be compelled to return reels to United to be rewound, and cites a Law Department opinion that such compulsion is legally possible, provided the spools are properly marked, though expressing doubt on its practicality. The second, dated March 1940, indicates abandonment of any attempt to enforce such return, and a practice of selling reels to the users. The final instance of possible technical tying refers to abrasives. Here a single document, a report on the use of abrasives in the shoe industry[54] dated May 1938, indicates the desirability of a development which would link abrasives to the machines so that United could enjoy a continuous market, and an increased revenue from the sale of abrasives. No indication of any action on this suggestion appears.

These three examples are similar in that they show at most an expression of desire to accomplish a tying result, which, if accomplished, would tend to exclude competition from the particular supply market in which the tie operated. In this weak sense, these expressions of desire may be identified with "intent" to monopolize particular supply markets. But whether this "intent" is or is not a "specific intent" seems an unanswerable question. If, for example, in the case of the plastic eyelets, the proposed new development had other advantages, such as producing superior eyelets, and the effect of monopolization was merely a by-product of the laudable aim of producing superior eyelets, would the end result, in the event of a successful development, be any less a monopoly in the eyelet field? The true force of these examples of the possibility of technical tying is not to show that United's intentions were not honorable, but to illustrate again the power in the supply field which United's machine position gives it. Were there not high barriers to entry in the machine field, a successful United development linking a particular supply to a machine which threatened to close the particular supply market to all but United would, in general, call forth a response in the way of another machine-supply combination which would compete with the one United offered. Given the present structure of the machine market, such a response is unlikely, and a successful machine-supply tie would in general result in United monopoly in the particular supply market.

[54] G-3994, XV, 172.

In summary, examination of the relations between machines and supplies shows that United can, in certain situations, gain advantages in the supply markets by pricing policies which make difficult the entry of rivals—specifically in situations where the offer of a supply and a machine which uses it is more attractive to the buyer than the offer of a supply alone, uncorrelated with the using machine. But consideration of both this advantage, and the possible gains of a technological link of machine and supply, point to United's power in the machinery market, rather than any specific practice in the supplies field itself, as the source of United's ability to use tying arrangements to restrict competition in particular supply markets.

4. RESEARCH IN THE SUPPLY FIELD

As in machinery, United's view of its own activities in the supply field places great emphasis on research and on the opportunities offered by the integration of machinery and supply activity in one enterprise for greater progress in both fields.[55] In general terms, the force of this argument is undeniable: that the development of new machines requires some coördinate work in developing supplies which are fed through the machines, and conversely, that the development of new supplies may require coördinate advances in the design of machines is perfectly clear. But, of course, this argument in general terms does nothing to indicate that one particular level of activity in supply manufacture rather than another is necessary to attain the benefits of complementary research in the two fields.

It is further clear that this argument applies only to those supplies which are related to machine functioning: 35 per cent of the total sales volume of United supplies is accounted for by items with no relation to machines at all (class D), another 46 per cent by shoe parts which are not themselves fed through machines (class C), and this leaves only 19 per cent which are either expendable machine parts or supplies fed through machines.[56] Thus the importance of integration to research is relevant for perhaps some half of United's supply business, broadly speaking (i.e., 19 per cent in classes A and B plus perhaps half the 46 per cent in C, using the factor of half to account both for supplies like shoe laces for which integration is of little or no significance and supplies like wood heels in which inte-

---

[55] See Dean, ch. ii.   [56] See pp. 212–213; Table 3, p. 218.

gration may have some significance, but for which it is certainly less than is the case in the class A and B items).

Evidence on the actual record of research in supplies is scattered, and is insufficient to permit a detailed analysis of research inputs and research results of the sort which was made on machinery research,[57] but the little available shows very wide variations in United performance from product to product, even within the group in which machine intimacy is high. On the one hand there is the example of the cement field, in which United efforts have been substantial, and important results have been achieved. The testimony of Nash[58] shows B.B. Chemical as spending currently some $400,000 per annum on research, about half of which comes from United's research budget and half from B.B. Chemical's own funds; a substantial part of this total goes to cements of all kinds. Tetlow testified that some $800,000 had been spent on research and development in cements in the period 1932–1951. During this time several major changes in cement technique were introduced by United, including better solvents for pyroxylin cements, and, most important, the introduction of synthetic cements—based on neoprene and nitrile rubber—which permitted much higher output rates in the cement-sole-attaching process by shortening the period required for bonding, the "time dwell" of the cement, as well as providing a better bond.[59] It is perhaps worth noting that the basic materials for these new developments were the result of work by Du Pont, and were provided to United, and later to other manufacturers, by Du Pont.

On the other hand, there are the examples of eyelets and machine needles and awls, on which very little or nothing in the way of improvement has appeared in a long period of time, and on which there is no indication of substantial research effort. Needles and awls, which are manufactured for United by Torrington, are a relatively unimportant supply item: in 1947f sales were less than $400,000 (compared with $1666 thousand for adhesives of all kinds), making them the 17th class of supply items among 33 in volume of sales.[60] The documentary evidence cited above[61] and the testimony of Ross, President of Torrington,[62] show that the needles United sold were no better than those produced by a very small competitor, that they

---

[57] See above, pp. 147–202.   [58] Tr. 7994–98.
[59] Tr. 9124–27, 8661–72, 9032–36.   [60] Table 2, pp. 216–217.
[61] See above, p. 246.   [62] Tr. 7000–7022.

were in no way patented, and that the specifications provided by United were not greatly different from the specifications furnished Torrington by Landis, Champion, and others. Further, the last general revision of United's specifications had occurred fifteen years ago. Eyelets, on the other hand, are a very important supply item. Shoe-trade sales in 1947f were more than $2 million, ranking fifth in importance in all supply items and second only to nails and tacks of items distributed by United's sales department.[63] The testimony of James, manager of the eyelet department,[64] and of Harrington, assistant director of research,[65] shows that there was no significant change in eyelets for nearly 25 years. United's competitors produce eyelets which function effectively in United machines; they are in general far inferior to United in research resources. James testified that the last important changes in eyelet design occurred about 1928; they were the introduction of rolled instead of scored eyelets, and the substitution of aluminum for brass as the nearly universal material for use in eyelets.[66] It is not clear from the testimony whether or not United introduced the rolled eyelet. As far as the substitution of aluminum for brass is concerned, this was a United development; but, inasmuch as the essential problem was the development of a suitable alloy, and as this problem was solved by United's supplier,[67] it is fair to conclude that United's role was that of pointing out the problem, rather than that of solving it, a task which another eyelet manufacturer may have been as well fitted to perform. Harrington testified to some efforts beginning in 1937 to develop plastic eyelets and appropriate machinery for inserting them in shoes. This development originally aimed at producing eyelets from the plastic material in the same machine that inserted and set them, or using semi-formed eyelets in sheets or string, which would be cut off and set by the eyeletting machine. One of the aims of these developments was the elimination of the pot and raceways now needed for handling the eyelets, which are brought to the machine competely formed and loose. The first goal was abandoned after a few conferences; about 1000 man-hours were expended on the second before it was abandoned.[68] An attempt to produce fully preformed plastic eyelet which

[63] Table 2, pp. 216–217.   [64] Tr. 7293–7334.
[65] Tr. 7214–7292.   [66] Tr. 7298–7301.
[67] Presumably Alcoa, although there is no testimony on this point.
[68] Tr. 7225–70.

would be inserted and set in a machine fundamentally similar to the presently used one has reached the stage where successful completion appears likely. Some $30,000 has been spent on this since 1937.[69] The successful conclusion of this project would be of much less significance than that of the abandoned project and, indeed, it is not at all clear that the substitution of plastic for metal promises any economies.[70] Altogether, neither results nor efforts in eyelets provide corroborating detail in support of a generalization on the beneficial effects of the machine-supply tie in stimulating technological progress.

As in the machinery branch of the case, the Government's view of the significance of United's research in the supplies field emphasizes research as an instrument of monopolization, and United "suppression" of research[71] rather than the quality of research and its results as a measure of United's market performance. As an example of "shelving" of research, and the use of simultaneous machine and supply developments as an instrument of monopolization, *inter alia,* the Government offers the development of the Griswold tape method of Economy insole reinforcing.[72]

The second of the Government's contentions—that the introduction of tape reinforcing methods simultaneously with the introduction of new machines, such as the Insole rib-reinforcing machine A, is a method of monopolizing the supply market—can be dismissed on logical grounds alone. In general, as well as in the particular case of tape reinforcing for welt insoles, the use of a new supply which is applied by machine requires the development of a new or the adaptation of an old machine to its application. Thus the commercial introduction of the supply implies a simultaneous introduction of the coöperating machine; without it, the supply would be useless. While it is undoubtedly true that the integrated supplier of machines and supplies has an advantage over the non-integrated supplier of either in introducing new materials, this advantage is an expression of the economies of integration which arise when there are close

---

[69] Tr. 7254–57, 7269.

[70] G-3905, XV, 41 ff., esp. para. 5, sec. 1, in the context of the whole document, and the previous document, G-3904; also testimony of James, 7313–17.

[71] See above, pp. 199–202.

[72] The evidence on this subject is contained in G-246, 280, 557, 558, 559 (II 399–402); G-172, 259, 2963, 78, 85, 4426, 4427, 4428 (XVII, 144–161); G-79 (XIV, 274); and the testimony of Nash (Tr. 8027–33; 8072–8111), and Roberts (Tr. 12526–33; 12559–81; 12595–623). A summary statement of the Government's contentions is given by Freed in Tr. 8110–1.

technical connections between machine and supply. It can hardly be considered as monopolistic per se, and any monopoly power in the supply field which such integration confers is a consequence of monopoly power in the machinery market. It is neither the result of a "specific intent" to monopolize the supply market, or evidence of such a "specific intent."

The Government's contention on the first point—the shelving of research—turns chiefly around the introduction of the Griswold tape method for reinforcing economy welt insoles to replace the overall method. According to the Government, it was in 1937 that United began its experiments on methods of tape reinforcing that required the use of two strips of canvas tape, covering only the inside of the upstanding rib and the area of the insole immediately adjacent to it, in contrast to the overall method in which the whole insole from rib to rib was covered. The efforts were moved by a desire to "insure" against the development of a commercially practicable substitute for B.B. Chemical's Bostik and Gold Top processes of overall reinforcement, which, at the time, were used for approximately 40 per cent of the welt shoes made. In particular, any generally applicable improvement on the reinforcing method then in use by the 4 or 5 largest welt-shoe manufacturers might provide such a substitute. That method differed from the Bostik and Gold Top methods chiefly in that the manufacturers coated their own canvas with latex, and then applied the second coat of adhesive to the insole directly, rather than to the dry, pre-coated canvas. Presumably, wide use of this process would provide much greater opportunities for competing suppliers of canvas and cements than currently existed when the two BB processes provided pre-coated canvas and cement to be applied to it as a single "package." But at the time, United feared that any improved process would yield less revenue than the current Bostik and Gold Top processes, and suggested that experiments should be carried out, but that any decision on demonstration and commercialization of an improved process should be deferred, since the present processes would be satisfactorily protected (in a patent sense) for some years, and the current competitive situation did not demand another method.[73] Development of the tape process proceeded, but

[73] For these contentions, the Government relies chiefly on G-4762, an experimental program committee report of May 1936, printed, and G-172, an EPC report of May 1937, XVII, 144 ff.

only the impact on United's marketing practices of the court decisions on B.B. Chemical Co. v. Ellis[74] led to its commercial introduction. The decision of the District Court, given on 24 April 1940, made United aware that it would face considerable competition from independent suppliers of canvas and cements on the overall process.[75] United's response to the decision was to bring out with great speed machinery and tape for practicing the tape process; the first insole rib reinforcing machine (IRR, A) was offered commercially in June 1940, and the use of the process grew rapidly thereafter.[76] The fact that it was the threat of competition, and not the normal course of development which was responsible for the commercialization of the tape process at that time, is shown by reference to contemporary documents which describe the new machine as "admittedly a temporary model, commercialized to facilitate the introduction of the Process,"[77] and which suggest that it has been subject to unusually high parts breakage and service demand.[78] Similar indications of poor performance and hurried commercialization for the insole rib cementing machine—A, another new machine required for the tape process—appear in a memo to the General Manager dated November 1941,[79] which indicates that the machine was put out commercially before terms had been set, and that its performance had been unsatisfactory.

United counters these arguments by asserting, through Nash and Roberts, that the tape-reinforcement process was simply the natural result of the continuous process of development which United had been and is carrying on in the field of welt insoles, and that it was commercialized when it was ready, independently of any possible consequences of the Ellis case for the market position of the overall method. Thus Nash testified that the work on the tape method was a response to shoemakers' demands for greater flexibility in welt in-

[74] 32 F Supp 690, 117 F2d 829, 314 US 495.

[75] G-4428, patent dept. memo., Feb. 1942, which says "it can be assumed that this (overall) method of reinforcing an insole may well be subject to considerable competition in view of the Ellis patent decision."

[76] G-246, II, 401 ff., Nash 12531–3.

[77] G-79, AR of Goodyear dept., dated 15 July 41, XIV, 274.

[78] G-246, PC report date April 41, II, 401; the report actually speaks of the hope that Model B will show smaller breakage rates and lower service requirements; viewed in the light of the other statement, this may indicate that these were unusually high but this is not a necessary inference.

[79] G-1967, II, 433 ff.

soles, which appeared in the middle thirties; that this work was carried out as fast as possible; and that the results were made commercial when they were ready.[80] Further, he failed to recollect any difference in the competition faced by Bostik before and after the Supreme Court decision in the Ellis Case.[81] This testimony was amplified by Roberts, who surveyed the whole history of welt-insole manufacture to show that tape was a natural step in the course of insole development. In particular, he indicated that many early attempts to do something like tape reinforcement had been made, citing patents to Keithe in 1895, Rollings in 1917, and Poole in 1936; in general, these failed because of the inadequacy of existing cements to make a sufficiently strong bond on a narrow surface.[82] Roberts also discussed the problem of flexibility, and various attempts by United and others, mostly United, to provide thinner insoles of sufficient strength. Two chief forms were the cemented rib, which required no channeling at all and therefore could use a very lightweight insole, and the Unichannel process, in which only a single lip was channeled, rather than two, as in the ordinary channeled insole. The cemented rib had had a long history, beginning in 1917 with the C-3 line experiments and extending to the present development of the Clark insole. In general, these experiments failed because a suitably strong rib which could hold the stitching was not provided; the Clark insole was expected to meet this problem. The Unichannel process was developed in 1936; it was technically successful, but its cost was too high to permit its wide use. The tape method was developed as another solution to the demand for flexibility; it proved to be successful.[83] On the whole insole development since 1917, United had spent about $1.1 million on new machines, and $0.6 million on improvements to existing machines, or about $60,000 per year on the average over the period.[84]

The testimony of United's officers makes a valid and important point—that there has been a history of experimentation and development in welt-insole construction and that any particular development must be seen in the context of that history, and the testimony provides in ample detail the appropriate context. But within that context, Roberts and Nash really fail to meet the specific thrust of the Government charges, namely that the rate of development and the

[80] Tr. 12526-8.   [81] Tr. 8087-90.   [82] Tr. 12559-61.
[83] Tr. 12567-71, 12580-1, 12595-603, 12612-23.   [84] Tr. 12621-22.

speed of commercialization of the tape-reinforced insole were sharply influenced by a change in the competitive position of the predecessor overall process. In fact, certain portions of their testimony support the Government interpretation of the history and reinforce the evidence of the documents listed above. The most direct support is provided by the development history of the insole reinforcing machine A, as sketched by Roberts.[85] Griswold designed and built the first hand-operated tape-laying machine in 1937. By November 1938, he had built the first power-operated machine, which was tried out in February 1939. In May 1939, another power-operated machine was tried out. Up to this point, the work had been done by B.B. Chemical Co.; at this point United's own Research Department entered into the work, and the machine was redesigned and the first commercial model A was out in June 1940. Thus the total development period was about three years, and the period from the last experimental model[86] to the first commercial model was 13 months. This period corresponds to the "testing period" which was discussed extensively in other testimony and in United exhibits. In comparison with the testing periods of two "simple" machines covered by the testimony and affidavits of Booma,[87] this period is rather short. The tack detector had a testing period from the research model to the first commercial model of fifteen months. Since the development period from the first successful idea to the research model in this machine was only seven months, it may be considered as representing a "simpler" problem than did the IRR-A, for which the corresponding period was over a year—from some time in 1937 to May 1939. The lacing machine A had a longer history. The first operating model was tested for three months, and then a second operating model was produced on the basis of these tests. Between the production of this second model and the adoption of the machine commercially, two years elapsed. The period from the first good idea (ignoring earlier failures) to the first operating model was about two years, so this machine may be taken to represent a somewhat harder problem than the tape-laying machine, but not greatly so. Thus, on the admittedly slim basis of comparison with two other machines, whose development histories were taken as "typical" by United, it appears that the last part of the IRR-A's development, from research model to commercialization, was shorter than might be expected.

[85] Tr. 12531–3.   [86] B.B.'s May 1939 model.   [87] Cf. above, pp. 162–163.

Further indirect support for the Government view is supplied by certain variances between different parts of Roberts' testimony on the subject. Thus Roberts indicated, as noted above, that development of the IRR-A was carried on entirely by B.B. until May 1939 or later.[88] In later testimony, Roberts spoke of United interest and participation in the Griswold tape development from the start, and said that he, Roberts, expected a hostile reaction to the process from shoe manufacturers.[89] This testimony is not strictly inconsistent with the earlier statement; but it tends to give a different impression of the degree of United's participation, and by itself is less consistent with the Government's view of an unusual change in the pace of the development process than is Nash's testimony. Another small variation in which Roberts' testimony at one point is less specific than at another arises in connection with the time at which difficulties with the tape method, due to warping of insoles, were experienced. Roberts speaks of "early experiments (which) showed that unless the tape was fed properly, . . . you would get warpage of the insole itself" in the context of a discussion of the development of the tape method.[90] In his earlier testimony, Roberts had described the deformation problem as one that arose after the model A had been commercialized in June 1940, and was solved by modifications in the model B, commercialized in 1941.[91] Again, the later testimony is less consistent than the earlier with Government's theory of hasty commercialization of the Griswold tape process under the impact of possible competition for the overall process. Finally, Nash was asked, in cross examination, about a 1936 Wagner patent (2,121,938), presumably reading on tape methods of reinforcing insoles, which United had acquired, and in particular why it was not further developed. He denied knowledge of the patent.[92] When the subject was brought up again, in Roberts' testimony, Roberts indicated that the Wagner patent covered basically an invention similar to the Unichannel insole, and that the rib of a Wagner insole could be either tape or overall reinforced, but failed to indicate which method of reinforcement in fact appeared in the patent, or to deal with the question addressed to Nash.[93] Nor is there further testimony on this point.

All these differences in testimony are minor, but they do support the general impression that United's response to the Government

[88] Tr. 12531–3.   [89] Tr. 12612–23.   [90] Tr. 12613.   [91] Tr. 12531–2.
[92] Tr. 8091.   [93] Tr. 1261.

charge on tape reinforcing was one of indirection, which failed to meet squarely the points made by the Government. These weaknesses in United's position, together with the documents offered by the Government, justify the conclusion that the introduction of tape-reinforced insoles presents another example of the responsiveness of the pace of United's research and development activities to variations in the pressure of competition in the market. Other similar examples, discussed above, included the heel seat laster E and the lacing machine A.[94] The comments there made apply here; namely, that, granting the fact of variation in speed of development, the Government's interpretation of this fact as evidence of intent to monopolize, or of the speeded-up commercialization as an instrument of monopolization, shows a misplaced emphasis and a confusion of causes and results. It is the existence of United's considerable market power which gives it scope to choose the pace at which new developments will be brought to fruition. What should be emphasized, therefore, is that an increase in the intensity of competition would serve to narrow that scope, and to create more cases in which competitive pressure forces United to act speedily and successfully, or lose out to competitors.

The economy insole problem deserves the extended discussion it has received here (and in the record) in spite of these essentially negative conclusions with respect to the contentions of both sides. It is precisely the negative conclusion on United's contention that is important: the fact that commercialization of new machine can be speeded up by competition tells heavily against the General United argument about the relations between successful research and United's position in the market.[95] This is true wether or not the particular instance of quickened development was in fact over-hasty, and led to less good results than could otherwise have been achieved, since it is only the absence from the market of sufficiently strong competitors that makes possible the successful marketing by United of an imperfect development.

In sum, the positions of neither the Government nor United on research in the supply field stand up under critical analysis. The Government is no more successful in praying that United's research activities were an instrument of monopolization, used with the

_____

[94] See above, pp. 199–201.   [95] See above, pp. 189–199.

specific intent to monopolize the various supplies markets than it was in proving its similar contention with respect to the shoe machinery market.[96] On the other hand, United fails to show either that its achievements in bettering supply items and introducing new ones are absolutely so great as to "justify" its substantial (though varying) degrees of market power in many of the supply markets, or that such technical advance as it clearly has sponsored is so intimately tied up with its market position, either in machines or in supplies, that any reduction in its market power would *pro tanto* threaten technical advance in the field.

5. SUMMARY: UNITED'S ACTIVITIES IN THE SUPPLIES MARKETS AND CONCLUSIONS ON LIABILITY

The foregoing analysis of United's activities in the field of shoe factory supplies, comprising a group of markets related with varying degrees of closeness rather than a single market, justifies a conclusion that these activities are illegal under the Sherman Act. This conclusion applies to United's supply business as a whole, rather than to specific practices, and it depends heavily on the context of United's market dominance in the shoe machinery market. United has substantial market power in many of the supplies markets; wood heels, last, shoe boxes, box toes, and shoe laces are important exceptions. In some markets, United's occupancy is nearly complete; in others, though it occupies only half the market or less, its competitors are so small and weak that it can still exercise considerable dominance. In every case, United's long line of supplies and the integration of its supply and machine businesses give it important advantages over competitors who are nearly all single-product or short-line suppliers, and offer no or little machinery. Acquisitions and exclusive marketing agreements have been important factors in the achievement of United's market position, and the "snowballing" effect of both the long line and integration has also been a significant factor in the growth process.

In itself, integration of supply and machine businesses, and of different types of supply businesses, is not "monopolistic," and should not be illegal. Such integration carries with it real social economies; it also involves advantages of a "headstart" variety, and purely private

[96] See above, pp. 199–202.

advantages of "insurance" by combining profitable and unprofitable or doubtfully profitable items which raise significant barriers to the entry of unintegrated rivals. The social advantages are not such as to suggest that United is a "natural monopoly" in the supply field. The fact that many of the advantages of integration to United stem from United's dominance in the machinery market—itself not the result of "natural monopoly"—further emphasizes the possibility that efficient producers and sellers of supplies can be of smaller size and degree of integration than United.

The use United has made of its market power has not been such as to "justify" it, either in terms of a "trusteeship" (good-monopoly) theory of the Sherman Act, or in terms of an economic argument of the benefits of scale. On the positive side, there has been no showing of research performance of high quality dependent on United's market position, which would alone serve as an economic justification for that position. On the negative side, the existence of quantity discrimination, the drive towards non-price competition, and the attempts to tie machines and supplies both through price discrimination and through technical ties, all tell against a performance justification of United's market position.

Here, as in the machinery market,[97] a finding of legal liability under the Sherman Act can be given economic content by the existence of feasible remedial measures which can be expected to lessen United's dominance in many of the supplies markets. These will be discussed in detail in the concluding chapter. It may be pointed out now that the most important part of the remedy in respect to supplies is the group of remedial measures taken to lessen United's power in the machinery market, since much of its power in supplies rests thereon. But not all, and other remedies than those applicable to the machinery field are necessary and will be suggested.

6. TANNING MACHINERY

The tanning machinery aspect of the case deserves only brief treatment: in a word, the Government fails to make its case. Its contentions were essentially two: first, that United intends to monopolize the tanning machinery field; second, that United, through its subsidiary, Turner Tanning Machine Company, already had a dominant

[97] See above, pp. 207–208.

position in the field.[98] For support of its first contention—intent to monopolize—the Government relies chiefly on three things: United's plan to institute a leasing system, United's initiation of an expanded program of research in the field of tanning machinery, and Turner's acquisition of three other tanning machinery companies—Carlton Ruhe in 1928; Whitney in 1929; Harding Engineering in 1936. United concedes its plan to introduce leasing into the industry[99] and agrees that it has planned an expanded research program in which United and Turner will share.[100] The acquisitions were not of great significance: that of Whitney was · substantial, involving $125,000, but Whitney was certainly in failing condition at the time of the acquisition;[101] the other two were too small to indicate any monopolistic intent in themselves.[102]

As has been argued extensively above, neither leasing nor research are in themselves illegal, or evidence of monopolistic intent. The illegality of leasing in the shoe machinery market arises from United's dominant position in that market; the problems of United's research activities exist in a similar context. Therefore the whole of the Government case rests on the validity of the second contention—that Turner already dominates the tanning machinery market. The Government argues that Turner's share of the market in or before 1940 was about 67 per cent,[103] relying on a letter from Rudebush, director of the tanning research program, to Roberts, dated February 1946,[104] in which the total value of tanning equipment in use in 1939 is estimated at $50 million, and the total value of the types produced by Turner at $33.5 million. It is clear from the language of the document and from the argument of Powers[105] that the Government has misinterpreted the sense of the statement, ignoring the appearance of "types" in the description of the category to which the figure $35 million is attached. No clear basis for a market share estimate exists in the record. Stephenson on cross-examination admitted having told Government attorneys that Turner machines probably accounted for

---

[98] See Complaint, para. 95, and GTB, Part I, pp. 565–9. Whether or not the Government presses these contentions is not clear, since its briefs on liability and on relief make no mention of Turner Tanning Machinery Co.; nonetheless, the few comments here are set down for the sake of completeness.   [99] Tr. 4768–76, Powers.

[100] Tr. 4723–96, Roberts, Stephenson, president of Turner.

[101] G-4521, XVII, 286, S-139.

[102] G-4457, 59, XVII 189–90; G-4460, XVII, 191.

[103] GTB Part I.   [104] G-4503, XVII, 263–6.   [105] Tr. 4683–5.

65 per cent of the equipment in tanneries in those fields in which Turner operates.[106] Applied to the 67 per cent of the total machinery value which is formed by types Turner produces,[107] this would give a market share of some 43 per cent. The Rudebush letter cited above quotes a Census estimate of $1.2 million annual production of "leather working machinery"; Turner's sales are about 14 per cent of this total. But the exact scope of the Census category is not clear, nor is there any positive showing that it includes only the class of machinery appropriate to a measurement of Turner's market share.[108] Even if the 43 per cent figure is taken as correct, this certainly is not a sufficient basis for a finding of market dominance, nor is there other evidence to fill in the picture.

Perhaps the strongest bit of evidence in favor of the Government's view is a series of letters from Rudebush to Knight, head of the Affiliated Program Committee, running from November 1938 to July 1940,[109] in which various calculations on the relative advantages of sale and lease of proposed new machines are shown. Underlying them all is the assumption that lease revenue will be some share (75 or 67 per cent) of the saving to the tanner made possible by the use of the new machine. This assumes, of course, a sufficient degree of market power to permit discriminatory pricing, such as United practices in the shoe machinery market. Whether this betrays an unconscious assumption of monopoly, a conscious wish for monopoly, or merely great faith in the strength of Turner's patents and great doubt as to the ability of any competitors to provide competing machinery is not clear. In any event, the wish for monopoly is not the same as the intent to monopolize, unless the means exist; and the Government has made no showing that Turner indeed has the means to monopolize the tanning machinery market. Lacking such a showing, and lacking any reliable estimate of Turner's present market position, the Government's contentions must fail.

[106] Tr. 4766.   [107] Cf. above.   [108] Tr. 4705–13, Rudebush.
[109] G-4480, 81, 82, 82, 82, XVII, 199–210.

Part Three

Remedies

VIII. Remedies

The end of an anti-trust action is relief: only the remedial decree gives the findings of liability content. By its nature, relief in an equity action brought by the United States under the Sherman Act must be forward looking, seeking to prevent future violations of the law rather than to recompense those who suffered from past violations. Remedy proposals thus are predictions; given the limited capacity of economists to predict in any but broad terms, such proposals cannot be expected to follow in detail the analysis of the functioning of the market which led to the conclusion of liability. Further, problems of practicability as well as problems of fairness place important limitations on what alterations in market structure or what restrictions on behavior may appropriately be recommended in an anti-trust decree. In general, both criteria lead to preference for a less over a more drastic remedy whenever the former promises to do the job. The same criteria favor broadly drawn decrees, with jurisdiction in the Court to modify them when necessary, rather than attempt at precise specification of how the defendant should conduct his business in the future.

Further there is an important standard of administrative feasibility—as distinguished from business practicability—which any remedial decree should meet. The Court should not be engaged in the continuous task of regulating the business of the defendant under the decree. Ideally, a decree should seek a once-and-for-all rearrangement of the defendant's business, after which he should be as free to operate as any other business. This ideal is almost never attainable: few (if any) decrees are without such items as reasonable royalty provisions or reasonable price provisions over which the Court again retains ultimate supervision. Nonetheless, it is worth emphasizing that the purpose of the remedy is the ultimate creation of a degree of competition in the relevant markets in which the defendant sells such that continued supervision becomes unnecessary, not the creation of a regulated industry with the Court sitting as Public Service Commission. Since this is an ultimate aim, it is to be expected that there will be a transition period during which a fair degree of "regulation" by the Court may be necessary. This is perfectly clear from the point of view of economic analysis in the present case, where the aim of the decree is to create the conditions that will make possible the growth of existing and the appearance of new competitors to an extent that will substantially reduce United's market power. After such conditions have been created, the actual appearance of competitors of sufficient strength and numbers to bring about this result is obviously not an instantaneous process. It is quite difficult to predict with any accuracy what time span is necessary; in general, by making generous allowances for the life of injunctive provisions and retaining the jurisdiction of the Court to modify them when appropriate, such predictions can be dispensed with.

The following pages will consider four major lines of remedial action: dissolution of United; forbidding leasing and certain associated injunctive provisions; divorcement of certain United subsidiaries and lines; and additional injunctive remedies directed to the supply markets. The last three of these are complementary to each other; the first, which is asked for by the Government as its primary remedy, is an alternative to the other three. In examining each one, appropriate consideration will be given to the rationale of the remedy in terms of its expected contribution to the creation of conditions favoring the growth of competition, its practicability in business terms and its administrative feasibility, its impact on the shoe industry, and its impact on United.

1. CORPORATE DISSOLUTION

The Government, in its Brief on Relief, requests the division of United into three full-line manufacturers.[1] Further, it requests the separation of all supply activities from the machinery business.[2] It is not clear from the Brief whether this request is made only if dissolu-

[1] Brief on Relief, pp. 43–6. [2] Ibid., p. 59.

tion is not granted, or whether it holds in any case; the oral argument fails to settle this doubt.[3] For the purpose of the present discussion this difficulty will be passed over, and the discussion of the appropriateness of complete divestiture of supply activity examined in section 4 below. The Brief speaks of the existence, at least for a transitional period, of a single research and development organization which will serve all three successor companies. The oral argument talks of three separate research and development departments, attached respectively to each newly created machinery company. Again, neither the Brief nor the oral argument makes clear whether the three successor companies would be permitted to market on a lease-only basis, or would be required to offer a sale option.

The center of the Government's proposal is the notion that United's major asset is its stock of outstanding leased machines—some 100,000 in number, which could easily be divided among three successor companies. While this stock of leased machines may well be United's most important asset in a balance-sheet sense, this view ignores the important going concern elements of United—the manufacturing plant which turns out new machines, the research and development department, the string of service establishments. The major obstacle to dissolution lies in the existence of a single manufacturing plant. This obstacle is especially significant if it is assumed that the successor companies are forbidden to operate on a lease-only basis. In this case, with the sale of most of the outstanding machines, two of the three successor companies would be in the position of having cash, executive officers, engineering and research personnel, branch offices and service personnel, all of which could be divided among the three with more or less facility, but no factories and no skilled labor force. The Beverly plant and its trained labor force, on the other hand, would be too big for the third company, and would be wastefully underutilized. While machines, and some workers, might be moved, this too would be an uneconomic operation, and it is doubtful to what extent workers in adequate numbers could be moved. Thus two of the three successor companies would be put at a serious disadvantage, namely of being out of the market with no new machines to sell for whatever period it took to set up a plant, train a labor force, and get into production—at least two or three years.

[3] Tr. 14129–66, Timberg, esp. 14159–65.

This disadvantage would be less serious if leasing were to continue, since the two new successors could still maintain customer contacts through service and perhaps parts operations in the transition period. But there are strong arguments against the continuation of leasing, even with three sellers, in that leasing would facilitate a division of the market among the three, each retaining his customers, with little competition among them—a result not made more unlikely if each of the three companies was staffed, as it would have to be, by United personnel.

It would be possible, of course, for Beverly to continue to provide machines for all three successor concerns during the transition period, thus removing the disadvantage of the two non-Beverly producers. But such a relation among the three would be a poor beginning to an effort aimed at creating competition among them. If it lasted until the two non-Beverly successors had achieved a high level of manufacturing skill it might last too long to permit the growth of healthy competition; if the supply relations were terminated as soon as the two concerns set up their own factories, they might suffer serious competitive disadvantages for some time until they achieved an appropriate level of experience and skill in manufacture.

The use by the three successor companies of a joint research and development staff for any extended period of time would also operate to inhibit competition among them, but there seems to be no reason why the present research division of United could not be divided in three.[4] The change between Brief and oral argument on this point may indicate that the Government repudiated this suggestion, and now stands on the feasibility of a tripartite division of United's research activities.

There is no precedent in previous anti-trust decrees for the breaking up of a single-plant firm, which is what United is, considered solely as a shoe-machinery manufacturer. Further, no economic discussion of anti-trust policy has ever led to the suggestion of breaking up a single plant. Even where it is clear that a smaller plant could be equally efficient, the diseconomies of trying to subdivide an operating technical unit—or, alternately, of condemning existing plant to idleness while at the same time encouraging the building of new plant—have precluded consideration of such dissolution as a practicable policy.

[4] See above, pp. 97–99.

In spite of the foregoing arguments, a proposal for splitting United in three might merit consideration if no other remedial measures promised to create conditions which would make more competition likely. Such indeed is the Government's view.[5] Is it justified? Two considerations support the contention that it is not. The first is the tremendous importance of leasing in the maintenance of United's dominance in the market; absent leasing, many avenues for competition now closed will be open. The second may be put in terms of the impatience of the Government: it is true that the day after the injunctive remedies discussed below—which are broadly similar, though considerably different in detail, to those asked by the Government— United's market position will be no less than it was the day before. But, if the argument below has merit, the means of maintaining that position will have been taken from United; and, with the passage of time, say five years, its position will have been considerably weakened. Given a justified expectation of results from weaker measures, a remedy which is drastic, unprecedented, and of doubtful practicability should not be tried.

2. AN END TO LEASING

The most important single alteration in the operation of the shoe machinery market leading to an increase in the degree of competition therein is the end of the lease method of marketing, and the dissolution of the lease bundle which United provides under that method. Together with certain alterations in United's patent policies and a ban on the expansion of United by acquisitions, this change may be expected to lower significantly the existing barriers to competition.

United should be enjoined from marketing machines by any other method than sale. All machines now in the hands of shoe manufacturers on lease from United should be purchased by the lessees or returned to United. Machines should be sold individually, at uniform prices to all buyers. United should be permitted to continue to provide service, either on United-made machines only or on all machines, at its discretion, but under a system of separate charges, so that service transactions are separate from machine sales transactions. This does not mean that United may sell service only on the basis of fees for each operation performed. If it desires, it may offer

[5] Brief on Relief, pp. 37–43.

annual service contracts, machine by machine, factory by factory, or manufacturer by manufacturer; but no service contracts should be permitted to extend for more than one year, and charges should be uniform for similar contracts with manufacturers in the same location. Geographical uniformity of charges, while permissible, should not be mandatory. Repair parts for United machines must likewise be made available on a non-discriminatory basis to all buyers, without tying them either to the purchase of new machines from United, or to the purchase of repair or other service from United. United may, of course, refuse to allow its servicemen to repair United machines with non-United parts;[6] but it must not condition the availability of its parts upon the utilization of its repair service facilities. Nor should United be permitted to create a parts-service tie through price discrimination: United parts must be available at the same prices to those using other repair service as to those using United repair service. Finally, marketing through sale will include conditional sale, but United should not be permitted to tie provision of finance to the machine, and equivalent terms should be offered those who use United's financing facilities, and those who use other finance facilities where they are available.

The aim of these measures is clear from the previous discussion of the importance of leasing in maintaining United's market share[7] and of the problems of equity and efficiency created by the lease-service bundle.[8] In brief, they will loosen the tie between United and the customer created by the present leasing system; they will lead to the growth of a second-hand market in shoe machinery, with all that that implies for the creation of competition; they will remove the tying effects of the present leasing system which tend to make a customer take all his machines from United; and they will eliminate the compulsory-pooling principle in the payment for service.

The desirability of a decisive move to terminate leasing, rather than making an arrangement which commands United to offer the shoe manufacturer the option of lease or purchase when he acquires a new machine,[9] whether that option shall present "economically equivalent terms" (as the Court phrased its question) or whether

[6] Cf. *Pick Mfg. Co.* v. *General Motors,* 80 F2d 641, affmd per curiam, 229 US 3.
[7] See above, pp. 64–73.   [8] See above, esp. pp. 134–146.
[9] Asked for by the Government, Brief on Relief, pp. 13–19; previously suggested as a problem worth exploring by the Court—see testimony of McNeill, cited below.

it shall be so designed as to favor purchase (as the Government requests), rests on several grounds. The most important one is that the way to deprive United of the barriers against competition provided by leasing is to terminate leasing, rather than to create an option which will reduce its use, but in an uncertain way, spread over a long period of time, and perhaps in a very uneven fashion over the shoe industry. Both practicability and administrative feasibility likewise tell against the use of a lease-sale option, if leasing on a unit-charge basis is allowed. The record is filled with recitals by United witnesses on the difficulties of prediction involved in getting "equivalent" lease and sale terms where lease charges are on the basis of use.[10] While Dean[11] expresses in substance the view that the purely formal difficulties of computing equivalent prices had been overstated by other witnesses, his testimony indicates that many operational difficulties would face United in marketing under an optional lease-sale arrangement. And it is further clear that, whether or not marketing under a lease arrangement is less or more costly per unit transaction than marketing by sale, an optional system would be more costly than either, since it would involve the record-keeping organization and sales efforts required for both. Moreover, the "equivalence" of lease and sale terms, or their departure from equivalence in a specified direction by a fixed amount, would vary with the cost of capital, the state of the shoe-manufacturing industry, and other aspects of the general business situation. Any continuing attempt to maintain a fixed relationship between lease and sale terms under an optional arrangement would require fairly frequent intervention by the Court, especially if the Government had the right, as it would, to raise the question of the maintenance of the relationship under changing conditions. Thus a lease-sale option would be inferior to an order prescribing sales on grounds of feasibility.

If unit charges were not continued, either on grounds of practicability or because they result in socially undesirable quantity discrimination,[12] and if service were separated from the lease bundle, it would be much easier to provide for optional lease-sale marketing of machines. But in such a case, United's interest in the continuance of leasing would be gone, since the chief virtues United finds in leasing

[10] See Tr. 12171–204, McNeill; 12343–400, Colloquy, Court and McNeill;12931–6, 12948–53, Merriam.
[11] Tr. 13095–115.   [12] See Kaysen Memorandum, Tr. 5249–53.

are bound up with unit charges and the provision of service in the bundle.[13] If allowed to offer a lease option on a monthly rental basis only, with service charged for separately, it seems safe to assert that United would prefer to move to a straight sales basis. However, the shoe manufacturers and Compo, United's most important present competitor, would prefer to see a lease-sale option, rather than a straight sales system, imposed on United by the Court. The testimony of the shoe manufacturers indicates unequivocally that they do not now desire a sales system;[14] while it is clear that Compo leases primarily because United does so, Compo's witnesses expressed themselves in favor of the leasing system.[15] Just how much weight the expressed interests of the shoe manufacturers and of United's competitors should carry is an arguable proposition. From one point of view, the Government may be seen as acting, in essence, in their behalf when it sues United under the Sherman Act. On this view, the imposition of a straight sale policy on United would be unfair, and the Court should refrain from so doing whatever the economic merits of the method. On the other hand, the economist is inclined to argue that the Sherman Act is aimed at promoting competition, and that the promotion of competition may harm specific competitors, and even specific customers in the competitive market. As the discussion above on the relations between United and the shoe manufacturers made clear,[16] United has exercised a sort of paternalistic despotism over the manufacturer; it is to be expected, then, that introduction of a more competitive, and more individualistic, regime in the machinery market will cause suffering among at least some of the shoe manufacturers. Similarly, the process of loosening United's grip on the machinery market may be not without pains to Compo and other competitors, whose business policies are naturally adapted to those of the dominant seller, and may have to change when change is imposed on him. It is clear that this is an issue which cannot be resolved purely on economic grounds. The additional remedies considered in Part III below, however, may provide a way of avoiding at least that part of the issue which relates to Compo; that part which relates to the shoe manufacturers must be faced.

It has been recommended that United be permitted to continue its service activities, provided that service charges are made separate

---

[13] See above, pp. 189–193.

[14] Above, p. 202.

[15] Tr. 10266–9, Smith.

[16] See above, pp. 202–206.

from machine transactions, are non-discriminatory among purchasers, and are not used as a method for tying machines or parts to
service. The Government requests that, if dissolution is not ordered,
United's service business be divested and operated independently.[17]
This appears both unnecessary and undesirable. It is undesirable
because of the real economies in the provision of service by the machine manufacturer, especially in relation to the flow of information
and suggestions which are relevant to the improvement of existing
and the development of new machines. It is unnecessary because the
chief evils the Government sees in the present integration of service
and machine business—what it calls commercial surveillance, and
the use of servicemen to promote the sale of United machines and
supplies—are really evils only in the context of United's market
dominance. Assuming the success of the remedies here recommended in substantially lessening that dominance, these activities
are reduced to their ordinary position of inevitable features of competitive business—keeping in touch with the activities of competitors
through customers, and using every (legal) means to promote the
sale of one's products.

The change from United's present marketing arrangements to a
sales system requires some transition period during which two re-
arrangements can be completed. The first is the internal rearrangement of United's marketing and service organizations which will
enable it to distribute new machines on a sales rather than a lease
basis and to charge separately for service; the second is the period
within which the disposition of machines now out on lease should
be completed. These two periods need not be the same, of course.
The following suggestions appear reasonable: (1) Within 18 months
of the effective date of a final decree, United should cease to lease
newly distributed machines, and offer them on a sale-only basis. In
the interim, machines distributed to shoe manufacturers should be
offered on one-year leases for straight monthly rentals, with provisions for applying the rentals to the purchase price, if the lessor later
buys the machines, and with provisions for handling charges if the
lessor returns the machine at the end of the lease period. These may
be included in the monthly charge, or appear as separate payments
on termination of the lease. (2) Within the same period, United
should cease to provide service as part of the lease bundle on out-

[17] Brief on Relief, p. 52.

standing leases. When this is done, payments under outstanding leases should be modified to reflect the change in the content of the lease. Such modifications should be made on the basis of United's average service costs for each machine type, since they will be temporary, lasting only until obligations under outstanding leases are liquidated. On temporary new leases which are made during this period, in accordance with (1), service should be charged for separately on the basis of costs plus a fair profit for United. If United and the lessee cannot agree on the basis of charging for service in this interim period, they shall refer their problems to an arbitration board, the composition of which will be described below. (3) All outstanding leases are to be liquidated, either by transfer of title to the lessee or by return of the machine to United within a period of four years from the effective date of the final decree, although some lessees may still be in debt to United after that time.

The substantive problems of arranging for the transition from lease to sale are pricing problems: on what terms should existing leases be liquidated? On what terms should new machines be sold? These two problems are not unrelated, but they present an important difference from the point of view of the Court. It is both feasible and appropriate for the Court to prescribe the former set of prices (on suitable advice, *vide infra*); the same cannot be said for the schedule of sales prices at which United offers its machines 18 months after the final decree. It might appear desirable for the Court to prevent the same kind of inter-machine discrimination in sales prices which now exists in lease terms,[18] and it would be possible to prescribe cost-plus-uniform-mark-up pricing for each machine, even though there are difficulties of cost allocations for such items as research and development. But, as has been pointed out in the discussion of price discrimination above,[19] some price discrimination is almost inevitable in a multi-product firm, and a changing pattern of discrimination is one of the most important means of competition in markets where multi-product firms compete. The freezing of United's price structure on a cost-plus basis would inject an element of rigidity into the market, instead of freeing it from such elements, and it would limit rather than invigorate competition. By the time United was selling its machines, a visible and growing stock of second-hand machines would have been created by the turnover of shoe manu-

---

[18] See above, pp. 73–78.   [19] Pp. 127–128.

facturers. These, plus the stock of old machines in the hands of shoe manufacturers, would already limit to some extent the degree of price discrimination that it would be feasible for United to practice. In time, as competition of all sorts increased, including the further increase in the stock of used machines, the copying of machines with poor or no patent coverage and the possible expansion of existing sellers into new fields, further limits would be put on United's ability to maintain a frozen pattern of inter-machine price discrimination, as it now does under leasing. It would appear preferable for the Court to rely on the growth of these restraints, rather than to attempt to determine United's price policy.

The appropriate instrument for deciding the terms on which current leases would be settled would appear to be a conference of representatives of the Shoe Manufacturers Association and of United, similar to the one which negotiated the new lease terms after the Clayton Act case. Such a conference should be supplemented with a Court-appointed panel of masters or arbitrators, who would have the power to make recommendations to the Court on points where United and the shoe manufacturers could not reach agreement. Such a panel might be composed of a retired officer of United, a retired shoe manufacturing executive, a public accountant with experience of the shoe-manufacturing business, a lawyer, and an economist, all selected by the Court, with appropriate advice from the parties, and the panel might be paid by United and the Shoe Manufacturers Association. The panel might also review the negotiations between United and the shoe manufacturers, and comment on the recommendations to the Court arising from them. On the basis of this or some similar mechanism for negotiating a settlement of the leases, the Court could issue an order providing settlement terms. The Court might provide guidance to the negotiators on some other matters than the time limit for settlements. One important point is that the terms on which the shoe manufacturers acquire title to machines that they now lease should give United at least its present return, since there has been no finding that United's overall profits have been excessive, and the lease settlements are an inappropriate means of attempting to redress the wrongs of previous inter-machine price discrimination—if they were suffered by the shoe manufacturer at all. In general, this might mean that United should get at least the average present value of payments expected under the lease (appropriately adjusted for the time distribution of actual payments under the settlement arrangement) plus something for the 12 per cent scrap value of the machine; the lessee should get full credit for his right-of-deduction-fund accumulations; and the inventory profits arising from the termination of leases drawn on pre-1950 terms (if any) should be divided between United and the shoe manufacturers. Just as fairness demands that United be permitted to recover something like its average returns from the transfer of ownership of leased machines to the lessees, it also demands that no shoe manufacturer who could afford to keep his machines under lease for the rest of the lease term be made unable to do so by the terms of settlement. To insure this may require that settlement terms vary from manufacturer to manufacturer. Either settlement terms which were related to the past lease payments of each manufacturer (or class of manufacturers), or funding arrangements which varied the time period for payment without varying the total payment might be used to insure the desired result. In other words, a system of leasing which has involved discrimination among lessees may quite naturally be expected to require lease-settlement arrangements which involve discrimination among the lessees-become-purchasers.

The order enjoining leasing and requiring sale of machines and provision of service on a basis of separate charges should run for a period of 15 years, or one-and-one-half lease lives. It may, of course, be sooner modified if the growth of competition warrants it and United, or even the Government, requests modification. By the end of that period the sales system will have become sufficiently well established in the industry to make the reappearance of leasing unlikely, whatever its significance for competition in the then-existing state of the market.

After the prohibition of leasing, the next restraint in terms of importance to be placed on United's business conduct is an injunction against the acquisition of shoe-machinery businesses, or stock interest in shoe-machinery businesses, or the assets of shoe-machinery businesses, for a period of ten years. This prohibition should be absolute, and extend even to acquisitions at bankruptcy sales. Its purpose is obvious; its effect will be to make it relatively easier for competitors of United to expand, and for potential competitors of United to enter the market, in part, at the cost of those businesses which sell out or go into bankruptcy, since the removal of United from the market will lower the prices paid, on the average, in such transactions. Again, this cost may be viewed as one of the costs of the restoration of competition, the incidence of which is beyond the control of the Court.

Similarly, and almost equally important, United should be enjoined from acquiring patents or patent applications or inventions not in the form of patents or patent applications by purchase from persons not in its employ. Ten years is again suggested as the life of this restraint. In those situations in which applications by others are in interference with United applications, or in which patents held by others block the use of United patents, United should seek settlements through methods other than purchase of the applications or patents. With respect to applications in interference with United applications, United might seek to compromise on the conflicting claims and get a non-exclusive license under the other patents. Similarly, where patents of others block United developments, United should seek non-exclusive licenses under the blocking patents. Perhaps, in the case of a mutual blocking, where the other party demands an exclusive license under United's patent(s), United should be allowed, in turn, to receive an exclusive license under the other's patent(s), although there is a danger that this proviso might lead to wide use of exclusive-licensing arrangements, since the existence or non-existence of mutual blocking is not objectively demonstrable in any simple fashion. When United is unable to negotiate an appropriate non-exclusive license (assuming the proviso above is not made), it will simply have to abandon the development. The result of this restraint will be to deprive United's large patent holdings of their snowballing effect, or at least reduce its magnitude appreciably,[20] and thus to reduce the patent barrier to the competitive offer of new machines, either by existing sellers or by new entrants. It is true that the pace of United development may be somewhat slowed by its failure in particular instances to secure licenses within the restraints of the decree on some patents which block its developments. Further, there may and probably will be a sub-class of these cases in which the owner of the blocking patent may fail to make the development United is prevented from making, because of mutual blocking, or lack of ability, or lack of interest in the particular field. But the negative effects of these factors will be offset, and quite possibly far outweighed, by the positive effects of stimulating

[20] Above, pp. 89–90.

new centers of development, and forcing outside inventors—in shoe factories, for instance—to turn to others than United as a market for their patents and ideas.

Third, United should be enjoined from acquiring second-hand shoe machinery for ten years. There must be two exceptions to this injunction: first, of course, where United sells under chattel mortgages, it must have the right to repossess its machinery for non-payment in the usual way; second, United should be allowed to purchase second-hand machines in such numbers as would be appropriate for experimental purposes. The purpose of this restraint is to facilitate the quick growth of a second-hand machinery market in which United is not the dominant factor. Once such a market has developed, there is no reason why United should not deal in it.

Finally, United should be required to license, at reasonable royalties, all presently held patents and all patents granted to it within the next five years reading on shoe machinery, shoe-making processes, shoe constructions, shoe parts, and shoe-factory supplies. Such licenses may be exclusive; but they must be individual licenses, not conditioned on the licensee's acceptance of licenses under other United patents; they may not be conditioned on the cross-licensing to United of either presently owned or future patents of the licensees; they may not be conditioned on territorial restrictions or pricing restrictions on the sale of the licensees' products. For all patents acquired after the five-year period (from the date of the decree), and for all patents in non-shoe machinery and supply fields, United shall be completely free of special restraints of any kind. Where a licensee under this order so requests, United should be required to furnish to the licensee such "know-how" with the patents—including drawings, metallurgical specifications, the advice of United engineers—as may be necessary to practice the patented invention. All such transfers of "know-how" should be compensated for at cost, including overheads, plus a reasonable fee.

The criterion of reasonable royalties should be development costs plus a fair profit, including in costs an appropriate allowance for the overheads of research and for the average costs of unsuccessful developments which must be borne by successful developments, rather than the maximum profit United could receive from the exploitation of a patent if it did not license. This criterion is probably not in fact important in the case of most patents which United would be called on to license, in view of their narrow scope.[21] Only the licensing of a relatively "important" patent would raise the possibility of a large (positive) difference between the maximum returns and cost standards of reasonable royalties.

The Government has requested that United be ordered to license its patents royalty free.[22] In addition to the lack of legal precedent for such a step, and the Hartford-Empire decision reversing a District Court which ordered royalty-free licensing, the reason for not requiring royalty-free licensing is simply that the significance of United's patents in maintaining its market position is not so great as to warrant such a drastic remedy. The Government, of course, takes a different view, but it has failed to sustain that view on the present record.[23] Whatever restraining force on entry United's patent holdings exercise seems to be sufficiently reduced by the licensing requirements suggested above as to cease to constitute more than a very minor barrier to competition. The non-cross-licensing provision is especially useful in this respect, since it provides an opportunity for United's rivals to catch up with United's present technology while not forcing them to sacrifice any advantages over United that they now possess or may acquire in the future.

The series of restrictions which this section has suggested should be placed on United's methods of doing business in the near and middle future can be expected to promote the growth of competition in a variety of ways. Competition in service, both from some shoe manufacturers providing their own, and from the growth of independent service agencies, will probably develop quickly. Equally rapid will be the competition to new machines provided by the existence of a second-hand machinery market. It is natural to expect that the provision of service, the sale of second-hand machinery, the sale of machine parts, and the distribution of shoe-factory supplies will in many cases be undertaken by a single enterprise. In time, some enterprises of this sort may begin to offer new shoe machinery, especially of the less complicated types. Through this process, some fairly substantial competitors may be expected to develop in time. These same factors, and the reduction of patent barriers and the prohibition of acquisitions by United, will operate to make it easier for existing competitors, like Compo, Atlas Tack Co., Boston Machine Works,

[21] See above, pp. 78–79.　　[22] Brief on Relief, pp. 19–28.
[23] See above, pp. 108–112, 199–202.

to expand. Neither of these processes is at all likely to create a competitor anything like United's size; but, taken together, they will go far to reduce the market power carried by United's still large market share. Some of the larger shoe-manufacturing enterprises may begin to produce, or at least have produced for them, some of their own shoe machinery, which will further weaken United's position in the market.

As a result of these changes, what can be expected to happen in the shoe-manufacturing industry? The end of United's protective domination of the market will certainly result in the requirement of more managerial skill for the shoe-manufacturing businesses. Problems of machine service, of the replacement of obsolete machinery, and of finance, that are now, in effect, dealt with by United, will become the responsibility of the shoe manufacturer. Though the actual initial capital required for entry will change little with the change from lease to sale,[24] the problems of cyclical fluctuation and the existence of fixed obligations under chattel mortgages may make the new firm in possession of greater capital more certain to succeed than the one which begins with the proverbial shoestring. All these changes will make entry somewhat more difficult, and will result in the failure of firms, because of poor management, which might succeed under the present system. This will hit the very small manufacturer relatively hard, as compared with his middle-sized and larger competitors. But, even with a substantial reduction in numbers, say 15 to 20 per cent, the factors which have operated to make the shoe industry competitive will continue to do so: entry will still be relatively free, economies of great scale will be largely absent, style factors and marketing factors will continue to be of great importance. Moreover, the changes brought about by relief will operate in some ways to increase the efficiency of shoe manufacturing, since machine utilization and machine service will now become a factor in competition among the shoe manufacturers. There is no reason, from the side of competition or from the side of efficiency, to expect the cost of shoes to increase as a result of the changes.

To be sure, there is the non-economic problem of the significance of the possible reduction in the number of independent businesses in the shoe industry, but the order of magnitude—200 to 300 firms—seems too small to make this a matter of major concern. And it will

[24] See above, pp. 203–205.

be counter-balanced to some extent by the creation of new firms supplying parts, service, second-hand machines, and shoe-factory supples.

The probable impact of a sales system and a second-hand market on research have been much discussed in the record. The most important arguments have been analyzed above.[25] Here only a few comments are necessary. First, it is clear that as a result of these remedies United will have less revenue to spend on research in shoe machinery than it now does. The whole industry may or may not have less revenue to spend in this way. Whether it does depends on the importance that quantity discrimination had in fact in extending the distribution of machines, a point which is hardly touched on in the record; and on the extent to which shoe manufacturers find it economical to extend the life of existing machines, both by holding on to machines they own for long periods of time, and by meeting expansion needs through the purchase of second-hand rather than new machines (of course, considering the industry as a whole, these two are the same thing). If the total available to the whole shoe machinery industry for research is less than what was available under unit-charge leasing, this means, as was previously pointed out, merely that the shoe manufacturers find it worthwhile to pay for less research, in a competitive market, than United was able to make them pay for through monopoly, quantity discrimination, and enforced obsolescence. This conclusion is subject to two qualifications. First, it might be that none of the new firms receiving revenue that formerly went to United will be large enough to spend any money on research, since there is some minimum size research unit required for efficiency. This seems unlikely, in view of the fact that Compo is already doing research work, and that even an independent inventor like Kamborian can make useful contributions. Second, United has argued that only by working continually on large variety of small improvements can a research staff be maintained, in order that it should be ready to make occasional big jumps when it is possible to do so. If, as a result of the end of leasing, many minor and less complicated machines are used over very long lives and effective research work on them is abandoned, and if minor improvements on major machines can no longer be sure of finding a market at a price sufficient to cover the costs of developing them,

[25] See pp. 189–199.

then it will be no longer possible to maintain a research staff of sufficient size to create big improvements. This is certainly a possibility. But it seems to represent an extreme one, and United's whole argument on this point has been qualitative, and in terms of absolutes, although it has dealt with a problem that is surely a matter of degree. It does not seem likely that the long-term result of the remedies will be to cut United's research efforts devoted to shoe machinery to much less than half their present size, yet at less than half its present size the research division functioned effectively in the past.[26] Moreover, other research efforts, including possibly quite large ones by some shoe manufacturers, will develop in the industry, and thus the assertion that the end of leasing must lead to a decline in research beyond that induced because of the economic inefficiency of spending more for research than shoe manufacturers are willing to pay for in a more competitive machinery market, does not appear warranted.

Finally, a few words on the impact of these measures on United is in order. The shoe-machinery market has not, in the past, been a growing one: increases in machine productivity have more or less kept pace with increases in shoe production, and the total number of shoe machines in factories has remained nearly constant in the last thirty years.[27] The same is probably not true for total value of shoe machinery, in constant prices, but no figures for this are available in the record. This trend may change, since there has been a sharp change in the rate of population growth in recent years,[28] and shoe production and machine demand may respond accordingly. But leaving aside such speculations, if the remedy measures are at all successful (and unless the market expands rapidly), they should result in a substantial diminution of United's income from shoe machinery and from shoe-factory supplies. Thus United's existing manufacturing, research, distribution, and service capacities may prove too large for its volume of business in these fields in the middle future. These idle resources may well provide a further stimulus to the one United alreadys feels (cf. its tanning-machinery activities) for applying its great talents to other fields than shoe machinery. The expansion of tanning-machinery activity is one such

[26] See Table 0, p. 150; Table 13, p. 169.   [27] Above, pp. 27–28.
[28] See Davis, *Am. Econ. Review,* June 1952.

field, the application of United skills to textile machinery, can-closing machinery, ordnance, might also be possible. Such expansions, provided they do not aim at monopoly, or employ illegal methods, will benefit the economy, as well as providing United with business to replace what it will undoubtedly lose in the shoe-machinery and supply fields.

3. DIVESTITURE OF CERTAIN UNITED ACTIVITIES AS A FURTHER STEP

In addition to the injunctive remedies examined above, aimed at creating conditions that would make it easier for competitors to grow vis-à-vis United in the machinery market, divestiture of certain United subsidiaries, branches, and machinery lines might be undertaken as a step to create new competition immediately. In particular, a new shoe-machinery and shoe-factory-supply producer could be created by divesting United of B.B. Chemical Corporation, its own Cement Shoe department, its two eyelet manufacturing branches, S.O. and C. Co. and J. C. Rhodes, and its Eyeletting department; setting up these plus suitable executive, research, manufacturing, and sales staffs as a separate corporation, and through stock sales such as described below, making this corporation independent of United. Such a measure can be seen as a step in the direction of recreating conditions similar to those which prevailed before the original mergers which created United's predecessor company. Or more directly, it would create a new competitor in the market, offering two lines of machines and several lines of supplies, about twice the size of Compo, and staffed by experienced and able personnel. While neither of its two machine lines would compete directly with the machines offered by United after the divestiture, there would be indirect competition between cement-shoe machines and bottoming machines for other processes, especially machines for making Little-way and slip-lasted shoes. Moreover, in time, the New Company might well expand its line; the more readily since it would contain some operating and research personnel familiar with other types of shoe machinery. And also United might in the future re-enter these fields, creating direct competition between itself and the New Corporation. Moreover, both cement-shoe and eyeletting fields are ones in which competition now exists—Compo and Atlas Tack, respectively, are the most important competitors—and there would therefore be no question of stifling competition by a tacit division of fields between United and the New Company.

In setting up the New Company, the B.B. Chemical Company, which already has a business organization and a corporate existence, might well be used as a vehicle. United would transfer to B.B. the appropriate additional personnel from Beverly, the Boston central office, and the branches, as well as the staffs of the two machine departments and the eyelet manufacturing plants. The transfer of assets should include all the patents reading on both machines and supplies which will be sold by the New Company; where these also read on items which remain in United's hands, some kind of royalty-free-licensing arrangement should be worked out. Also among the transferred assets should be the existing stocks of parts for the machines distributed by the two departments, as well as drawings, tools, and fixtures peculiar to those machines, and the trademarks, except the trademark "United," on all items which the New Company would distribute. After the transfer, the B.B. Chemical Co. might well call itself the B.B. Chemical and Shoe Machinery Company, as a way of retaining a share of the United good will in the products which have previously borne its name. United would then distribute the shares of the New Company to its shareholders in proportion to their United holdings. Each holder of more than 5 per cent of United's outstanding stock would then be required to dispose of either his United or his New Company holdings, disposition to be made through the agency of a Court-appointed trustee, who would hold shares without voting them until they were sold, with a three-year limit on the holding period. The officers and directors of United and the New Company, who would form two separate, non-overlapping groups, would not be given an option, but would be required to dispose of their New Company and United holdings respectively, and would be enjoined from reacquiring stock in the other company for ten years, or so long as they held offices or directorships.

Since United, in organizing the New Company, would be acting for the benefit of its stockholders, United's best efforts in organizing, staffing, and launching the New Company could confidently be expected. The greatest handicap the New Company would face would be its lack of machinery-manufacturing facilities. But since it would have trained technical personnel, stocks of machine parts, the title to the machines now out on lease in the fields in which it would operate, and a substantial income (see below) from its going non-machinery activities, this handicap should not be too difficult to overcome. Moreover, the machines it would manufacture are not among the more complicated machines now produced by United, and thus its position in every respect would be different from the difficult one of the successor companies created by a complete three-way split of United which was discussed above.[29]

The viability of the New Company would be all but guaranteed by its possession of the B.B. Chemical and eyelet supply business. In 1947, these amounted to some $7.5 million per year.[30] Moreover, a substantial part of this business, about half the eyelet volume and about an eighth of the B.B. Chemical volume is outside the shoe trade, so that the New Company might be in a position to expand in other fields than the shoe field. In addition to the supply business, the 1947 lease revenue of the two machine fields amounted to some $1.3 million.[31]

The feasibility of small-scale, short-line operations in the cement-shoe and eyeletting fields, as well as in associated supply fields, is demonstrated beyond doubt by the successful operations of Compo and Atlas Tack, as well as by the existence of other smaller competitors. The technical feasibility of this particular divestiture recommends itself because for both B.B. Chemical and the eyelet plants there exist functioning business organizations, not directly part of United proper, that possess separate manufacturing facilities. B.B. Chemical has distribution and research facilities as well. The further expansion of personnel and facilities that these organizations would require to manufacture cement-shoe and eyeletting machinery does not seem too difficult, especially in view of their acquisition of trained personnel of all sorts.

A further advantage of this divestiture would be its results in the supply fields. It would reduce United's shoe-factory-supplies business (including that of the other subsidiaries) by about 15 per cent in total volume. Five of the 36 classes of merchandise distributed to the shoe trade by United and its subsidiaries[32] would go to the New Com-

---

[29] See above, pp. 272–275.

[30] B.B. Chemical sales about $5.5 million, Tr. 8034 ff., Nash; eyelet sales about $2 million, Tr. 7295, 7323, James.

[31] G-4725 for cement shoe; James Tr. 7323, for eyeletting.

[32] See Table 2, pp. 216–217 above.

pany: eyelets; waxes; adhesives; liquids, including finishes; fillers; softeners, etc.; and insole reinforcing. Given the importance of a long line in competition, and the relative advantages the long-line seller has in adding another item over the single line seller,[33] the diminution of the length of United's line and the creation of a fairly large new multi-product seller in the supplies field will add a very important element of competition to the whole supply field. It may be expected that United will re-enter certain of the fields which the New Company occupies. Thus the reinforcing of welt insoles, which would go to the New Company, might be taken up again by United rather soon because of the technical importance of the insole characteristics in the design of welt sewing, outsole stitching, and lasting machinery for welt shoes, all fields which are major revenue producers for United. On the other hand, until United re-entered the cement shoe field, it would hardly be expected to re-enter the field of adhesives, even though cement lasting and other cement operations are important for other shoe constructions.

If a New Company operating in the cement shoe, eyeletting, and supplies fields were created by divestiture, the question arises, which, if any, of the restrictions set out under (3) above should apply to it, and in particular whether or not it should be permitted to continue to operate on a lease basis, with service in the lease bundle. There are strong arguments pro and con on this question. First, the New Company as a newborn innocent may be presumed to be free of the sins of its parent and thus it may be argued that the Court has no power to impose on it restrictions which it can impose on United only because of the latter's liability for violation of the Sherman Act. The invalidity of this argument will be assumed without discussion, as the problem seems purely formal; but it may have legal substance. Secondly, the New Company is being launched into a machinery market in which a substantial degree of competition already exists: it will have, at the outset, less than 50 per cent of the cement-shoe-machinery market and some 80 per cent of the eyeletting-machinery market.[34] Since leasing per se is not illegal, but becomes bad only in the context of market domination, it would not be necessary to impose a sale policy on the New Company to keep it from violating the law. Further, as indicated in the discussion above,[35] Compo would probably desire to continue leasing. If the New Company is

[33] See pp. 229–231 above.   [34] See Table 4, p. 45.   [35] Above, p. 278.

forced to sell only, Compo might find itself forced to do likewise; if not, Compo can continue its present marketing policies undisturbed.

On the other side, the desirability of eliminating leasing from the market to the extent possible, in view of its history, argues for the imposition of the prohibition. Further, the not entirely remote possibility of non-competitive market sharing between the New Company and Compo and non-re-entry on the part of United into the cement-shoe field should be guarded against by providing the same kind of competition from second-hand and copied machinery that which a sales market creates in this field as in other shoe machinery fields. This argument is reinforced by the fact that leasing probably operates to facilitate a live-and-let-live market-sharing policy, with neither Compo nor the New Company making much effort to attract customers away from the other, because of the strong customer-distributor tie which prevails under a lease-bundle system. Certainly, if leasing is allowed, modifications of the lease, by the removal of full-capacity clauses and termination charges, and shortening the term to five years, should be ordered so as to reduce the strength of the tie of lessee to lessor. Finally, it is not clear that the imposition of a sales policy on the New Company will cause Compo to follow suit. This would most probably be the case if Compo were facing United; with a rival more nearly its own size, Compo might try to compete against a sales marketing policy with service sold separately by continuing to offer shoe manufacturers the lease bundle. In fact, it is not unlikely that, in the first instance, such competition would create some difficulties for the success of the New Company's sales policy, though in the longer run this need not be the case, especially as the shoe manufacturers become accustomed to buying their other machines.

On the whole, the weight of the economic argument seems to be in favor of preventing the New Company from leasing; not so considerations of equity, especially if Compo's views and the testimony of the shoe manufacturers are accorded much importance. There seem to be no good reasons for imposing on the New Company the other restrictions which were recommended to be imposed on United with respect to acquisitions, dealings in second-hand machinery, and patents. In general, it would appear inequitable and undesirable to create restrictions on the New Company which would operate directly to favor Compo at its expense, since there would not be the same disparity of an order of magnitude in size between the two that there is between United and its competitors, not to speak of the disparity in market position in the total shoe-machinery market. The only serious problem of future behavior of the New Company in respect to competitive policy, that it might merge with Compo, appears to be amply guarded against by Section 7 of the Clayton Act (as amended in 1950, 64 Stat. 1125).

Several transition periods would be involved in the formation of such a New Company. Some time would have to be allowed for its organization and the process of stock distribution, say eighteen months. Together with the three-year limit suggested above (1) for the separation of ownership of the New Company and United, this would mean nearly five years before the New Company was set up and operating with complete independence of United. The same period should provide a sufficient transition time for the New Company to move from a lease to a sale basis in its machinery operations, if such a change is required; and it would be more than ample for the revision of its lease terms in accordance with the previous suggestions, if sales are not required. If sales are required, whatever arrangements are provided for in the general lease-settlement negotiations[36] can be applied to machines to which the New Company acquires title, since these settlements will have been determined before the New Company actually starts operations.

4. ADDITIONAL REMEDIES IN THE SUPPLY FIELD

If both the injunctive and the divestiture measures set out in sections 2 and 3 above are put into effect, a considerable lessening of United's dominance in the field of shoe-factory supplies will occur. This diminution will arise chiefly from the divestitures proposed under (3); all that would be done by the injunctive measures proposed under (2) is the creation of enterprises which might profitably undertake to distribute shoe-factory supplies under certain conditions—namely, second-hand machinery dealers and machine-repair enterprises. United would still remain far and away the most important distributor of shoe-factory supplies and the most important producer of many of them, and it would continue to dominate

[36] Above, pp. 279–282.

the markets for many categories of supplies. The additional remedies suggested below aim at a further reduction of United's power in
the supplies field, and, in particular, are designed to provide the newly
created distributive outlets described above with something in the
way of supplies to distribute. The argument for applying these additional remedies becomes even stronger if the divestiture discussed
in (3) is not ordered.

The first restriction which should be laid on United's activities in
the supply field is an injunction prohibiting United from acting as a
distributor of supplies that it does not manufacture, for a period of
ten years. This injunction would reduce the volume of United's supply business by about a further $4 million per year: $1.4 million of
items for which United acts as exclusive distributor, $1.6 million of
items made to United's specifications by other manufacturers, and $1
million of items in neither category.[37] Enough has been said above[38]
to indicate the appropriateness of grouping the "United-specification"
items with the "exclusive-distributorship" items. The main result of
this injunction would be that these goods would tend to flow to the
shoe manufacturers through the distributive machinery which would
be created by the results of the orders under (2) above, as has been
indicated previously. This suggests that some transition period, say
two years, be allowed, within which United has to break off its
distributorship arrangements. With respect to some items in which
there is a high degree of machine intimacy, such as needles and awls,
it may be expected that United itself will undertake manufacture of
them: this is perfectly appropriate, since it would result in an increase
of competition in the sale of such items.

The second restriction should be a ban on acquisition of businesses, stock interests in businesses, and assets in the supply field,
similar to the one proposed in the machinery field. In logic, this
should be extended to require United to dispose of its stock holdings
in Tubular Rivet and Stud and Torrington; but, since it would be
required to cease acting as distributor for their products, the divestiture hardly seems important enough to justify the injunction. This
ban should terminate in ten years, and it should extend to fields of
shoe factory supplies which United does not now distribute, as long
as they are shoe factory supplies. The ban should not be interpreted

[37] See Table 2, pp. 216–217 for a list of all the items involved and the sales volume
of each in 1948f.   [38] See above, pp. 219–221, 230–231.

to prohibit United's entry into the tanning business, or United's entry into the manufacture of synthetic leather or leather substitutes of a new kind, if United chooses to direct some of its released resources to these fields. The purpose of the order is obvious: it neutralizes some of United's headstart advantages and its natural tendency to grow whether real social economies are involved or not,[39] and it allows other suppliers in the field a chance to achieve such growth as might put them on a more equal competitive footing with United in the future.

Finally, United's present system of quantity (actually volume) discounts on certain supplies[40] should be enjoined, and only such quantity (not volume) discounts should be permitted as can be justified in terms of direct cost savings. The quantity discount now operates to give low prices to very large manufacturers, who in its absence might be inclined to become self-suppliers, either through manufacture or through contracts with manufacturers, of some of the items to which the plan applies. Its continued existence would tend to maintain these buyers as customers of United and make it difficult for new sellers to reach them, since the new sellers might not yet find it possible, in terms of their costs and the volume of their business, to offer the kind of discounts offered by United. The standard of direct cost benefit used as a test for justification of any new quantity discount is somewhat more stringent than the usual Robinson-Patman Act standard of cost saving,[41] but it is the only meaningful one from an economic point of view. Since this injunction goes beyond what is ordinarily demanded by the law, it should be limited to a ten-year term, and thereafter United would be bound only by the standards of the Robinson-Patman Act.[42]

Assuming that these restraints on United's supply activities are ordered, and that the divestiture described in (3) is carried out, there appears to be no warrant for any further divestiture in the field of supplies. In particular, the complete divorce between machine and supply activities which the Government has requested (in the absence of a tri-partite dissolution of United's machine business?)[43] is unnecessary and inequitable. In the first place, there has been no

[39] See pp. 229–230 above.   [40] Above, pp. 247–250.
[41] See Note: "Proof of Cost Differentials under the Robinson-Patman Act," 65 *Harv. law. rev.* 1011.
[42] Incidentally, it is fairly clear from the evidence that United's present discount system does in fact violate the Robinson-Patman Act.   [43] See above, pp. 272–275.

showing of market power, or of any live current intent to monopolize for several important supply fields, particularly the activities of
United's three subsidiaries which distribute independently: Hoague-
Sprague, shoes boxes and box-forming machinery; United Last Co.,
lasts; and F. W. Mears Co., wood heels. Together these account for
about a third of United's total supply business.[44] Second, it seems
difficult to devise a practicable plan for divorcing United's sales
activities, given the United manufacture of the products, and the
existence of a substantial network of field offices needed for servicing. The economies of selling the supplies United and some of its
branches and subsidiaries manufacture through this organization
are obvious; they will be increased when United needs a field sales
organization for machinery sales. Further, the genuine technical and
research economies in integrating the production of machines and
some supplies are ignored. Finally, the remedies already suggested
have a great enough likelihood of success to make dubious the propriety of imposing so drastic a remedy as the complete divorce of
supply and machine operations.

5. TANNING MACHINERY: THE OUNCE
OF PREVENTION

Economists rush in where lawyers fear to tread (and judges need
not follow). In spite of the negative conclusions on liability in tanning machinery reached above[45] and the apparent abandonment by
the Government of this part of the Complaint,[46] is there some reason
and some legal basis for ordering United to abandon its attempts
to institute leasing on a unit-charge basis in the field of tanning
machinery, especially if it is expected that, as a result of the rest of
the decree, United will increase its activities in that field?

The reason for such an order is that, even though the Government failed to provide enough evidence to prove its contention that
Turner Tanning, United's subsidiary, had a position of market
dominance in the industry, what evidence there was in fact pointed
to this conclusion. The verdict should be "not proven," rather than
"not guilty." Turner's market share, on one estimate, appeared to be

---

[44] See Table 4, pp. 222–223 for market share, volume of business, and conclusions
on market power; pp. 232–243 for discussion of intent.
[45] Pp. 266–268.
[46] It is not discussed in the Government *Briefs* on Liability and Relief.

43 per cent. Turner advertised itself as the "largest concern in the world devoted to the manufacture of hide-and-leather-working machinery" in its 1950 catalogue.[47] Such other companies as appear in the evidence are for the most part considerably smaller than Turner. S-339 a and b purport to show that Turner manufactured 22 machine types, half of which were made by 6 or more other manufacturers; 7 major competitors manufactured from 3 to 17 types; there were 8 minor competitors. On this basis, and the general history of the drive toward monopoly in United's shoe machinery operations, as well as the assumption that monopoly is necessary, which underlies United's arguments about leasing and research, is it safe to allow the introduction of leasing by United, especially if it succeeds in coupling all the new types of machinery in the market to the leasing system? Or is it wise to try to prevent this development now, at the point at which United energy will probably be directed into tanning-machinery research whether or not it can operate under lease arrangements?

On the other side are several points. First, the United documents cited by the Government reveal much resistance to leasing among the tanners and even among the officers of Turner.[48] Second, the exemplary effect of the shoe-machinery decree may well be sufficient to make United change its mind about the virtues of leasing. Third, the road to acquisition of competitive tanning-machinery companies has been closed by the amendment of Section 7 of the Clayton Act; this road was open for United in the shoe-machinery field.

As for the legal basis, there is the discretion of the Trial Court and the much quoted words of Mr. Justice Cardozo in United States v. Swift and Company[49] which couple the dangers of size and a past history of abusive use of power. Those words were used as an argument against modifying a decree; will they serve to justify drawing one? Or are remedies without wrongs not ghosts, but hobgoblins in the law?

[47] S-132.   [48] G-4503, XVII, 263 ff., G-4505, XVII, 267 ff.
[49] 286 US 106 at 116.

Part Four

The Outcome of the Case:
Some Lessons from It

IX. The Outcome
of the Case

1. THE OPINION OF THE DISTRICT COURT

Five years and two months after the Government filed its complaint, the District Court of Massachuetts handed down its opinion and decree in the case of the United States *v.* United Shoe Machinery Corporation.[1] The Court found United liable under Section 2 of the Sherman Act in monopolizing the shoe machinery market, and in monopolizing the markets for some shoe machinery supplies. The other important charges of the complaint—that United was attempting to monopolize the shoe machinery market, that United was attempting to monopolize the markets in shoe machinery supplies other than the ones it already dominated, and that United was attempting to monopolize the market in tanning machinery—were dismissed. The first was dismissed as having no validity separate from the actual monopolization;[2] the second and third as not supported by the evidence.[3]

The flavor of the opinion can be illustrated by quoting three passages from the Court's own summary. First, on United's market power:

United Shoe Machinery Corporation manufactures all the principal types of machines used in all the major processes of shoemaking. It distributes the more important types only through leases. These leases have many "partnership" features which go beyond insuring United prompt,

---

[1] The opinion was handed down on 18 February 1953; it is reported in 110 F Supp. 295. References here are to the pages of the pamphlet copy.

[2] P. 107.   [3] P. 108.

periodic payment of rent. Through these leases United maintains contacts with approximately 90 per cent of all shoe factories. It supplies more than 75 per cent of the demand for shoe machinery (excluding dry thread sewing machinery). From these and other facts, such as analysis of United's pricing practices and a comparison between United and its competitors in terms of financial resources, of facilities, of accumulated experience, and of variety of machines offered, it appears that United has such substantial market power as to give it effective control of the shoe machinery market.[4]

Second, on the sources of United's power:

United's market control is attributable first, to the company's original constitution, approved in 1918 by the Supreme Court, second, to the company's superior products and services, and third, to the company's business practices. Of these practices, the most important have been the leases already mentioned. . . . Though these practices and methods have not been predatory, immoral, nor, on their face, discriminatory as between different customers, they have operated as barriers to competition. United's market strength has also been increased to some extent by its acquisitions of patents and its purchases, for scrap, of second hand machines.[5]

Finally, on the law of monopolization under Section 2 of the Sherman Act:

Since Judge Learned Hand's opinion in 1945 in *United States* v. *Aluminum Company of America,* 2nd Cir., 148 F. (2d) 416, and the 1948 opinion of the Supreme Court in *United States* v. *Griffith,* 334 US 100, that provision of #2 of the Sherman Act addressed to "every person who shall monopolize . . . any part of" interstate commerce has been so interpreted as to reach any enterprise that has exercised power to control a defined market, if that power is to any substantial extent the result of barriers erected by its own business methods (even though not predatory, immoral, or restraining trade in violation of #1 of the Sherman Act), unless the enterprise shows that the barriers are *exclusively* the result of superior skill, superior products, natural advantages, technological or economic efficiency, scientific research, low margins of profit maintained permanently and without discrimination, legal licenses, or the like.[6]

In its discussion of the law of monopolization, as applied to shoe-machinery market, the Court extended the doctrines of *Aluminum* in an important way.[7] Like other writers and judges, the judge saw

[4] P. 1.   [5] P. 2.   [6] P. 2.   [7] This discussion occupies pp. 97–107 of the Opinion.

Aluminum[8] as marking a turning point in the interpretation of #2 of the Sherman Act. He found that "comparable principles" were applied by the Supreme Court in the *Griffith, Schine, Paramount,* and *Columbia Steel* cases, and that "the technique and the language of Judge Hand were expressly approved" in the *Tobacco* case.[9, 10] In these decisions the judge saw three related but distinct strands: an enterprise which acquires or maintains a power to exclude others by methods involving unreasonable restraints of trade in violation of #1 violates #2 of the Sherman Act (the traditional view); an enterprise which has the power to exclude competition, and either exercises it or has the power to do so violates #2 whether or not any restraints illegal under #1 are involved (*Griffith*); an enterprise which has acquired an overwhelming share of the market "monopolizes" by virtue of that fact, unless it can fairly be said that its monopoly has been "thrust upon it," or is attributable to nothing more than "superior skill, foresight, and industry" (*Aluminum*). Hand's definition of the "thrust upon" exception was broadened by Wyzanski to exempt a defendant who could show that it owed its monopoly:

solely to superior skill, superior products, natural advantages, (including accessibility to raw materials or markets), economic or technological efficiency (including scientific research), low margins of profit maintained permanently and without discrimination, or licenses conferred by, and used within, the limits of law (including patents on one's own inventions, or franchises granted directly to the enterprise by a public authority).[11]

The first ground of decision was not open to the Court, since the lease arrangements—which might be viewed in their context as contracts in restraint of trade in violation of #1—had been earlier approved by the Supreme Court, in decisions not yet overruled. The Court found both the second and third grounds of decision applicable to the facts of the present case, and did not distinguish between them. "The facts show that (1) defendant has, and exer-

---

[8] *United States* v. *Aluminum Co. of America*, 148 F (2d) 416.

[9] Opinion, p. 99.

[10] The citations are: *United States* v. *Griffith*, 334 US 100 (1948); *Schine Chain Theatres, Inc.* v. *United States*, 334 US 110 (1948); *United States* v. *Paramount Theatres, Inc.*, 334 US 131 (1948); *United States* v. *Columbia Steel Co.*, 334 US 495 (1948); and *American Tobacco Co.* v. *United States*, 328 US 781 (1946).

[11] Opinion, p. 101.

cises, such overwhelming strength in the shoe machinery market that it controls that market, (2) this strength excludes some potential, and limits some actual, competition, and (3) this strength is not attributable solely to defendant's ability, economies of scale, research, natural advantages, and adaptation to inevitable economic laws."[12] Thus the legal test of monopoly contained in the District Court can be summed up in the slogan: the achievement or retention of dominant market power by business methods which are more restrictive than necessary is monopolization under Section 2 of the Sherman Act.

With respect to shoe machinery supplies, the Court found that United's power in supplies markets rested on its power in the machinery market. The supply fields in which United was dominant were identified as cutters and irons, nails and tacks, eyelets, and wire, in each of which United's market share was over half. In the other supply fields—shoe boxes, lasts, wood heels, shanks, adhesives, finishes, and reinforcing materials—in which United's market share was less than half, it had only such power as flowed from its long line, its business relations with shoe manufacturers, and the comparative weakness of its competitors. This did not justify a finding of monopolization in these fields.

2. THE APPEAL

United appealed the District Court's decision on 16 April 1953, taking all but full advantage of its 60-day allowance. The main argument on which it based its appeal was one of law: the District Court had not correctly interpreted the sense of #2 of the Sherman Act in applying it to the facts which it had found.[13]

[12] Pp. 101–2.

[13] See *Brief for Appellant,* in the Supreme Court of the United States, *United Shoe Machinery Corporation* v. *United States,* Oct. Term 1953, No. 3494. The *Brief* is dated April 1954.

To be sure, United challenged the Court's findings of fact on many points as well, but the thrust of the Brief lies in its argument on the law. The oral argument by United's counsel before the Court makes this clear.

The major arguments on the facts contained in the Brief were: (1) Leasing was neither restrictive nor exclusionary, and the Court erred in so finding; pp. 64–68. (2) The lease "bundle" was not a barrier to competition; pp. 68–70. (3) The concept of a "market for shoe machinery" underlying the Court's conclusion on United's market share is fallacious; pp. 70–73. (4) The conclusions on United's power in the supplies markets are erroneous, since they rest only on findings of market share, which should be viewed in historical perspective, and in the context of United's business; pp. 73–75.

United's counsel contended that Section 2 of the Act made illegal monopolizing *conduct,* not merely situations in which a firm could be shown to have a dominant share of some market.[14] The District Court had explicitly stated that United's conduct did not fall within the ban of the law;[15] the same course of conduct and the same business practices had been twice approved by the Supreme Court. How could there then be a finding of liability, based "solely on economic considerations"?

In the words of the Brief:

The invalidity of the criteria adopted by the Court below is forcibly illustrated by applying them to the circumstances of the case at bar. . . .

What should United have done? In this background should it immediately after the decision in the Sherman Act case have discontinued its system of distribution which the Court then said had "become so widely and firmly established as to render the substitution of a different system practically impossible" or should it have made such a substitution immediately after the Court decided in the Clayton Act case that certain provisions of its leases did not offend that Act as substantially lessening competition and tending to create a monopoly? And if it should not have changed its practices then, when should it have done so? No such time can be set, for the position of United and its practices have never created a situation in which there was any more warrant for demanding a change than there was when those cases were tried and decided. The Court below did not attempt to set the time at which United first violated the Act, and pointed to no change in practice which would establish that time.

The result of adopting the criteria laid down by the Court below would be that a concern having that percentage of a "market" which may be considered as showing that it has "market control" would be obliged to employ only such practices as would encourage and promote competition with it to the fullest extent. . . .

It is incredible that the statute was ever intended to have such a meaning.

It is one thing to limit by law the individual's freedom of choice in the

---

[14] The argument is summarized in *Brief for Appellant,* pp. 52–62.

[15] See District Court Opinion, pp. 105–6. "It is only fair to add that the more than 14,000 page record, and the more than 5,000 exhibits, representing the diligent seven year search made by Government counsel aided by this Court's orders giving them full access to United's files during the last 40 years, show that United's power does not rest on predatory practices. Probably few monopolies could produce a record so free from any taint of that kind of wrongdoing. The violation with which United is now charged depends not on moral considerations, but solely on economic considerations."

interest of others. It is quite another thing to leave the individual ostensibly free to choose among several courses, none of which is proscribed by the positive or even the moral law, and then to make a case against him because his actual choice is deemed by a court not to be "economically inevitable."

The rule of reason still applies to Section 2 as it does to Section 1. The same rule of reason which leaves scope for ordinary economic motivations and business behavior under Section 1 must also leave room for the pursuit of the "normal business purpose" (citing Columbia Steel).

It still must be true that the law "trusts to its prohibitions" and does not affirmatively "compel competition nor require all that is possible." (Citing *US* v. *United States Steel Corporation*, 251 US 417 at 451 (1920)). Its prohibition against "monopolizing" must not be perverted into a positive requirement of conducting business in a fashion which creates a maximum of opportunities for competitors to take it away. This would be contrary to all known laws of economics and to fundamental principles of competition.[16]

Acting perhaps in accord with the legal saw that it is the holding and not the opinion which is significant, the Supreme Court upheld the court below, *per curiam* and without opinion, on 17 May 1954.[17] Thus it left unresolved some of the important doctrinal problems raised both by Judge Wyzanski's definition of the "thrust upon" exceptions in the Hand doctrine of liability under Section 2 of the Sherman Act, and by United's objections to the whole theory on which the decision rested.

3. THE DECREE

The substantive provisions of the decree can be grouped in seven categories[18]

(1) Lease or sale option (paragraphs 5 and 7). United must offer for sale any machine it offers for lease. Lease and sale terms must be such

[16] *Brief,* pp. 57-59.   [17] The decision is reported in 347, US 521.

[18] The full decree, as modified, is reproduced as Appendix B. All references are to the numbered paragraphs of that Appendix.

The original decree was part of the Opinion, dated 18 Feb. 1953. This was modified by two orders of the Court. The first, dated 12 July 1954, modified paragraphs 12 and 13 of the original decree to allow the bona fide sale of or assignment of patents, to define the time scope of patents included under the provisions of 12 more clearly, to define employment in 13 more clearly, and to add "patent applications" wherever "patents" appeared. The second, dated 17 September 1954, modified paragraphs 2 and 10 of the original. "Grommets and hooks" were deleted from both paragraphs, and paragraph 2 was modified to permit the defendant freedom of action outside the fields of shoe machinery and shoe factory supplies.

"as do not make it substantially more advantageous for a shoe factory to lease rather than to buy a machine." The Court will not supervise the terms, but if they fail to meet the criterion, the Government may intervene and ask for further relief. United may not refuse to lease or sell any machine to a prospective customer, if that machine is being commercially offered for lease or sale, except for good cause. Anyone refused a machine shall have the right to intervene and have the Court hear his claim; in that case United shall be required to justify its refusal.

(2) *Lease terms and lease practices (paragraphs 6 and 8)*. New leases must be of no more than five years' duration, and after one year must be terminable at will by the lessee. On such termination the lessee can be required to pay all rentals already due, shipping charges, costs of broken and missing parts, and three months' additional monthly rentals (but not unit charges). No difference in return terms may be made when return is due to replacement by a competitive machine though terms may be more favorable to the lessee if return is due to machine defects, customer abandonment of operations, or customer dissatisfaction after a trial period. No other return charges or deferred payments are permissible. Leases may include unit charges as well as monthly rentals, or either alone; but no monthly minima on unit charges may be set. No leases may contain a full capacity clause. Each lease must state explicitly what services and privileges it covers. No right of deduction fund or similar provision is permissible. Service must be charged for separately, if United wishes to continue to provide service. Service charges may be on an operation-by-operation basis, or an annual contract basis (but no longer), and any economies in annual contracts over other arrangements may be reflected in the tariff of service charges. Charges must be uniform as between lessees and purchasers of machines. Travel time may be billed separately, and thus service charges may vary for factories in different locations. United shall not be required to give service in connection with machines or parts manufactured by others. Parts must be made available on the same terms to all customers, whether they own or lease machines, and whether or not they use United's service facilities. United may provide up to 30 days' free installation, instruction and repair services with any machine; or 60 days' free services under a trial rider to the lease.

United may vary the substance of lease forms, except for the actual pricing provisions, only with the Court's approval. United is not required to present to the Court its methods of arriving at pricing provisions, but they must be non-discriminatory as between customers of the same general class, except for deposit provisions, which may vary from lessee to lessee.

(3) *Settlement of outstanding leases (paragraph 9)*. United must con-

fer with the Government, with representatives of the National Shoe Manufacturers association, and with any lessees who have formally asked to be consulted (by becoming intervenors in the case) and prepare a plan for terminating all outstanding leases. The plan must make non-discriminatory provisions whereby, within a reasonable period of time, lessees under existing leases may buy or lease under the new leases those machines now in their factories. These arrangements must be at least as favorable to the shoe factories as the new lease terms and schedule of sales prices.

(4) Reorganization of United's supply business (paragraphs 10 and 11). United must dispose of its business and the business of its subsidiaries in the manufacture and distribution of tacks, nails, and eyelets. United must cease to distribute any supplies not manufactured by itself or a corporation in which it owns at least 20 per cent of the Common Stock.

(5) Restraints on acquisitions (paragraphs 13, 14, 15, 16). United may not acquire any shoe machinery or shoe factory supply business, or any stock in such business, if the transaction involves more than \$10,000. United may not acquire any patent or patent application except those arising from the work of its employees unless it agrees to license the acquired patents on a reasonable royalty basis for use in shoe machinery manufacture or shoe manufacture (see below). United may not acquire an exclusive license under any patent unless it receives the right to sub-license, and agrees to do so as with acquired patents. United may not buy any second-hand shoe machinery, except for no more than \$25,000 worth per annum for experimental purposes. But its right to repossess its own machinery sold under conditional sales agreements is retained.

(6) Patent licensing (paragraph 12). United must give any applicant a non-exclusive license on a non-discriminatory reasonable royalty basis on any patent held by it at the time of the beginning of the Decree's operation, or any patent resulting from an application filed by that time. The licenses may restrict the use of the patent to the manufacturer and sale of shoe machinery, shoe factory supplies, and the like. The licenses must provide for access by the licensee to United's technical information, at a reasonable charge.

(7) Quantity discounts (paragraph 17). Any discount system used in the sale of supplies must comply with the Robinson-Patman Act.

The major jurisdictional provisions of the decree are:

(1) The decree goes into effect on 1 January 1955, and will be subject to general review on 1 January 1965, when both parties shall report on its effects. At that time, either party may petition for its modification, in view of the then state of the industry, and United's market power at the

time. (Paragraphs 1, 18, others *passim*.) Except as noted in (2) below, United's obligations under the decree begin on 1 January 1955.

(2) United has till 1 April 1955 to file a plan for settling outstanding leases, and a plan for disposing of its business in tacks, nails, and eyelets. It has till 1 January 1958 to stop distributing supplies not of its or its subsidiaries' manufacture. (Paragraphs 9, 10, 11.)

(3) The provisions of the decree are limited to United's activities in the fields of shoe machinery and shoe factory supplies or in relation to the shoe manufacturing industry. (Paragraph 2.)

(4) The provisions of the decree are limited to United's activities in the United States. (Paragraph 22.)

(5) The Court retains jurisdiction, and either party may apply as appropriate for modifications of the decree. (Paragraph 23.)

4. THE DECREE: THE SETTLEMENT OF OUTSTANDING LEASES

The first problem which arose under the Decree was the settlement of the outstanding leases under the provisions of paragraph 9. Negotiations between United and the National Shoe Manufacturers Association, representing the lessees, began in September 1954; agreement for a plan for settlement was finally reached, not without pressure from the Court, nine months later, and was embodied in an Order of the Court dated 1 June 1955.[19]

---

[19] The basic documents covering this negotiation are:

    i. Exhibits N-1 and N-2, Transcripts of two conferences between representatives of United and of NSMA, the first held 14 September 1954; the second, 15–16 December 1954.

    ii. United's proposal for settlement dated March 30, 1955.

    iii. Government's objections to United proposal, dated 29 April 1955.

    iv. NSMA objections to United proposal, dated 29 April 1955.

    v. New England Shoe and Leather Association objections to United proposal, dated 2 May 1955.

    vi. Transcript of Hearing, 7 March 1955 (pp. 1–77).

    vii. Order of Court, 8 March 1955.

    viii. USMC, *Explanatory Report of Basic Material Used in the Determination of Optional Sales Prices for Outstanding Machines as Contained in the Plan Filed 30 March 1955* (dated 9 March 1955). Prepared by Joel Dean Associates, Filed 20 April 1955.

    ix. NSMA, *Sales Prices for Outstanding Shoe Machinery, A Basis for Negotiation* (dated 7 May 1955). Prepared by Andrews, Anthony and MacLean. Filed 13 May 1955.

    x. USMC Plan for Terminating Form A Leases (revised), dated 16 May 1955.

    xi. Transcript of Hearing, 17 May 1955 (pp. 1–47).

    xii. Order of Court, dated 1 June 1955.

The important issues arising in the settlement proposals were three: what options is the lessee to have with respect to continuing to hold the machine under lease and on what terms, purchasing it and on what terms, returning it and on what terms; what is done about service for these machines; what happens to the lessee's credits in the Right of Deduction Fund.

United's first plan[20] offered lessees four options:

(i) to terminate the lease in accordance with its old provisions;

(ii) to purchase the machine, at a price based on the new sales price and the age of the machine (the age-price formula is shown in Table 1 below);

(iii) to terminate the old (Form A) lease and retain the machine on a new (Form B) lease, in which case United waives deferred payments due under the Form A lease, and initial payments (if any) due under the Form B lease, and makes available the lessee's credit balance in the Right of Deduction Fund to be applied to his payments under the Form B lease, spread equally over its five-year term;

(iv) to continue to hold the machine on a Form A lease until its expiry.

In each case, service arrangements would follow the form of the option: service would continue to be provided without separate charge under the fourth option, and would be provided at the lessee's election, according to the tariff of service charges, under options two and three. The Right of Deduction Fund credits would be available to the lessee only under the third option.

This plan drew objections from all the other parties concerned: the Government, the National Shoe Manufacturers Association, and the New England Shoe and Leather Association, which had also become an intervenor.[21] All thought the sales prices too high, all objected to the continuation of Form A leases with their original provisions, all objected to the restrictions placed on the lessee's use of his credits in the Right of Deduction Fund; all objected to the requirement of deferred payment if the leases were terminated and its waiver if they were transformed into Form B leases. The NESLA thought the age-price formula did not decline rapidly enough as machine-age increased. The Government objected to the use of the new sales prices as a basis for the sale of the outstanding machines. Instead it

[20] Dated 30 March 1955.
[21] See their respective Objections, filed 29 April, 29 April, and 2 May 1955.

proposed the old sales formula used by United for General department machines: factory cost plus development expenses plus 100 per cent. To this basis, a steep declining balance curve should be applied to get an age-price formula.

It is inappropriate to characterize this first proposal as the result in any sense of negotiation between United and the lessees' representatives. It was simply a unilateral proposal by United. At the meeting of 14 September, United merely presented an outline of the settlement proposals without discussing any figures, since it had not yet announced either its new sales prices or its new lease terms. There was debate, not entirely cordial, between United and counsel for the NSMA, and other NSMA representatives on the "illegality" of existing leases, on ownership rights in the Right of Deduction Fund, and on other similar matters. There was also some unfavorable comment on United's ability and willingness to provide some prices as a basis for discussion. President Brown of United told the shoe manufacturers that United had suffered very substantial increases in its manufacturing costs since the last increase in lease terms in 1950.[22] At the second meeting, on 15, 16 December 1954 Professor Dean, United's consulting economist, outlined the methods for finding the sales price equivalent to the lease return, using the Rex pulling-over machine as an example. Again, the shoe manufacturers were voluble in their criticism. They thought the price of used machines much too high and they objected to the new lease terms as well. The NSMA counsel requested the tabulations and computations underlying the figures presented at the meeting; these President Brown refused to give.[23] Finally, the figures for used machine prices presented at the

[22] See Transcript, Ex. N-1, *passim*. Especially noteworthy was the sharp tone of Johnson, President of Endicott-Johnson Co., United's third largest customer. He asserted (p. 76) that of his approximately 5000 leases, nearly half had run more than 20 years, before 1945.

Winslow, United's Board Chairman, flatly stated that the principles of lease sale equivalency, which, on United's formula, underlay the sales prices for outstanding machines, were not a matter for discussion with the NSMA. They were up to United, and, ultimately, to the Court (pp. 80–81).

[23] Transcript, Ex. N-2.

McAllister's (NSMA counsel) request and Brown's refusal are on pp. 111–16. Again, the whole proceeding was marked by something less than good temper. Johnson was particularly sharp again, so were several others. The tone of the shoe manufacturers in their discussions at these two meetings presents an interesting contrast to the tone of the testimony of the shoe manufacturers—a different group of persons—in the course of the trial. See above, pp. 202–203.

meeting were only very little different from the figures incorporated in United's 30 March proposal.

As a result of United's refusal to disclose the basis of Dean's computations, there was a hearing on 7 March 1955; this was followed by an Order, dated 8 March, requiring United to furnish the information requested. During the Hearing, the Court indicated some dissatisfaction with the course and pace of the negotiations,[24] and the Order also contained some language which might be expected to stimulate the parties to move toward agreement.[25]

United finally made available the computations underlying its proposals, and the NSMA prepared a detailed criticism of them.[26]

The United document first derives a sales-price equivalent to the new Form B lease terms, then takes this as the zero-year price for a formula relating prices of outstanding machines to their ages. The equivalent sales price is calculated as follows. The extra flow of payments a manufacturer holding a machine under lease over its entire economic life beyond that which he would make if he owned the machine is estimated. The chief element in this flow is of course the payments under the lease; others are differences in taxes, in insurance costs, and the salvage value which an owner would receive at the end of the machine's economic life, but which a lessee would not. Some items, such as service, or associated wage costs, are the same

[24] Hearing, Transcript, p. 22: "Moreover, if it takes too long to work out the decree in detail, and too many hearings are involved, and the practical value of the decree seems as though it will be lost, the Court will feel bound to move more drastically in amending the decree than it did in preparing the decree. . . . If it (the optional system) turns out to be unpractical, I know which of the two alternatives I shall follow."

[25] Order, p. 1, 2: "If the parties are unable substantially to agree upon all major features of a plan, it may turn out that the Court may have only three practical alternatives:

(1) to leave the existing leases to run their course,
(2) to terminate without financial adjustment all outstanding leases on the ground that they are unlawful, or
(3) to impose a less than subtle formula but one that can be made effective promptly enough to have practical consequences. This third is much the most likely course, and the formula would probably be drawn from the testimony heretofore given."

[26] United's analysis was prepared by Prof. Joel Dean of Columbia University School of Business and the staff of Joel Dean Associates. The NSMA criticism and counterproposals were prepared by Messrs. Anthony, Andrews, and MacLean of Harvard Graduate School of Business Administration, with the assistance of some other members of their faculty, and some of the Economics Department of Massachusetts Institute of Technology. The full titles of the two documents are shown as items (viii) and (ix) of the list contained on p. 309 above, footnote 19.

under ownership or lease, and thus cancel out of the computation. A suitable discount rate is then applied to the dated items in this flow, and its present value computed. This present value is the "economically equivalent" sales price of the machine.

The basic elements in the estimate are: the lease terms, the discount factor, the economic life of the machine, the rate of use of the machine, the salvage value of the machine at the end of its economic life, and the age-price formula for outstanding machines. On all these points, the United estimates were severely criticized by NSMA. On the whole, the criticisms appear sound. It was not the case, however, that the alternate method for estimating each particular element proposed by NSMA was itself free from criticism. In the following paragraphs, the conflicting views are present briefly.

United used the new Form B lease terms as its basis for computing equivalent sales prices, and thus the price of outstanding machines. NSMA pointed out that on a crude estimate, this basis placed a value of approximately $225 million on the stock of leased machines, compared with their 1954 balance sheet value of $53.5 million at cost, and $28.1 million depreciated. On the basis of the old General department formula of manufacturing cost plus development expense plus 100 per cent, the machines outstanding, if new, would sell at $120 million. NSMA asserted that between January and May 1955 United shipped 1000 new machines, mostly under lease, indicating the lack of "equivalence" in the sales prices. NSMA argued that since the shoe manufacturer, if he continued to lease the machines he then held, would do so largely under Form A leases of various dates, the lease basis for the computation should be some average of the Form A rates of the relevant time periods.[27] The question at issue here was how should the inventory profits of the machine revaluation implicit in the new prices be divided between United and its lessees. The United formula claimed them all for United, on the ground, presumably, that the machines were United's property. NSMA appeared to claim them all on behalf of the shoe manufacturer, presumably on the ground that he would have liked to have them. While the property argument, narrowly viewed, is correct, and the Court explicitly denied itself the power to fix the level of prices,[28] it still can be argued that a broad view of the equities required some division of these profits between United

27 See NSMA, pp. 1–14.   28 See the Decree, para. 5 particularly, and generally.

and the lessees. After all, the revaluation itself arose from the anti-trust decree, absent which the lessees would have gone on enjoying the preëxisting Form A rates for many years. Indeed, given the record of United's sluggishness in revising prices, the 1950 rates might well have persisted for a decade or even two.

Both United and NSMA agreed that the appropriate discount factor to apply was some figure for the shoe manufacturer's cost of capital. United interpreted this to mean the cost of capital for the shoe industry, in the aggregate; or, put another way, the cost of the representative dollar of capital to the shoe industry. United estimated this cost at 10 per cent. NSMA argued that the appropriate figure was the cost of capital to the representative shoe manufacturer—either the median shoe manufacturer, or the manufacturer of the median shoe. Since the representative shoe manufacturer (in either of these senses) is much smaller in size than the firm owning the representative dollar (i.e., the firm in the asset size array within which the median dollar falls), the appropriate capital cost is much higher. NSMA estimated it at 20 per cent, made up of 18 per cent experienced capital cost plus 2 per cent for "machinery risk" which the shoe manufacturers had not previously borne, but would bear for machines which they purchased.[29] NSMA's contention as to the appropriate concept of the cost of capital seems the correct one. In addition the United estimate was full of technical errors, and the NSMA estimate appeared free from them.[30] United estimated the capital cost for a company with some $70 million total assets, while the median shoe manufacturer has some $½ million total assets, and the manufacturer of the median shoe, $3-4 million. It is noteworthy that the United estimate of the cost of capital to the shoe manufacturer makes it about the same as

[29] The two sets of estimates are discussed in detail in United, Appendix III, and NSMA, Annex I, respectively.

[30] These errors were pointed out in the NSMA criticism. United included Goodyear, Goodrich and U. S. Rubber in its sample; these are not shoe manufacturers, except incidentally, and the cost of capital to them reflects the risks of tire manufacturing, not shoe manufacturing. The inclusion of these firms prevented United from observing the true relation of capital cost and size of firm, and justified the use of a sample of 25 large firms, including the three rubber companies. United failed to make as good use of its data as was possible: it utilized an average cost of capital to the firm over the period of observation for each, thus getting only 25 observations. It could have used each year's capital cost for each firm as a single observation, and corrected for serial correlation, yielding a much larger number of points in the sample. United used SEC data on flotation costs for large companies, without taking into account SEC data showing the relations between size and flotation cost.

the estimate of United's own earnings rate, as shown by the Dean study.[31]

United estimated the economic life of shoe machines as varying from 8 to 26 years, at "birth." It estimated that ⅓ of the active machines had "long" lives, averaging 16 years; ⅓, "medium" lives, averaging 12 years, and ⅓ "short" lives, averaging 8 years. Machines then inactive (no longer manufactured) were estimated to have economic lives averaging 6 years. NSMA attacked both the estimates and the methods of producing them, which involved statistical analyses of United's records of shipments and returns of machines in the past. NSMA, basing its own figures on the consensus offered by eight industry experts, gave the following as the estimated economic lives of thirty selected important machine types:

Years	Number of Machine Types
10	15
8	3
5	11
3	1

In the NSMA view, the inactive machines were all obsolete already, and therefore their estimated economic life was zero.[32] NSMA's method of estimation is of doubtful value. The industry experts can hardly be free from all bias, especially in the context of the case. But its criticisms of United's estimates appear to be sound. Both United's experience, as shown in the record, and United's recently negotiated BIR depreciation rates show an average life for leased machinery of 10 years. It is probably true that under the new situation in the industry, obsolescence will be somewhat more rapid than it has been in the past, and therefore historical experience cannot be applied without modification to predict the future economic life of shoe machinery.[33]

United's estimate of expected machine utilization was the result of a complex series of calculations. In general, it involved taking historical records of machine usage, and adjusting them for underutiliza-

---

[31] See p. 115–116 above.

[32] These points are discussed in detail in United, App. I, and NSMA, Annex III.

[33] In addition to these general criticisms, the NSMA report presented certain detailed criticisms of the statistical techniques involved in the United estimates. These were valid; in particular the criticism of the very small and erratic samples on which the later years of turnover-method estimates of economic life were based.

tion in the past, due to the lack of incentive for high utilization under the previous leases. United anticipated some 35 to 45 per cent higher machine utilization in the future than the average experienced in the period 1950–1954, a period of high shoe production. NSMA attacked these figures as too high, and offered figures some 25 to 35 percentage points lower, based on the judgment of shoe manufacturers. These appear unduly subjective, unless some technique for relating judgment to past experience is shown, as it was not in the NSMA document. But the United estimate does appear too high. It incorporated the doubtful assumption that every machine of a particular type in a factory could produce as much as did the best machine of that type in a past historical period. In addition, the United computations subjected the data to many rather arbitrary manipulations, so that the element of judgment played a large role in the final result.[34]

The two studies again differed sharply when it came to the estimate of salvage value. United defined it as the resale value, on an "as is" basis, of a machine at the end of its economic life. It estimated resale value from data available to it on second-hand sales of optional terms machinery. A scatter of machine age against resale price as shown in these sales provided the basis for a curve relating age to price, moving from 65 per cent of the new price for 2-year-old machines, through 35 per cent for 10-year-old machines and 14 per cent for 30-year-old machines to a low of 6 per cent for 40-year-olds.[35] NSMA offered a flat estimate of 15 per cent of the original price as the salvage value.[36] The United sample appears a poor one as a basis for predicting resale values of used major machines, when they come into the market in significant numbers. The

[34] For the detailed discussion, see United, App. II, and NSMA, Annex IV. Again the NSMA report presents a great deal of detailed technical criticism. The criticism of the United sample of shoe factories on which the estimate was based was particularly cogent. Though the sample contained 42 factories, the number represented for any particular machine type varied from 29 to as low as 9. In addition, the sample was stratified by factory size (10 cells) and process groups (8 cells); but other equally important variables determining machine utilization, such as location, price-line, frequency of product change, and the like, were uncontrolled.

[35] See United, Appendix IV. The curve was fitted freehand, and gave a very bad fit to the scatter, in the writer's judgment. A crude test made by fitting a freehand curve to the means of several subgroups of the data showed little consistent slope and no relation which appeared statistically significant.

[36] NSMA, p. 54. No argument is presented in support of this figure.

15 per cent figure suggested by NSMA seems not too far out of line with 12 per cent salvage value which United realized on the average by tearing down machines at the end of their lease lives. On the one hand, the parts are worth less than a functioning machine; on the other, the value of the parts to United may be high because of United's superior ability to recondition them and to salvage usable parts from a machine which cannot function efficiently as a whole.

The five factors examined above provided a basis for estimating the "equivalent sales price" for a new machine. To pass from this to the sales price for an outstanding machine required some formula for depreciating the price of the machine with time. United proposed a formula for active machines which went on a straight line basis from 90 per cent of the new price for 1-year-old machines to 15 per cent of the new price for 40-year-old machines. All older machines were treated as 40 years old. For inactive machines, the cut-off age was 26 years. NSMA proposed three formulae, moving on a declining balance basis from the zero year price to cut-off points of 15 per cent of the zero year price at ages 25, 20, and 15 years, corresponding to its estimates of different economic lives for various machine types.[37] NSMA rightly criticized the straight line relation between age and price relative to new price used by United. As the NSMA document argued at some length, wide experience in many second-hand markets shows a much faster rate of decline in value in the early years of a machine's life than in the later ones.

Finally, on 16 May 1955, the parties agreed on a compromise formula for settling the leases. The sales price terms of the agreed formula are shown for selected machine ages in Table 1 below. Table 1 also shows United's original proposal of 30 March, and the NSMA counter offers of 7 May. It is clear from the Table that the final compromise came much closer to the NSMA proposals than to those of United. How much of this was the result of the superior bargaining skill of the NSMA representatives, how much the result of the pressure placed on United by the remarks of the Court as to what might happen in the absence of agreement[38] is not known. It is clear from the statements of United counsel at the final hearing

[37] See Table 1 for the figures for both the United and NSMA proposals. For the detailed discussion, see United, Appendix VIII, and NSMA, Annex VI.

[38] See above, p. 312, footnotes 24 and 25.

TABLE 1
Prices for the Sale of Outstanding Machines:
United and NSMA Proposals and Final Agreed Compromise
Ratio of Machine Price at Indicated Age to Zero Year Price

Machine Age (Years)	Percentage Factor					
	(1)	(2)	(3)	(4)	(5)	(6)
0	*See below	92.0%	*See below	96.6%	95.8%	94.6%
1	90.1%	88.0	82.4%	89.9	87.7	84.3
3	86.4	80.0	73.8	77.9	73.5	67.0
5	82.6	72.0	65.7	67.5	61.6	53.3
7	78.9	64.0	58.5	58.5	51.6	42.3
10	73.2	55.0	48.8	47.2	39.7	30.0
12	69.5	50.0	43.0	40.9	33.2	23.8
15	63.8	42.5	35.8	33.0	25.5	16.8
17	60.1	37.5	31.4	28.6	21.4	15.0
20	54.4	30.0	26.2	23.1	16.4	
21	52.6	27.5	24.8	21.5	15.0	
25	45.1	17.5	19.8	16.1		
28	39.4	15.0	17.2	15.0		
30	35.7	.	16.0			
32	31.9		15.0			
35	26.3					
40	16.9					
41+	15.0					

(1) USMC proposal, 30 March 1955, active machine types.
(2) USMC proposal, 30 March 1955, inactive machine types.
(3) Compromise agreed on by parties and approved by Court, 17 May, 1955.
(4) National Shoe Manufacturers Association proposal for machines with cut-off points of 25 years.
   Note: On May 6, 1955, National Shoe Manufacturers Association offered to accept the 25-year cut-off point for all machines.
(5) National Shoe Manufacturers Association proposal for machines with cut-off points of 20 years.
(6) National Shoe Manufacturers Association proposal for machines with cut-off points of 15 years.
   *Purchase price for machines held on Request for Loan of Machines executed on or after May 17, 1954 that are less than 1 year old is the full sale price of the machine less any initial payment already paid.

that United viewed the results as a matter of bargaining, not as the fruit of an agreement on principles.[39]

The final agreement also met the manufacturers' objections to United's earlier proposal in respect to other aspects of the settlement. Under the plan of 16 May, the lessee was given the following options:

(i) To terminate the Form A lease and return the machine. He will be required to pay shipping costs, and the cost of broken and missing parts, but deferred payments will be waived.

(ii) To terminate the Form A lease and purchase the machine, in accordance with age-price schedule set forth. (Table 1 above, column 3.) Deferred payments are waived. Any credits in the Right of Deduction Fund may be applied against the purchase price of the machine, at the lessee's options.

(iii) To terminate the Form A lease and retain the machine under a new Form B lease. Both deferred payments due under the Form A lease, and initial payments, if any, due under the Form B lease will be waived. Any credits in the Right of Deduction Fund may be applied by the lessee against his lease payments, spread out over the 5-year lease term in equal monthly installments. If the option to terminate the Form B lease is later exercised, the remaining credits may be applied to the charges then falling due, whether the machine is purchased or returned at the time.

(iv) To retain the machine under the Form A lease until its termination.

Under the first three options, United made service available in the new way, according to the service tariff. Under the fourth option, the lessee could continue to get service with the lease, at no separate charge, or he could, if he chose, relinquish his right to free service and pay the lease charges less 13.3 per cent.[40] Credits in the Right of Deduction Fund were to continue to accrue under Form A leases until 31 May 1955. After 1 January 1955, the credits were to be applicable only in accordance with the proposals of the 16 May plan. Any balance in the Fund remaining to the credit of a lessee after the

[39] Hearing, 17 May, Transcript, p. 11. Salinger, of United's legal department, described the table of the final proposal as "compromising neither Dr. Dean's conclusions nor the proper interpretation, as we see it, of Para. 9 of the Decree. . . . (It) is the result of plain dollars-and-cents bargaining." Of course, this statement must be interpreted in the light of United's position on lease-sale equivalency, and its continued maintenance of prices for new machines based on Dean's estimates.

[40] This figure apparently represents the ratio of service expenses to lease revenues for fiscal 1947. See above, p. 119, Table 1, Ch. IV.

termination of his Form A leases was to be earmarked for him in a Special Fund. Balances in this Fund could at any time be applied to the purchase price of new machines bought from United, or to lease payments on new machines leased from United. The credits so applied were limited to 10 per cent of the purchase price of new machines, or 5 per cent of the lessee's aggregate monthly lease charges.

In a Hearing on 17 May 1955, this settlement was approved by the Court, after the NSMA, the NESLA, and the Haverhill Shoe Manufacturers Association indicated their approval of it, and the Government made no objection.[41]

The Order of June 1, recording formally the agreement of the Hearing, added three points to the agreed settlement. First, the terms applied only to paragraph 9, and had no value as a precedent in interpreting other paragraphs of the decree. This, of course, represented the desire of both United, on the one side, and the NSMA and the Government, on the other, to make sure that Court approval of the agreement did not determine the Court's attitude toward United's sales prices for new machines. Second, United was ordered to report, semi-annually till 1 January 1954, the number of machines sold and leased by machine type, new or used, and age groups, 1–3, 3–8, . . . etc., by five-year intervals. The reports would be held confidential unless otherwise ordered by the Court. Third, the full capacity clause was ordered stricken immediately from all outstanding Form A leases.[42]

What can be said of this settlement? On the whole, its terms seem fair, and the balance appears to swing in favor of the shoe manufacturer rather than United.[43] The options and conditions of termination are reasonable. It is perhaps worth commenting on the persist-

---

[41] There were no intervenor shoe manufacturers other than the three associations. The NSMA represented 330 members, producing 85 per cent of the total shoe output, and well distributed geographically. (Transcript, pp. 24–5.) The NESLA represented 276 members, most of them New England shoe manufacturers with 500 or fewer employees. (Transcript, p. 31.) The Court commented on the lack of other intervenors, and on the meetings, circulars, and other devices used by the NSMA to canvass non-member manufacturers, and make them aware of their rights to intervene. (Transcript, p. 42.) The Court indicated that it was "merely approving a bargain between the parties which seems to me to have been fairly arrived at." It also noted that the approval of an agreed settlement deprived any party to the agreement of standing to appeal, and thus prevented further delay in the execution of the decree. (Transcript, p. 44.)

[42] Order, dated 1 June 1955.

[43] But this is a difficult judgment to make. While the age-price formula for machine sales represented a clear gain from United's original proposals, it is difficult to tell what

ence with which United hung on to any ties it could continue to maintain with its lessees. An imposed settlement might well have made different provisions with respect to lessees' credits in the Right of Deduction Fund, so that they had the option of receiving some lump sum settlement, rather than continuing to apply them in payment of purchases from United over some indefinite future period. But the practical considerations in favor of an immediate (at last), and agreed settlement cited by the Court certainly outweigh in importance the undesirability of allowing United to fight to the last to maintain the remaining milligausses of the magnetic field of lease arrangements in which its customers were formerly held.[44]

5. THE DECREE: NEW LEASE TERMS AND SALES PRICES

The new leases followed quite closely the provisions of paragraphs 6 and 8 of the Decree. On 27 November 1954, United announced its terms under the new Form B leases and its sales prices, effective 1 January 1955.[45] The new and the old terms are compared for the twenty-five machines which have been United's largest revenue producers,[46] in Table 2. The sales prices are also shown. The new terms show much higher monthly rentals—since charges for less than minimum use are no longer permitted, and somewhat lower unit charges. Deferred payments have been abolished, in accordance with the Decree; they have been replaced by initial payments only in the case of the two monthly-rental-only machines, the clicker-C and the Universal slugger. The median ratio of new monthly rentals to old monthly rentals (for the twenty machines which had monthly

---

"bargaining discount" should be applied to them. And given the prices taken as a starting point, it is difficult to see just how the inventory revaluation profits have been divided between United and its lessees.

[44] In this connection, it is noteworthy that United did fight to the last on every point. Thus the NSMA and Government requests in the 17 May Hearing that the full capacity clause be struck from existing leases was met by a determined plea in their favor, although an observer might have seen the conclusion as foregone.

[45] Two United documents show these terms. One, dated 27 November 1954, is entitled "Comparison of Shoe Machinery Form A Lease Terms currently in effect with the Form B Lease Terms Effective January 1, 1955." The second, bearing no date, is headed, "Shoe Machinery Lease Terms and Sale Prices, referred to in our letter to shoe manufacturing lessees of November 27, 1954."

[46] See above, Table 3, p. 34. In the case of the ORL-O, the two machines which have succeeded it, the GIS-B and OSA are included in the table for comparative purposes.

TABLE 2

COMPARISON BETWEEN TERMS UNDER FORM A LEASES (1950 TERMS) AND NEW FORM B LEASES
Most Important Machine Types in Terms of Annual Revenue

Machine	Monthly Rental $/mo. A	Monthly Rental $/mo. B	Ratio (2/1)	Unit Charge ¢/pr. or ¢/M st. A	Unit Charge ¢/pr. or ¢/M st. B	Ratio (5/7)	Minimum Use 1000 pr. or M st.	Minimum Charge $/mo.	Deferred Payment $ A	Initial Payment $ B	New Sales Price $100
	(1)	(2)	(3)	(4)	(5)	(6)	(7)	(8)	(9)	(10)	(11)
Outsole Stitcher A	—	40.00	—	9(M)	5(M)	.56	—	—	—	—	112.5
Goodyear inseamer B	—	47.85	—	14(M)	9(M)	.64	600(M)	18.00	500		150.0
Outsole rapid lockstitcher O	3.50	20.00	5.7	6(M)	3(M)	.5	800(M)	20.00	250		59.5
Welter K	2.00	45.75	22.8	12(M)	8(M)	.67	500(M)	10.00	250		80.8
Rex C, D	avg. 5.35	27.50	5.1	.8	.6	.75	4	14.00	250		79.5
Laster 6, 7	avg. 2.75	avg. 28.00	10.2	.1	.1	1.00	1.8	9.00	125		45.0
Side Laster B	2.25	23.00	10.2	.75	.425	.56	4	12.00	150		53.3
Universal Rounding & Channeling	6.00	22.25	3.7	.35	.275	.65	—	—	100		52.0
McKay Automatic Heel Loading & Attaching	5.50	47.50	8.6	.5	.425	.85	10	20.00	250		86.8
Goodyear Automatic Sole Leveler	5.50	47.50	8.6	.5	.475	.95	—	—	225		94.5
Heel Seat Laster E	25.00	42.50	1.7	1.0	.8	.8	9	36	600		90.3
Cement Soler	13.00	50.00	3.8	.6	.375	.63	10	24	700		179.5
Wood heel nailer	—	27.50	—	.625	.475	.76	12.5	31.25	1000		73.5
Goodyear Sole Layer	5.00	14.75	2.9	.25	.2	.8	—	—	100		42.0

TABLE 2—Continued

COMPARISON BETWEEN TERMS UNDER FORM A LEASES (1950 TERMS) AND NEW FORM B LEASES
Most Important Machine Types in Terms of Annual Revenue

Machine	Monthly Rental $/mo. A	B	Ratio (2/1)	Unit Charge c/pr. or c/M st. A	B	Ratio (5/4)	Minimum Use 1000 pr. or M st.	Minimum Charge $/mo.	Deferred Payment $ A	Initial Payment $ B	New Sales Price $100
	(1)	(2)	(3)	(4)	(5)	(6)	(7)	(8)	(9)	(10)	(11)
Goodyear Insole Trimmer	8.00	18.50	2.3	.2	.175	.88	—	—	125		45.8
Consolidated Hand Method Lasting Machine (McKay)	2.50	20.00	8.0	.4	.35	.87	4	7	150		36.0
Loose Nailer	2.50	55.00	22.0	.25			8	8	125		42.5
*Clicker C	10.00	14.50	1.5	—	—	—	—	—	100	130	13.0
Staple Sole Laster C	2.75	23.00	8.4	.75	.65	.87	3	9	200		49.0
USMC Sole Stitcher	3.75	32.25	8.6	8(M)	5(M)	.63	500(M)	15	300		66.8
Toe Laster C	—	40.00	—	1.25	1	.8	5	25	700		110.0
Wood Heel Attacher B	—	15.75	—	.625	.475	.76	5	12.50	300		41.8
USMC Sole Layer	9.75	40.00	4.1	.875	.6	.59	5	17.50	700		92.5
Stitchdown Thread Laster	2.25	11.25	5.0	4(M)	3(M)	.75	900	18.00	200		38.3
*Universal Slugger	15.00	18.75	1.2	—	—	—	—	—	125	236.25	15.8
Fiber Fastener	3.25	25.25	7.7	.3	.275	.92	8	12.00	150		43.8

* Monthly Rental only.

rentals under the Form A leases) was 5.4.[47] The weighted mean of the ratios, using 1947 machine type revenues as weights, was 9.3. The median ratio of new units charges to old unit charges (for 23 machines) was 0.76, and the weighted average 0.70.[48] Monthly rentals were increased some 540 to 900 per cent, while unit charges were decreased some 24 to 30 per cent, on the average. But, of course, unit charges were much more important revenue producers under the old leases than were monthly rentals,[49] so that these figures, in themselves, do not show how the cost of leasing has changed.

The NSMA made a study of the expected increase in leasing costs under the Form B lease, based on responses by 250 shoe manufac-

TABLE 3

PERCENTAGE INCREASE IN LEASING COSTS: FORM B LEASES *v.* NEW (1950 RATES) FORM A LEASES AND ACTUAL 1954 LEASING COSTS (BASED ON A SAMPLE OF 250 FIRMS)

	Form B *v* new Form A	Form B *v* actual 1954
All factories		
Median	37.6	60.3
1st quartile	22.3	42.8
3rd quartile	53.1	86.2
By size (medians only)		
Small (less than 1800 pr./day)	49.3	74.1
Medium (1,800 to 3,600 pr./day)	40.5	65.0
Large (more than 3,600 pr./day)	30.7	57.1
By shoe construction (medians only)		
Goodyear welt	33.0	49.1
Cement	34.6	75.9
Lockstitch	36.5	58.5
Slip lasted (California)	60.0	113.4
Stitchdown	31.2	61.5

[47] Excluding the two machines without unit charges, the median ratio was 6.7. The quartiles of the array of ratios were:

	20 machines	18 machines
first q.	8.6	8.6
third q.	3.4	3.8

[48] The quartiles were 0.87 and 0.64.

[49] See S-246, which shows that in the period of the trial, unit charges were about four times as important as rentals in *all* revenue from leased machines. For the machines shown in the tabulation above, this relation would be even greater.

turers to a questionnaire.[50] This study compared leasing costs, exclusive of service under the Form B leases, with net leasing costs (after an allowance for service costs) actually experienced in 1954, and with net leasing costs which would have been experienced under the 1950 Form A lease rates, if the manufacturers had held no machines under leases of earlier date. The results are shown in Table 3.

Compared with the costs which the representative manufacturer would have been experiencing under 1950 rates on the Form A leases, the new Form B leases imposed costs more than a third again as great. But, since in 1954 most manufacturers held a substantial proportion of their machines on leases which antedated 1947, the leasing costs which the manufacturers actually experienced in 1954 were lower than they would have been had they been based on new Form A rates. Compared with his actual 1954 experience, the representative manufacturer could have expected to pay 60 per cent more for leased machinery, net of service costs, under the new Form B leases. The average increases would have been greater for smaller and less for larger manufacturers, and would vary substantially among manufacturers making shoes of different constructions.

The figures above refer to the cost of leasing exclusive of service costs. The new tariff of service charges was filed in the Court on 20 November 1954.[51] The record shows the service experience of a selected group of Milwaukee factories under the old arrangements.[52] An application of the new rates to the experience of these factories

---

[50] *A Survey of Shoe Machinery Leasing Costs* (mimeo., no date), prepared by Andrews, Anthony, and MacLean. The questionnaire was circulated to the whole membership of NSMA.

[51] The basic rate for service by roadmen was $4.80/man/hour, applicable both to factory time and travel time. The minimum time was one half-hour factory time, and time over the minimum was computed to the nearest 6 minutes (0.1 hrs.). Overtime and Saturdays were paid for at time-and-one-half, Sundays and holidays at double-time. The standard work week was five 8-hour days; overtime was payable only on factory time. In addition, whenever overnight trips by a service man were involved, the shoe factory must pay living expenses, which were calculated as an addition to the basic rate varying from 65¢ to 88¢ per hour, depending on the service district. For multiple calls, travel time and living expenses were reduced, in a manner depending on the average experience of the service district.

Service provided by the Boston office was more expensive. Service by the operating departments, the planning, and shoe -ex departments was charged at the basic rate of $60/man/day, with a minimum time of 1 day and time calculated to the nearest 2 hours (¼ day). In addition, actual travel and living expenses are charged. Service by the machine-development department carried a basic rate of $73.50/man/day.

[52] See above, pp. 135–145.

suggests service costs under the new tariff of the order of 2.5¢ per pair for welts, and 2.1¢ per pair for cements and stitchdowns.[53] These figures can be compared with estimates of median per pair costs under Form B leases of 15.9¢ for welts, 6.4¢ for cements, and 5.1¢ for stitchdowns given in the NSMA survey.[54] Taken together, the two sets of figures suggest estimates of service costs under the new leases running from 13.7 per cent of total lease and service costs for welts to 27.9 per cent for stitchdowns. This compares with the estimated 13.3 per cent of total lease costs for service under the old leases. But these estimates are crude, and not too much reliance can be placed on them.[55] And further, it is clear from the discussion of service under the old leases that incentives to economize on the use of service did not exist, and service was in fact quite wastefully used. Thus it is likely that the actual service costs under Form B leases will be lower than the costs suggested by the experience of companies under Form A leases.[56]

Sales prices for the most important machines are contained in Table 2 above.[57] The basis for computing the sales prices has already been examined in the preceding section, and the views of the Government and the shoe manufacturers that the prices were "too high"

[53] These figures were derived as follows. Only service by roadmen was included. It was assumed that 80 per cent of the service time was at standard rates, 10 per cent at time-and-one-half, and 10 per cent at double-time, giving a per-hour cost of $5.50. This might be high, but it is compensated for by the omission of any Boston office service, at higher rates. This figure was then applied to the median figure of service hours/1000 pr. of shoes shown on p. 136 above.

[54] Survey, Table IV, p. 16.

[55] The estimates are based on a comparison between median lease costs under Form B leases for a national sample of 250 shoe manufacturers, and median service costs (constructed from median service hours per 1000 pair of shoes) for a sample of 34 factories in the Milwaukee district. The ratio of two such medians, assuming the samples are drawn from the same universe, is a very unreliable statistic, subject to wide fluctuations.

[56] Of course, this observation in no way applies to the usefulness of the figures—within the limits of their reliability—as an index of the increase in the price of service relative to other lease costs. The per pair service costs can be compared with the Survey figures for per pair lease costs on the new Form A leases (Survey, loc. cit.) to give another indication of the increase in the price of service. The proportions of calculated median per pair service costs on the new tariff (as above) to median per pair leasing costs under new Form A leases were: welts 20.7 per cent; cements, 43.0 per cent; stitchdowns, 47.9 per cent. Since the Milwaukee sample contained 22 welt factories, but only 7 cement and 5 stitchdown factories, the first figure is probably more reliable than the other two. These figures for the increase in service "prices" are not far out of line with the figures above for increases in leasing costs net of service.

[57] Pp. 322–323.

were noted there. The Court stated that the only real test of "equivalence" was whether or not machines were in practice sold,[58] and the
reporting machinery provided for in the Order of 1 June[59] would
reveal whether or not machines were in fact sold. Two comparisons
are available as tests for the sales prices, each of some—if limited—
value. A comparison of the sales prices with prices based on the old
United sales price formula for General department machines shows,
for the important machines listed in Table 2 above,[60] that the new
sales prices were on the average about 4 times the formula sales
price.[61] Comparisons with Compo's sales prices can be made for a
few machines. These fall into two groups, the cement process machines in which Compo and United have been competing for some
time, and the Moenus machinery, of German manufacture, which
Compo has recently begun to distribute in the United States.[62] The
United and Compo prices for machines in the first group are fairly
close together, with neither consistently higher. For the two machines
in the second group, United's prices are some twice as high as
Compo's.[63] The closeness in the first case is to be expected: the ma-

[58] Hearing of 7 March, pp. 22–3. See passage cited above, p. 312, note 24.
[59] See above, p. 320.   [60] Pp. 322–323.
[61] The formula, it will be recalled, is factory cost plus development cost plus 100
per cent. While figures for factory cost plus development cost were not available,
figures for insurance value were. In general, this is slightly larger than factory cost
plus development cost. (See above, p. 204). The ratios of new sales price to twice
insurance value for the 18 machines for which data were available were: median,
4.0; first quartile, 6.0; third quartile, 3.3.

To be sure, the insurance values are based on manufacturing costs of various previous dates, reaching far back into the past. But even if they are based on twenty-five-
year-old costs, there is room for a good deal of cost inflation in the ratios shown.

[62] See below, pp. 331–332.   [63] The comparisons are:

	USMC	Machine, Model, Price		Compo	Machine, Model, Price	
1st Group						
	Sole cementer B		$730	Sole cementer A, AM, AW		$505
		C	915		AK, AMK	565
					J, JM	905
	Bottom cementer B		1,075	Bottom cementer K		1,565
	Cement sole attacher C		7,350	Compomatic press A-10,		
				A-15, A-70		7,295
2nd Group						
	Rex pulling over C		7,950	Pulling over (Moenus)		4,545
	Auto heel seat laster E		17,950	Auto heel seat laster		
				(Moenus) MOH		6,900

I am indebted to Compo Shoe Machinery Corporation for their courtesy in furnishing
catalogues and price lists. The prices are those announced in the Compo price list effective
7 April, 1955.

chines are fairly similar, and the trade is familiar with their performance, etc. Moreover, Compo may be following United's prices, with appropriate differences for differences in machine specifications and performance. Such followership is to be expected in the present market situation. The differences in the second group are all the more striking, therefore. The Moenus machinery is of high quality, and has been characterized as comparable to or superior to United's by competent observers.[64] But the definite test of the market must wait the passage of time. It is clear that the market test is the only finally meaningful test of "equivalence" of lease and sale terms, and again, only the passage of time will reveal what the shoe manufacturers think of United's sales prices in practical terms. Only this test can show whether the Court's attempt to avoid the inequities to other shoe machinery manufacturers and to shoe manufacturers which might have been created by a Decree ordering United to end all leasing and sell machines was in fact practical.[65] In the meantime, however, some speculation on the level of prices and United's policy in setting them is not entirely amiss. The evidence assembled in the pages above makes it plain that the new terms represent a substantial increase in prices over the pre-decree level.[66] One possible interpretation of the new price level is that it arises from a decision by United to make the most of its market power while it lasts. In the past, United's markups, overall, have not been high;[67] perhaps its executives have decided that they might well enjoy more directly the fruits of the firm's market power while they still can. The increases in earn-

[64] See the testimony of Smith, Compo's machine designer on Moenus, Tr. 10289–92, 10326–35, 10338–40. Compo was not at this time distributing Moenus machinery, and Smith's discussion of Moenus, in the context of his attributing to United superiority over most but not all European machinery, may be taken as disinterested. See also a series of articles by the technical editor of the *Shoe and Leather Reporter* in the issues of 16 May 1953, 27 June 1953, 31 October 1953, 27 February 1954, 5 June 1954, and 18 September 1954, concerned with foreign shoe machinery, in which Moenus machines are mentioned among the foreign machines of proved quality. Also, the article "Outlook for Foreign Shoe Machinery" in *Leather and Shoes,* 7 March 1953, which expresses similar views.

[65] See the Opinion, pp. 114–15.

[66] Although there had been some increases in costs over the period from July 1950 (the date of the last terms change) and January 1955, these were much smaller in magnitude than the price increases. The BLS average for hourly earnings in the machinery industry increased about 25 per cent in the period, and the BLS index of the wholesale price of steel about 20 per cent; machinery prices in general, as recorded in the BLS wholesale price index, increased about 12 per cent over the period.

[67] See above, pp. 115–116.

ings this policy would provide would be welcome not only in themselves, but also as a means of financing the diversification of production into new (and perhaps riskier) fields which United appears to be undertaking.[68] Further, while the high level of prices might in general be expected to encourage the growth of competitive firms, and will probably do so, there is an important offsetting factor arising from the special character of the shoe machinery market. For some time to come, the most important kind of competition for United in respect to many machine types will be that provided by its own second-hand machines, since there are no other sellers in the market offering comparable machines. The high level of sales prices will discourage sales; to this extent they will retard the growth of this particular form of competition.[69] On balance then, the new prices might well help to delay the erosion of United's market power, as well as permitting United to profit from it while it can.

6. THE DECREE: OTHER PROVISIONS

Paragraph 10 of the Decree requires United to divest itself in due course of its manufacturing and distributing activities in tacks, nails, and eyelets. Accordingly, United filed a plan, agreed to by the Government, to dispose of this part of its business.[70] United will discontinue the manufacture of eyelets at its S. O. and C. Company branch plant. By October 1956 it will sell the stock and/or assets of W. W. Cross and Co. (a subsidiary) and J. C. Rhodes Co. (a branch plant). If it has not succeeded in so doing it will notify the Court, and by July 1957 United will create a new subsidiary corporation owning these assets, and distribute its shares proportionately among its own stockholders. All sales or transfers of these assets must be completed by 1 January 1958; until that time, United may continue its business

[68] See below, pp. 330–331.

[69] Further, markups for machine types without effective competitors may well be much higher than for those in which other sellers now offer adequate substitutes. I.e., the price discrimination policy embodied in United's leases can, and logically should, be carried over into its sales prices. Thus, for example, the decrease in the unit charge on the cement sole attaching machine was above the third quartile decrease for the whole distribution, while decreases in unit charges on the lasting machines and pulling over machines were at the other end of the distribution. (See Table 2 above.) And note the discrepancy between United-Compo price comparisons in the cement-shoe machinery field and in the lasting and pulling over machines which United has so long dominated.

[70] The stipulation reporting the agreed plan was filed 11 May 1955, and the plan was embodied in a Court Order dated 13 May 1955.

in nails, tacks, and eyelets, as long as the transfers have not been completed. If a new corporation is formed, it may have United as its distributor until 1 January 1958.

Paragraph 11 of the Decree requires United to cease to distribute shoe factory supplies manufactured by others after 1 January 1958. This process appears already to have begun by the time of the final negotiations about the decree. The *Shoe and Leather Reporter* carried a news note stating that Compo had initiated negotiations with all principal supply manufacturers who had distributed through United, seeking to become their distributor to the shoe trade.[71]

Again, here as elsewhere, the provisions of the decree will operate to change the structure of the market and the behavior of United only after some lapse of time, and a judgment of its effects must wait.

7. CONTEMPORARY DEVELOPMENTS IN THE TRADE

United's operations in the shoe machinery and supply markets did not change immediately; there was little attempt to anticipate the provisions of the decree, or to move before movement was compelled. United's sales and earnings during the period since the start of the trial showed a course not visibly influenced by its events.[72] But other reactions were visible. In particular, indications of an effort by United to diversify its operations, and move into markets unrelated to shoe manufacture, began to appear after the appeal was lost. The 1954 Annual Report announced the formation of an Ordnance Division within the Research Department to do research and development work on contract for the Armed Services, and the 1955 Report again mentioned the activity of this Division.[73] The company began to develop two new lines of machinery: automatic assembly machinery for electronic components, and portable, hand-held, pneumatic tools for feeding and inserting tacks, nails, and screws. One type of automatic assembling machine was already in the testing stage in 1955, and was used in the production of over 400 thousand units in radio and television manufacturing; others were still in the developmental stage. In addition, the B.B. Chemical Company was testing the application of a new quick-setting thermoplastic adhesive to the manu-

---

[71] *Shoe and Leather Reporter*, 18 September 1954.

[72] See United's *Annual Reports,* dated 1946 through 1955. Each covers the fiscal year ending 28 February of the year it is dated.

[73] 1954 Report, p. 9; 1955 Report, p. 9.

facture of paper milk cartons, paper bags, fiber cans, and for use in packaging machinery.[74]

Contemporaneous issues of trade journals in the shoe field gave the impression of another United reaction to the anti-trust suit: an increase in the frequency of United ads in these journals, and a greater emphasis on United's progressiveness and research resources in its advertising.[75] This may indicate an expectation by United of an increasing degree of competition in the shoe machinery market, after the decision in the District Court.

There were other and more important signs of the development of alternative sources of supply to United. Most of the new suppliers were foreign. The trade press cited above was full of accounts of foreign shoe machinery, and the shoe factory management conferences at the time featured large exhibits by distributors of imported machines.[76] The most important development in this respect was the arrangement between Compo and Moenus which made Compo the American distributor for Moenus machinery. This put a technically good line of shoe machinery in the hands of the largest and most successful of United's competitors, and added to Compo's line machines which it would have been difficult for Compo to develop for itself in a short period of time. The 1955 Compo catalogue offered four Moenus machines: a staple tacking machine, a pulling over machine, a tack side lasting machine, and an automatic heel seat lasting machine, all on sale terms only.[77] These signs of activity offer no

---

[74] 1955 Annual Report, pp. 8 and 9. The electronic assemblers were apparently the first results of United research into automation, looking forward to the ultimate design of fully automatic shoe machinery.

[75] This impression is based on an examination of the *Shoe and Leather Reporter* and *Leather and Shoes* for the year preceding the decision of the District Court, and the period since the decision to June 1955.

[76] See particularly: Brady (technical editor) in *Shoe and Leather Reporter*, 31 October 1953, "Foreign Shoe Machines in America"; Brady, *ibid.*, 27 February 1954, "Technical Progress at Cincinnati," an article describing the Shoe Factory Management conference of that month; Brady, *ibid.*, 5 June 1954, "New Machines for the Shoe Industry"; an article entitled "Outlook for Foreign Shoe Machinery," *Leather and Shoes*, 7 March 1953, which talks about the great stimulus to the use of foreign machines given by the European trip in 1952 of a committee of NSMA; *ibid.*, 27 February 1954, describing new machines exhibited at the Management Conference; and *ibid.*, 12 February 1955, an issue devoted to an account of the Factory Management Conference of that year, which forecasts the trend in shoe machinery.

[77] *Shoe and Leather Reporter*, 25 April 1953, had a news note stating that Compo intended to exhibit an outsole stitcher for Goodyear welts, a rotary pounder and an upper leather trimmer of Moenus manufacture at the Factory Management Confer-

basis for a quantitative judgment of the importance of foreign shoe machinery. In 1955 it must still have been very small, and problems of service and parts would limit its market growth, unless through arrangements like that of Compo-Moenus. Other distributors of foreign shoe machinery at the time, such as Herman Schwabe in New York,[78] were not themselves manufacturers, and did not have service organizations. The author of the article on "Outlook for Foreign Shoe Machinery" quoted above[79] estimated that in the five years from March 1953 foreign machines would supply 5 to 15 per cent of the market.

Compo built up its competitive position in other ways than through arrangement with Moenus. In May 1953 it acquired the Quirk Machinery Company[80] and it subsequently offered a Quirk heel-building machine. At the same time it acquired the United Wood Heel Co. of St. Louis.[81] In December 1954, Compo became the distributor of Norton and Behr-Manning abrasives to the shoe trade.[82] It is clear that Compo has tried to offer the shoe manufacturer alternatives to United in as many products as it possibly could. In another move, to be classified perhaps under the head of "search for new financing," Compo filed a triple-damage suit under Sections 4 and 5 of the Clayton Act, claiming damages of $10 million.[83]

All in all, there appear to have been stirrings in the industry indica-

---

ence, as well as the machines listed. By 1955 they had not yet been offered commercially.

For a discussion of the quality of Moenus machines, see above, p. 000. The agreement between Moenus and Compo was announced in April 1953 (*Shoe and Leather Reporter*, 25 April 1953) and the first machinery was offered for sale the following September. (*Ibid.*, 5 September 1953.)

[78] His 1955 catalogue, No. 53, listed clickers, insole channelers, pulling over machines, inseam trimmers, heel seat lasters, toe lasters, staple side lasters, rough rounders and channelers, outsole stitchers, sole levelers, sole attaching presses, among others. It is not clear that all of these were of foreign manufacture. All were offered for sale.

[79] P. 526, footnote 71.

[80] *Shoe and Leather Reporter*, 9 May 1953.

[81] *Ibid.*

[82] *Ibid.*, 4 December 1954.

[83] The suit was filed 28 May 1955 in the District Court of Massachusetts. The Complaint simply recited the charges and the findings in the Government case, and then alleged that by the same acts and practices United had injured Compo to the tune of $10 million.

A similar suit was filed by Allied Shoe Machinery Company, in the same Court, on 18 October 1954. In both cases plaintiffs were represented by counsel who had tried the Government's case, including the leading Government counsel.

tive of the growth of competition, most of which began after the Government won its case. No doubt there were also other factors contributing to these developments, but the prospect of a relaxation of United's grip on its shoe manufacturing customers was certainly one important one.

X. Some Reflections on the Standards and Administration of the Anti-Trust Laws

The usual way of generalizing from a sample of one is to denominate it a "case study," and speak of the insights into or suggestions about the problem at hand which can be drawn from it. We shall follow this procedure, and attempt to set down some broader reflections on the anti-trust laws which the United Shoe Case suggests.

1. ECONOMISTS AND LAWYERS

The adversary process is the traditional legal instrument for the discovery of truth. In its application to the kind of economic truths which are relevant to the decision of anti-trust cases (and other problems which turn on economic facts and economic conclusions), it has been as much criticized by economists as it is usually admired by lawyers. And indeed, this criticism appears justified. To spend, as in the present case, the time of perhaps a dozen lawyers, a judge, and at least again as many officers and employees of United for most of five years to gather, evaluate, and organize the information for what amounts to a study of the American shoe machinery industry, appears extravagant, even to an economist who has made an industry study. Less cumbersome techniques than the interrogatory, the Court order, oral testimony, and cross examination might, it would appear, do the job equally carefully and far more economically. For example, an examination of United's records and documents by two or three trained economists in the employ of the Government; the production therefrom of a report, the criticism of the report by another group of economists on behalf of United; and the ultimate evaluation of the report and the criticisms by a judge or an expert commission, would seem to be capable of producing a thorough study of United's relation to the industry without reducing the process to an *ex parte* determination, and would take far less time and resources.

This criticism of the trial process in anti-trust "big cases"[1] with their thousands of exhibits and ten thousands of pages of testimony taken in hundreds of days of hearings is certainly justified. The problem, however, lies not in the procedural limits imposed by a trial in a court, which, as the United case has shown, are as flexible as an imaginative judge can make them.[2] It lies rather in what the Government typically tries to show, and what defense counsel, therefore, must refute or cast doubt on, in the big anti-trust trial. This in turn, reflects the state of the law, as it is now interpreted by the Courts. The typical "big case" involves a complaint under Section 2 of the Sherman Act; frequently, to be sure, in addition to complaints under Section 1. In proving monopolization, the Government typically relies heavily on evidence of "intent," and defendants, correspondingly, strive to show the purity of purpose of their business practices. The law of monopolization under #2 requires a showing that the defendant has power over price or power to exclude competition, and something more—"an element of deliberateness."[3] Evidence, pro and con, on the existence of "something more" occupied a disproportionately large part of the United Shoe trial. Much of the government documentary evidence consisted of individual letters, reports, and like papers from United's files, selected more to show United's evil intentions than to depict the pattern of United's business practices. Indeed, it is no exaggeration to say that an overall view of the market and United's position in it hardly emerged from the Government's presentation of its case at all, so heavily was it pointed toward "intent." United, likewise used most of its presentation for material of the same kind. While the documentary evidence offered by United contained many admirable summary analyses of United's

[1] See B. P. McAllister, "The Big Case, Procedural Problems of Anti-Trust Litigation," 64 *Harvard Law Review* 27.

[2] *Vide* the calling of Compo executives as the Court's witnesses to give expert testimony, the direction of the Court to the parties to carry out a sample study of the suppliers of machines in a randomly selected group of shoe factories, the liberal admission of corporate documents in evidence.

[3] See *Report* of the Attorney General's National Committee to Study the Anti-Trust Laws (1955), p. 43. Also the discussion, pp. 43–60.

business practices, prepared for the purposes of the case, the oral evidence of United's officers and employees was devoted largely to explaining United's intentions in specific transactions or to a detailed and repetitive exegesis of United's business philosophy. Material of these types filled up perhaps two-thirds of the record of oral testimony.

If the law of monopolization dealt squarely with the business situation, and left "intent" in however shadowy a form to one side, the way would be cleared for a better-focused and briefer presentation on the substantive issues around which a Section 2 suit would then revolve. These would be: delimitation of the relevant market in which the defendant does business, measurement of the defendant's market share, examination of the power of other suppliers to offer alternatives to purchasers, and examination of the bases on which the defendant's dominant position, assuming it exists, rests—economies of scale, business practices, ownership of scarce raw materials or other bottleneck facilities, patents, agreements with others not to compete, etc.

Once it was well understood by counsel on both sides that these were the issues which had to be examined, at least some of them could be dealt with in relatively brief compass. Both market definition and market share should be susceptible either of stipulation, or of presentation in terms of sharply stated alternatives, between which the trier could choose on the basis of evidence and argument contained in briefs, with need for little oral testimony and cross-examination. By comparison, in the United case, the Government presented a clearly stated but poorly argued measure of market share, with no explicit discussion of how the market was properly defined; while United put into the record a great mass of material, including several volumes of unsummarized raw data resulting from the Court-ordered survey of a sample of shoe factories, designed to cast doubt on the accuracy of the Government figures (and perhaps to confuse the Court by sheer bulk), but devoid of positive statements of United's view of the definition of the market and its occupancy therein.[4]

The other issues listed are more complex than those of market definition and market share, and the last really contains the heart of a

[4] This comment is intended in no way to reflect on United's counsel, who undoubtedly considered this presentation as best suited to the interests of their client, and thus appropriate. It is made to point up the kind of waste motion (from the standpoint of the writer) which now fills up trial time, and which could be avoided with a different legal focus for the proceedings.

monopolization case. It is thus not to be expected that there will be any significant pre-trial agreement on them. Even so, however, discussion of them can be much more focused when the parties deal directly with them, under the guidance of a judge who knows that it is the answers to these questions which he seeks to find, than they will be when the presentation wanders freely from discussions of the economic context of defendant's behavior and its economic effects to an examination of the "intent" which underlay defendant's actions.

It is on the Government, primarily, that the power to reform the conduct of Section 2 cases in these respects rests. There is an anterior problem of what the law is, and whether the Wyzanski formulation rules out "intent" in any sense by speaking of methods more restrictive than necessary. But putting this aside,[5] and assuming that the kind of presentation sketched above is legally sufficient, it is the Anti-Trust Division of the Department of Justice which largely determines the shape of a trial. To be sure, a brave—or rash—defense counsel might brush aside the Government discussion of injudicious letters, repeated patent infringement suits, and the like as unworthy of notice, and concentrate his efforts on showing that his client occupied only a small share of the relevant market,[6] but it is rare that the situation permits such conduct on the part of counsel who must be mindful of his client's interests. This leads to the observation that the social marginal productivity of the application of trained economists to the anti-trust process is much higher if their skills are used by the Government in the organization and presentation of cases, as well as earlier in the process of selecting cases for trial, than if the same skills are used by the defense alone, or even put into the service of the Court, in assisting it to organize and evaluate economic evidence. Ideally, the Government, in a Section 2 suit, should present, through appropriate and competent evidence, the equivalent of a summary study of the defendant's industry, and defendant's place therein. In practice, limitations on information available to the Government at the commencement of a case will prevent this aim from being fully realized. Nonetheless, it remains a useful target for the Anti-Trust Division to hold before itself. So far as the preparation and presenta-

[5] See Section 2 below. Moreover, to a great extent, what the anti-trust law "is" at any moment depends to a substantial extent on the issues which the Government has but before Courts in previous cases. Thus even in this sphere, the Government has an important measure of initiative.

[6] See *U. S.* v. *Du Pont* (Cellophane), 118 Fed. Supp. 41.

tion of the United Shoe case is characteristic, the Government has as yet made no attempt in this direction.[7] Once the Government moved in this direction, defense counsel would follow suit perforce.[8] Such changes in the strategy of preparation and trial would go far to removing the limitations of the judicial process as a method for discovering the kinds of specific economic truths that are relevant to the enforcement of the anti-trust laws.

2. THE STANDARDS OF THE LAW: MARKET POWER v. MARKET PERFORMANCE

At the outset of this study, the author set forth his views on the relation between the concept of market power and the standard of liability he, as an economist, would consider appropriate in the enforcement of the anti-trust laws.[9] The major point of that discussion was to identify "monopolization" of Section 2 of the Sherman Act with the existence, in some market, of a firm (or group of firms) with persistent market power which was not justified by economies of scale alone, or in combination with the geography of production and the level of transport costs. Another possible view, that "monopolization" should be identified with lack of workable competition, and the latter, in turn, defined in terms of standards of acceptable performance with respect to profits, efficiency, and progressiveness, was rejected. In particular, a standard of workable competition (or, as it has been sometimes called, workable monopoly) which rests on the proposition that competition is workable in a particular market if no change that can be made by the action of a court can be counted on to improve the functioning of the market was rejected.[10]

These standards were dismissed on the grounds that no tests were available by which an objective evaluation of certain ingredients of

---

[7] This statement does not rest on the single example alone. Other recent cases, including Cellophane, *U.S.* v. *Du Pont* (General Motors), and the remedy proceedings in the Alcoa case, show the same defects in this respect.

[8] Further, it is the author's view, based on information from private sources, that defendants are already ahead of the Government in utilizing economists in assisting in the preparation of anti-trust cases.

[9] Above, pp. 16–20. The discussion applies chiefly to the concept of monopoly, and does not touch on the problem of *per se* violations, or how broadly the area of "incipient monopoly" should be delimited in the application of statutes like the Clayton Act and the Federal Trade Commission Act.

[10] See the literature of the "New Competition," esp. A. D. H. Kaplan, *Big Enterprise in a Competitive System* (Brookings Institution, 1954) and D. Lilienthal, *Big Business, a New Era* (Harper & Brothers, 1953).

performance—especially performance in research and progressiveness—could be made; and further, no weighting scheme which would tell a court how to combine low scores in one aspect of performance —say price-cost margins—with high scores in another—say activity in research and development—could feasibly be provided by law. Nothing in the analysis of the case as it has been unfolded appears to detract from the force of these arguments.[11]

A standard which equates monopolization with persistent market power not resting on scale economies implies the abandonment of "conduct" as the determining criterion of the defendant's liability, and instead, rests the judgment entirely on "situation." The standard of liability under Section 2 of the Sherman Act set forth in the Court's opinion does not reach quite so far. It exempts from the ban of the law not only market power achieved by the exploitation of economies of scale, and market power conferred by legal license, but also market power arising from superior skill, superior products, etc., or from low margins of profit maintained permanently and without discrimination. Conceivably, the first entrant to an expanding market, if well-supplied with capital, could maintain low margins of profit, expand rapidly with the market, and grow to such size, absolute and relative, as would discourage other would-be entrants from competition, yet possess no real cost advantages over a smaller potential competitor. The case of superior skill, superior products, and the like presents something of an economic puzzle. In general, it is to be expected that others can copy—where they are not protected by patents—the fruits of the superior firm's skills, either directly, or by hiring personnel away from it. Thus superior skill is unlikely to confer permanent advantage, unless buttressed by barriers to entry which preclude the appearance in the market of the successful imitator. Practically, in particular instances, the interval between the leader's new idea and the successful imitations of the follower is variable, and may be long enough to create a continuing lead for the innovator.[12]

---

[11] I.e., the author remains convinced. For the readers who were and remain unconvinced on these points, a rereading of Ch. v, Sec. 1, and Ch. vii, Sec. 4 is suggested.

[12] The ability of a firm to dominate a market solely by the exploitation of superior skills involves the appropriation by the firm of at least part of the rents which are imputable to the individuals, executives, scientists, or craftsmen, in whom the skills reside. Otherwise, the firm could not achieve a cost advantage over its rivals offering

Both these exemptions temper the situational rigor of the Court's standard, and give it some color of being based on conduct, conduct more restrictive than necessary. But their practical importance may be questioned on two grounds. First, neither represents a situation likely to be encountered, especially if the language of the Opinion, which speaks of market power deriving *solely* from the conduct exempted, is read literally. Second, defendants will find it very difficult to prove that they fall within the exemption. The task of demonstrating superior skill is not unlike the task of demonstrating outstanding performance in research and development in the absence of an objective standard by which achieved results can be measured. Permanently low and uniform profit margins in the context of changing market situations and sales in separated markets typical of most large sellers are unlikely ever to be encountered. Almost every multi-product and multi-market seller practices price discrimination to some extent, even if unwittingly.[13] It may be that the formulation of the Court comes as close to the economic standard suggested above as is possible, in view of the character of the statute. The Sherman Act, as a criminal statute, must forbid some kinds of conduct on the part of those to whom it applies.[14] Perhaps a different kind of legal mechanism is needed if the legislature wishes to reform certain business situations, irrespective of the conduct which led to them.

3. CAN COURTS FRAME EFFECTIVE ANTI-TRUST DECREES?

The aim of anti-trust proceedings is the creation of competitive conditions in markets where they were previously absent. In Section 2 proceedings this can be done—if at all—only by the remedial decree; a finding of liability in itself has no virtue in promoting competition.

---

the same product, and would have to offer superior products at prices sufficiently higher to offset their superiority in the eyes of buyers. The bureaucratic structure of large modern firms, emphasizing promotion from within, greatly lessens the ability of the possessors of scarce skills to demand their full market rents. Further, to the extent that the skills inhere not in the individuals alone, but in some kind of organized team, dependent on the organizational pattern of the firm, some of the rents perhaps should accrue to the firm itself, rather than to the individual members of the team.

[13] See above, pp. 126–128.

[14] It was the contention of United on appeal that the Court had already abandoned this aim in formulating the law as it did, and that United had no way of obeying the law as so interpreted.

The ability of courts to frame effective decrees is limited in two important ways: their natural conservatism which makes really radical structural reorganization of markets, achieved by divorcement, divestiture, and dissolution of defendant firms, rare; and the limitations on the information available to them, on the basis of which decrees must be drawn—ignorance reinforces caution. Do these limitations preclude hope of achieving significant results in reducing positions of market power through anti-trust action?[15]

Courts are essentially conservative institutions, conditioned to be so by the very nature of their functions. Though they make as well as interpret law, their legislative activity is interstitial, usually small in scope, and undertaken with caution.[16] In our democratic society, broad legislative power is given to representative legislatures; unrepresentative, professionalized bodies such as courts do not and cannot legislate in the same bold way.

A remedy order in an anti-trust case—especially one brought under Section 2 of the Sherman Act—is a piece of legislation, writing, for a limited period of time, new rules of conduct for defendant firms not imposed on others, and, sometimes, even requiring their reorganization. It is to be expected that this legislative power will be used with the caution characteristic of courts as legislators. The nature of the restraints which a District Judge feels when he writes a decree is forcefully stated in the Court's Opinion in the present case.

Judges in prescribing remedies have known their own limitations. They do not, *ex officio,* have economic or political training. Their prophecies as to the economic future are not guided by unusually subtle judgement. They are not so representative as other branches of the government. The recommendations they receive from government prosecutors do not always reflect the over-all approach of even the executive branch of the government, sometimes not indeed the seasoned and fairly informed judgement of the head of the Department of Justice. Hearings in court do not usually give the remote judge as sound a feeling for the realities of a situation as other procedures do. Judicial decrees must be fitted into the framework of what a busy, and none too expert, court can supervise. Above all, no matter with what authority he is invested, with what facts

[15] For a pessimistic view of the recent performances of courts in this respect, see W. Adams, "Dissolution, Divorcement and Divestiture: The Pyrrhic Victories of Anti-Trust," XVII *Indiana Law Journal* 1 (Fall 1951), and "The Aluminum Case: Legal Victory, Economic Defeat," XLI *American Economic Review* 915 (Dec. 1951).
[16] Indeed with such caution that many judges deny that it is ever done.

and opinion he is supplied, a trial judge is only one man, and should move with caution and humility.

That considerations of this type have always affected anti-trust courts is plain from the history of the Standard Oil, American Tobacco and Alcoa cases. To many champions of the anti-trust laws these cases indicate judicial timidity, economic innocence, lack of conviction, or paralysis of resolution. In the anti-trust field the courts have been accorded, by common consent, an authority they have in no other branch of law. Indeed, the only comparable examples of the power of judges is the economic role they formerly exercised under the Fourteenth Amendment, and the role they now exercise in the area of civil liberties. They would not have been given, or allowed to keep such authority in the anti-trust field, and they would not so freely have altered from time to time the interpretation of its substantive provisions, if courts were in the habit of proceeding with the surgical ruthlessness that might commend itself to those seeking absolute assurance that there will be workable competition, and to those aiming at the immediate realization of the social, political, and economic advantages of the dispersal of economic power.[17]

Judicial caution is not the only limitation which constrains the form of a decree. Anti-trust remedies affect others than defendants, and an equity court must consider whether its decrees are fair to all who feel their impact. In the Shoe Machinery Case, the Court decided not to impose a requirement that United cease absolutely to lease on grounds of fairness.

United is free to abolish leasing if it chooses to do so, but this Court hesitates to lay down an absolute ban for two reasons. First, if a ban were immediately applied, a substantial number of shoe factories would probably be put out of business, for they have not the assets, nor the capacity to borrow, requisite to purchase machines, even on conditional sales agreements. Second, if this Court forbade United to lease machines, it could not apply a similar ban to its competitors. This would constitute for United a major not a minor competitive handicap, if one accepts the testimony of the large number of shoe manufacturers who have already expressed their preference for leasing rather than buying machines. How deeprooted this preference is might be disputed; but it cannot be denied that virtually all the shoe manufacturers who took the stand, and the 45 shoe manufacturers who were selected as a sample by the Court, expressed a preference for the leasing system. . . . Moreover, Compo, which is United's chief rival, and which the Government claims was a chief victim of United's policies, favors the leasing system, and might encourage shoe factories to continue leasing.[18]

A further consideration is that the Government did not request that leasing be enjoined, and the Court is unlikely to go beyond what the Government requests.[19] The defendant has the opportunity to comment on the Government's requests for relief. Those that originate in the judge's chambers cannot be similarly examined.

The natural tendencies of courts to be cautious in their approach to anti-trust remedies is reinforced by the ill-considered and poorly presented plans which are often the contribution of the Government to the proceedings on relief. In the present case, for example, the Government presented a request for the dissolution of United into three competing companies as its major proposal for relief. The difficulties of this proposal have been examined in sufficient detail above.[20] What is appropriate to the present context is that the Government's argument in favor of this remedy was sketchy, poorly prepared, and failed to come to grips with any of the problems involved.[21] To convince a judge that so drastic a step was required would need a fairly detailed plan, well-supported by evidence, not 10 pages of generalities and citations from legal authorities, supported by 10 minutes of oral presentation.[22]

In part, the poor preparation of the Government arose from the fact that intent and conduct were uppermost in the minds of the lawyers who tried the Government case. Proof of liability in terms of an inappropriate standard, rather than the underlying economic situation, was the focus of the Government's efforts in the case. And again, this is typical. But this is not all. Resource limitations are also of great importance. The transcript suggested that the Department of Justice attorney who presented the arguments for dissolution really

---

[18] Opinion, pp. 114–5.

[19] Perhaps no more than this need be said with respect to the writer's suggestion of the creation of a New Company from B.B. Chemical and the Cement Shoe and Eyelet departments. See above, pp. 289–294.

[20] Pp. 272–275.

[21] See Brief for the United States on Relief, pp. 36–46, and Tr. pp. 14141 and 14159.

[22] This example is not unique. In the Alcoa remedy proceeding, Judge Knox refused to grant a Government prayer for dissolution because he was skeptical of the plan proposed. Yet here a good case could have been made, but the Government failed to present it. See U. S. v. Aluminum Co. of America, 91 F Supp. 333, Secns. 41–43.

had not had time to prepare himself thoroughly on the record of the case, no doubt because of other commitments. Moreover, an effective remedy presentation requires more than legal skills alone: the skills of economists and industrial engineers should also be drawn upon.

But even a large[23] increase in the budget of the Anti-Trust Division, spent on the hiring of appropriate professionals, will not remedy the problem of the drafting of effective relief decrees. In general, the kind of working knowledge of a business which is prerequisite to the successful and efficient performance on it of more or less drastic surgery is possessed mainly by the personnel of the firm itself, and not by any outsiders. The problem of improving decrees is in part the problem of making this knowledge available to the Court or other authority presiding over them. The present procedure of anti-trust trials does nothing toward this end. Again, if the standards of the law were revised to focus on situations rather than conduct, then a step in the right direction would be taken. Trials could then focus on an examination of the operations of the firm in its market context, rather than an attack on and defense of its aims in the transaction of a series of specific dealings with customers, suppliers, rivals, and thus the trial would stimulate the parties to produce the kind of information on which a decree could rest.

This same change in the law, if made explicit by legislation, would also do something to remove the judicial inhibitions on remedial action. If Congress were to tell the Courts that it was their function to change business situations whenever they permitted a firm or group of firms to have substantial market power, Courts would feel freer to exercise their discretion than they do now, when their concern is so much with the wrongfulness of business conduct. But whether the administration of such a statute is an appropriate task for Federal Courts, or whether a revision of the law incorporating a market power standard explicitly is at all likely are other questions, to which the experience of the Shoe Machinery Case cannot suggest answers.

[23] And visionary?

Appendix A

In the District Court of The United States for the District of Massachusetts

★

Civil No. 7198

United States of America, *Plaintiff*

v.

United Shoe Machinery Corporation, *Defendant*

★

COMPLAINT

The United States of America by its attorneys, acting under the direction of the Attorney General of the United States, brings this action against the United Shoe Machinery Corporation and complains and alleges, on information and belief, as follows:

JURISDICTION AND VENUE

1. This complaint is filed and these proceedings are instituted against the United Shoe Machinery Corporation under Section 4 of the Act of Congress of July 2, 1890, c. 647, 26 Stat. 209, as amended, entitled "An Act to Protect Trade and Commerce Against Unlawful Restraints and Monopolies," said Act being commonly known as the "Sherman Act," in order to prevent continuing violations by the defendant, as hereinafter alleged, of Sections 1 and 2 of said Act.

2. The defendant transacts business in the District of Massachusetts and may be found within said District.

DESCRIPTION OF THE DEFENDANT

3. The defendant is a corporation organized on May 2, 1905, and existing under the laws of the State of New Jersey and having its offices and principal place of business at 140 Federal Street, Boston, Massachusetts. Said corporation is the successor of United Shoe Machinery Company of New Jersey which was incorporated on February 7, 1899, under the laws of the State of New Jersey. Upon its incorporation, the defendant acquired substantially all the capital stock of United Shoe Machinery Company of New Jersey, and, on December 1, 1917, said company was merged with the defendant. Both corporations will sometimes be referred to hereinafter as United.

NATURE OF TRADE AND COMMERCE INVOLVED

4. In 1946 over 525,000,000 pairs of shoes, including all types of footwear, valued at about $1,500,000,000 were manufactured in the United States. These were made in approximately 1,400 shoe factories situated throughout the United States. About 25 per cent were made in factories in the State of Massachusettts.

5. While there are a multitude of shoe types with numerous variations upon each type, all shoes fall into three classes depending upon the method by which the outsole is attached to the rest of the shoe. These are sewed shoes, cement shoes, and nailed shoes. Sewed shoes account for about 59 per cent of the total number of shoes produced annually in the United States, cement shoes for about 38 per cent, and nailed shoes, consisting almost entirely of men's work shoes, for about 3 per cent.

6. The most important kinds of sewed shoes are the Goodyear Welt, McKay, sewed, lockstitch, pre-welt, and stitchdown. The Goodyear Welt embodies a system of construction regarded by the industry as the premier method of shoemaking. This system consists essentially of the use of an insole with an upstanding rib and superimposed welt which permit the stitching of the insole and outsole to the shoe in such a way that the stitching does not penetrate through the insole. About 30 per cent of the shoes manufactured in the United States, including virtually all men's dress shoes, are Goodyear Welts.

7. In McKay sewed and lockstitch shoes the outsole is attached to the insole by chain or lock stitching which passes through the insole.

These types are principally women's shoes and account for about 12 per cent of the shoes manufactured in the United States.

8. The stitchdown and pre-welt, like the Goodyear Welt, are constructed so that the inside of the shoe is not penetrated by stitching. They are usually infants', children's, and juvenile shoes and comprise about 14 per cent of the shoes sold in the United States.

9. The soles of cement shoes are usually attached by pyroxylin cement. This shoe was first commercialized in the United States about 1928 and has since gained wide popularity. Approximately 90 per cent of all cement shoes are women's, and the great bulk of those consist of low-priced dress shoes, sandals, sport shoes, slippers, platform shoes, and play shoes.

10. Until about 1860 shoes were made almost entirely by hand. Beginning about that time various machines were introduced to perform certain of the operations in the shoemaking process. As shoe-machine technology developed, more and more of the hand operations on shoes were supplanted by machines, so that today most of the operations of importance in the making of shoes are done by machine. As a consequence, the modern shoe factory employs numerous machines in the manufacture of shoes, and no manufacturer can engage in quantity production of shoes without such machinery. Machinery used in the manufacture of shoes is known in the shoe trade and referred to herein as shoe machinery in contradistinction to machinery used in the repair of shoes and known as shoe-repair machinery.

11. The principal procedures involved in the manufacture of shoes are known as upper cutting, upper fitting, stock fitting, lasting, bottoming, and making. Each of these includes various major operations performed by machine, which may be briefly described as follows:

12. Upper cutting and fitting consist of cutting, preparing, assembling, and uniting the various parts of the shoe upper. The parts of the upper are usually died out from leather and fabric by a clicking machine, and are sewed together on an upper stitching machine. In most shoes eyelets are inserted by eyeletting machines.

13. Stock fitting involves the cutting and preparation of the bottom stock of the shoe. Insoles and outsoles are frequently cut on cutting presses, known in the trade as dinking machines.

14. The lasting of a shoe is one of the most important steps in shoemaking. On most shoes it consists of a series of operations in

which the upper and lining are drawn over a wooden last and attached to the insole. The upper is initially stretched over and positioned on the last by a pulling over machine; a lasting machine then draws the upper over the last, conforms it snugly and smoothly to the profile of the last, and affixes it to the insole. Some lasting machines last the entire upper; others last only a part of the upper, such as the sides, toe, or heel.

15. Bottoming and making refer to the operations in which the outsole and heel are attached to the shoe. The outsole is initially affixed to the insole by an outsole laying machine, the edges of the outsole are rounded and trimmed by a rough rounding machine, and the sole is ironed by an outsole leveling machine. The outsoles of all shoes, except welts, are permanently attached by McKay sole sewing, loose nailing, or cement sole attaching machines. In welt shoes the welt is sewed to the insole by a welt sewing machine, the upstanding rib and surplus upper margin below the welt stitching are trimmed off by an inseam trimming machine, and the outsole is stitched to the welt by an outsole stitching machine. The part of the outsole to which the heel is attached, known as the heel seat, is usually fastened to the shoe by fiber fastening or loose nailing machines, and heels are attached by heel attaching and slugging machines.

16. The shoe machines described above will sometimes be referred to hereinafter as major machines. In addition, there are numerous other machines used in shoe factories which are more particularly identified in Appendix A attached hereto and expressly made a part hereof, and which will sometimes be referred to hereinafter as minor machines. A few of these are used only in the manufacture of rubber soles; all of the others are either auxiliary to major machines in the sense that their functions are immediately related to those of major machines, or they perform work independent of that done by major machines but of somewhat less importance in the shoemaking process. For example, prior to lasting, the insole and upper must be attached to the last. This is usually accomplished by machines auxiliary to lasting and pulling over machines, known as insole tacking and assembling machines. As previously explained, in welt shoes the welt is sewed to the upper and an upstanding rib on the insole by a welt sewing machine. The upstanding ribs on the insoles of most welt shoes are constructed by a group of machines auxiliary to the welt sewing machine, known as scoring, channeling, lip turning and setting, lip

and rib cementing, and reinforcing machines. Certain so-called metallic fastening machines, such as staple fastening and wiring machines, are used to fasten parts of the shoe together temporarily at various stages in its manufacture. Numerous other minor machines perform the various shoemaking operations known in the trade as lacing, buffing, skiving, cementing, folding, edging, roughing, trimming, conforming, splitting, cutting, molding, pounding, ironing, finishing, etc.

17. Continuously since 1899 United has been engaged in the manufacture and distribution of shoe machinery. Immediately upon its formation in 1899 United acquired most of the capital stock, business and assets of the Consolidated and McKay Lasting Machine Company, McKay Shoe Machinery Company, Goodyear Shoe Machinery Company, and Eppler Welt Machine Company, each of which was engaged in the manufacture and distribution of shoe machinery in the United States. The purpose of the merger, as set forth in a circular to stockholders of the Goodyear Shoe Machinery Company, was to realize "the great advantages to be secured by the control in one corporation both in the United States and foreign countries of the efficient types of shoe machinery. . . ." The effect of the merger was to consolidate in United the companies manufacturing practically all the welt sewing, outsole stitching, lasting, metallic fastening, and heel-attaching machines then being manufactured and distributed in the United States.

18. Since the merger United has continued to manufacture and distribute shoe machines of the type manufactured by its constituent companies to the extent that such machines have been in demand by shoe manufacturers, and from time to time since 1899 has embarked upon the business of manufacturing and distributing numerous other types of machines. At present United manufactures and distributes all types of major machines, except upper stitching machines, and all types of minor machines of importance, including each of those listed in Appendix A hereof.

19. Most of the shoe machinery made by United is manufactured in its principal factory at Beverly, Massachusetts; a substantial part is manufactured in factories of branches of United known as Booth Brothers Company, at Rochester, New York, and O. A. Miller Treeing Machine Company at Plymouth, New Hampshire. The distribution of its shoe machinery is handled almost entirely by

various so-called operating departments of the company known as the Lasting-Heeling, Eyeletting, Goodyear, Rubber Shoe, Fitting Room, Cutting Die, Littleway, Cement Shoe, and General Departments.

20. United is the only company in the United States which can completely equip a shoe factory with its necessary machinery, exclusive of upper stitching machines. The principal competitor of United is the Compo Shoe Machinery Company, and its operations are, with unimportant exceptions, confined to the manufacture and distribution of cement sole attaching machines and their auxiliaries. All other competitors of United manufacture only a single type or a few types of shoe machines. By reason of this, some or most of the machinery of all shoe manufacturers in the United States has been manufactured by United.

21. Most major machines and numerous minor machines manufactured by United are supplied to shoe manufacturers only on lease; the rest of its machines are made available by United to shoe manufacturers on sale terms only, or on sale or lease terms at the option of the shoe manufacturer. United's gross income from its leases in 1946 was $21,504,541. Its gross income from the sale of machines was $507,036. Over 80 per cent of the United machines now in use in shoe factories were distributed by United on lease as distinguished from outright sale.

22. United requires that all machines on lease to shoe manufacturers be serviced, and repaired by United. In part to provide this service, United maintains numerous branch offices throughout the United States conveniently situated near the various shoe production centers of the country. Approximately 900 roadmen are assigned to these offices for the ostensible purpose only of servicing shoe machinery in the possession of lessees. By reason of United's repair service, its roadmen have ready access to virtually all shoe factories in the United States.

23. United manufactures and sells shoe machinery parts and maintains depots for spare parts conveniently located to meet the demands of shoe manufacturers for such parts. United's gross income from the sale of parts in 1946 was $3,513,074.

24. United is engaged in the sale to shoe manufacturers of shoe factory supplies consisting of materials used in conjunction with various types of shoe machines; parts of shoes or materials from

which shoe parts are made; chemical compounds used in shoemaking; and shoemaking tools, findings, and miscellaneous equipment and accessories. Its gross income from the sale of shoe factory supplies in 1946 was over $25,000,000. Seventy-five per cent of the dollar volume of shoe factory supplies sold by United is manufactured in its main factory at Beverly and in factories of branches, subsidiaries, and affiliated companies of United, and 25 per cent by manufacturers in which United has no stock interest and from which United purchases supplies for resale. Such branches, subsidiaries, and affiliated companies of United and the shoe factory supplies manufactured by them are as follows:

Name	Principal Place of Business	Relation to United	Products
B. B. Chemical Co.	Cambridge, Mass.	Subsidiary	Cements, stains, waxes, leather finishes, reinforcing tapes for insoles.
W. W. Cross & Co., Inc.	East Jaffrey, N.H.	do	Tacks, nails.
S. A. Felton & Son. Co.	Manchester, N.H.	do	Hand and power brushes.
Hoague-Sprague Corp.	Lynn, Mass.	do	Boxes, box blanks, paper and fiber board, box forming machine.
Fred. W. Meers Heel Co., Inc.	Boston, Mass.	do	Wood heel block.
Shoe Form Co., Inc.	Auburn, N.Y.	do	Plastic shoe and hosiery forms.
Shoe Lace Co.	Lawrence, Mass.	do	Shoelaces, trimmings.
United Last Co.	Brockton, Mass.	do	Lasts.
Binghampton Die Plant	Binghamton, N.Y.	Branch	Cutting dies.
Booth Bros. Co.	Rochester, N.Y.	do	Accessories.
Hughes Eyelet Co.	Taunton, Mass.	do	Eyelets, accessories.
O. A. Miller Treeing Machine Co.	Plymouth, N.H.	do	Shoe trees, shoelaces.
J. C. Rhodes & Co., Inc.	New Bedford, Mass.	do	Eyelets, accessories.
The S.O. & C. Co.	Ansonia, Conn.	do	Do.
St. Louis Die Plant	St. Louis, Mo.	do	Cutting dies, accessories.
United Awl & Needle Co.	West Medway, Mass.	do	Awls, drivers, fibre fastening material, accessories.
United Shank & Findings Co.	Whitman, Mass.	do	Wood, steel, and combination shanks.
Celastic Corp.	Arlington, N.J.	Jointly owned by United and E.I. du Pont de Nemours Co.	Box toe material, celastic softener.
Tubular Rivet & Stud Co.	Wollaston, Mass.	25% of stock owned by United.	Hooks, rivets, grommets

25. Continuously since about 1951 shoe manufacturers have been engaged in the tanning of hides for shoe leather in tanneries owned or operated by said manufacturers. Approximately 25 per cent of the shoe leather presently made in the United States is manufactured in tanneries of shoe manufacturers. For many years United, through a wholly owned subsidiary known as the Turner Tanning Machinery Company with its principal place of business at Peabody, Massachusetts, has been engaged in the manufacture and sale of tanning machinery used by tanneries in the manufacture of shoe leather.

26. A substantial part of the shoe machinery, shoe machinery parts, shoe factory supplies, and tanning machinery hereinbefore described, including such machinery, parts, and supplies manufactured by or for United, is distributed in interstate commerce from the state of its manufacture, principally the State of Massachusetts, to shoe manufacturers in numerous other states throughout the United States.

OFFENSES CHARGED

27. Continuously from the year 1912 to the date of the filing of this complaint the defendant, United Shoe Machinery Corporation, has been violating Section 2 of the Sherman Act by:

(a) Monopolizing interstate trade and commerce in the shoe machinery industry of the United States;

(b) Monopolizing the manufacture and distribution in interstate commerce of all major shoe machines, except upper stitching and cement sole attaching machines, and attempting to monopolize the manufacture and distribution in interstate commerce of cement sole attaching machines;

(c) Monopolizing the manufacture and distribution in interstate commerce of numerous minor shoe machines of the type manufactured by it, and attempting to monopolize the manufacture and distribution in interstate commerce of all other such minor shoe machines;

(d) Monopolizing the manufacture and distribution in interstate commerce of parts used in shoe machinery leased by United;

(e) Monopolizing the distribution in interstate commerce of numerous of the shoe factory supplies of the type sold by it, and attempting to monopolize the distribution in interstate commerce of all other such supplies; and

(f) Attempting to monopolize and monopolizing the manufacture and distribution in interstate commerce of tanning machinery used in the manufacture of shoe leather.

In furtherance thereof, the defendant has combined and conspired with others to monopolize, and has entered into numerous contracts, agreements, and understandings in restraint of, the manufacture and distribution in interstate commerce of shoe machinery, shoe machinery parts, shoe factory supplies, and tanning machinery, in violation of Sections 1 and 2 of the Sherman Act. The defendant threatens to continue and will continue the offenses herein alleged unless the relief hereinafter prayed for is granted.

28. The defendant has attempted to monopolize and has monopolized the shoe machinery industry and the manufacture and distribution of shoe machinery, shoe machinery parts, shoe factory supplies, and tanning machinery, as hereinbefore alleged, by:

(a) Eliminating and disabling its actual and potential competitors engaged, or proposing to engage, in the development, manufacture, and distribution of shoe machinery, by acquiring their assets and employing their keymen;

(b) Inducing companies engaged in the manufacture and distribution of shoe machinery and shoe repair machinery to confine their operations to certain machines, to distribute their machinery to shoe factories exclusively through United, and to refrain from selling shoe repair machinery to shoe factories;

(c) Pursuing a manufacturing and marketing policy designed to prevent the installation in shoe factories of all competitive shoe machinery and to displace with United machinery all competitive shoe machinery installed in shoe factories;

(d) Engrossing patents and inventions relating to the manufacture of shoe machinery and using such patents and inventions to prevent competitors from manufacturing and distributing shoe machinery;

(e) Preventing the distribution of second-hand shoe machinery;

(f) Requiring lessees to purchase from United all parts for shoe machinery leased by it;

(g) Acquiring the capital stock and assets of corporations engaged in the manufacture and sale of shoe factory supplies;

(h) Inducing manufacturers engaged in the manufacture and sale of shoe factory supplies to market such supplies to the shoe trade exclusively through United;

(i) Using its monopoly of shoe machinery as an instrument to monopolize the distribution of shoe factory supplies; and

(j) Acquiring the capital stock and assets of corporations engaged in the manufacture and sale of tanning machinery.

The aforesaid monopolization and attempts to monopolize, and the acts, acquisitions, contracts, agreements, and understandings which formed a part thereof and were used in effectuation thereof, are hereinafter more fully set forth and described.

I. SHOE MACHINERY

A. Disabling actual or potential competitors by the acquisition of their assets and the employment of their keymen

29. To eliminate and restrict competition in the manufacture and distribution of shoe machinery United has from time to time acquired assets, including patents, machinery, models, and plant equipment, of numerous companies and individuals engaged, or proposing to engage, in the development, manufacture, and distribution of shoe machinery. United has also from time to time attempted to engage, and has engaged, in its employ inventors and other keymen of competitors for the purpose of restricting competition by depriving competitors of the services of such personnel. By means of the foregoing, United has suppressed the competition of numerous companies engaged in the manufacture and distribution of shoe machinery and has prevented other companies from entering into the business of manufacturing and distributing shoe machinery in competition with United. The transactions of this nature now known to plaintiff are hereinafter more fully described.

General Shoe Machinery Company

30. General Shoe Machinery Company was formed in 1917 by certain shoe manufacturers, including International Shoe Company, the largest manufacturer of shoes in the United States, to engage in the shoe machinery business in competition with United. During the period from 1917 to 1923 General engaged in the development of certain major machines and in the manufacture and sale of certain minor machines, principally treeing and finishing machines. By 1923 major machines of General were being used successfully for the manufacture of shoes and were ready for commercial exploitation.

31. In 1923 United agreed with certain of the stockholders of General, including International Shoe Company, to acquire the assets of General upon assurances sought by United that said stockholders would cooperate with United to prevent prosecution of it

under the antitrust laws for said acquisition. Pursuant to the agreement, General assigned to United for the sum of $400,000 its principal patents and applications for patents on shoe machinery, and United engaged the principal inventor of General in its employ. Thereupon, General discontinued its development work on shoe machinery, declined to lease or sell the major machines which it had developed, and proceeded to confine its shoe machinery business to treeing and finishing machines.

32. In 1928, pursuant to the aforesaid understanding reached in 1923, United acquired the remaining assets of General, including its treeing and finishing machine business, under a subterfuge adopted by it with the connivance of stockholders of General to hide the fact that United was acquiring the assets of one of its principal competitors. United induced International Shoe Company to purchase all assets of General not acquired by United in 1924 and simultaneously caused International to transfer said assets to United for the sum of $150,000. General was thereupon dissolved. The purchase of General's assets by International Shoe Company was not in good faith but was instigated by United to cloak an intentional violation of the antitrust laws.

Reece Shoe Machinery Company

33. Reece Shoe Machinery Company, a wholly owned subsidiary of Reece Buttonhole Machine Company, was engaged during the period between 1911 and 1934 in the shoe machinery business in competition with United. During said period the company developed and marketed clicking machines and various minor machines and was engaged in developing and attempting to commercialize lasting, outsole stitching, and welt sewing machines.

34. In or about 1928 United sought to employ the principal inventor of Reece Shoe Machinery Company who was then engaged in developing its outsole stitching and welt sewing machines. In 1934 United acquired for the sum of $55,000 all assets of the Reece Shoe Machinery Company, except those used in the manufacture of clicking machines. Said assets included all patents, models, and plant equipment used in the construction of the lasting, outsole stitching, and welt sewing machinery which Reece Shoe Machinery Company was then engaged in developing for commercialization. In 1935 Reece Shoe Machinery Company was consolidated with its parent

company which at all times thereafter has confined its shoe machinery business to the manufacture and sale of clicking machines.

Charles C. Blake and C. C. Blake, Inc.

35. C. C. Blake, Inc. was engaged during the period from about 1913 to 1932 in the development of automatic shoe machinery and succeeded in obtaining patents upon, and in constructing experimental models of, such machinery, including automatic welt sewing, outsole stitching, lasting, rough rounding, and channeling machines. In the year 1932 United acquired for the sum of $15,000 all assets, including shoe machinery patents, of said company and engaged its principal inventor in United's employ. United has never commercialized the automatic shoe machinery acquired from C. C. Blake, Inc.

Alexander E. Little and the Littleway Process Co.

36. Prior to 1924 Alexander E. Little developed and patented a process of lasting and outsole stitching known as the Littleway process, and staple lasting and lockstitch sole sewing machines to be used in said process. By 1924 the machines were being used successfully in the manufacture of shoes and were sufficiently developed for commercialization.

37. In 1924 United and Little entered into and thereafter carried out a contract providing as follows:

(a) That Little would cause to be incorporated a company to be known as the Littleway Process Company;

(b) That Little would assign to United 49% of the capital stock of the Littleway Process Company for the sum of $1,000,000 and would hold the remaining 51% in escrow subject to a five-year option of United to acquire said stock for the sum of $2,000,000;

(c) That Little would assign all patents covering the Littleway process to the Littleway Process Company which would thereafter engage in the business of licensing shoe manufactures to use the process;

(d) That Little would transfer to United its staple lasting and sole sewing machines, and patents and applications for patents upon such machines, and that United would thereafter engage in the manufacture and distribution of such machine;

(e) That for a period of ten years Little would not engage in any business competitive with the Littleway Process Company or United.

In 1927 United acquired from Little for the sum of $1,400,000 the remaining 51 per cent of the stock of the Littleway Process Company.

38. Continuously since 1927 the Littleway Process Company has been engaged, as a wholly owned subsidiary of United, in the business of licensing shoe manufacturers to use the Littleway process, and United has been the sole manufacturer and distributor of staple lasting and McKay lockstitch sole sewing machines used in said process. In 1946 over 50,000,000 pairs of shoes were staple lasted by the Littleway process and over 10,000,000 pairs were both staple lasted and stitched by said process.

Jacob S. Kamborian and Northern Machine Company

39. Northern Machine Company was formed by Jacob S. Kamborian and Albert Bancroft in 1930 to manufacture and commercialize irons, known as hot plates, invented and developed by Kamborian for use in cement lasting. In 1932, while Northern Machine Company was manufacturing and selling hot plates, United offered to purchase the company for $75,000 and sought to engage Kamborian in its employ. Upon the rejection by Northern Machine Company and Kamborian of said offer, United caused to be issued to it a British patent reading upon the Kamborian hot plate.

40. Between 1930 and 1932 Kamborian developed and patented in the United States a cement side lasting machine. During negotiations between United and Northern Machine Company for the sale of said company, Kamborian, at United's request, demonstrated his lasting machine to United. Thereafter, United caused to be issued to it a British patent reading upon Kamborian's lasting machine.

41. In 1935 United purchased from Kamborian his cement side lasting machine and patents upon said machine for the sum of $50,000. As a condition of said purchase imposed by United, Kamborian accepted employment with United as an inventor upon a three-year contract. While employed with United Kamborian was required by United to confine his work for Northern Machine Company to the development and exploitation of Kamborian hot plates, and at all times during said employment the business of Northern Machine Company was limited to the manufacture and sale of said hot plates. United has never commercialized the cement side lasting machine acquired from Kamborian.

Napoleon A. Monfils and Monfils Shoe Machinery Company

42. Monfils Shoe Machinery Company was a partnership formed in 1935 by Napoleon A. Monfils and Albert Meyers to manufacture, in a machine shop owned by Monfils, and sell a heel attaching machine developed by Monfils. In 1936 United engaged Monfils in its employ and acquired his machine shop, shoe machinery patents, and the rights of the Monfils Shoe Machinery Company in the heel attaching machine then being manufactured and sold by it. Upon agreeing to accept employment with United, Monfils caused Monfils Shoe Company to be dissolved.

Pincus Brauner and Brauner Manufacturing Company

43. Between 1934 and 1937 Pincus Brauner and the aforesaid Meyers caused the Brauner Manufacturing Company to be incorporated and to engage in the manufacture and sale of cement shoe machinery and in the development of a heel attaching machine. In 1937 United induced Brauner to accept employment with it and to transfer to United models and patterns of said heel attaching machine. Thereafter, United obtained a patent upon said machine.

William P. Egan and General Machine Sales Company

44. During the period from 1910 to 1938 William P. Egan and John F. Sheehan were partners in the business of manufacturing and selling shoe machinery, principally reconditioned second-hand machinery, said business being known after 1935 as General Machine Sales Company. In 1938 United induced Egan to withdraw from the partnership and accept employment with United. Thereafter, the business of General Machine Sales Company declined substantially, and the company was liquidated upon the death of Sheehan in 1942.

Barge Electric Shoe Cement Press, Inc.

45. Between 1932 and 1937 Barge Electric Shoe Cement Press, Inc., was engaged in the manufacture and distribution of sole cementing presses. In 1937 United acquired from Barge Electric Shoe Cement Press, Inc., for the sum of $45,000 the patents upon said presses and all jigs, tools, patterns, and other equipment used in their manufacture. Thereupon, Barge Electric Shoe Cement Press, Inc., ceased doing business.

Fitchburg Engineering Corporation

46. Prior to 1935 Fitchburg Engineering Corporation developed and patented a sole tempering machine and marketed said machine through the American Shoe Machinery Company. In 1935 United caused American Shoe Machinery Company to acquire the patents upon said machine from Fitchburg Engineering Corporation and to assign said patents to United. Thereupon, Fitchburg Engineering Corporation ceased manufacturing sole tempering machines.

Barbour Welting Company

47. Prior to 1928 Barbour Welting Company was engaged in the manufacture and distribution of a patented welt tempering machine. In 1928 United acquired from Barbour Welting Company for the sum of $5,000 all outstanding machines on lease by it and patents thereon, and Barbour Welting Company ceased the manufacture and distribution of such machines.

Safety Utility Economy Company

48. Prior to 1924 Safety Utility Economy Company was engaged in the manufacture and sale of electrical heating devices for use in the manufacture of shoes. In 1924 United acquired from said company the patterns, tools, and other equipment used in the manufacture of said devices, and Safety Utility Economy Company ceased the manufacture and sale of such devices.

Standard Shoe Tying Machine Company

49. Prior to 1924 the Standard Shoe Tying Machine Company was engaged in the manufacture and distribution of shoe tying machines. About 1924 United acquired from said company its assets, including jigs, tools, patterns, parts, and other equipment used in the manufacture of shoe tying machines, and said company ceased doing business.

Naumkeag Buffing Machine Company

50. Prior to 1920 Naumkeag Buffing Machine Company was engaged in the manufacture and distribution of buffing machines. About 1920 United acquired the assets of said company, and said company ceased doing business.

Gimson Shoe Machinery Company

51. For many years prior to 1930 Gimson Shoe Machinery Company was engaged in the manufacture of shoe machinery at Leicester, England, and in the export of such machinery to the United States through sales agents located in the United States, including Reece Shoe Machinery Company. In February, 1930, the assets of Gimson Shoe Machinery Company were acquired by British United Shoe Machinery Company, a subsidiary of United, and Gimson Shoe Machinery Company was liquidated. At the same time Gimson Shoe Machinery Company assigned to United all United States patents and pending applications relating to shoe machinery and held by said company.

B. Restrictive agreements with competitors

52. United has from time to time entered into agreements and understanding with various manufacturers of shoe machinery and shoe repair machinery designed to restrict, curtail, and prevent their competition in the manufacture and sale of such machinery. Under the terms of said agreements with United said manufacturers have confined their manufacture of shoe machinery to certain kinds, marketed their machinery exclusively through United, and refrained from distributing shoe repair machinery to shoe factories. The agreements and understandings of this nature now known to plaintiff are hereinafter more fully described.

Singer Manufacturing Company

53. For many years Singer Manufacturing Company has manufactured and sold most of the upper stitching machines, many of the buttonhole machines, and certain miscellaneous equipment used by shoe manufacturers in upper fitting. Between 1912 and 1920 Singer caused the Hamel Shoe Machinery Company to be organized and to engage, in competition with United, in the manufacture and sale of shoe machinery, other than upper stitching machines. Said company was at all times owned, controlled and financed by Singer.

54. Upon its formation, Hamel acquired four shoe machinery companies which were actively engaged in the development, manufacture, and distribution of shoe machinery. Thereafter, Hamel manufactured and marketed machinery of the type made by said com-

panies. In addition, Hamel expended large sums of money in extensive developmental work on shoe machinery, other than that made by the companies acquired by Hamel, and in the acquisition of patents upon said machinery, and manufactured and sold certain types of machinery thus developed by it. By 1920 numerous shoe machines of Hamel were being used by shoe manufacturers, and in some instances shoe factories were completely equipped with shoe machinery made by Hamel.

55. Throughout the period from about 1920 to the date of this complaint, United and Singer have been parties to an agreement and understanding, the substantial terms of which have been that United would refrain from manufacturing and distributing upper fitting machinery, including upper stitching and buttonhole machines, and equipment of the kind manufactured by Singer, and that Singer would not engage in the manufacture and distribution of any other type of shoe machinery. Said agreement has been and is being carried out by Singer and United, and in furtherance thereof the parties thereto have done the following:

(a) Singer caused the Hamel Shoe Machinery Company to cease doing business in 1925 and to assign its shoe machinery patents to Singer.

(b) Singer from time to time transferred to United by license and agreement, in some instances for no money consideration, all patents acquired by Singer from Hamel and other shoe machinery patents held by Singer.

(c) Singer has at all times since the liquidation of Hamel refrained from manufacturing and selling shoe machinery, other than upper stitching and buttonhole machines.

(d) During the period between 1936 and 1946 United withdrew from the manufacture and distribution of buttonhole machines and induced its customers to substitute Singer machines for United machines.

(e) United has at all times refrained from manufacturing upper stitching machines and upper fitting equipment of the kind manufactured by Singer, and, when requested by shoe manufacturers to supply upper fitting equipment of the kind manufactured by Singer, has purchased such equipment from Singer for resale to shoe manufacturers.

(f) United and Singer have from time to time collaborated in developmental work upon their respective lines of machinery.

(g) United and Singer have continuously collaborated in the preparation of shoe factory layouts under arrangements providing that Singer limit shoe factory layouts prepared by it to fitting rooms and that United induce shoe factories for which it prepared layouts to acquire from Singer upper fitting machinery and equipment of the type manufactured by Singer.

The Lamson Company

56. Prior to 1934 the Lamson Company sold and installed in shoe factories shoe conveyor systems patented and developed by it. In 1934 Lamson and United entered into, and have since continuously carried out, the following agreement:

(a) That United should be the exclusive agent for Lamson in the United States for the distribution and maintenance of shoe conveyor systems;

(b) That the normal method of marketing shoe conveyor systems should be by lease and not by sale, and that shoe conveyor systems should not to be sold except with the consent of United;

(c) That United should pay to Lamson the sum of $220,000 in partial settlement of United's share in patent and developmental costs of shoe conveyor systems;

(d) That Lamson and United should share equally in the manufacturing costs of shoe conveyor systems and in the income from leases of said systems;

(e) That Lamson should appear as lessor in all leases of shoe conveyor systems and that no publicity should be given to the aforesaid agreement nor to United's interest in shoe conveyor systems.

Tubular Rivet & Stud Company

57. Tubular Rivet & Stud Company has been engaged for many years in the manufacture of hook setting machines. Continuously since 1912, pursuant to agreement between Tubular Rivet & Stud Company and United, United has been the exclusive agent of Tubular Rivet & Stud Company for the distribution of such machines to shoe factories. Since the execution of said agreement, all hook setting machines of Tubular Rivet & Stud Company installed in shoe factories have been distributed by United pursuant to said agreement.

Breuer Electric Manufacturing Company

58. Prior to 1936 Gordon A. Brawley developed a heat blower for removing wrinkles from shoes and induced Breuer Electric Manu-

facturing Company to manufacture the blower and to distribute it exclusively through a company formed by Brawley, called Gordon A. Brawley & Associates. In 1935 United caused to be assigned to it a patent issued to one Sandt, and thereafter demanded that Brawley & Associates desist from distributing the heat blower on the ground that it infringed the Sandt patent. In 1936 United purchased from Brawley & Associates its agency for the distribution of said blower and the good-will of its business in heat blowers. At all times since 1936 United has been the exclusive agent of Breuer Electric Manufacturing Company for the distribution of heat blowers.

Landis Machine Company

59. For many years Landis Machine Company has been engaged in the manufacture and sale of shoe repair machinery. About 1936 Landis, under threat of infringement suit by United, agreed with United to refrain, and has refrained, from soliciting the business of shoe manufacturers for machinery manufactured by Landis.

C. The pursuit by United of a manufacturing and marketing policy designed to restrict and eliminate competition

60. To forestall, restrict, and eliminate competition in the manufacture and distribution of shoe machinery United has continuously pursued a policy of (a) distributing most of its machinery upon leases which are intended to, and do, prevent shoe manufacturers from using competitive machinery; (b) adopting charges and other lease and sale terms for its machinery calculated to prevent the installation or cause the removal of competitive shoe machinery, and modifying said charges and terms for said purpose; (c) preëmpting the market for new and improved shoe machinery by introducing such machinery when competition arises or is anticipated, and by developing and distributing new and improved machinery similar to or duplicating such machinery introduced by its competitors; (d) distributing "fighting" machines to replace and prevent the installation of competitive machines; and (e) refusing to sell parts and equipment for use in or with competitive shoe machinery. In furtherance of this policy, United has instituted and used a system of policing shoe factories which has enabled it at all times to know the amount, kind, and source of all competitive machinery in all shoe factories in the United States.

1. *United's leasing policy*

61. For many years United has declined to sell most of its shoe machines and has made such machines available to shoe manufacturers only upon leases which reserve to United the sole and exclusive property in the machines and which grant to lessees the right to use the machines only for the purposes specified in the leases. United offers certain of its machines upon lease or sale terms at the option of shoe manufacturers but has followed the practice of establishing such alternative terms of sale and lease as will cause shoe manufacturers to lease such machines. As a consequence, most machines offered by United on optional terms are leased by shoe manufacturers.

62. At present United offers on lease only all of its major machines, except sole cutting and certain leveling machines; all minor machines handled, with a few unimportant exceptions, by its Lasting-Heeling, Goodyear, Littleway, and Cement Shoe departments; and various minor machines handled by its other departments. It offers on sale and not on lease a limited number of unimportant shoe machines handled, principally, by its General Department. All other shoe machines are offered on optional lease or sale terms. As a consequence of the foregoing, of the 123,000 United machines in shoe factories today only 21,000, or approximately 17 per cent, are owned by shoe manufacturers.

63. United's leases for most of its machines provide for the payment by shoe manufacturing lessees of flat rental charges or of so-called unit charges based upon the number of shoes upon which the machines are used or upon the number of operations performed by the machines. Leases for the rest of its machines provide for the payment of both rental and unit charges. Where unit charge machines are adaptable for more than one kind of operation separate charges are assessed by United for each kind of operation.

64. All leases of United have for many years, and do now, contain the following provisions which, along or in combination with one or more of the other, are intended to, and do, deter and prevent shoe manufacturing lessees from replacing with a competitive machine each of the shoe machines leased from United:

(a) That the lessee shall use the machine for not less than a term of five or ten years, depending upon the type of machine and the date of execution of the lease; that the lease may be cancelled during said term only by United; and that, thereafter, the lessee shall continue to use the machine indefinitely subject to the right of United or the lessee to terminate the lease upon 60 days' notice;

(b) That the lessee of each unit charge machine shall use the machine each month upon a stipulated minimum number of pairs of shoes, and shall pay to United a stipulated sum of money at the conclusion of each month during which the machine is not used upon said minimum number of pairs of shoes;

(c) That the lessee of each unit charge machine shall use the machine to its full capacity upon all shoes made by the lessee upon which the machine is capable of being used.

(d) That upon termination of the lease the lessee shall surrender the machine to United in good order and condition, shall reimburse United for the cost of all broken or missing parts, and shall pay to United a stipulated sum of money varying according to the machine leased from about 20% to 85% of the value of the machine.

United has from time to time invoked said lease provisions to prevent shoe manufacturers from replacing United machines with competitive machines.

2. *The adoption and modification of lease and sale terms to eliminate competition*

65. United has from time to time upon the introduction by it of shoe machinery adopted terms for such machinery, including rentals, unit charges, and selling prices, calculated to cause the machinery to supplant competition in its field. In numerous instances where competition of importance has developed with respect to shoe machinery then being manufactured and distributed by United, United has attempted to stifle such competition by modifying its lease and sale terms in the following respects, among others:

(a) Granting extended free trials of machinery;
(b) Waiving initial payments, monthly payments for use less than minimum, and lease termination charges;
(c) Loaning machinery to shoe manufacturers on a short-term basis for the manufacturers' so-called peak load operations;
(d) Reducing rental, unit, and sale charges;
(e) Substituting rental for lease charges; and
(f) Substituting sale terms for lease terms.

By means of such marketing tactics United has intentionally driven out of business numerous shoe machinery companies, including the B & W Shoe Machinery Company and the H. Gordon Co., Inc., and has attempted to frustrate, and has frustrated, the manufacture and distribution of shoe machinery of various types by numerous companies, including Compo Shoe Machinery Company, Hamlin Machine Company, and Brethols Manufacturing Company.

3. Preëmption of the market for new and improved shoe machinery

66. United has continuously sought to anticipate all demands of the shoe industry for improved or new machinery and, where such demand appeared to invite competition, to forestall such competition by manufacturing and distributing such machinery. In numerous instances United has adopted improvements, or purported improvements, in shoe machinery for the purpose of eliminating competition encountered by old and unimproved shoe machinery of United. By virtue of this, to the extent that new and improved shoe machinery has been developed by United since 1912, United has usually been able, as intended by it, to entrench itself in the fields of such machinery before competition could develop.

67. In all instances where new or improved shoe machinery of importance has been introduced by competitors of United, United has developed and introduced similar machinery of its own for the purpose of displacing from shoe factories such machinery of its competitors and preventing its installation. United has thereby eliminated or substantially restricted installations of competitive shoe machinery by numerous companies, including, among others, Compo Shoe Machinery Company, Hamlin Machine Company, International Shoe Machinery Company, and Peerless Machinery Company. The attempts by United to suppress the competition of said companies by manufacturing and distributing machines of the kind introduced by them are hereinafter more fully described.

Compo Shoe Machinery Company

68. The most important development in the shoe industry since 1912 has been the introduction of the cement shoe and machinery for its manufacture. For some time prior thereto United has refrained from introducing such machinery for fear of displacing other

machinery manufactured by it. The first commercially successful cement shoe machinery was offered to the shoe industry in the United States in 1928 by Compo Shoe Machinery Company, and until 1931 virtually all cement shoes were bottomed on such machinery. Upon the development of the Compo machinery United offered to purchase such machinery and the patents thereon for $55,000. Said offer was rejected, and United thereupon commenced the development of machinery similar to that of Compo. In 1931 United introduced its line of cement sole machinery, and since that time has progressively increased the volume of cement shoes bottomed on its machinery. In 1946 approximately 52 per cent of all cement shoes were bottomed on machinery of United manufacture.

Hamlin Machine Company

69. About 1929 Hamlin Machine Company commercialized a heel flap trimming machine developed and patented by Nicholas W. Mathey. Upon the acceptance and use of the machine by shoe manufacturers, United introduced a similar machine in 1931 and distributed said machine until 1940 on terms calculated to prevent the distribution of Hamlin's machine. In an action for infringement by Mathey against United, the United States District Court for the District of Massachusetts found that United had intentionally infringed Mathey's patent, and that United "knew or must have known" that the effect of the terms established by it on its heel flap trimming machine "would ruin the plaintiff as its only competitor in a distinctive field." By reason of the intentional infringement by United of Mathey's patent, the terms established by United upon its machine, and the employment by United of tactics designed to harass Hamlin in doing business, Hamlin was forced out of the business of manufacturing and marketing heel flap trimming machines.

International Shoe Machinery Company

70. About 1940 Jacob S. Kamborian developed, patented, and commercialized through the International Shoe Machinery Company the first successful side lasting machine to perform a continuous lasting operation. Upon the acceptance and use of the machine by shoe manufacturers, United introduced in 1943, and has since been distributing, a similar machine which it at all times

knew to infringe, and which the United States District Court for the District of Massachusetts has found infringes, Kamborian's patents upon his side lasting machine.

Peerless Machinery Company

71. About 1914 the Peerless Machinery Company developed, patented, and commercialized a device to be used upon eyeletting machines for setting invisible eyelets in shoes. Upon the acceptance and use of the device by shoe manufacturers, United introduced, and has since been distributing, an identical device. In an action for infringement filed on behalf of Peerless against United, the United States District Court for the District of Massachusetts found that United had infringed the Peerless patent and that "the infringement was willful, deliberate, and intentional."

4. Policing of competition

72. For many years United has employed its 900 roadmen to police all installations of competitive shoe machinery in the United States. Although such roadmen are granted access to shoe factories by shoe manufacturers solely for the purpose of servicing United machinery, United has required its roadmen to, and they do, systematically detect and report to United all installations and removals of competitive shoe machinery. United maintains a current file of so-called outside machine installation and removal reports of its roadmen for the purpose of enabling it to ascertain at all times the nature of the competition which each of its machines encounters. United has at all times used said reports as a basis for determining the methods to be employed by it to suppress the competition revealed by said reports. When United embarks upon a program to eliminate a competitive shoe machinery line it causes its roadmen to make periodic checkups in shoe factories and reports to United concerning the competitive machinery involved to enable United to appraise the success of its program.

D. Engrossing shoe machinery patents and inventions to suppress competition

73. United has been for many years, and is now, engaged in a program of engrossing all patents and inventions of importance relating to shoe machinery for the purpose of blanketing the shoe

machinery industry with patents under the control of United and thereby suppressing competition in the industry.

74. Since 1920 United and its subsidiaries have acquired 6,712 United States patents, the vast majority of which relate to shoe machinery. 4,172 of these patents, including 3,777 standing in United's name, have issued since January 1, 1930. In addition, United has acquired by licenses, some of which are exclusive, the right to use 108 other patents. On January 1, 1947, United's Patent Department had 857 inventions "on hand," of which 400 were the subjects of patent applications pending in the United States Patent Office.

75. United has for many years maintained large staffs of research and patent experts to develop and process all patentable ideas relating to shoe machinery for the purpose of causing patents to issue to United. Its Research Division employs about 500 men, has a current annual budget of $3,000,000, and has spent $20,000,000 since 1930. United's Patent Department has a staff of 28 full-time lawyers who work in close collaboration with the Research Division. The Research Division has employed, at one time or another, most inventors skilled in the shoe machinery art under contracts binding the inventors to assign all inventions to United not only during the inventors' terms of employment, but also for stipulated periods thereafter.

76. United has instituted and conducted a campaign in the shoe industry to cause the industry to pass on to United all shoe machinery patents, improvements, and inventions. By means of this campaign United has inspired the industry to believe that United represents the only market of importance for shoe machinery inventions. Since 1930 United has acquired 325 patents and 200 inventions, some of which were later patented by United, from persons and companies unaffiliated with United.

77. By its aggregation of shoe machinery patents United has prevented all others, including its competitors, from exploiting the progress in the shoe machinery art represented by said patents. United has licensed others (exclusive of its machinery customers) to use only 208 of the 4,172 patents acquired by United and its subsidiaries since 1930, and has refrained from licensing the use of all other such patents.

78. By depriving its competitors of the art covered by its blanket of patents, United has arrogated to itself the power to determine to what extent new and improved machinery covered by patents held

by United shall be offered to the shoe industry, and has exercised this power to promote the continued use of machinery of United which has been on the market for many years. Of the 3,777 patents acquired by United since 1930, aside from those of its subsidiaries, 2,729 are "paper" patents which United has never purported to commercialize. Many of these paper patents cover machinery which, if built, would compete with outstanding United machinery, but which United has refrained from developing and offering to the shoe trade.

79. Only a limited number of the 1,048 patents which were acquired by United since 1930 and which United claims it has commercialized cover new machinery or improvements of substantial importance. United has out on lease today and has sold since 1930, 554 models of machines. 462 of these were in use prior to 1930; the balance, amounting to 92 models, have been adopted since 1930 and are claimed by United to be covered by 363 of the patents acquired by it since 1930. Thus, of United's 3,777 post-1930 patents no more than 363 have been commercialized through new machine models adopted by United since that time and offered by it today.

80. United has purported to incorporate a few of the remaining 685 commercialized patents in machinery which is no longer being offered to the trade and most of the rest in currently offered machinery which was placed on the market by United prior to 1930. A substantial number of such patents are employed by United to enable it to claim patent protection upon machinery which has been on the market for many years and on which all basic patents have expired. United has thereby caused its competitors to refrain from marketing similar machinery for fear of infringing United's post-1930 patents claimed by it to read upon such machinery.

81. The complexity of the patent structure erected by United, its size, and the obscurity of its boundaries which United has intentionally fostered, have, as intended by United, operated to deter others from developing machinery beyond the range of United's patents. In addition, United has employed its patents to fence in competitors by preventing them from developing and using improvements upon their machinery, to block developments in important fields of shoe machinery, to compel the assignment of related patents and inventions, and to tie the use of United machinery to shoe processes controlled by United.

82. United has invoked its patents in numerous instances where

competitors have sought to market shoe machinery. Its Patent Department systematically reviews all outside machine installation reports submitted by roadmen to detect all instances where claims might be made by United that competitive machinery infringed United patents. In numerous instances United has attempted to prevent, and has prevented, the distribution of competitive machinery by threatening to institute, and instituting, infringement proceedings.

E. Preventing the distribution of second-hand shoe machinery

83. United has at all times sought to prevent its shoe machinery from being reconditioned and sold by other companies as second-hand shoe machinery. For said purpose, United has insisted upon the return to it of all leased machinery when shoe manufacturers have discontinued its use. United has induced shoe manufacturers to lease machinery offered on optional lease or sale terms partly to enable United to recapture such machinery from shoe factories for the purpose of preventing its distribution as second-hand machinery. United has from time to time engaged in programs to recapture machinery sold by it by buying used United machinery and by granting to shoe manufacturers trade-in allowances on new machinery in exchange for used United machinery. All shoe machinery thus recaptured by United has been reconditioned and distributed as new machinery or scrapped.

84. To restrict the competition of second-hand shoe machinery United has from time to time acquired by outright purchase or by granting trade-in allowances on new machinery, and has scrapped used shoe machinery made by competitors of United, and has declined to sell shoe machinery parts to second-hand shoe machinery dealers.

F. The monopoly of shoe machinery achieved and maintained by United

85. By means of the unlawful conduct hereinbefore described, United has placed in shoe factories most of the shoe machinery used in the manufacture of shoes in the United States. Over 85 per cent of the total number now in use in all shoe factories of each of 16 types of major machines, and over 90 per cent of each of 14 types of such machines, have been manufactured by United. The number in shoe factories of each type of major machine manufac-

tured by United and the percentage represented by United machines of the total number of each type of all makes in shoe factories are as follows:

Major Machine	Number of United Machines in Shoe Factories	Percentage of Total Number of Machines in Shoe Factories Represented by United Machines
Clicking	16,408	97
Lasting	12,554	94
Eyeletting	7,299	93
Outsole stitching	3,537	92
Heel attaching	3,169	93
Pulling over	3,145	99
Welt sewing	1,470	97
Rough rounding	1,430	98
Loose nailing	1,224	98
Outsole leveling	1,082	97
Outsole laying	1,029	96
Slugging	881	87
Cement sole attaching	870	40
Cutting press (dinking)	756	72
Inseam trimming	595	99
McKay lockstitch sole sewing	581	91
McKay chainstitch sole sewing	498	88
Fiber fastening	472	100

86. By reason of the foregoing, most major operations on most shoes manufactured in the United States are performed by United machines. In particular, United pulling over machines are employed on virtually all shoes in which the upper is initially pulled over the last by machine; United machines perform the lasting on all men's and women's shoes with insignificant exceptions and on most children's and juvenile shoes; over 90 per cent of the soles of all sewed shoes are attached by machines of United make; the outsoles of all work shoes are nailed on United machines; and the bottoming of virtually all Goodyear Welts is done by welt sewing and outsole stitching machines of United manufacture.

87. Appendix A hereof sets forth the number in shoe factories of

each type of minor machine handled by each of United's operating departments and the percentage represented by United machines of the total number of each type of all makes in shoe factories. The composite figures for each of United's operating departments are as follows:

Department	Number of Minor Machines of United in Shoe Factories	Percentage of Total Number of Machines in Shoe Factories Represented by United Machines
General	20,183	71
Fitting room	13,982	57
Lasting-heeling	14,107	86
Goodyear	7,857	87
Cement shoe	3,415	66
Eyeletting	839	100
Littleway	716	93
Rubber shoe	709	64
Cutting die	673	89

88. As reflected by Appendix A hereof, United has placed in shoe factories 500 or more machines of each of 38 minor types. Over 80 per cent of the total number now in use in all shoe factories of each of 29 of said machine types, and over 90 per cent of each of 18 of said machine types have been manufactured by United.

II. SHOE MACHINERY PARTS

89. United has at all times embodied in its leases, and enforced, a provision requiring its lessees to purchase from United all duplicate parts, extras, mechanisms, and devices of every kind needed or used in operating, repairing, or renewing leased machinery. In addition, United has continuously designed its machines in such manner as to require parts of off-standard specifications which can only be obtained from United. By virtue of the foregoing, United has at all times sold all parts for its leased machinery purchased by shoe manufacturers and is the only company in the United States engaged to any substantial extent in the manufacture and sale of shoe machinery parts.

III. SHOE FACTORY SUPPLIES

90. For many years United has been engaged in a program designed to enable it to provide all shoe factories in the United States with all shoe factory supplies required by them. In furtherance thereof, United has acquired, either directly or through its subsidiaries, capital stock in numerous companies engaged in the manufacture and sale of such supplies. Said companies, their principal places of business, the dates of the acquisitions by United of a majority of their capital stock, and the products manufactured by them are as follows:

Name	Principal Place of Business	Date of Stock Acquisition	Products
B. B. Chemical Co.	Cambridge, Mass.	1928	Cements, stains, waxes, leather finishes, reinforcing tapes for insoles.
Celastic Corporation	Arlington, N.J.	1925	Box toe material, celastic softener.
Conway Wood Heel Co.	Conway, N.H.	1922	Wood heel blocks.
Fellows Wood Heel Co.	Brentwood, N.H.	1928	Wood heel blocks.
Framingham Last Co.	Brockton, Mass.	1925	Lasts.
Hoague-Sprague Corp.	Lynn, Mass.	1925	Shoe boxes, shoe box blanks, paper and fibre board, box forming machines.
Hughes Eyelet Co.	Taunton, Mass.	1918	Eyelets, accessories.
Maple Wood Heel Co.	Newburyport, Mass.	1922	Wood heel blocks.
Fred W. Mears Heel Co., Inc.	Boston, Mass.	1922	Wood heel blocks.
Merrimack Wood Heel Co.	Boston, Mass.	1927	Wood heel blocks.
Shoe City Wood Heel Co.	Lynn, Mass.	1930	Wood heel blocks.
Shoe Form Co., Inc.	Auburn, N.Y.	1934	Plastic shoe and hosiery forms.
Shoe Lace Company	Lawrence, Mass.	1936	Shoelaces, shoe trimmings.
Slipper City Wood Heel Co.	Salem Depot, N.H.	1922	Wood heel blocks.
Star Wood Heel Company	Brooklyn, N.Y.	1925	Wood heel blocks.
United Last Company	Brockton, Mass.	1916	Lasts.
United Shank & Findings Company	Whitman, Mass.	1920	Wood, steel and combination shanks.

Each of the above companies, except Celastic Corporation, is a subsidiary of United or has been merged with United or one of its subsidiaries. United owns approximately 50 per cent of the capital stock of Celastic Corporation and markets exclusively all shoe factory supplies made by said company.

91. In furtherance of the aforesaid objective, United has entered into arrangements with numerous manufacturers of shoe factory supplies to sell their products to shoe factories. In many instances said manufacturers have agreed to distribute their products to the shoe trade exclusively through United. The companies distributing their shoe factory supplies exclusively through United, their principal places of business, and the shoe factory supplies made by said companies are as follows:

Name	Principal Place of Business	Products
American Brass Co.	Ansonia, Conn.	Staple lasting & toe wire.
American Steel & Wire Co.	Worcester, Mass.	Staple lasting & toe wire.
E.I. duPont de Nemours Co.	Wilmington, Del.	Synthetic leather, insole & midsole material.
Endicott-Johnson Corp.	Endicott, N.Y.	Fibre blocks.
Hyde Manufacturing Co.	Southbridge, Mass.	Machine knives.
Independent Nail & Tacking	E. Bridgewater, Mass.	Wire nails.
Marstin Adhesive Co.	Lynn, Mass.	Glue.
Snell-Atherton-Norcross Co.	Brockton, Mass.	Hand tools.
Mullen Brothers, Inc.	Brockton, Mass.	Finishes.
Thompson Manufacturing Co.	Lynn, Mass.	Roll covers.
Union Paste Co.	Medford, Mass.	Glue.

92. United has continuously employed its dominance of the shoe industry achieved through its monopoly of shoe machinery, hereinbefore alleged, to further its business of selling shoe factory supplies. By means of its influence and prestige in the shoe industry created by its shoe machinery business United has induced numerous shoe manufacturers to rely upon United as a single or principal source of supply for both machinery and shoe factory supplies. In addition, United has sought to persuade, and has persuaded, shoe manufacturers to use United supplies with United machines by:

(a) Representing to shoe manufacturers that United machines give superior performance when used with United supplies;

(b) Causing its roadmen responsible for servicing United machines to promote the sale of United supplies used in such machines and to police sales of competitive supplies;

(c) Specifying United supplies for use with its machinery upon the submission to shoe manufacturers of factory layouts prepared by United;

(d) Introducing shoe factory supplies simultaneously with the introduction of shoe machines with which such supplies are used;

(e) Establishing such terms upon United machines requiring United supplies as will induce shoe manufacturers to install such machines in preference to others which do not require United supplies;

(f) Correlating prices for shoe factory supplies with charges for machines in which such supplies are used.

93. Until 1920 United leased its eyeletting and metallic fastening machines on condition that the lessees purchase from United eyelets and metallic fastening materials, such as nails and tacks, used in said machines. By means of said leases United achieved a monopoly in the distribution of such supplies to shoe factories. Pursuant to a decree of the District Court of the United States for the Eastern District of Missouri in 1920 United cancelled said leases, but its monopoly of interstate commerce in eyelets and metallic fastening materials used in said machines has been preserved, and has not been dissipated by the cancellation of the leases.

94. By means of the unlawful conduct hereinbefore described, United has established itself as the only company in the United States distributing a full line of shoe factory supplies. United sells about 40 per cent of the dollar volume of all shoe factory supplies of the kind marketed by it and its subsidiaries and used in shoe factories. It supplies at least 73 per cent of each of the various kinds of metallic and fiber fastening materials incorporated in shoes by machine, that is to say, 95 per cent of the eyelets, 100 per cent of the fiber fastening materials, 75 per cent of the nails, 85 per cent of the tacks, 73 per cent of the screws, and 97 per cent of the wire. United also supplies over 90 per cent of the perforating awls and drivers, stitching needles and awls, rolls and wheels, cutters and irons, sharpening stones and wheels, knives, and brushes, used in shoe machinery; 99 per cent of the celastic material, 50 per cent of the shoe shanks, 35 per cent of the wood heel blocks, and 40 per cent of the lasts, used in the manufacture of shoes; and at least one-third of most of the chemical compounds, including 40 per cent of the solvents, 90 per cent of the celastic softeners, 40 per cent of the finishes, and 75 per cent of the thread waxes, used in shoe factories.

IV. TANNING MACHINERY

95. Turner Tanning Machinery Company has been engaged for many years in the manufacture and sale of tanning machinery. Upon

the entrance by shoe manufacturers into the field of shoe leather tanning, Turner supplied to such manufacturers a substantial part of the machinery used in tanneries owned by them. To preëmpt the demand of shoe manufacturers for tanning machinery, United during the period between 1920 and 1931, acquired, and now holds, substantially all the capital stock of Turner. By virtue of said acquisition, United, through Turner, manufacturers and sells 75 per cent of the tanning machinery used in tanneries in the United States, including those owned by shoe manufacturers.

96. Until 1929 Whitney Machine Company was engaged in the manufacture and sale of tanning machinery in competition with Turner. In said year United caused Turner to acquire the assets of Whitney and to engage in its emply the president and principal inventor of Whitney. Thereafter, Whitney ceased doing business.

EFFECTS OF THE VIOLATION OF LAW

97. The aforesaid monopolization and attempts to monopolize and the acts, acquisitions, contracts, agreements, and understandings used in effectuation thereof, have had the following effects as intended by the defendant:

(a) The defendant controls and dominates the shoe machinery industry of the United States and has the power to exclude all others from said industry.

(b) The defendant has the power arbitrarily to determine who may engage in the manufacture of shoes in the United States, the extent to which machinery shall be used in the manufacture of shoes in the United States, and the kinds of shoes which shall be manufactured in the United States.

(c) The defendant has retarded and forestalled the development and introduction of new and improved shoe machinery, including automatic shoe machinery, thereby compelling shoe manufacturers to continue to use machinery of the defendant which has been on the market for many years, retarding the introduction of mass production techniques in the manufacture of shoes, restricting the productivity of labor in shoe factories, and preventing reductions in shoe manufacturing costs by the use of new and improved machinery.

(d) The defendant has collected excessive, arbitrary, and noncompetitive charges for its products and services and has thereby made excessive and unreasonable profits from the manufacture and distribution of shoe machinery, shoe machinery parts, shoe-factory supplies, and tanning machinery.

(e) The defendant has exacted from shoe-manufacturing lessees for the use of shoe machinery of the defendant large sums of money in excess of the reasonable value of such machinery and of the service rendered by defendant upon said machinery.

(f) The supply of shoe machinery in the United States has been restricted and curtailed, thereby causing from time to time serious shortages of shoe machinery and retarding the operation and expansion of the shoe industry.

(g) The second-hand shoe machinery market in the United States has been forestalled and destroyed.

(h) Competition among shoe manufacturers in shoe machinery technology has been curtailed and eliminated.

PRAYER

Wherefore, the plaintiff prays:

1. That the Court adjudge and decree that the aforesaid monopolization of the shoe machinery industry of the United States and of interstate trade and commerce in shoe machinery, shoe machinery parts, shoe factory supplies, and tanning machinery, and the aforesaid attempts to monopolize, and contracts, combinations, and conspiracies to monopolize and restrain, interstate trade and commerce in said products, are in violation of Sections 1 and 2 of the Sherman Act.

2. That the Court adjudge and decree that the defendant has monopolized and attempted to monopolize the shoe machinery industry of the United States, and interstate trade and commerce in shoe machinery, shoe machinery parts, shoe factory supplies and tanning machinery, and has combined and conspired to monopolize, and has contracted, combined and conspired to restrain, interstate trade and commerce in said products in violation of Sections 1 and 2 of the Sherman Act.

3. That the defendant and its directors, officers, agents, representatives, and all persons or corporations acting on behalf of the defendant be perpetually enjoined from continuing to carry out, and be required to desist and withdraw from, said monopolization and attempts to monopolize, and said contracts, combinations, and con-

spiracies and be perpetually enjoined from in any way monopolizing, attempting to monopolize, and combining or conspiring to restrain, interstate trade and commerce in shoe machinery, shoe machinery parts, shoe factory supplies, and tanning machinery in violation of Sections 1 and 2 of the Sherman Act.

4. That the Court adjudge and decree that the aforesaid contracts and agreements between the defendant and Singer Manufacturing Company, The Lamson Company, Tubular Rivet and Stud Company, Breuer Electric Manufacturing Company, and Landis Machine Company, are in violation of Sections 1 and 2 of the Sherman Act; and that the defendant be required to cancel said contracts and agreements.

5. That the Court adjudge and decree that each of the aforesaid leases of shoe machinery between the defendant and shoe manufacturers is in violation of Sections 1 and 2 of the Sherman Act; and that the defendant be required to cancel each of said leases.

6. That, upon the election of any lessee of the defendant and under such conditions and on such terms as the Court shall determine and order with due consideration for the rental and unit charges heretofore paid by such lessee to the defendant for the use of shoe machinery of the defendant, the defendant be required to sell to said lessee and divest itself of its entire right, title, claim, and interest to and in shoe machinery on lease to said lessee.

7. That the defendant be required to offer to sell at reasonable prices all shoe machinery manufactured and commercialized by it and be enjoined from leasing shoe machinery except upon terms and conditions approved by the Court.

8. That the Court adjudge and decree that the defendant has engrossed shoe machinery patents and inventions and has used said patents and inventions to monopolize and attempt to monopolize interstate trade and commerce in shoe machinery, as aforesaid, in violation of Section 2 of the Sherman Act.

9. That, under such conditions and on such terms as the Court may deem appropriate and necessary to dissipate the effects of the unlawful conduct herein alleged and to establish free and unfettered competition in interstate trade and commerce in shoe machinery, the defendant be required to make available to all applicants therefor all patents and inventions relating to shoe machinery now or here-

after owned by the defendant and its subsidiaries and all models, drawings, plans, patterns, and specifications of shoe machinery embodying said patents and inventions; and that the defendant be enjoined from asserting any rights under said patents and inventions until the effects of the unlawful conduct herein alleged have been dissipated.

10. That, under such conditions and on such terms as the Court shall determine and order, the defendant be required to sell and divest itself of its entire stockholdings in Turner Tanning Machinery Company and its entire right, title, claim, and interest to and in the manufacturing plants and other properties and assets of the branches of defendant known as Booth Brothers Company and O. A. Miller Treeing Machine Company.

11. That the defendant be enjoined from engaging in the manufacture or distribution of shoe factory supplies.

12. That the Court adjudge and decree that each of the aforesaid exclusive contracts between the defendant and manufacturers of shoe factory supplies is in violation of Sections 1 and 2 of the Sherman Act; and that the defendant be required to cancel each of said contracts.

13. That, under such conditions and on such terms as the Court shall determine and order, the defendant be required to sell and divest itself of its entire stockholdings in B.B. Chemical Co., Celastic Corporation, W. W. Cross & Co., Inc., S. A. Felton Son Co., Hoague-Sprague Corp., Fred W. Mears Heel Co., Inc., Shoe Form Co., Inc., Shoe Lace Company, Tubular Rivet & Stud Company, and United Last Company.

14. That, under such conditions and on such terms as the Court shall determine and order, the defendant be required to sell and divest itself of its entire right, title, claim, and interest to and in the manufacturing plants and other properties and assets of the branches of defendant known as Binghamton Die Plant, Hughes Eyelet Company, J. C. Rhodes & Co., Inc., the S. O. & C. Company, St. Louis Die Plant, United Awl & Needle Company, and United Shank & Findings Company.

15. That the plaintiff have such other further and general relief as may be just and proper.

16. That the plaintiff recover the costs of this suit.

Frank W. Kelleher,
Special Assistant to the Attorney General.
C. Worth Rowley,
Alfred Karsted,
Edward M. Feeney,
Roy N. Freed,
Special Attorneys.

Tom C. Clark,
    Attorney General
John F. Sonnett,
    Assistant Attorney General
Holmes Baldridge,
    Special Assistant to the Attorney General
William T. McCarthy,
    United States Attorney.

Appendix B

Revised Final Decree

Filed October 6, 1954

FINAL DECREE, February 18, 1953, as modified by orders of the COURT, July 12, 1954 and September 17, 1954.

This cause having come on to be heard, and the Court having fully considered the evidence and arguments, and having filed its Findings of Fact, and Opinions on Violation and Remedy, it is hereby

ORDERED, ADJUDGED, AND DECREED that:

1. As used in this Decree:
   "A Day" means January 1, 1955.
   "B Day" means April 1, 1955.
   "C Day" means January 1, 1965.

"Shoe Machinery" means all types of shoe machinery distributed to shoe factories for use in the manufacture or repair of footwear, except dry thread sewing machines.

The words "machine type," "machines" and "machine" as used in this Decree mean "shoe machinery" as defined herein.

The word "supplies" as used in this Decree means all products, when distributed by defendant for use or consumption by shoe factories, of the types heretofore classified by the defendant as sales merchandise.

The word "patent" as used in this Decree means a United States patent for an invention relating to the manufacture, use or sale of footwear, shoe machinery or supplies.

2. Defendant violated §2 of the Sherman Act, 15 U.S.C. §2, by monopolizing the shoe machinery trade and commerce among the

several States. Defendant violated the same section of the law by monopolizing that part of the interstate trade and commerce in tacks, nails and eyelets, which is concerned with supplying the demand for those products by shoe factories within the United States. The other charges of violation of the Sherman Act set forth in the complaint are dismissed with prejudice. No obligation of the Defendant under this Decree shall apply to its manufacturing, distribution, service, patent or other activities in any industry other than shoe machinery and supplies or in relation to any industry other than the shoe manufacturing industry.

3. Defendant, its subsidiaries, and each of their directors, officers, agents, and employees, and, all persons acting for them, are hereby enjoined and restrained from further monopolizing those parts of the trade or commerce among the several states which have been referred to in the previous paragraph.

4. All leases made by defendant which include either a ten-year term, or a full capacity clause, or deferred payment charges, and all leases under which during the life of the leases defendant has rendered repair and other service without making them subject to separate, segregated charges, are declared to have been means whereby defendant monopolized the shoe machinery market.

5. After A Day, defendant shall not offer for lease any machine type, unless it also offers such type for sale. Defendant, if it offers any machine type for lease, shall set such terms for leasing that machine as do not make it substantially more advantageous for a shoe factory to lease rather than to buy a machine. Defendant shall not be required to secure advance judicial approval of the financial terms in sales or lease contracts. But if any lease or contract substantially discriminates in favor of leasing, plaintiff may apply to this Court for further specific relief.

6. Before A Day, defendant, if it desires to continue to lease any shoe machinery, shall file in this court a standard form of lease that meets the following directions. Other standard forms of lease shall be filed in this Court by defendant promptly as they are printed and before defendant places them in use.

a. The maximum term for either an original or renewal lease shall be five years.

b. Provision shall be made that a lessee shall have the right to return the leased machine at any time after one year, on paying all rentals already accrued, the shipping charges, the cost of broken and missing parts, and in adddition, no more than the equivalent of the monthly (not the unit) payments which would have been due had the lessee kept the machine for an additional three months. The lease may provide for return on terms more favorable to the lessee if the return is due exclusively to defects in the machine, or customer dissatisfaction after a trial period, or customer abandonment of operations. But no return charge shall discriminate on account of the substitution of a competitive machine.

c. The new forms of lease shall not include any return or deferred payment charges other than those specified in the previous paragraph. But they may include provisions for initial charges and deposits.

d. Defendant may, if it sees fit, use a unit charge in addition to, or as an alternative to, monthly rental charges. But such unit charges shall have no minimum.

e. After A Day, defendant shall not include within any lease, whether unit charges are used or not, a full capacity clause, or any equivalent.

f. After A Day, defendant shall not include either in the terms of, or the application of, any lease any plan similar to the right of deduction fund which it has heretofore established, or the 1935 Plan which it adopted for lessees desiring to return machinery.

g. Defendant shall not be obliged to present to the Court a statement of what will be the amount of, or method of calculating, its rentals, its charges, deposits, or like financial terms. But, after A Day, in preparing, executing, or applying its leases, defendant shall not discriminate between customers of the same general class, except that defendant may make different deposit provisions for different persons, upon an individual basis.

h. Defendant may propose various uniform lease riders to provide for peak-load or trial installations. Defendant may also use various loan forms to cover installation of experimental or other machines for which commercial terms have not been adopted. All such riders and forms shall comply with the preceding paragraphs.

i. Each lease shall expressly state what services and privileges it covers. After A Day, defendant may render, without separate charges, instruction services, installation services, repair services, or other services, during a period of 30 days, exclusive of Saturdays, Sundays and holidays, after the machine has been first installed and set up in line for use in shoe manufacture. After such 30-day period, defendant shall not provide any such services for a machine covered by a lease, except during the first 60 days, exclusive of Saturdays, Sundays and holidays, of a trial installation period covered by a lease trial rider as above provided, other than upon the basis of separate and reasonable charges for the services rendered, and the permission to render service for machines covered by lease trial riders herein contained shall be subject to the condition that similar service is made available for trial installations of machines whether to be leased or to be sold.

j. Defendant shall not vary the substance of the forms of lease submitted to the Court, without the Court's approval, but defendant may, without submitting them to the Court, use such special forms of lease or loan agreements as may be appropriate to the requirements of Federal, State or local governmental agencies and of educational institutions not engaged in the manufacture of footwear for profit. This provision shall not be interpreted as requiring defendant to secure advance judicial approval of the dollars and cents figures used in setting monthly rental charges, unit charges, deposits, or other specifically fiscal aspects of the lease.

7. Except for good cause, defendant shall not after A Day refuse a prospective customer's request to lease or buy a machine, of a type which defendant is at the time of such request offering for commercial lease or sale. In the event that a prospective customer is refused the privilege of buying or leasing a machine, he shall have the right to intervene in this case in this Court to have his controversy adjudicated, and in such proceedings, defendant shall have the burden of proving that there is good cause for refusing to make the sale or lease.

8. Before A Day, defendant shall present to the Court, if it desires to continue to render repair and other services, a tariff of the charges which it proposes to apply for rendering service. This service tariff shall have uniform charges for leased and sold machines. It may take into account travel time as well as time used in making repairs or rendering other services. It may recognize any economy defendant actually realizes in its business on a quantity basis, or any other economies in servicing customers of a particular type, or customers who commit themselves for particular periods of time, in any event, however, not exceeding twelve months at a time. Neither the tariff nor this Decree shall be interpreted as requiring defendant to render services in connection with machines, or parts, not of its manufacture. The tariff shall provide that parts shall be made available on the same terms to customers receiving services, customers not receiving services, and any other person; provided, however, that defendant shall not be obliged to furnish parts to a customer to help him construct an entire new machine out of assembled parts.

9. Before B Day, defendant, after conferring with plaintiff, with

representatives of The National Shoe Manufacturers Association, and with any lessees who previous to B Day have intervened in these proceedings, shall present to the Court a detailed plan for terminating all outstanding leases. This plan shall make appropriate non-discriminatory financial provisions for defendant's rights and each lessee's rights in connection with the termination of existing leases. It shall also make non-discriminatory provisions under which, within a reasonable period, lessees under leases existing before B Day may buy or lease those machines which have been installed. Such provisions shall be at least as favorable to shoe factories as the provisions in the new lease and sale forms.

10. Before B Day, defendant shall submit a plan for disposing of such parts of its business and the business of its subsidiaries as are concerned with the manufacture or distribution of tacks, nails and eyelets.

11. Beginning three years after A Day, defendant shall not distribute any supplies not manufactured by itself or a corporation in which it owns at least 20 per cent of the Common Stock, provided that this shall not apply to supplies acquired by United before then.

12. Defendant shall grant to any applicant, except a deliberate infringer, a non-exclusive license under any or all patents now held by defendant on reasonable non-discriminatory royalty terms. Such licenses may, however, be limited to the manufacture, use, and sale of shoe machinery, shoe supplies, and like products used in shoe factories. Such licenses may contain a provision for the inspection of the records of the licensee by an independent auditor who shall report to the licensor only the amount of royalty due and payable and no other information. Such licenses shall contain a provision for imparting in writing, at a reasonable charge by the licensor to the licensee, the methods and processes used by defendant as of the date of this Decree in its commercial practices under the patents licensed. This Court reserves jurisdiction to pass upon the reasonableness of any royalty or charge herein directed to be reasonable. Nothing in this paragraph applies to patents issued upon the basis of applications filed later than A Day, nor shall anything herein prohibit the defendant from making a bona fide sale or assignment from time to time of any patent held by it.

13. After A Day, defendant shall not acquire any patent or patent applications except patents or patent applications acquired by reason

of bona fide employment of the inventor by it or by a subsidiary unless defendant files in this Court an agreement to license that patent or patent application as provided in the previous paragraph with respect to patents it now owns.

14. After A Day, defendant shall not acquire any exclusive license under any patent unless such exclusive license grants defendant the right to license others and defendant promptly files in the Court an agreement to license as provided in Paragraph 12 of this Decree.

15. After A Day, defendant shall not acquire any shoe machinery business, any business manufacturing or distributing supplies for shoe factories, or any part thereof, or any stock therein, if the transaction involves more than $10,000 or its equivalent.

16. After A Day, defendant shall not buy or acquire any second-hand shoe machinery manufactured by it or any other person except for experimental or like purposes. The total acquisitions under this paragraph in any one year shall not represent an expenditure of more than $25,000, or its equivalent. Nothing in this paragraph shall be construed to apply to such rights as defendant may have to repossess, or to acquire at public auction, machines which it has conditionally sold and which the purchaser has lost the right to retain.

17. After A Day, defendant shall not continue any plan for quantity discounts in connection with any of its supplies, unless such discount system complies with all applicable laws.

18. On C Day, both parties shall report to this Court the effect of this decree, and may then petition for its modification, in view of its effect in establishing workable competition. If either party takes advantage of this paragraph by filing a petition, each such petition shall be accompanied by affidavits setting forth the then structure of the shoe machinery market and defendant's power within that market.

19. Defendant shall pay the costs of this case.

20. On or before October 1, 1954, defendant shall send to each of its then lessees a written copy of this Decree as modified prior to the date of mailing.

21. Nothing in this Decree shall impose any obligation on defendant until three months before A Day.

22. Nothing in this Decree shall impose any obligation on defendant or its subsidiaries to do or omit any action outside the United States.

23. Jurisdiction of this cause is retained for the purpose of enabling either of the parties to apply to this Court at any time for such further orders and directions as may be appropriate for the correction, construction, or carrying out of this Decree, and to set aside the Decree and take further proceedings if future developments justify that course in the appropriate enforcement of the Anti-Trust Act.

Index